The Hypothetical Mandarin

MODERNIST LITERATURE & CULTURE

Kevin J. H. Dettmar & Mark Wollaeger, Series Editors

Consuming Traditions
Elizabeth Outka

Machine-Age Comedy
Michael North

The Hypothetical Mandarin
Eric Hayot

The Art of Scandal
Sean Latham

The Hypothetical Mandarin

Sympathy, Modernity, and Chinese Pain

Eric Hayot

OXFORD
UNIVERSITY PRESS
2009

OXFORD
UNIVERSITY PRESS

Oxford University Press, Inc., publishes works that further
Oxford University's objective of excellence
in research, scholarship, and education.

Oxford New York
Auckland Cape Town Dar es Salaam Hong Kong Karachi
Kuala Lumpur Madrid Melbourne Mexico City Nairobi
New Delhi Shanghai Taipei Toronto

With offices in
Argentina Austria Brazil Chile Czech Republic France Greece
Guatemala Hungary Italy Japan Poland Portugal Singapore
South Korea Switzerland Thailand Turkey Ukraine Vietnam

Published by Oxford University Press, Inc.
198 Madison Avenue, New York, New York 10016

www.oup.com

Library of Congress Cataloging-in-Publication Data

Hayot, Eric, 1972–
The hypothetical mandarin : sympathy, modernity, and Chinese pain / Eric Hayot.
p. cm.
Includes bibliographical references and index.
ISBN 978-0-19-537796-5; 978-0-19-538249-5 (pbk.)
1. Europe—Civilization—Chinese influences. 2. China—In literature. 3. Sympathy—Moral and ethical aspects—History. I. Title.
CB203.H39 2009
940—dc22 2008041918

9 8 7 6 5 4 3 2 1

Printed in the United States of America
on acid-free paper

Acknowledgments

Words do the best they can, how they can. To respect them is to behold their noematic, vigilant arrangement of life and death, so different from the photograph's, in its own way just as curious and obscene. But prose's long exposures seep relentlessly, against the grain of memory, into the forgotten and the unconscious, and are encoded there against the promise of future reactivations. Each reactivation in turn recalls memory's unhurried rush toward oblivion.

Likewise, in the doubled frame of memory and forgetting, the help that made this particular act of writing possible, translating animation into animation, and into this text's body. So that:

I wish to thank my family for their love and support.

The conception of this book owes a great deal to Judith Green, who invited me to give the talk that became its major idea. I wrote *The Hypothetical Mandarin's* first outline in Tucson, where countless hours spent with Charlie Bertsch and Greg Jackson taught me lessons in friendship and intellectual life. I gained much, while at the University of Arizona, from a group of tremendous students (Christine, Baumgarthuber Sean Cobb, Matt Cook, Amanda Gradisek, Megan Massino, Sally Northmore, Sarah Osment, Helena Ribeiro, Sam Schwartz, Jack Skeffington, Mark Sussman, and Julie Ward), and from colleagues (Susan Aiken, Ed Dryden, Bill Epstein, Larry Evers, Stephanie Pearmain, and Susan White). Some of the research for chapter three was supported by a Career Development Grant awarded by the University of Arizona's College of Humanities, which gave me time to travel to the Wason Collection on East Asia at Cornell University's Kroch Library.

Most of the manuscript was written in Los Angeles, where for two years I was supported by a Global Fellowship at the University of California at Los Angeles's

International Institute, in a program whose director, Françoise Lionnet, serves the profession as an exemplar of sustained, generous mentorship. I am grateful to my fellow fellows, especially Nitsan Chorev, Liz DeLoughrey, Nate Jensen, Smitha Radhakrishnan, Nina Sylvanus, Jeff Timmons, and Yiman Wang, to German Esparza and Takamasa Imai, and to Ron Rogowski, who made the International Institute such a rewarding place to write and think. In and around UCLA, I also benefited from conversations with Ali Behdad, Michael Heim, Neetu Khanna, Chris Looby, Jessica Pressman, Marcia Reed (of the Getty Institute), David Schaberg, Michael Szalay, Shu-mei Shih, and John Williams, all of whom generously read or responded to parts of the manuscript. Among friends in and around Los Angeles I am especially grateful to Michelle Clayton, Paul Gilmore, Mark Goble, Yogita Goyal, Eleanor Kaufman, Mark McGurl, Sianne Ngai, Sharon Oster, Elisa Tamarkin, and Julie Townsend; together they made those two years the most intense and exciting experience of intellectual and personal friendship I've had so far. Research for chapter two was supported by a Mellon Foundation grant from The Huntington Library, where Meredith Berbee, Juan Gomez, and Kate Henningsen provided invaluable assistance. With funding from the International Institute, I made several visits to the Medical Historical Library at Yale University, where Toby Appel guided me through the labyrinths of the Peter Parker collection.

The manuscript was revised, edited, and otherwise polished in State College, Pennsylvania, which my colleagues Gabeba Baderoon, Tom Beebee, Hester Blum, Chris Castiglia, Liana Chen, Jon Eburne, Michael Elavsky, Carey Eckhardt, Charlotte Eubanks, Alexander Huang, Djelal Kadir, Brian Lennon, Sophia McClennen, Henry Morello, Daniel Purdy, Chris Reed, Amit Schejter, Rachel Teukolsky, and Reiko Tachibana make such an exciting, interesting place to be. I am grateful to my research assistants, Bunny Torrey and Grace Wu, and to the administrative staff of Penn State's Department of Comparative Literature, including Cindy Bierly, JoElle DeVinney, Phyllis Favorite, Irene Grassi, Sharon Laskowsky, Mona Muzzio, Bonnie Rossman, and Lynn Setzler, for their support.

Audiences at UCLA's Center for Chinese Studies, Cambridge University, University of California at Berkeley, Arizona, Yale, University of Wisconsin, Tsinghua University, University of California at Irvine, University of Pennsylvania, Princeton University, and three meetings of the American Comparative Literature Association gave me incisive and invariably helpful hearings. I have been lucky to have had conversations with and received advice from Emily Apter, Bill Brown, David Damrosch, Rey Chow, Susan Stanford Friedman, Robert Kern, and Lydia Liu, and a long friendship with Jane Gallop. Jennifer Lee, David Eng,

Lindsay Waters, Josephine Park, Soo La Kim, Carlos Rojas, Wai Chee Dimock, Paul St. Amour, Eileen Chow, and Jing Tsu all helped clarify and expand my thinking, as did Ted Wesp and Kelly Klingensmith. My editor at Oxford University Press, Shannon McLachlan, was the Hüsker Dü to this project's Minneapolis. I am thankful to her assistants Chrissy Gibson and Brendan O'Neill, and to series editors Kevin Dettmar and Mark Wollaeger, these latter for seeing how this project might fit within the optic of their series and for showing me how to see that as well.

I want to acknowledge, finally, the people who constitute the first concentric circle of my address: Timothy Billings, Christopher Bush, Pericles Lewis, Colleen Lye, Haun Saussy, Rebecca Walkowitz, and Steven Yao. Our collective catalog of expenditure and exchange operates at the limit of reciprocal economy, and from there works its slow magic on my life. I dedicate this book to Chris, my most intense interlocutor, the one whose prose, whose conversation, and whose friendship most intensely continue to teach me how to be the person I am trying to become.

A version of chapter 3 appeared in *Representations* 99 (summer 2007) as "Chinese Bodies, Chinese Futures"; a version of chapter 5 appeared in *Modern Chinese Literature and Culture* 18:1 (2006). I am grateful for the permission to reprint that material here.

Contents

Series Editors' Foreword

With Eric Hayot's *The Hypothetical Mandarin: Sympathy, Modernity, and Chinese Pain,* the Modernist Literature & Culture series for the first time steps noticeably outside of its "comfort zone"—even, one might argue, eschews its stated goal of exploring the cultural bearings of literary modernism. To such a charge, we can only plead "guilty": a book as wide-ranging and thoughtful, as well as thought-provoking, as *The Hypothetical Mandarin* is bound to unsettle comfortable visions of period, field, nation, and method, making the series' founding logic somewhat strange to itself. For Hayot takes as his object of inquiry not modernism per se, but the Western project of modernity writ large—and yet zeroes in, with uncanny precision, on one of its most persistent and disturbing topoi: the figure of the suffering Chinese subject, and its relationship to two hundred years' worth of Western discourse about human sympathy and human rights.

The book opens—in its very first sentence—with reference to Adam Smith's *Theory of the Moral Sentiments* (1790), which includes a excursus Hayot calls "a remarkable thought experiment" (and from which he derives his title). It's an apt description of this text, as well: experimental in method and form, bold and risk-taking, conveying all the excitement of an *essai,* a trial: a tenacious tracking of cultural traces according to their own sinuous logic, a trail that leads inexorably back, across two centuries, to that hypothetical, unseen, suffering Chinese stranger. In this sense, Hayot's is a postmodern investigation of a constituent aspect of our modernity; as Jean-François Lyotard suggests in his evocation-cum-description of "the postmodern" writer, "the text he writes, the work he produces are not in principle governed by preestablished rules, and they cannot be judged according to a determining judgment, by applying familiar categories to the text or to the work. Those rules and categories are what the work of art itself is looking for."[1]

Amongst other things, *The Hypothetical Mandarin* is a reflection on the status of the example and the anecdote in contemporary literary and cultural theory, especially in light of the prominence they have been given in New Historicism and cultural studies. The persistent way in which Chinese "examples" turn up in over two hundred years of Western efforts to articulate a discourse of critical distance and human sympathy—"the sustained and persistent appearance of the Chinese under the sign of sympathy, and of sympathy under the sign of the Chinese"—begins, in Hayot's analysis, to look rather suspect, and rightly changes the very way in which he understands and deploys the "example" in his own critical narrative (most evident, perhaps, in the book's closing pages, in which three different examples would seem to present three equally plausible attempts at closure). Examples, one might say, always point in two directions: shoring up the writer's argument, yes, but inevitably unmasking the ideological motivation of that argument at the very same time. Hayot's, then, is a symptomatic understanding of the example.

And yet within this broad and compelling historical and theoretical inquiry, Hayot also makes an important contribution to ongoing conversations in modernist studies about center and margins, cosmopolitan metropole and provincial town: about whether, at this stage in modernist studies' growth as a discipline, it is still possible to displace the reigning, even unconscious, paradigm of Anglo-American modernism from a new modernist studies that palpably desires to globalize itself. For scholars of modernism, then, Hayot's most important contribution may be his call to globalize the field more thoroughly: to develop a nuanced historical, geographic, and linguistic model of modernism that doesn't simply decenter a putative London-New York axis, but troubles the very notion of centrality. This Hayot does by importing from astronomy the diagnostic notion of the "ecliptic"—"the universal," Hayot defines it at one point, "construed in relation to a false sense of centrality."

If the structure or logic of this move looks deconstructive, it is—as is Hayot's refusal to substitute, in any simplistic way, China for Great Britain or the United States as the more adequate center of a properly understood transnational modernism. But it is not the older, linguistically self-absorbed version of decon-

[1] "Answering the Question: What Is Postmodernism?" trans. Régis Durand, in *The Postmodern Condition: A Report on Knowledge*, trans. Geoff Bennington and Brian Massumi (Minneapolis: U. Minnesota Press, 1984), p. 81.

structive thinking from the 1970s and 80s. Ultimately, Hayot asks us to understand sympathy as both deeply human and as a culturally determined, linguistic construction, arguing that "sustained attention to the *making* of sympathy" might help to "undermine the normalizing assumptions about its naturalness that make it so hard to imagine why someone else doesn't feel about suffering the way you do." Hayot suggests a picture of Anglo-American modernism with its Chinese "other" always already lodged deep, even preconsciously and prelogically, within: "What effect does the use of China as an *instrument of measure*," he forces us to ask, "have on what it serves to measure?"

The Hypothetical Mandarin thus moves an implicitly Anglo-American model of modernism from the center of Modernist Literature & Culture by interrogating the very logic of the series itself; if the series is able to survive the challenge this book represents, it will be the better for it. And either way, we'll be in Eric Hayot's debt.

KEVIN J. H. DETTMAR AND MARK WOLLAEGER

The Hypothetical Mandarin

Introduction

The Hypothetical Mandarin

---

1. The Mandarin (First Appearance)

In the substantially revised and expanded sixth edition of *The Theory of Moral Sentiments*, published shortly before his death in 1790, Adam Smith added a remarkable thought experiment to his discussion on "the influence and Authority of Conscience." The experiment had to do with the effects of physical distance on moral judgment. Having suggested that any moral adjudication between two parties must proceed as though it were made "from the place and with the eyes of a third person," who could judge impartially between them, Smith went on to remark how infrequently such judgments actually appear in practice.[1] If the "great empire of China" were suddenly destroyed by an earthquake, for instance, how would an average European react to the news? Though he might, in the initial shock, "make many melancholy reflections upon the precariousness of

[1] Adam Smith, *The Theory of Moral Sentiments*, eds. D. D. Raphael and A.L. Macfie (Indianapolis, 1984), 135. Further references in the text are cited as *MS*. Raphael and Macfie note that though Adam Smith wrote the following passage in 1760, it did not appear in print until the 1790 edition; they also suggest that his choice of an earthquake owes something to the famous earthquake of 1755, which killed as many as ninety thousand people and destroyed the city of Lisbon (see 134n*a*, 136n*j* and 141n*x* for more extensive bibliographic information). The entire section "Of the Influence and Authority of Conscience" appeared only for the first time in the second edition of 1760, which substantially revised the text of the first 1759 edition. Smith's book remained more or less unchanged until its sixth edition, printed in 1790.

human life," or in a soberer moment consider "the effects which this disaster might produce upon the commerce of Europe," he would eventually return to his normal life "with the same ease and tranquility, as if no such accident had happened" (*MS*, 136). Out of sight, out of mind; the death of distant millions would in the long run fail to register its fated and objectively terrifying imprint on his conscience. But consider, Smith writes, that

> the most frivolous disaster which could befal himself would occasion a more real disturbance. If he was to lose his little finger to-morrow, he would not sleep to-night; but, provided he never saw them, he will snore with the most profound security over the ruin of a hundred millions of his brethren, and the destruction of that immense multitude seems plainly an object less interesting to him, than this paltry misfortune of his own. To prevent, therefore, this paltry misfortune to himself, would a man of humanity be willing to sacrifice the lives of a hundred millions of his brethren, provided he had never seen them? (*MS*, 136–37)

With this last hypothetical question, which pits the value of the lives of millions of Chinese against the loss of an individual finger, Smith formulates for the first time a philosophical conjecture that has remained, in a variety of derivative forms, a crucial figure of European thought over the last two centuries: What is the relative worth to you of harm done to a Chinese stranger?

The hypothetical's classic formulation appears in Balzac's *Le Père Goriot* (1835), in a conversation between Rastignac and Bianchon:

> "Have you read Rousseau?"
>
> "Yes."
>
> "Do you remember the passage where he asks the reader what he would do if he could make a fortune by killing an old mandarin in China by simply exerting his will, without stirring from Paris?"
>
> "Yes."
>
> "Well?'
>
> "Bah! I'm at my thirty-third mandarin."
>
> "Don't play the fool. Look here, if it were proved to you that the thing was possible and you only needed to nod your head, would you do it?"
>
> "Is your mandarin well-stricken in years? But, bless you, young or old, paralytic or healthy, upon my word—The devil take it! Well, no."[2]

[2] Balzac, *Le Père Goriot*, in *Oeuvres Complètes, Scènes de la vie privée VI* (Paris, 1949), 361.

By the end of the nineteenth century, this passage in Balzac was well enough known to generate entries under "*tuer le mandarin*" (to kill the mandarin) in the *Littré* dictionary of 1874, defined as "to commit an evil action in the hope that it will remain unknown"; the phrase also appeared in the eighth edition of the dictionary of the *Académie Française* (1932–35), as an idiom for "killing, with certain impunity, a complete stranger in the expectation of some advantage." In the intervening years, it has become a staple figure of the philosophical problem of moral distance, holding pride of place, for instance, in Carlo Ginzburg's essay, "To Kill a Chinese Mandarin: The Implications of Moral Distance," which puts it in a historical trajectory that ranges from Aristotle to David Hume, from Smith and Balzac to Walter Benjamin, and opens up the history of the putatively "natural" feeling of human sympathy by showing how philosophical articulations of compassion's necessities have shaped, and drawn on, the eras to which they belong. Along the way Ginzburg points out that the passage Balzac refers to never actually appears in Rousseau.[3]

How does spatial distance affect one's moral responsibility to others? Is it worse to allow a stranger to starve on your doorstep than to allow one to starve halfway across the world? How, historically, have societies drawn the line between the doorstep and the world, teaching their inhabitants where moral responsibility ends and indifference begins? And why, finally, did Balzac's misremembered story of a mandarin become a figure for these philosophical problems, which are at the

[3]A version of the passage can be found in François-René de Chateaubriand's *Le Génie du Christianisme* (1802), where it takes this form: "If, merely by wishing it, you could kill a man in China and inherit his fortune in Europe, being assured by supernatural means that the deed would remain forever unknown, would you allow yourself to form that project?" (Carlo Ginzburg, "To Kill a Chinese Mandarin: The Moral Implications of Distance," in *Wooden Eyes: Nine Reflections on Distance*, trans. Martin Ryle and Kate Soper [New York, 2001], 164.). Ginzburg suggests that Chateaubriand's story draws from an episode in the work of Denis Diderot dating from 1773, in which a European murderer "transported to the coast of China" is too far from his crime to feel its sting on his conscience (165). But there may be a simpler explanation, as Smith's version predates Chateaubriand's by twelve years in print. Given that Chateaubriand began writing *Le Génie* while in England in 1799, his source for the hypothetical's basic structure may have been Smith rather than Diderot. Chateaubriand's passage is discussed by Paul Ronai, "Tuer le Mandarin," *Revue de littérature comparée* 10 (1930), 520–23. The mandarin hypothetical appears in a variety of literary sources over the years; for a listing of mostly European sources see Laurence W. Keates, "Mysterious Miraculous Mandarin: Origins, Literary Paternity, Implication in Ethics," *Revue de littérature comparée* 40.4 (1966), 497–525. As for why Balzac might have misremembered Chateaubriand as Rousseau (or indeed intentionally confounded them), Haun Saussy suggests to me that the "general will" Rousseau theorized, of which the neo-royalist Balzac would have been deeply suspicious, might have been perceived by the latter to operate with the same implacable randomness and violence that characterizes Bianchon's hypothetical murder.

heart of the sympathetic transformation of human life that founded modernity's dream of a universal subject?

Let us begin by locating Balzac's hypothetical, along with Smith's example of the Chinese earthquake, within that humanitarian transformation, which since its inauguration in the sympathetic revolution of the eighteenth and nineteenth centuries has gone on to remake the social, cultural, and political faces of Western life.[4] Drawing on religious and philosophical doctrines that would have been nearly incomprehensible to their historical forbears, Europeans and Americans in that period dramatically expanded the human and geopolitical space toward which the average member of their societies was presumed to be emotionally responsible, and toward which both the individual and the state were supposed to direct their attention and care.[5] By the middle of the nineteenth century, sympathy, and the moral responsibility that abetted it, found itself engaged in social reform movements designed—at least in their public, self-conscious discourse—to establish affective and material relationships with a wide variety of living beings, including the poor, the mentally ill, prisoners, slaves, foreigners, and even animals, whose troubles had not been the subject of serious institutional or personal concern only a century or two earlier.[6] This groundswell of humanist

[4]See for instance Thomas Bender, ed., *The Antislavery Debate: Capitalism and Abolitionism* (Berkeley, 1992); Shirley Samuels, ed., *The Culture of Sentiment: Race, Gender, and Sentimentality in Nineteenth-Century America* (New York, 1992); Elizabeth Barnes, *States of Sympathy: Seduction and Democracy in the American Novel* (New York, 1997); Ian Baucom, *Specters of the Atlantic: Finance Capital, Slavery, and the Philosophy of History* (Durham, N.C., 2005); Benjamin Daffron, *Romantic Doubles: Sex and Sympathy in British Gothic Literature, 1790–1830* (New York, 2002); Joseph Fichtelberg, *Critical Fictions: Sentiment and the American Market, 1780-1870* (Athens, 2003); Mary Lenard, *Preaching Pity: Dickens, Gaskell, and Sentimentalism in Victorian Culture* (New York, 1999); Dana D. Nelson, *The World in Black and White: Reading "Race" In American Literature, 1638–1867* (New York, 1993); and Gonzalo Sánchez, *Pity in Fin-de-siècle French Culture: "Liberté, Égalité, Pitié"* (Westport, 2004).

[5]On the incompatibility of doctrines of sympathy with earlier models, see R.S. Crane, "Suggestions towards a Genealogy of the 'Man of Feeling'" *ELH* 1.3 (Dec. 1934), 206–07.

[6]On slavery, see Thomas Bender and Baucom; on the mentally ill, see Michel Foucault, *The Birth of the Clinic: An Archaeology of Medical Perception*, trans. A.M. Sheridan Smith (New York, 1973) and *Madness and Civilization: A History of Insanity in the Age of Reason*, trans. Richard Howard (New York, 1965); on torture, see Edward Peters, *Torture* (London, 1985); on prison reform see Norval Morris and David J. Rothman, eds., *The Oxford History of the Prison: The Practice of Punishment in Western Society* (New York, 1995) and John B. Bender, *Imagining the Penitentiary: Fiction and the Architecture of Mind in Eighteenth-Century England* (Chicago, 1997). On animals, see James Turner, who writes that Europe's "flood of sympathy, embracing all people, could hardly fail to overflow its original bounds and brush with pity the sufferings of other sentient beings. Particularly at a time when scientific discoveries suggested a closer kinship between men and beasts … animals began to benefit from this exuberance of compassion" (*Reckoning with the Beast: Animals, Pain, and Humanity in the Victorian Mind* [Baltimore, 1980], 7.).

reform, an "immense cultural revolution" involving what Charles Taylor has called "the affirmation of ordinary life," borrowed its philosophical justifications from thinkers like Francis Hutcheson, David Hume, and Smith, and took its religious ones from liberal Anglicanism, whose preachers urged parishioners to visit the sick, care for the poor, and to experience the "'pleasing Anguish, that sweetly melts the Mind, and terminates in a Self-approving Joy' which is the chief earthly reward of persons who indulge their naturally good inclinations" toward benevolence.[7] It found literary expression in the great eighteenth-century novels of sensibility, which praised "a generous heart" and a "capacity for refined feeling," encouraging moral growth in those new bourgeois subjects to whom appeals for compassionate reform were so frequently addressed—effectively schooling generations of gentlemen and gentlewomen in the observation of sympathetic scenes and the performance of the emotions appropriate to them.[8] By 1811 this earnest moral education had become common enough for Jane Austen to critique the fad in the name of a more down-to-earth "sense." And when, sixty years after Austen, Gustave Flaubert lampooned with his usual clear-eyed cruelty Frédéric Moreau's romanesque fantasies in *L'Éducation Sentimentale,* he only confirmed the nearly universal approbation conferred on the self-consciously progressive, humanitarian spirit that defined his era.

[7] Charles Taylor, "Conditions of an Unforced Consensus on Human Rights," in *The East Asian Challenge for Human Rights,* Joanne R. Bauer and Daniel A. Bell, eds. (Cambridge, 1999). The second citation is from Crane, who is quoting the Scottish moralist David Fordyce, writing in 1754 (227). A great deal of work has been done to debunk the notion that the rise in compassion resulted from the general moral improvement of humankind; on this subject see especially Thomas Haskell, "Capitalism and the Origins of Humanitarian Sensibility," parts 1 and 2, in *The Antislavery Debate: Capitalism and Abolitionism,* ed. Thomas Bender (Berkeley, 1992). For philosophy, see David Hume, *Treatise of Human Nature* (New York, 1978) and Francis Hutcheson, *Essay on the Nature and Conduct of the Passions and Affections* (Gainesville, 1969); see Alexander Broadie, "Sympathy and the Impartial Spectator," in *The Cambridge Companion to Adam Smith,* ed. Knud Haakonssen (Cambridge, 2006), for an essay describing Hutcheson and Hume's influence on Smith's theory of sympathy. On liberal Anglicanism, see Gerald Cragg, *From Puritanism to the Age of Reason: A Study of Changes in Religious Thought within the Church of England, 1660 to 1700* (Cambridge, 1966).

[8] Janet Todd, *Sensibility: An Introduction* (London, 1986), 8. Todd identifies sentimental literature's heyday as the period from 1740 to 1770, tracing its decline through adjectives applied to the term "sensibility" (see 7–8). She writes that Smith's *Theory of Moral Sentiments* was the "end to a line of British moral philosophy" that admitted "the sentimental aim of trying systematically to link morality and emotion" (27). The long-term implications of this sentimental education, though no longer explicitly articulated in philosophical terms, continued to operate through the humanitarianism that bears their dreams into the nineteenth and twentieth centuries. On the literature of sensibility, see also Barbara Benedict, *Framing Feeling: Sentiment and Style in English Prose Fiction, 1745-1800* (New York, 1994).

2. The Chinese Ecliptic

From inside the phenomenological framing provided by the great cultural and narrative project that remade the emotional life of ordinary Europeans and Americans, a narrative hypothetical in which one resisted the temptation to murder a Chinese mandarin established itself as a generic philosopheme for the question of how best to be, or to become, a modern, sympathetic human being. It is the opening premise of this book that China's appearance inside the two-centuries long discourse on the relation between sympathy and humanity makes a difference to the history of Western thought—though what kind of difference, exactly, remains to be determined. It follows from this premise that no history of modernity will be complete if it cannot account for the habit of this reference, for the sustained and persistent appearance of the Chinese under the sign of sympathy, and of sympathy under the sign of the Chinese. Its historical expressions, mechanisms, and topographies unfold like so many accordions in the pages that follow, illuminating there the specific outlines of the difference they make.

The particular analysis of China's place in the history of sympathy and suffering will be shaped by a more general sense of the role China has tended to play in Western history and thought. There, "China" has been most consistently characterized as a limit or potential limit, a horizon neither of otherness nor of similarity, but rather of the very distinction between otherness and similarity, and thus, because what is at stake in the era of modernity in the West is the dream of the universalization of culture, as a horizon of the very idea of horizons, a horizon, that is, that marks the limit of the universal as a transcendental field. "China" has been, in short, not just one name for the line that delimits inside from outside, one form of the concept of totality, but rather a *form* of all forms of totality, a figure against which other forms of totality have been measured. This is true insofar as "China" has fulfilled a generic ideal of the ethnic other, particularly of that type of other known as the Oriental.[9] But it is also particularly true of China, whose longstanding status as the place one gets to

[9]Whose history became visible so clearly for the first time in Edward Said's *Orientalism* (New York, 1979), and whose analysis has been extended by so many others since then. As an instance of a case in which Chineseness seems interchangeable with a generic barbarism of the other (which may not even be "Oriental"), consider that the painful twisting of the skin on the forearm, known in the United Kingdom as a "Chinese burn," is called an "Indian burn" in the United States. In either case, the association with a particularly inventive small cruelty is associated with an "other," but it clearly does not matter much which one; or rather, the other chosen depends on local historical factors and not on the perpetual stability of a stereotype.

by digging through the center of the earth reflects the ways in which Chinese otherness differs from a generic Oriental otherness under whose aegis it sometimes appears.

China's unique mythology in Western history is the product of two major historical facts: first, that modern Europe encounters China as the first contemporaneous *civilizational* other it knows, and not as a "tribe" or nation whose comparative lack of culture, technology, or economic development mitigated the ideological threat it posed to progressivist, Eurocentric models of world history. China's status as an actively competing civilizational model stands in stark contrast to the modern European encounters with, say, the civilizations of ancient Egypt (long gone), the Indian subcontinent (colonizable), the Ottoman Turks (declining), or the Aztec empire (destroyed). Though each of these was absorbed as a historical and ideological force into the European generation of its self-image, and differently each time, it would be a mistake to fold the Chinese example entirely into a generically postcolonial one with which it has much in common. Second, for much of the period that modern Europe has known China—especially in the seventeenth and eighteenth centuries—the latter had significant economic and technological advantages over Europe in the manufacture of certain especially desirable goods, most notably tea, silk, and porcelain, whose exchange dominated, financially and figurally, the maritime economies of the eighteenth and nineteenth centuries. This importance has not widely been recognized in the fields of literary and cultural studies, at least partly because these fields have not tended to address questions of political economy. Thus it takes an economic historian, Kenneth Pomeranz, to assert that it is "China, *more than any other place*, that has served as the 'other' for the modern West's stories about itself, from Smith and Malthus to Marx and Weber," a claim whose truth-value interests me less than the fact that such a thing would be impossible to say in literary studies, my native field.[10]

The features that made China such a challenge to the European idea of modernity have tended to be erased by the historical and sociological accounts of China written in the nineteenth and twentieth centuries. The sense of that empire as a historically immobile, stagnating, underdeveloped and despotic space

[10] Kenneth Pomeranz, *The Great Divergence: China, Europe, and the Making of the Modern World Economy* (Princeton, N.J., 2000), 25 (emphasis mine). Chinese advantages in industrial manufacture led to what can only be called from our present perspective "industrial espionage"; for a particularly compelling reading of the work of Daniel Defoe as a figure for what one might call Europe's "industrial desire," see Lydia Liu, "Robinson Crusoe's Earthenware Pot," *Critical Inquiry* 25.4 (Summer 1999).

developed by thinkers like Smith, Hegel, or Marx has only in the economic histories of recent years been seriously challenged, and the implications of those challenges for the notions of historical development that follow from the work of these important thinkers have yet to be fully elaborated. The dismissal of Chinese legitimacy, and the forgetting of its massive impact on the European economy and imagination in the seventeenth and eighteenth centuries is at least partly an effect of the dramatic rise of European economic power, whose growth line crosses that of China somewhere around 1815, when Europe took the lead that came to subtend the modern world system.[11] (As we will see, however, a general anxiety about the sheer numbers of Chinese people and, indeed, an ongoing tendency to see China as an immanent horizon of the capitalist market, persisted well through the nineteenth century and beyond.)

The combination of these historical facts gives China and the idea of China a unique, if hardly paradigmatic, place in the record of European historiography and economic thought, not to mention in the forms of literature and culture that operated under the umbrellas of European-driven imperialism and economic globalization. Here one might note that the *absence* of China from the field of postcolonial studies feels like the symptomatic expression of its strange relationship to contemporary scholarship on the relation between the West and its others. Partly this absence has to do with the fact that China was never quite colonized, of course, but the fact of not having been colonized, rather than being understood as a crucial event in the history of colonialism, has instead become the implicit justification for China's exclusion from the postcolonial field. As though the failure to belong to a model were not in and of itself an important expression of logic of the model. It is precisely by virtue of being on the margins of the postcolonial that China can contribute to the historical and theoretical work in the field.[12]

I begin, then, by noting that China's function as a horizon of horizons stems directly from its "civilizational"—that is to say, its cultural, economic, and technological—challenge to Europe, and from the historical and material

[11] The date comes from Andre Gunder Frank, *ReOrient: Global Economy in the Asian Age* (Berkeley, 1998), 283.

[12] On this same subject, some fifteen years ago, Rey Chow, arguing that the question should be "how, *in spite of* and perhaps because of the fact that [East Asia] remained 'territorially independent,' it offers even better illustrations of how imperialism works—i.e., how imperialism as ideological domination succeeds best without physical coercion, without actually capturing the body and the land" (*Writing Diaspora: Tactical Interventions in Contemporary Cultural Studies* [Bloomington, 1993], 7–8).

relations that have brought the two in contact with one another (and, at times, kept them from each other).

In what follows, I will occasionally call this function "ecliptical" or "ecliptic," using a term borrowed from the field of astronomy to refer to the larger relational structure and history I have described so far. The *ecliptic* is the path of the sun seen from the surface of the Earth. For most of human history it was a measure of astronomical space and worldly time; in the ecliptick, as Geoffrey Chaucer wrote in 1391, "is the longitude of a celestiall body rekned, evene fro the heved of Aries unto the ende of Pisces," from, that is, one spring equinox to the next, *yonge sonne* to dissipated one.[13] The ecliptic was essentially the measure of the universe as clock, a frame for the metronomic motions that guided astrological predictions, the science of astronomy through Copernicus, mythological narratives, and the rhythms of agricultural life. The later revelation that the path of the sun seen from the surface of the Earth is not *the* path of the sun, but (a) an artifact of the Earth's own path around the sun, and (b) therefore simply *a* path of the sun seen from a certain perspective, has not cured ordinary life of ecliptic language, which tends still to refer the sun as "high" or "low" in the sky.

The ecliptic thus names a particular kind of relationship between the local and the universal: the universal as it is imagined from a particular perspective, one whose locality is named and defined by the universal it declares. As far as the actual ecliptic goes, its "universal" figure, namely the sun, was as universal a figure as it was possible to think in the chasm between Ptolemy and Copernicus, when the solar system was the only universe anyone knew, and the night sky's stars realms for the gods to play in. Its perspectival relation was therefore universalizing (its perspective quite literally the perspective of the entire planet) and localizing (from other planets or other solar systems our sun follows an entirely different path across the local sky) all at once. It was a figure for the *virtually* universal, the *virtually* local—the universal construed in relation to a false sense of centrality rather than the universal as such. From the perspective of this book, this history makes the ecliptic an especially useful figure for the relation between "China" and "the West": it is a figure of the relation between two things rather than a sign for one or the other of them; it is the figure, I repeat, of a *relation*, and not of the things related. Much of this book will be concerned with tracing the history of that relation, recognizing the ways in which a Western

[13]"And his latitude is rekned after the quantite of his declynacioun north or south toward the polys of this world," Chaucer added in his *Treatise on the Astrolabe* (originally ca. 1391–92; Norman, 2002).

perspective oriented around China helps establish the centrality of the West to the history it writes, even as it writes—with its other "hand," as it were—a more local history of the geopolitically limited landmass it calls "China."

I discuss the ecliptic idea along two major lines of advance. First, the book reads the consistent appearance of the Chinese example in relation to the general development of the idea of the modern human being, attending particularly to the ways in which the seemingly arbitrary choice of China shapes the thought that underlies it, and the ways in which the ecliptic relation between China and the West helps the West understand itself as a civilization and as modern (just as people on Earth have imagined the being and significance of the Earth in relation to the presence of a single, "rotating" sun). How does the cultural baggage that comes along with the Chinese example shape or articulate the history of the human to which it belongs? What effect does the use of China as an *instrument of measure* have on what it serves to measure? And how does this rhetorical, philosophical figure—never independent from China's position in global history, its relations to trade or emigration, to imperialism, to globalization—modify some imaginary and fully neutral theory of the human that would never have required the Chinese example, or even used it? In what sense, that is, is the conception of the modern sympathetic human being that the West represents to itself in some sense already—from the very beginning—"Chinese," and what would it mean for it to be so? These questions, which bear immediately on the historical and philosophical value of the examples this book discusses, also raise the more general problem of the relation between the example and its illustrated rule, the "for instance" and the principle it sustains; here *The Hypothetical Mandarin* will engage, though at some remove, the ongoing attempt to think the tension between the supplemental and the necessary, the transient and the exigent, as they operate in action and in thought. More on this in a moment.

The second line of advance reverses the frame of this initial orientation, abandoning China's influence on the history of sympathy to attend to the latter's effects upon the history of the Western experience of China.[14] It thus flips the

[14] Against whatever initial revulsion will refuse, seeing the braided pair under the microscope here, to acknowledge that they are objects of the same order—that persists in believing that sympathy is a word-concept and thus very much subject to this sort of representational history, while "China" is something else entirely, I will simply say that the difference between sympathy and China along the axis of reality is of degree not of kind. "China" operates simultaneously as a contested name for an Asian landmass with a particular national and cultural history, *and* as a rhetorical-epistemological figure that refers to the cultural travels of that landmass, neither of these—the landmass or the

terms of the ecliptic while remaining focused on its relational structure as such; instead of showing how this ecliptic relation taught the West about itself, it relates what it taught the West about China. This generates the following problems: How does the intertwining of the dual problems of "China" and "sympathy" affect the place of China in Western history, sociology, medical science, philosophy, and literature? How does the availability of "China" as a certain kind of representational figure correspond to and shape its undeniable presence in the world that represents it, and what kinds of effects does this availability and shaping have on such things as international diplomacy, the treatment of Chinese immigrants, or theories of universal history? As it responds to these questions, the book intervenes in the larger project of writing the global history of "China," to which such scholars as Timothy Billings, Christopher Bush, Rey Chow, Lydia Liu, Colleen Lye, David Palumbo-Liu, David Porter, Haun Saussy, Shu-mei Shih, and Steven G. Yao, among many others, have contributed in recent years.

Though *The Hypothetical Mandarin* concerns itself extensively with representations of China, the quantity of this attention never suggests that its dismantling of a Eurocentric conception of European history ought to be replaced by a sinocentric picture that restores China to its rightful place at the core of a world history that would be, as in some nationalist or ethnically empowering imaginary, "proper" to its status as a great civilization. Much of this work will undermine, not for the first time, the fantasy that there ever existed a pure and unadulterated "West" that was the source of the civilizational tradition that some thinkers in the United States and Europe routinely claim for it. But the book will also propose, obliquely, that such an undermining operates with respect to China as well (where fantasies of cultural uniqueness and historical time sustained by the "person" of the Yellow Emperor console the ideological brethren of the

---

figure—operating independently of one another, but in dialogue, just as someone with a reputation for bluffing at cards might successfully play a game completely "straight," deliberately taking advantage of the relation between concept that names her and the fact of being, more or less simply, not identical with it (this is a case in which the player's resistance to interpellation is empowering; the historical record on interpellation is bleaker, as its theorization by Louis Althusser suggests). As in the case of the poker player, the recursive interactions between "China" as fact and "China" as figure makes one of the subjects of negotiation the very notion of authenticity that would appear to divide them from one another, because once the player plays it straight in relation to a prior reputation for bluffing, any question about whether she is truly a bluffer "at heart" must establish a *relationship* between the figural and the factual dimensions of her personality and thus theorize, however unconsciously, a more general relation between facts and figures. Haun Saussy, Steven Yao, and I have made this argument at more length, minus the poker example, in the introduction to *Sinographies: Writing China* (Minneapolis, 2007).

American neo-conservatives). I do this work, however, not to produce this undermining effect but because I am trying to understand what is historically true. That truths occasionally destabilize the self-aggrandizing delusions of patriots is a happy side effect of their pursuit.

3. Empire of Cruelties

For some time now China has been a privileged object of European and American discourse on cruelty. Its role there as a horizon of horizons is one feature of its participation in a longer discourse on sympathy and humanism in which it has only recently taken up a speaking part. Consider for instance the following sentence, which appeared in the pages of *The New Republic* a year after the People's Republic's murderous suppression of the student movement in Tiananmen Square in 1989: "No better proof could be imagined for Nietzsche's insight that cruelty is the great festival pleasure of mankind than the torment inflicted by the Chinese people on one another for the last 400 years."[15] This is by all rights a fairly astonishing thing to say, given the breadth and import of the historical claim it makes: no better proof, Andrew Nathan writes, for human pleasure in cruelty than the Chinese of the last four centuries. And not just no better proof in actuality, but no better proof anywhere: no better proof could be *imagined* than the self-inflicted torment of the Chinese.

The exceptional quality of the Chinese is confirmed, it seems, by the adjective that precedes "proof": "better" becomes, thanks to the "no" that precedes it, an idiomatic superlative. But this grammatical exceptionalism undoes itself just as it breaches Chinese shores: by the end of Nathan's sentence, we learn that the hyperbolic pleasure in cruelty of the Chinese illustrates Nietzsche's judgment on all of "mankind." Thus are the exceptional Chinese returned to the family of man, their torment an instance of a more general human rule. A rule to which the sentence's Chinese find themselves subjected even as they, in the best imaginable way, instantiate it: from the outskirts of the human, they assure the reliability of the category.[16]

[15] Andrew Nathan, *China's Transition* (New York, 1997), 15.

[16] The connection between Chinese history and cruelty that Nathan outlines is an impolite version of the claim that there is a special connection between Chinese culture and violence. Note for instance the parenthetical that follows the opening lines of Stevan Harrell's introduction to *Violence in China:* "Why does a culture that condemns violence, that plays down the glory of military exploits,

This is not a new story: the movement whereby the exceptional object, rejected, excluded, and marginal, comes through its very marginality to provide the support for the structure from which it has been removed lies at the very core of philosophy, and its critique belongs to the tradition called "deconstruction." Located in a worldly perspective, stated with reference to a combination of geography and truth, the process through which the particular example guarantees the universal category is precisely what I intend to name with the word "ecliptic": the Chinese serving as a measure of the species. But Nathan's sentence above is also important because it presents us with the other major feature of the discursive network that brings together China, sympathy, and the universal subject of modernity, namely the idea that the Chinese are unusually or especially cruel. The historian Jonathan Spence identifies the European origins of that proposition in the middle of the sixteenth century, when he finds a Portuguese traveler reporting that the Chinese have a remarkable capacity for cruelty.[17]

---

awards its highest prestige to literary, rather than martial, figures, and seeks harmony over all other values, in fact display such frequency and variety of violent behavior, that is, of the use of physical force against persons? (Whether Chinese culture is more violent than other cultures is difficult to judge, but it is visibly not less violent than many.)" (*Violence in China: Essays in Culture and Counterculture*, ed. Jonathan N. Lipman and Stevan Harrell [Albany, 1990], 1.). What is so strange about this parenthesis is that it gives what would otherwise be a book on the sources and structures of violence in Chinese culture—a perfectly reasonable project, if it were the sort of thing people studied in all cultures—the comparative edge hinted at but unelaborated in the first sentence. The difference between such a project and something like David Der-wei Wang's *The Monster that is History* is that Wang frames the history of violence in China within a larger philosophical and cultural framework that keeps the Chinese example from becoming exceptional (*The Monster That is History: History, Violence, and Fictional Writing in Twentieth-Century China* [Berkeley, 2004]).

[17] Spence discusses narratives by the sailor Galeote Pereira and the Dominican monk Gaspar da Cruz in his book, *The Chan's Great Continent: China in Western Minds* (New York, 1988). Pereira, a soldier and trader, spent four years in Chinese prisons after being caught smuggling goods off the coast of Fujian in 1549. His account of his treatment is, all things considered, fairly even-handed. But consider the use made of that same material in da Cruz's 1569 *Treatise, in which the things of China are related at great length, with their particularities, as likewise of the kingdom of Ormuz,* which gives its chapter on Chinese judicial punishments, whose content is taken almost entirely from the accounts of Pereira and his fellows, the following subtitle: "this is a notable chapter" (*he capitulo notauel*). Given that no other chapter in his account has a subtitle at all, the chapter is indeed "notable," just as much for its subtitle as for the way in which it raises the emotional stakes of Pereira's reports and the critique of the Chinese far beyond the levels apparent in the earlier narrative. The difference between Pereira and da Cruz may not be, however, the site of a historical break or rupture beyond which the take on the Chinese relation to suffering is inevitably negative; it seems, rather, an early example of cultural intolerance not yet fully hooked into, as are the texts I examine in this book, the discourse on sympathy and humanity that so consistently framed discussions of China from the late eighteenth century onward.

The stereotype has been reinforced over the years in a wide variety of genres and figures, including illustrated guides to Chinese punishments, photographs of Chinese executions, sociological accounts of "Chinese characteristics," Harry Houdini's performances of his "Chinese Water Torture" box, cartoonish villains like Ming the Merciless or the notorious Doctor Fu Manchu, and exposés of the *laogai* prison system in the People's Republic of China, to give only a partial accounting.[18] Its mythology presents us with evidence for the generalized perception of a difference in cultural relationships to sympathy and suffering, the representation of an abyss above which civilization and barbarism sway in a precarious balance.

In the countless reproductions of this stereotype, which circulated with only the barest regard for the reality to which they referred, we witness the West affirming the phatic and ceaselessly necessary production of its unique difference, naturalizing the "Chinese" position on cruelty to the point that it could, by the end of the nineteenth century, be imagined to speak in its own defense. So that in 1899 a Chinese torturer appearing in a French novel could answer "back" to Europe on cruelty's behalf, grousing to a European visitor to his bloody workshop about the damage done by "occidental snobbism that invades us, with its ironclads, its rapid-fire canons and long-range rifles, its electricity, its explosives, in short, everything that makes death collective, administrative, and bureaucratic."[19] The complaint, which appears in the anarchist Octave Mirbeau's *Torture Garden* (*Le Jardin des supplices*), suggests that one way for anticapitalist anarchism to make common cause with a Romantic defense of craft labor against a reformist, sympathetic era that had outlawed torture, remade the prisons and hospitals,

[18] In *Death by a Thousand Cuts,* Timothy Brook, Jérôme Bourgon, and Gregory Blue note the long history of Chinese cruelty in the West and remark that especially in the post–1945 period, jokes about the Chinese affinity for torture allowed the postwar generation to distance themselves from an allegedly premodern past (Cambridge, Mass., 2008). On Houdini, see Ruth Brandon, *The Life and Many Deaths of Harry Houdini* (New York, 1993); on *laogai* prisons, remark the subtitle of Harry Wu and George Vescey's *Troublemaker: One Man's Crusade Against Chinese Cruelty* (New York, 1996); on Fu Manchu and other stereotypes, see Sheng-Mei Ma, *The Deathly Embrace: Orientalism and Asian American Identity* (Minneapolis, 2000) and Robert G. Lee, *Orientals: Asian Americans in Popular Culture* (Philadelphia, 1999). The other examples are discussed at more length in the chapters to come.

[19] Octave Mirbeau, *Le Jardin des supplices* (Paris, 1957), 187 (translation mine). The torturer goes on with great pleasure to describe to his guests a torture he'd invented in which a frenzied rat eats its way into the body of the condemned, before complaining that a panel of judges had denied its use: "I was bringing them something infinitely glorious . . . a unique example of its type, and capable of firing the imaginations of our greatest artists . . . but they didn't want it . . . [. . .] These are the symptoms of our decadence . . . Ah! We are a defeated people, a dead people! The Japanese can come . . . we can no longer resist them . . . Farewell, China!" (193, translation mine).

substituted machine guns for crossbows, and replaced the festival scene of the public execution with the prospect of total panoptic sovereignty, was to travel through the realm of the imagination Europe called "China."[20]

The justifications for soft imperialism and modernization create histories of the rectification of cruelty, its socialization and control, and its elimination as a legitimate form of the expression of state power. As Mirbeau's torturer suggests, the bureaucratic modernization of violence and the increased importance of sympathy reached well beyond the boundaries of Europe, as European colonizers instituted policies in other countries designed to adjust local norms relating to violence and suffering, or simply asserted in the field of international diplomacy the philosophical fact of their sympathetic difference.[21] Talal Asad has referred to this practice as "humanizing the world," the process whereby a locally particular relationship to sympathy and suffering universalized itself in the guise of a civilizing modernity. The elimination in the colonies of "customs the European rulers considered cruel," Asad argues, derived from the need "to impose what they considered civilized standards of justice and humanity on a subject population—that is, the desire to create new human subjects," this latter task in the elevation of barbarians to global citizenship one of the major side projects of the imperialist adventure. (Allegedly humanitarian efforts were also, sometimes, genuinely humanitarian in intention or in effect; this is history, not a cartoon, and its engagement with the fact and the idea of violence is complex.) As Asad remarks, the forms of sympathy and humanity so allowed did not require the elimination of all pain (lamentably, civilization so often has to be imposed at gunpoint) but rather the eradication of those kinds of suffering deemed barbaric or gratuitous, and the retention of "suffering that was necessary to the process of

[20] Let us not pass over in silence, however, the ways torture becomes erotic in both Mirbeau's novel and in the period more generally. Karen Haltunnen has explicitly linked the rise of a European interest in forms of sadomasochistic pornography to rise in humanitarian sensibility of the late eighteenth century in "Humanitarianism and the Pornography of Pain in Anglo-American Culture," *The American Historical Review* 100.2 (April 1995). My penultimate clause refers to the well-known opening to Foucault's *Discipline and Punish*, where the difference between the public drawing and quartering of Damiens the regicide and the private, reformist incarcerations of a few decades later marks the shift from the feudal to the modern state (*Discipline and Punish: The Birth of the Prison*, trans. Alan Sheridan [New York, 1979]).

[21] Even as, in Europe and the United States, the increasing importance of sympathy led to the production of "sensationalist" images and narratives in the penny press, as though the disappearance of torture as a form of state punishment simply forced a reappearance of scenes of torture marked as illegal. Haltunnen reproduces an 1848 woodcut of "Michael McGarvey beating his wife to death" whose appeal is as much to voyeuristic pleasure as to sympathetic outrage (313).

realizing one's humanity—that is, pain that was adequate to its end, not wasteful pain."[22]

Because, as Asad argues, "pain does not simply constitute irrefutable evidence of the corporeal ground of experience, [but] is also a way of constituting the epistemological status of the body," what was at stake in the transformation of pain and suffering—and what was *lost* in that transformation, very much in the sense that Mirbeau articulates it—was one particular use of the body as an epistemological heuristic, as, that is, a way of knowing the world and a way of grasping the body's relation to it.[23] Whether the delegitimation of that way of knowing constitutes a tragedy is not the question here. Important rather is an understanding of suffering, its recognition and its classification, as epistemological processes, *as mechanisms for the production of social truth and for the location of self in relation to world*, and thus an awareness of the body's paradoxical status as both "mode and object of knowing."[24] When normative assumptions about the proper relation to sympathy and suffering dominate a cultural discourse as completely as do the ones that drive the modern discourses on humanity and human rights, it is easy to lose sight of the cultural and historical production of those relations, easy to imagine that these universal norms have allowed us finally to reach the unmediated ground of humanity's corporeal existence, from which one might then deduce the laws and habits that ought to govern ordinary life. Looking at the way that this network of sympathy, suffering, and exchange has developed returns its cultural project and epistemological implications to the foreground of thought. This not simply to criticize that project for being particular, or complicit with imperialism or global capital, as though there were today a relation to sympathy or suffering that could somehow operate outside the framework of cultural particularity or the history of imperialism and globalization. The point is rather to understand how these mechanisms operate *within* the fields of imperialism and globalization, and thence to grasp how their production through a variety of cultural objects and in a number of different cultural moments has shaped the thought patterns of the world in which we currently live. If, as Asad suggests, modernity is first and foremost a "*project*—or rather, a

[22] Talal Asad, *Formations of the Secular: Christianity, Islam, Modernity* (Stanford, 2003), 109, 111. For an articulation of the way the logic of "necessary pain" appears in decisions made by the International Monetary Fund, see Joseph Stiglitz, *Globalization and its Discontents* (New York, 2003), 119–22.

[23] Asad, 92.

[24] Susan Stewart, *On Longing: Narratives of the Miniature, the Gigantic, the Souvenir, the Collection* (Durham, N.C., 1993), 131.

series of interlinked projects—that certain people in power seek to achieve," then the stakes of thinking through the form of humanity in whose name that project has been carried out should have profound implications for the collective and incorporated futures that we can imagine for the planet and the species.[25]

Nowhere have these implications been clearer in recent years than in the "Asian values debate" on human rights. This debate, which represents the "most prominent contemporary attack on what for the last two decades most states and human rights activists have taken to be authoritative international standards," originated in the early 1990s from the leadership of three prominent East Asian economic success stories—Malaysia, Singapore, and the People's Republic of China.[26] Despite a general recognition that the initial impetus for the debate stemmed largely from attempts by authoritarian regimes to justify their continued rejection of international standards regarding political speech and legal protections, by the late 1990s it was the case, as Joanne R. Bauer and Daniel A. Bell write in their introduction to *The East Asian Challenge for Human Rights*, that "East Asian" views on human rights were "contributing to a genuine dialogue that goes to the heart of the debate [on] the meaning of 'universality' and the areas of justifiable [cultural and political] difference."[27] The debate has since drawn in such international organizations as the United Nations, local and transnational nongovernmental organizations, philosophers, historians, and political theorists, and grown to encompass discussions on whether temporary restrictions on civil and political rights can be justified by the need for the expansion of social and economic ones, on the possibilities of building a transnational Rawlsian consensus, and on the contributions Confucian values might make to a new and more fully universal definition of the human being, particularly one that abandons the weaknesses of Western-style "individualism."[28] The most powerful international expression of the debate's geopolitical

[25] Asad, 13.

[26] Jack Donnelly, "Human Rights and Asian Values: A Defense of 'Western' Universalism," in *The East Asian Challenge for Human Rights*, Joanne R. Bauer and Daniel A. Bell, eds. (Cambridge, 1999), 64.

[27] Bauer and Bell, 4. Errol Mendes also refers to the debate as "more apparent than real" as he searches for common ground between East and West (he finds it in Canada), but the fact that he participates in the debate at all suggests that though it may be unreal in the arena of international political maneuvering, it is real enough in the realm of political philosophy ("Asian Values and Human Rights: Letting the Tigers Free," in *Asia Pacific Face-Off*, eds. Fen Hampson, Maureen Molot, and Martin Rudner [Ottawa, 1997], 176.).

[28] On Rawls, see Onuma Yasuaki, "Toward an Intercivilizational Approach to Human Rights," in Bauer and Bell; on Confucian values, see Joseph Chan, "A Confucian Perspective on Rights for

legitimacy was the 1993 Bangkok Declaration on Human Rights, jointly signed by the governments of the entire Asian region, which asserted that "while human rights are universal in nature, they must be considered in the context of a dynamic and evolving process of international norm-setting, bearing in mind the significance of national and regional particularities and various historical, cultural, and religious backgrounds"—a phrase whose initial "while" opens a substantial philosophical attack on the universality it goes on to affirm.[29] The declaration's effects on the concept of human rights today have been extremely powerful: it has inaugurated the only significant contemporary critique of the concept of human rights to emerge from an explicitly *national* or *regional* perspective, and it has articulated from that perspective a theory of a universal, culturally located, and post-Western subject of modernity.[30]

There exists, I will say right now, surprising no one, no such subject except in the imagination. But the imaginative possibility of such a subject, the idea that there is or could be a kind of human or a kind of humanity that would allow us

---

Contemporary China," in Bauer and Bell, and Tu Weiming, "Implications of the Rise of 'Confucian' East Asia," *Daedalus* 129.1 (Winter 2000). Tu in particular picks up on critiques made by former Singapore Prime Minister (PM) Lee Kuan Yew and former Malaysian PM Mahathir bin Mohamed about the social problems allegedly produced by Western individualism, writing that a need for a new theory of "togetherness" is obvious "in light of the danger of social disintegration of all levels, from family to nation" (179).

[29]The Bangkok Declaration was issued in March 1993 as the Asian region's contribution to the Second World Conference on Human Rights, which was held in Vienna in June 1993. It is reprinted in *Negotiating Culture and Human Rights*, eds. Lynda S. Bell, Andrew J. Nathan, and Ilan Peleg (New York, 2001), and I am citing from its appearance there (394). For a reading of the declaration as far more coincident with existing universalist notions of human rights than it initially appeared to be, see Michael Dowdle's essay in that volume; for more on these "Asian values debates" in general, see also the essays in Bauer and Bell; Michael C. Davis, ed., *Human Rights and Chinese Values: Legal, Philosophical, and Political Perspectives* (Hong Kong, 1995); and Chad Hansen, "Do Human Rights Apply to China? A Normative Analysis of Cultural Difference," in *Constructing China: The Interaction of Culture and Economics*, eds. Kenneth G. Lieberthal, Shuen-fu Lin, and Ernest P. Young (Ann Arbor, 1997).

[30]The other major challenge to the concept of universal human rights comes from feminism; see for instance Robin West's influential "Jurisprudence and Gender," which argues that the presumptive human subject of law is, by virtue of its theorization as physically separate from other such subjects, exclusively masculine (*The University of Chicago Law Review* 55.1 [Winter 1988]). Feminist critiques of human rights also appear within the governmental framework of the United Nations, as in the Fourth World Conference on Women, held in Beijing in 1995. Lynn Hunt's history of human rights is sensitive to this terrain, while ignoring the Bangkok Declaration (and indeed the question of cultural difference) entirely (*Inventing Human Rights: A History* [New York, 2007]). On the relation between "women" and "Asian values," however, see Norani Othman, "Grounding Human Rights Arguments in Non-Western Cultures: *Shari'a* and the Citizenship Rights of Women in a Modern Islamic State," in Bauer and Bell, and Anne-Marie Hilsdon, ed., *Human Rights and Gender Politics: Asia-Pacific Perspectives* (London, 2000).

all finally to get along—if everyone would just stop being such assholes—remains a vital part of contemporary political life at the tactical and philosophical levels.[31] Such a subject, whose invention and articulation would gather all cultural differences under the umbrella of a universal and "capital-H" Humanity has until recently been the exclusive dream of the European Enlightenment, its invention one of the major achievements of the last few centuries which, having seen the violent and deliberate deaths of human beings in appalling numbers, finally produced the near-universal adoption of the United Nations' Declaration of Universal Human Rights in 1948. The construction of a *theory* of human being-ness that could and should apply to every single member of the species relied upon, as Lynn Hunt has recently argued, the concomitant invention of a new sort of human subject defined by an "imagined empathy" toward the suffering of others of the type we see developing in Smith and Balzac. From the historical dawning of this human subject to the present day marks only a fractional shift in the planet's geologic time. For the evolved apes subject to the declarative lightning bolts of 1776, 1789, or 1948, however, the moment has been defined by ceaseless efforts and ferment, hypocrisies and disappointments, in the project of thinking the human subject defined by such an empathy, and, with greater difficulty, that of living up to the promises projected forward by such a thought.

It may feel like a historical accident that the foremost revisionary challenge to these European promises in the last two decades comes from precisely that geographic region whose importance to the development of the concept of the human it is *The Hypothetical Mandarin*'s task to demonstrate. But it feels like less of one if one recognizes that the "Asian values" whose legitimacy is asserted in the human rights field gain almost all of their rhetorical force from the economic success of the East Asian countries in the late 1980s and early 1990s. The structure of the contemporary debate thus reproduces the one that allowed Europe to export its culture through cultural and military imperialism over the last few centuries, and not incidentally to place its values at the center of the 1948 Universal Declaration: the right to assert the potential

[31] As should be the case, despite the criticisms leveled at the concept and its pretensions. I follow Inoue Tatsuo in believing that "sovereignty needs human rights not just as a functional compensation for what it undermined but also as a positive justification for its emergence," and thus that in a world defined by state sovereignty the language of human rights remains crucial to both the rhetoric and thinking of anyone seeking to abridge or limit that sovereignty in any way ("Liberal Democracy and Asian Orientalism," in Bauer and Bell, 30.). As for what might happen if sovereignty as we understand it disappears, see Michael Hardt and Antonio Negri, *Multitude* (New York, 2004).

universality of one's cultural values derives almost directly from the perceived ability of those values to sustain economic development, and thus, given the history we have, on a relationship to capitalism. (This is why culturalist arguments against civil and political rights made by third-worldist movements in the 1960s, or three other recent declarations—the Cairo Declaration of 1990, the Tunis Declaration of 1991, and the San José Declaration of 1993—did not generate anything like the philosophical response that the Bangkok Declaration did.) Recognizing the degree to which the legitimacy of any given piece of state-generated human rights discourse relies on the success of its economy allows us to see that the entire question of universal rights cannot be thought outside the process of industrial and postindustrial modernization.[32] From that larger perspective the apparent civilizational divide separating the two behemoths, East and West, facing each other across the Viennese tables of the 1993 World Conference on Human Rights, coalesces into a deeper affinity produced by the "subtending line of force of global capital" that joins them, as Pheng Cheah has argued, "*against* the possibility of other alternatives of development, feminist or ecological-subalternist."[33]

Noting the coincidental development of the concepts of human rights with the dramatic historical increase in the range and power of capital, Cheah goes on to remark that the concept of the "human" grounding rights talk takes as its most fundamental value the inexchangeability of the human being. This inexchangeability—a resistance to commodification that allows the human being to retain a fundamental (or "inalienable") separation from the circulation of capital—was framed by Immanuel Kant in his 1785 *Groundwork of the Metaphysics of Morals* as a question of the difference between price and dignity: "What is related to general inclinations and needs has a *market price* [*Marktpreis*]," he noted, "but that which constitutes the condition under which alone something can be an end in itself has not merely a relative worth, that is, a price, but an inner worth [*einen innern*

[32] Which explains why the debate faltered at the geopolitical level following the 1997 Asian financial crisis. For a longer discussion of the relation between the economics of international trade and the history of human rights, see Susan Koshy, "From Cold War to Trade War: Neocolonialism and Human Rights," *Social Text* 58 (Spring 1999).

[33] Pheng Cheah, *Inhuman Conditions: On Cosmopolitanism and Human Rights* (Cambridge, 2007), 148–49; further references in the text are cited as *IC*. Let us remark one crucial feature of the "Asian values debate" that retains the East/West divide even under the guise of a mutual recognition: it consistently opposes Asian *values* to Western *philosophy*. Such a structure picks up (probably inadvertently) on the *zhong xue wei ti, xi xue wei yong* (Chinese learning for essential things [*ti*], Western learning for practical matters [*yong*]) formula adopted by Chinese modernizers in the early twentieth century, though its repetition in this case seems as much tragedy as farce.

Wert], that is, *dignity*" (*IC*, 155).[34] For Cheah the presence of the discourse of the market at the core of the theorization of the universal subject of modernity suggests that the entire notion of human rights is caught up from the beginning in the market to which it is so often rhetorically opposed. The history of human rights, in which the human being's inalienable distance from the process of exchange functions as the counterweight to the ever-broadening commodification of human life, is in such a conception not so much the refusal of global capitalism as one of its dialectical supports: what Cheah rather bleakly calls capitalism's "product-effect" (*IC*, 166).[35]

The intimacy between the rhetoric of capitalism and the Asian values controversy appears most visibly when political figures argue that the adoption of the full civil and political rights agenda favored by the West would hamper the economic growth and development needed to provide a way out of poverty and access to the other universally recognized social goods necessary in modern states (schools, medical care, and the like).[36] Consider former Singapore Prime Minister Lee Kuan Yew: "*It is not enough to have sympathy*... Freedom, human rights, democracy, when you are hungry, when you lack development, when you lack basic services, does not add up to much" (*IC*, 233; emphasis

[34]This distinction between price and dignity should recall Smith's speculations on the Chinese earthquake, with which it shares the potential exchangeability of human life and human suffering. By the time Chateaubriand presents, probably for the first time in print, the dilemma of the fortune and the mandarin, the scene of moral decision has all the philosophical force of a Kantian imperative. No matter how much he imagined the mandarin afflicted with disease or sorrows, in order to make it easier to kill him, Chateaubriand writes, he "heard in the depths of my heart a voice crying out so strongly against the simple thought of such a supposition, that I could not doubt even for an instant the reality of conscience" (*Le Génie du christianisme*, as cited in Keates, 505 [translation mine]). In Chateaubriand's text, the wrongness of the proposed exchange between the fortune and the mandarin reproduces exactly the difference between *Marktpreis* and *inner Wert* that allows Kant to establish the human being's ontological resistance to commodification—even if he happens to be far away, or sick, or Chinese.

[35]I would not be quite as bleak as Cheah. By reversing his point of view, we can see that the idea of the "market" as we understand it operates in the social imaginary as a dialectical effect of the notion of the "human" that is technically excluded from it; as well to say, then, that the market is humanism's "objectivity-effect" as that humanity is the market's "product-effect." We are dealing here not with a base (the market) and a superstructure (the human) but with a system structured around a mutually constitutive dialectic, of which the distinction between economic base and humanist superstructure is a *feature* of a system that may not have constitutive *parts*.

[36]This is the thinking behind the Bangkok Declaration's investment in recognizing the "interdependence and indivisibility of economic, social, cultural, civil and political rights, and the need to give equal emphasis to all categories of human rights" (Bell et al 392); the first three categories aim to undermine the centrality of the latter two to Western rights talk. The United States remains one of the few nations to have refused to sign the International Covenant on Social, Economic, and Cultural Rights adopted by the United Nations in 1965.

mine).[37] Though "not much of a case *against* democratic rights can be established on the basis of their allegedly negative effects on economic growth," as Amartya Sen has argued, the general sense that human rights grounded in sympathy and economic growth have *something* to do with each other appears on the American side of this divide as well, where the assumption of the Clinton administration seemed to be that the East Asian economies would grow their way out of authoritarianism into fully "civilized" democracies sometime shortly after enough people had television and ate at McDonalds.[38] It is this last position that has been undermined by the philosophical and political arguments "for" Asian values that, by suggesting that economic growth is possible without what the West calls "freedom" (never mind McDonalds), attempt to separate economic from noneconomic modernization, the capitalist legacy of the Enlightenment from its philosophical one. This new Asian modernity would in theory derive its rights and its theory of the human from a "nondichotomous thinking" that encourages "organic solidarity" and emphasizes the role of the "family as the basic unit of society."[39] The conjunction of its fantasy of development with the one originating in New York and Washington I take to be evidence of what Arif Dirlik means when he writes that the idea of alternative or multiple modernities "legitimizes the most fundamental assumptions of modernization by rendering them globally valid, forecloses serious consideration of alternatives to modernization, and reintroduces Eurocentrism by the back door," since the concept's culturally pluralist pretensions are impoverished by the paucity of economic choices it offers.[40] In a post-Fordist world, everyone can have whatever

[37] As Koshy has noted that statements like these offer "an alibi for authoritarianism" does not change the fact that they also expose "Western pseudouniversialism" (24).

[38] Amartya Sen, "Human Rights and Economic Achievements," in Bauer and Bell, 93. The word "civilized" comes from Jack Donnelly, who reinforces the universalist, progressivist position when he writes that "a society in which the self must always be categorically subordinated to other simply cannot be considered 'civilized' in the late twentieth century" (Bauer and Bell, 78). As for McDonalds and the televisions, let us update the dream for this century's American bourgeoisie: locavore cuisine and wireless hotspots.

[39] Tu Wei-ming, 205. Elsewhere, Tu writes of the Chinese contribution to a mode of national belonging for the twenty-first century: "The modern West's dichotomous world view (spirit/matter, mind/body, physical/mental, sacred/profane, creator/creature, God/man, subject/object) is diametrically opposed to the Chinese holistic mode of thinking," a sentence whose own reliance on dichotomy ("diametrically opposed") is curiously, well, Western (201).

[40] Arif Dirlik, *Global Modernity: Modernity in the Age of Global Capitalism* (Boulder, 2007), 14. For a useful introduction to "multiple modernities," see Stephen R. Graubard, "Preface to the Issue 'Multiple Modernities,'" *Daedalus* 129:1 (Winter 2000), as well as the other essays in that issue.

modernity they'd like, as long as what they'd like is a modernity of the capitalist type (which is to say: modernity).

Though this book does not directly address the "Asian values debate," the historical work it pursues ought to modify some of the premises of the debate as it is currently articulated. Most important, the sense that East Asia has only recently arrived on the scene of human rights discourse is undermined by the recognition that though it is only in the 1990s that East Asia enters the debate as a *speaking subject*, it has for a much longer time been one of the debate's privileged referential *objects*. Though the difference in grammatical position matters, it is nonetheless a misreading of the historical record to imagine that an Asian "arrival" on the scene of philosophical modernity dates back only to the moment when it acquires the economic right to speak. The appearance of the mandarin and the "Asian values debate" at either end of this historical process—and indeed continually throughout it—suggests rather that any attempt to seriously consider the relation between China and human rights must begin at the moment when China first enters Enlightenment discourse on the human, with the recognition that the Asian "challenge" to human rights has been operating on the *inside* of a larger discourse on humanity for at least two centuries now, and that this discourse exerts some major effects on the ways that the Asian values debate is articulated and received. At least in the history of the imagination, which is the history of life lived in an ideological world. Which is the kind of history that concerns us here.

4. The Example-Effect

Though all books address, one way or another, the theories of culture, of evidence, or of historical causality that hold them together, such an address seems especially necessary for this one, where from the beginning the relationship between the book's major historical elements—sympathy, the human, and China—has been shadowed by the potentially accidental, coincidental relationship that links China to the former two. It would be needlessly reductive to assert that no difference exists between the invention of the modern human, on one hand, and its references to China, on the other, between the well-nigh ontological importance of the primary historical event and the rhetorical or cultural material that accompanies it. Instead, it seems crucial to recognize that whatever twines these objects does so only insofar as it recognizes and takes advantage of the "generic" difference between them; to recognize, that is, that the grammar of this relationship depends on the differing cultural and epistemological roles played by the *idea* ("the invention of the sympathetic human") and the *example* to which it refers ("China"). An explicit recognition of that difference will be needed if the book is to tell the story of what is after all an imaginary and seemingly arbitrary relation, even if that relation continues to haunt, in the precarious lives of those hypothetical Chinese victims, contemporary accounts of the future of human rights and the political possibilities of globalization.[41]

A book that claimed that China was simply extraneous or supplemental to the main direction of, say, Smith's theory of moral philosophy or Balzac's characterization of Rastignac—or that simply ignored the appearance of China in these contexts, which is how most people handle it—would have a lot less work to do. Here we confront the fact that though the exemplarity of examples is a problem for any work that relies on them, for a book that is precisely *about* the history of a certain kind of example and a certain kind of exemplarity (the kind, that is, that does not "feel" exemplary) the question of the example becomes a particular and pressing problem. No dawn for this darkness can appear solely as a second-order, metadiscursive discussion of the generic problem, or as an attempt to argue theoretically for the importance and reality of cultural connections and social imaginaries, even if it is clear that part of the issue here has to do with the epistemological status of the overdetermined, overimbricated cultural object and its relation to history. Because the very heart of the method stems from the difference between the "first" and "second" order of things, the "truly" historical and the "merely" coincidental, and thus the degree to which any discussion can or should be held historically or philosophically responsible for the qualities of its content—whether, that is, one can separate something like the central or

[41] Hunt's 2007 history of the human rights, for instance, refers to Smith's earthquake as it imagines the challenges facing the future of that powerful, utopian discourse (210). Likewise, K. Anthony Appiah's 2006 *Cosmopolitanism*, whose goal it is to articulate an intellectual and political "attitude" toward this era which continually announces itself to us as global, makes Balzac's mandarin a feature of its final chapter on "Kindness to Strangers," though it does not mention his Chineseness (*Cosmopolitanism: Ethics in a World of Strangers* [New York, 2006], especially 155–58; for a discussion of the status of the philosophical example in that book, see Bruce Robbins, "Cosmpolitanism: New and Newer," *boundary 2* 34:3 [2007], 59). Another recent philosophical discussion of the mandarin that makes no mention of his Chineseness appears in Iddo Landau's "To Kill a Mandarin," *Philosophy and Literature* 29 (2005). Only Keates in 1966 seems to find the mandarin's national origin interesting, writing that for Europeans in the nineteenth century "the rich citizen of the Middle Kingdom was yet a citizen of an alien and *remote* society; indeed, the plurality of the worlds discovered in the Renaissance has still to be fused into a new unitary world. The only unity is moral, *in the limited sense* that our Chinaman-mandarin belongs to humanity [emphasis mine], and a crime or sin against him, as it concerns the *mens rea*, would be as grievous as one against our next door neighbor" (504).

necessary features of an articulation of the nature of human sympathy from the apparently arbitrary choice of a Chinese mandarin as its avatar—then any discussion that would simply articulate as though at a *remove* from the argument the theory that subtends it would wind up reproducing the very problem it meant to diagnose. If your point is that the rhetoric of an idea matters—that the choice of examples, for instance, makes a difference to the philosophy of it, or that a set of referential habits and historical occurrences that might not have happened nonetheless exert some kind of effect on the shape of the habits or histories in which they appear—then it would seem especially short-sighted to make your claim while holding it fully separate from the examples that contextualize it and that make it comprehensible. Or, to put things more plainly: you can't argue that the *example* matters to the *idea* without acknowledging that the *examples* you use to show that examples matter to the idea matter to the *idea* that examples matter to the idea. (The fact that China functions as a particular kind of example adds another layer of complexity to this project.[42])

In what follows, I will be calling the force of Chinese exemplarity its "example-effect." The phrase gestures toward Roland Barthes' well-known notion of the fictional "reality-effect," which argues that details that serve no narrative function—details that are seemingly useless—have a special importance in the development of modern fictional realism, since they testify to the presence of a world out "there," beyond the narrative necessities of a given story, that subtends the novelistic world.[43] Likewise the example-effect produced by "China" creates the *possibility* of philosophy by appearing as a seemingly arbitrary historical or political detail whose value lies precisely in its having "nothing" to do with the philosophical material it illustrates. Why should we pay attention to the fact that the earthquake happens in China, when the real issue is that Smith is inventing the moral tradition that will change Europe, and everyone knows he was writing about the Lisbon earthquake anyway? And the mandarin, well, he could just as well have been Japanese, Aztec, or Lithuanian—in fact, in an early children's novel

[42] As it does in the American context, where attempts to discuss anti-Asian racism run into the fact that once you get past the 1960s so much of the Asian stereotype is positive; to think about the history of Asian Americans as an instance of American race relations thus requires thinking about how the particular relation of Asian Americans to exemplarity itself constitutes part of the history that one wishes to address. One way to frame that address *thematically* is the idea of the "model minority"; for an overview of that subject, see Robert Lee, *Orientals: Asian Americans in Popular Culture* (Philadelphia, 1999), 145–203.

[43] Roland Barthes, "The Reality Effect," in *The Rustle of Language*, trans. Richard Howard (Berkeley, 1989).

of Balzac's, that same hypothetical appears, and the person being murdered is from New Holland![44] Let's focus on the real issues, and drop all this cultural nonsense. . . .

Well, yes, kind of. But if the murdered person's nationality didn't matter, why did Balzac bother changing it? And how do we account for the actual history of the planet, in which the mandarin hypothetical becomes a phrase common enough to enter the dictionaries? Likewise for Smith's earthquake: if he was thinking of Lisbon, why didn't he say so? And why hasn't his mention of an Indian earthquake in *The Wealth of Nations* (1776) caused contemporary philosophers to cite and recite it as they attempt to think through questions of moral distance?[45] And why has it been so easy, somehow, to perform that same dismissive operation on all kinds of historical interferences produced by East Asia, including, for instance, the importance of Asian Americans to the history of the United States (which has only recently begun to be recognized[46]), the series of technological innovations at the heart of modern seafaring, warfare, and media culture, Asia's role in the economic transformation caused by modern capitalism, and so forth? Against the temptation to simply dismiss the Chineseness in this or any other instance—a dismissal that can only be made on the grounds of a sureness about what "matters" for real history that I do not share—this book traces the history of a particular social and intellectual form: the example or instance that has traditionally been considered extraneous to the ideas it illustrates and explains.[47] To take this form seriously requires among other things taking it seriously *as an example*: recognizing that part of how it functions in

[44] See Ronai, who notes, however, that it is only with the word "mandarin," "through its association with exotic treasures," that the figure passes into common usage (521; translation mine).

[45] India has a "very singular government in which every member of the administration wishes to get out of the country, and consequently to have done with the government, as soon as he can, and to whose interest, the day after he has left it and carried his whole fortune with him, it is perfectly indifferent though the whole country was swallowed up by an earthquake," Smith wrote (New York, 2000), 692.

[46] See for instance Erika Lee, *At America's Gates: Chinese Immigration during the Exclusion Era, 1882–1943* (Chapel Hill, N.C., 2003), and Mae Ngai, *Impossible Subjects: Illegal Aliens and the Making of Modern America* (Princeton, N.J., 2005).

[47] This kind of exemplarity is intimately connected to what I've been calling the ecliptic. It's precisely at the boundary line of the universal or the horizon that the particular example slides most easily into the general, as, for instance, in the ways that discussion about the sun (which is, after all, a particular star) tends by the very fact of calling it "the" sun to make it a universalizing figure and the absolute horizon of all human experience. Presumably people living in orbits around the three stars that make up Alpha Centauri would mean something completely different when they referred to "the sun."

culture is precisely as the kind of thing that does not matter very much to the generality it illustrates, and which is consumed or interpreted by the vast majority of readers as the kind of arbitrary reference that might just as well have referred to something else.

Much of the work to elaborate the significance of the example-effect happens in the book's first chapter, which involves a sustained attention to one recent discussion of an experience of Chinese suffering. As that chapter will make clear, I conclude that no ethical argument about an experience that arrives to us as a text can be made in a manner that separates it from its examples, and thus that any evidentiary argument belongs at least partially to the examples on which it draws—*even or perhaps especially when those examples present themselves as arbitrary.* Such an approach has some interesting effects on the role of the examples themselves, since it is only through a sustained critical engagement with their particular language, their historical context, and the forms of their mediatic circulation that the arguments acquire the momentum they need to theorize themselves "away" from the examples, without for all that ever escaping their gravitational pull. The examples in this book thus acquire a strange mixture of particularity and generality. Though such a mixture obtains for all examples everywhere—the function of examples is, after all, to be exemplary—in this case, I have tried to halt the normal and normalizing transition from the particular to the general, the instance to the instantiation, that makes the example that which "illustrates, or forms a particular case of, a general principle, rule, state of things."[48] The chapters that follow suspend that process at precisely the moment at which the individual anecdote, citation, sentence, or episode threatens to cross over into general principle, there to be replaced by a rule or state of things that effectively erases the anecdote's or citation's importance *qua* itself—that is, its existence as something other than an example of some idea. The examples thus tend to *exemplify* the claims I am making in this introduction without becoming for all that *exemplary*, without constituting the total apprehension of the cultural network or habit whose story the book writes. Instead, they indicate points at which that network can be said to have "touched down" with particular force, while retaining a remainder that has in some cases very little to do with their exemplification, but whose presence must be respected if one wishes to avoid dismissing that remainder as accidental and thus irrelevant to the general project. If that incompleteness can be recuperated for the book as a whole, it is because it

[48] *Oxford English Dictionary*, example, n., 1.a.

figures (though necessarily incompletely) the general awkwardness of the Chinese reference in European history, which it thus attempts to think in terms of its example-effect.[49]

5. Outline

The chapters follow. The first presents an attempt to work out the principles organizing the methodology of the book through an example particular to it. A reading of Stephen Greenblatt's analysis of the 1606 account of the torture of a Chinese goldsmith in Java accompanies a discussion of the status of the new historicist "anecdote." The anecdote's relation to language and history has allowed it to become the privileged epistemological form of much contemporary literary criticism. In a gesture typical of the method of the book as a whole, the chapter applies to the theory of the anecdote it finds the principles of anecdotality it articulates and generates from that operation some guidelines for the methodology of the subsequent chapters: the evidentiary material that sustains any general or theoretical conclusion (be it anecdote or description, novel or poem, photograph, medical case study, or union pamphlet) must exert both formal and thematic pressures on the theory that it comes to sustain. This sentence's applicability to the general field of the example-effect outlined above generates the major methodological task of this book, which is to think the relation of exemplarity to history within the general fields of literary and cultural criticism.

Chapters 2 through 7 do not so much exemplify the methods outlined in the first chapter as test it in particular cases. Much of the historical argument of the

[49] Because their historical range is extensive (the earliest example dates from 1606, and the latest from 2006), their geographic and linguistic range reasonably broad (most of the material is in English, but some is in French, German, or Chinese), and their genres diverse (travel narrative, medical case study, photograph, novel), the examples discussed in the chapters that follow do have the advantage of indicating a wide set of possible forms that the discourse on Chineseness, suffering, and the human can take. They do not, however, define the entire range of discursive possibility. Among the many things I do not discuss are the history of footbinding and the dramatic increase in recent decades in the international adoption of Chinese children, two major sites for the expression and indeed the lived, embodied production of the discourse on China and human life. On footbinding, see Dorothy Ko's excellent *Cinderella's Sisters: A Revisionist History of Footbinding* (Berkeley, 2005), and Wang Ping's *Aching for Beauty: Footbinding in China* (Minneapolis, 2000). On adoption, see Vincent Cheng, *Inauthentic: The Anxiety over Culture and Identity* (New Brunswick, 2004), particularly chapter 4; David L. Eng, "Transnational Adoption and Queer Diasporas," *Social Text* 21.3 (Fall 2003); and Toby Alice Volkman, ed., *Cultures of Transnational Adoption* (Durham, N.C., 2005).

book takes place through the accretion of these examples, their accumulated weight finally enough to assert the simple fact that China has consistently been thought, in the space between sympathy and cruelty, as the ecliptic of the modern human. Beyond that weight, however, each chapter also explores through its major examples one possible mode of the Chinese ecliptic. So that chapter 2, on George Henry Mason's *The Punishments of China* (1801) reads the internal logic of Mason's literary production—its figuration of type and example, its address to its reader, its justifications for its project, its arrangement of word and image—against the double themes of sympathy and exchange that have organized this introduction. And chapter 3, largely a discussion of the medical case histories and oil portraits produced in and around the first Western missionary hospital in China (1838–52), finds in the paintings and the reports a studiously neutral relation to Chinese suffering that plays against the pressing possibilities of national allegory and the individual resistance to the language of pain. Asad's notion of suffering as epistemological process returns heavily there, as it does again, though less explicitly, in chapter 4, in which the particularly American fantasy of a Chinese future defined coextensively with industrialization becomes fodder for the paranoid and, as the chapter argues, ultimately utopian imaginings of an early American science fiction novel (1890). Together these three chapters constitute the first part of the book, which focuses particularly on questions of exchange. They show how the history of Chinese suffering and sympathy in the West has been dominated by perceived threats emerging from China as a market (especially in chapters 2 and 4), and they illustrate the ways in which such a domination can nonetheless fail, despite the presence of all its most conventional markers, to determine the full field of representational and experiential possibility (chapter 3).

The second part of the book, chapters 5, 6, and 7, addresses questions of representation and representability. Chapter 5 centers on a reading of Bertrand Russell's 1922 trip to China, which it discusses in relation to Russell's theory of sensibilia and the more generally modernist investment in the discrete experience of objects. In order to highlight the generic difference between "life" and "literature" elided in a micro-genre like the anecdote, the chapter narrates Russell's experience as though it were a novel, and uses this narration to reflect on the relation between coincidence and significance, literature, and history. More broadly, however, it is a chapter on the field of modernist studies, an attempt to think about how or why the "problem" of China that Russell identifies in 1922 continues to seem extraneous to the philosophical project of modernist representation, and a proposal for how to read those things—China and representation—together through the epistemological aperture of Russell's theory of sensibilia.

That aperture is literalized, embodied, and violated in the subsequent chapter. Chapter 6 provides a reading of images of surgical operations in 1970s China, which leads to a long investigation of the relation between pain and the aesthetic, suffering and anesthesia, these latter figured in a Benjaminian critique of photography as a medium and given an embodied force through a lengthy discussion of the photograph of the flayed body of an executed Chinese prisoner. That photograph, taken in the early years of the twentieth century, is best known for its appearance in Georges Bataille's 1961 *Larmes d'Eros*, and the chapter spends much time parsing the difference between the image that appears in that book and the photograph owned by Bataille. All this ultimately allows the chapter to produce a retheorization of the materiality of the photographic object, a theorization that it applies, in a final turn inward, to the representation of Chinese surgeries with which it began.

The operating room's appearance in the Bataille chapter recalls and reflects on the material about surgical theaters that features heavily in chapter 3. Indeed, by chapter 6, it will have become clear that the entire question of sympathy with which we began has transformed itself into an interest in the relation between suffering and representation, aesthetics and anesthetics, as those terms play themselves out continuously in the images and descriptions of Chinese bodies the book reproduces and reads. Chapter 7, the concluding chapter, clarifies this transformation. It follows a brief review the first part of the book, focused on the relationship between sympathy and economic exchange, with a more lengthy discussion of the second, focused on the relation between suffering and representational exchange. In so doing, it shows how these four key terms—sympathy, suffering, economic exchange, and representational exchange—establish the semiotic network that frames the historical discourse on China, sympathy, and modernity (while stopping just short, probably to the great relief of most readers, of filling out the entire Greimasian semiotic square they create). It does so with reference to three major examples: Peter Handke's *The Chinaman of Pain* (*Der Chinese des Schmerzes*, 1983), Lu Xun's preface to *A Call to Arms* (*Nahan*, 1922), and the wildly popular contemporary museum exhibitions of plasticized corpses, whose startling exemplifications of the "human" bring together in one final, jarring prosopopoeia the unifying themes of this study. The book's last section opens, speculatively, onto the imaginary field of "sympaesthetics." Its final sentences attempt, in the spirit of that speculation, to hold open the shuttering window of the book's closure.

6. The Mandarin (Return)

By their appearance the plasticized corpses establish an anthropomorphic counterpart for our hypothetical mandarin, against whose imaginary life the rickety consciences of the West shore their unquiet incertitudes. A little attention to his specificity is, thus, in order. In addition to being Chinese, he is, let us note, a mandarin, not a peasant or a seamstress, a scholar whose Kantian *innerer Wert* depends at least partly, we might imagine, on the commodifiable *Marktpreis* of his earned knowledge and social position. Mandarins were, as Balzac knew, state functionaries chosen through an extensive examination process largely focused on philosophy and literature; in the European imaginary, they functioned as expressions of a form of governmentality whose power derived from rote memorization and imitation of the Chinese classics, and which oversaw a state committed to the relentless reproduction of its own social and governmental form. By the mid-1800s widespread historical and philosophical attacks on Asia's historical immutability from figures like Smith or Hegel made the mandarin a figure for stagnation in its broadest possible meanings: historical stasis (and hence no progress), economic stasis (hence no class mobility), and the stasis of capital, this latter the necessary form of "a despotic state machine cornering the bulk of the surplus and functioning not merely as the central apparatus of repressing of the ruling class, but as its principal instrument of economic exploitation."[50] To exchange a Chinese mandarin for a European fortune was thus, essentially, to exchange stasis for movement, or, to put things in more explicitly economic terms, to exchange noncirculating capital for its circulating cousin. From this perspective Balzac's hypothetical grasps the social imaginary binding China to the West far more clearly than Smith's does, because in the former's proposed exchange, the figuration of a particular kind of life as *resistant* to market pricing (the mandarin's fortune, like China's history, fails to circulate) becomes through the act that kills him a mobile inheritance whose assent to the market depends on the fact of it already having been exchanged, once, for a life.[51]

[50] Perry Anderson, summarizing Karl Marx's theory of the Asiatic mode of production, in *Lineages of the Absolutist State* (London, 1974), 483.

[51] To the mandarin's role as a figure for a certain model of capital circulation, one can further adduce a linguistic dimension: among the definitions the *OED* gives for "Mandarin" is "any obscurantist, esoteric, or exclusive variety of a language," which borrows from the mandarin's economic and governmental stereotype the sense of mobility without movement, or activity without change (mandarin, n., 2.b).

Other figures might have suggested to their auditors a different answer to the question of exchange: would you accept the death of a slave or two in return for cane sugar and cheap cotton?[52] Would you, today, admit that the miner occasionally maimed in an industrial accident is the unfortunate compensation for reduced prices on computer motherboards? Most people alive in the past two centuries have answered yes to questions like those, if only by the passive fact of living in an economic system devoted to the production of surplus value. These rewritten versions of the hypothetical will thus not fail to reveal the embarrassing complicity of all consumers with a certain statistical violence.

This allows us to understand more clearly why the mandarin is a mandarin, and why he is Chinese. His rhetorical function is to move the question from the realm of *politics* to the realm of *philosophy* by screening the addressee from the recognition that his or her life has already, and for a long time, benefited from the exchange between life and capital proposed in the trade between mandarin and fortune. The mandarin is just far away enough, one might say, that the real effects of his role in the European world that imagines him can be ignored, shifting the modal tenor of the question from "what *should* you do?" to "what *would* you do?," the latter obscuring behind the screen of its implied protasis (its "if" clause) the fact of decisions already taken and made.[53]

Such a concealment is ideological in the most fundamental of senses, deeply complicit with the production of a mythology of imperialism (and indeed of capital more generally) that aims to divorce its all-too-predictable consequences from its life as an ideal.[54] That said, we should also recognize that the removal of this decision to the realm of the imaginary opens a potential space of resistance or revolutionary possibility. In philosophical space, life has not yet been commodified, and the

[52] Remembering that Toussaint Louverture died in a French prison in 1803.

[53] In this sense, the hypothetical of the murdered mandarin can be compared to that other great nineteenth-century hypothetical question, "What would Jesus do?" (i.e., if you were Jesus, what would *you* do?) whose formal operations and cultural history have been discussed at length in Gregory S. Jackson, "'What Would Jesus Do?': Practical Christianity, Social Gospel Realism, and the Homiletic Novel," *PMLA* 121.3 (May 2006). Another project would connect the hypothetical as narrative form to the work done in fiction by the rise of the scientific *hypothesis*, which John Bender has argued shares with novelistic fiction an affinity for knowledge production based on "cases," that is, "causal and narrative sequences" that share "basic technologies of world making and sense making" ("Enlightenment Fiction and the Scientific Hypothesis," *Representations* 61 [Winter 1998], 15).

[54] Much the same way civilian casualties caused by modern warfare, as predictable as they are to anyone who has been paying the slightest bit of attention, are nonetheless understood to be extraneous to the *ideal* of modern warfare and thus remain in some sense excusable, this even though the stated ideal has never existed, and never will.

addressee is not yet complicit in the system that has commodified it. The hypothetical's philosophical space permits its addressees to free themselves from the cognitive dissonance established by the fact that they have in some sense already decided this question, and thus allows them to discover and affirm for themselves the moral ground upon which the current political and economic situation might be resisted. The question posed by the mandarin hypothetical thus produces via its forgetting the philosophical space necessary for thought to consider life from "the place and with the eyes of a third person, who has no particular connexion with either," as Smith had proposed of moral judgments in 1790 (*MS*, 135). Here again we see how the example-effect of "China" (as race, as nation, as culture) reproduces the problem of exemplarity and idea that surrounds China's historical relation to the invention of the modern human: it matters that the mandarin is Chinese, because his being Chinese means that his being Chinese doesn't matter. The function of Chineseness is thus, paradoxically, to force the ecliptic transformation of the instance into a universal *that retains the instance in fossil form*. It appears by disappearing; it disappears by appearing. Grasping this ghostly, shifting figure in all its holomorphic complexity is the task of the pages that follow.

1 Anecdotal Theory

Edmund Scott, Exact Discourse *(1606); Stephen Greenblatt,* Learning to Curse *(1990)*

Form is neither the external and superficial mold into which content is poured nor the inner truth of the text, expressed in its organic shape. It is neither an icon nor a fixed or static structure; it is in the most fundamental sense "not given."

—Ellen Rooney, "Form and Contentment," *MLQ* 61.1 (March 2000), 37

Why mightn't there be, somehow, a new science for every object?

—Roland Barthes, *Camera Lucida: Reflections on Photography*

Toward the end of the introduction to *Learning to Curse,* Stephen Greenblatt cites a long passage from Edmund Scott's 1606 *Exact Discourse of the Subtilties, Fashions, Pollicies, Religion, and Ceremonies of the East Indians.* The passage tells the story of Scott's torture of a Chinese goldsmith in Java, whom Scott believed had participated in the theft and arson of the English "house," or "factory." Under questioning, however, the goldsmith "would tell us nothing":

> Wherefore, because of his sullenness, I thought I would burn him now a little (for we were now in the heat of our anger). First I caused him to be burned under the nails of this thumbs, fingers, and toes with sharp hot iron, and the nails to be torn off. And because he never blemished [i.e., turned pale] at that, we thought that his hands and legs had been numbed with tying; wherefore we burned him in the arms, shoulders, and neck. But all was one with him. Then we burned him quite through the hands, and

> with rasps of iron tore out the flesh and sinews. After that, I caused them to knock the edges of his shin bones with hot searing irons. Then I caused cold screws of iron to be screwed into the bones of his arms and suddenly to be snatched out. After that all the bones of his fingers and toes to be broken with pincers. Yet for all this he never shed tear; no, nor once turned his head aside, nor stirred hand or foot; but when we demanded any question, he would put his tongue between his teeth and strike his chin upon his knees to bite it off. When all the extremity we could use was but in vain, I caused him to be put fast in irons again; where the emmets [ants] (which do greatly abound there) got into his wounds and tormented worse than we had done, as we might well see by his gesture. The [Javanese] king's officers desired me he might be shot to death. I told them that was too good a death for such a villain.... But they do hold it to be the cruellest and basest death that is. Wherefore, they being very importunate, in the evening we led him into the fields and made him fast to a stake. The first shot carried away a piece of his arm bone, and all the next shot struck him through the breast, up near to the shoulder. Then he, holding down his head, looked up on the wound. The third shot that was made, one of our men had cut a bullet in three parts, which struck upon his breast in a triangle; whereat he fell down as low as the stake would give him leave. But between our men and the Hollanders, they shot him almost all to pieces before they left him.[1]

These lines present Greenblatt with an interpretive dilemma. "What are we to do with such a passage?" he asks. "What is history to make of it? what kind of story do we want to tell about Scott and his victim—or not to tell about them?" (*LC*, 12). We might, as others have, locate such a story inside a broader history of capitalism, imperialism, or torture, allowing its specificity to push us toward a theory that subsumes it. But such a reading moves too quickly from instance to abstraction, Greenblatt argues. And in its haste, it misses what really matters about this story, he writes. Though "the link between capitalism and imperialism *does* manifest itself in Scott's writing and his actions, ... we may doubt that this link is sufficient to explain either the writing or the actions or doubt that its history is the history that it most behooves us to tell when we read those terrible sentences" (*LC*, 13). Though Greenblatt will finish the introduction a few pages later with an

[1] *Learning to Curse: Essays in Early Modern Culture* (New York, 1990), 11–12. Further references in the text are cited as *LC*.

assured, definitive sense of the interpretive challenge he faces, here the word "doubt" articulates his sense of the limitations of historical approaches: there seems to be, on the edges of Scott's narrative, something that escapes the pallid glance of a universalizing history. Something about the terror of the sentences generates, in the middle of this doubt that history's eye has seen it all, the need to tell another version of the story: the story it "most behooves us" to tell.

That story depends on a particular attachment to the literary status of Scott's prose, paired with a willingness to read "all of the textual traces of the past with the attention traditionally conferred only on literary texts" (*LC,* 14). Whatever story we tell cannot ever quite be a conventionally disciplinary *histoire* because, as Greenblatt writes, "what is unbearable about Scott's passage exists for us *in the text,* and not only in his complacent acceptance of his own acts. There is something about *the sentences themselves* that is horrible" (*LC,* 14; emphasis mine). Something "in the text" can be held apart from the historicity of Scott's acts and his acceptance of them; something in the text escapes conventional modes of historical perception. Attention solely to the referential facts obscures the medium of their arrival; something in the text—in the textuality of the text—remains a crucial part of what makes it unbearable.

One sees the importance of this insistent textuality in the movement from "passage" to "text" in Greenblatt's phrase "What is unbearable about Scott's *passage* exists for us in the *text,*" where the distinction marks, however slightly, the difference between something one moves through to history or meaning and the tactile material of the words themselves, which impedes and detains us in a passage whose either end opens to the light of history and event. It is in the context of the "horribleness" of Scott's particular language "that the victim's silence—the torturer's inability to turn pain into a manifestation of his power, to extort so much as a scream that he could then record—takes on whatever meaning it has" (*LC,* 14). The agon of torture that binds Scott to the goldsmith simultaneously realizes and allegorizes a battle over signification and absence, language and silence. Only in the context of the passage's own language, of language in general, can a critic acquire the measure of its meanings. Ignoring the language in which the story is told, barreling from event to history, obviates the very thing that the story is *about.*

Greenblatt titles the section in which he cites Scott's passage, "Fiction and Reality." Its principal argument is that the poststructuralist erasure of the boundary between fiction and nonfiction proves "inadequate" to the task of interpreting a text like Scott's (*LC,* 15). Remembering the difference between fiction and nonfiction "alters our mode of reading . . . texts and changes our ethical position toward them," Greenblatt writes. "Our belief in language's capacity for reference is part of our contract with the world; the contract may be playfully suspended or broken altogether, but no abrogation is without consequences and there are circumstances where the abrogation is unacceptable. The existence or absence of a real world, real body, real pain, makes a difference" (*LC*, 15). The difference between fiction and reality, on which "any history and any textual interpretation worth doing" depends, thus hangs on the fact of real bodies and real pain, on the insistent reality of bodies and pain that cannot simply be reduced to language. At the site of a body in pain, Greenblatt finds the theoretical limit to the erosion of "traditional paradigms for the uses of history and the interpretation of texts" (15). The articulation of this limit—conceived with explicit reference to poststructuralist theories of language—is the major goal of Greenblatt's introduction.

My purpose in this chapter is to argue against this claim of Greenblatt's while remaining fairly close to the arguments that lead up to it. Rather than take up and defend the simpleminded version of poststructuralism to which he alludes, or rehearse yet another time the "debate" between the new historicist method Greenblatt helped make famous and the deconstructive critiques of it by such figures as J. Hillis Miller, I want to stay firmly within the ambit of Greenblatt's thought and attempt to open there a space for a more generous theory of language than Greenblatt seems to allow, without then having to claim that I have demonstrated the superiority of language over reference or the final enculturation of the actual. I will proceed, accordingly, by reading Scott's passage and Greenblatt's citation of it, and by using that reading to advance, however slightly, beyond the theoretical structure within which the introduction to *Learning to Curse* first appeared. The limit of that advance should establish a methodological framework for the chapters that succeed this one, just as the introduction that preceded this chapter framed the thematic and historical presumptions and preoccupations of the book as a whole.

1. Narrative Grammar

Readers familiar with new historicism will recognize in the sentences of the goldsmith the presence of the most privileged epistemological feature of new historicist reading, namely the "anecdote." Indeed, in the earlier sections of the introduction to *Learning to Curse*, Greenblatt discusses at length Joel Fineman's essay on "the theoretical implications of new historicism's characteristic use of anecdotes" (*LC*, 5).[2] As "the narration of a singular event," Fineman had written, the anecdote is "the literary form or genre that uniquely refers to the real" (*HA*, 56). Greenblatt elaborates: "The anecdote has at once something of the literary and something that exceeds the literary, a narrative form and a pointed, referential access to what lies beyond or beneath that form. This conjunction of the literary and the referential, Fineman argues, functions in the writing of history not as the servant of a grand, integrated narrative of beginning, middle, and end but rather as what 'introduces an opening' into that teleological narration" (*LC*, 5).

By occupying a middle ground between reference and literature, the anecdote resists the narratives of traditional history in favor of what Fineman calls an "opening" that "exceeds" the literary by virtue of its "narrative form" and its referential access to something "beyond or beneath" it. In other words, as a "narrative form" specifically dedicated to the real, the anecdote binds story to history. And, in this binding, the anecdote—here Greenblatt cites Fineman again—"produces the effect of the real," but "only in so far as its narration both comprises and refracts the narration it reports," that is, only insofar as its narration in some sense reports the story it tells and reports itself reporting that story, indicating its referential content and its narrative structure all at once (*HA*, 61). The anecdote, one might say, is a passage sentences linger in, an alleyway whose dual openings toward history and language illuminate the interior geography of its form.

The rest of this chapter examines the process whereby Scott's passage becomes Greenblatt's anecdote. I argue that the appearance of the anecdote in Greenblatt's text—the "becoming-anecdote" of these sentences—does not happen by itself or self-evidently, but occurs through a set of processes having to do with citational practice, racial stereotype, and narrative form. These in turn operate inside historical networks that have taught us how to think about the relationships between pain, language, and Chineseness. The attention paid to these processes and these relationships aims to undermine the grounds whereby Greenblatt theorizes the anecdote, and through the anecdote, the relationship between historical reality and language. This should, when it comes, feel like progress.

[2] Joel Fineman's essay appeared in the first of the two collections of work in new historicism edited by H. Aram Veeser ("The History of the Anecdote: Fiction and Fiction," in *The New Historicism*, ed. H. Aram Veeser. [New York & London, 1989]); further references in the text are cited as *HA*. Stephen Greenblatt refers to Fineman again in one of the two chapters devoted to anecdotes and anecdotality in *Practicing New Historicism* (Chicago, 2000), which he co-wrote with Catherine Gallagher (49–52). That Gallagher and Greenblatt refer to their two chapters on anecdotes as being "about" new historicism, by contrast to the four chapters that are examples "of" new historicism, suggests something of the anecdote's continuing importance for theorizing new historicist work.

In Scott's *Exact Discourse*, the goldsmith's torture belongs to a much longer story, in which thieves dig a tunnel under the warehouse set up by Scott and his mission. In the process of the underground transfer of the Englishmen's goods to the building next door, one of the thieves accidentally starts a fire. The resulting conflagration draws the attention of the Englishmen, who rush in to save their goods and discover the tunnel. They follow it to the building next door and detain everyone they find. One of the men they catch "confesses" under torture and names the goldsmith as an accomplice.

Greenblatt cites Scott's narrative as it appears in a version edited by William Foster and published for the Hakluyt Society in 1943. That version differs in several small but important ways from Scott's original text, which is available as a facsimile reprint from 1973.[3] Among these differences is that the passage Greenblatt cites ends in the Hakluyt edition at the end of a paragraph, whereas in Scott's original the narrative continues for another ten lines:

> ...they shot him almost all to pieces before they left him [end of citation in Greenblatt, and of the paragraph in Hakluyt]: now in this time the Admiral and the Sabindar sent us a guard of men every night, for fear the Chinese would rise against us, but we feared it not: yet we kept four of the men to be witnesses, that whatsoever we did (if they should rise) was but in our own defense: after I had kept this fellow of Jortan [a place name; this man had been held by Scott, and tortured and questioned in the case of the theft] nine or ten days, and could prove nothing against him, I gave him a piece of stuff [cloth] to make him a suit, and set him free. So soon as he was out of our gates, every one that met him took him by the hand, and greatly rejoicing would say, that now they saw the Englishmen would do no more but justice. (*ED*, F3; spelling modernized)[4]

[3] Sir William Foster, ed. *The Voyage of Sir Henry Middleton to the Moluccas, 1604–1606* (London, 1943); Edmund Scott, *An Exact Discourse of the Subtilties, Fashions, Pollicies, Religion, and Ceremonies of the East Indians, as well Chinese as Javans, there abiding and dwelling* (London, 1606); reprinted from the copy of the Bodleian Library, Oxford as *The Subtilties...of the East Indians* (Amsterdam, 1973); further references in the text are cited as *ED*.

[4] Scott at one point refers to the "fellow of Jortan" as a "Chinese born, but now turned Javan" and says that he is a beloved member of the community (*ED*, F; spelling modernized). He also describes the Javanese community's pleasure in his execution of the Chinese goldsmith. The phrase "Chinese turned Javan" suggests that the fellow of Jortan is a *peranakan* Chinese, a member of a diaspora that began in the tenth century. Ien Ang writes that "between the sixteenth and nineteenth centuries Chinese trading quarters in cities such as Bangkok, Manila, and Batavia became large and permanent, aided by the

Though Scott does not explicitly connect the threat of anti-European violence and his public performance of English justice, their narrative proximity indicates the degree to which the culture of European trade throughout the seventeenth and eighteenth centuries, which depended on the deployment of physical power against potentially aggressive foreign competitors, attempted also to produce cultural structures that might defuse such aggression in advance. Scott's gathering of "witnesses" to the English's self-defense against potential violence extends the juridical map of crime, questioning, and punishment that organizes the narrative of the burning warehouse to the more general context of the complex social scene that surrounds the English presence on Java. His *Exact Discourse,* which is designed to assure the East India Company's directors of his surehanded direction of its financial fortunes, also testifies to his attempts to produce in Java the cultural mythology of Englishness (one he presumably believed in) that would help distinguish the Company and the English from the other European traders with whom they competed.

Though Scott's awareness of his potential vulnerability to both physical violence and a more general cultural contempt participate in his projection of imperialist power and self-justification, and are therefore of a piece with his violent torture of the goldsmith, they nonetheless mitigate the devastating narrative closure of Greenblatt's citation, which ends with the goldsmith in pieces—a conclusion not without self-reflexive narrative effects of its own. Its truncation effectively organizes the anecdote as a story with a fixed beginning ("he would tell us nothing"), middle, and end, shaping it as what the *Oxford English Dictionary* calls, in its definition of the anecdote, a "narrative of a detached incident, or of a single event, told as being in itself interesting or striking."[5] It is indeed the singularity of the event, the self-enclosing quality of the citation in Greenblatt, that prompts the set of interpretive questions he asks and determines the intensity of the passage's relation to reference.

That referential intensity—the passage's anecdotal status, in other words—depends as well on two other citational decisions Greenblatt makes. His unmarked modernization of the spelling in the Hakluyt edition erases one

ascendancy of European colonialism in the region" (*On Not Speaking Chinese: Living Between Asia and the West* [New York, 2001], 47). The simultaneously racial and cultural politics of Scott's situation can thus be seen to include at least four groups: the English, the community of native Javanese, the *peranakan* community, and recently arrived Chinese who do not yet qualify as having "turned Javan." For more on the cultural politics of contemporary *peranakan* Chinese, see Ang, chapters 1–3.

[5] *Oxford English Dictionary,* anecdote, n. 2.a.

potentially alienating barrier to rapid and complete understanding, the real body and real pain in the text now appearing in our English, not Scott's.[6] And his citation of the passage as a single block of text allows its visual form to reflect the singular anecdotality of its narrative. One need only imagine the effect of these same sentences cited and commented on separately over the course of a few pages to get some sense of how the experience of these sentences as a "single event" depends on the way in which Greenblatt cites them and makes them such a shocking, powerful thing to read. My own citation of Greenblatt's citation must be understood, therefore, as a reproduction not simply of the language he takes from Scott but also as a citation of the physical and visual arrangement of that language in his own text. What I am responding to includes both Scott's sentences, then, and Greenblatt's use of them in *Learning to Curse.*

So: to recognize that Greenblatt's citation of Scott's text creates the passage as anecdote is to understand that the passage operates referentially in two different contexts simultaneously. While from Scott's perspective, this episode might be said to have no real anecdotal status—it might, that is, be understood as not yet separated from a broader narrative context in which Scott attempts to impress the directors of the Company that sent him to Java—its citation in *Learning to Curse* disconnects it from that context, giving it an ontological status of its own. These sentences become visible as a single thing, gain their being as a single story through Greenblatt's citation. And it is through that citation that the anecdote acquires a narrative structure that will become familiar over the course of this book, in which a third observer located slightly to the side of the narrative frame—a bystander, of sorts—becomes the source of a moral evaluation of the referential events that the story presents.[7] The gap between Greenblatt's position and Scott's, the former's identification with the goldsmith's pain twinned with a critique of the latter's insensibility, generates this triangular narrative structure.

This is at least partially a historical claim. Though these sentences would have shocked many of Scott's contemporaries, and would strike some of ours as business as usual, the difference between Scott's position and Greenblatt's, or rather, the development of a critique of Scott's position as consistent with a

[6]The spelling in the Hakluyt Society edition already modernizes the original, but Greenblatt brings it further up to date.

[7]There is, to be sure, a distance between the narrator and the protagonist in Scott's passage, made by the temporal gap between an "I" that narrates the past history of a protagonist and the "I" of the protagonist himself, but that temporal difference does not produce any moral or experiential distance (narratologically: the narrator, the focalized agent, and the subject agent are the same).

"horror of cruelty," as Greenblatt puts it, occurs somewhere inside a matrix that includes the major shifts in cultural understandings of the meaning and value of the human, of sympathy, and of suffering that occurred in the eighteenth and nineteenth centuries.[8] The appearance of this narrative triangle and its moral position on cruelty marks, therefore, one node of a transhistorical matrix with especially complex etiologies.

In the Chinese case, these include the themes of endurance and silence: "Yet for all this he never shed tear; no, nor once turned his head aside, nor stirred hand or foot."[9] Though the uncanniness of endurance in torture speaks to a general economy of bodies, violence, and pain, in which the body is simultaneously the instrument of its person and the weapon with which a person can be driven out of his or her body, the endurance of this particular goldsmith does not occur outside the anthropological history in which he appears. Consider for instance the following passage from Bertrand Russell's 1922 *The Problem of China:* "I do not think that, in comparison with the Anglo-Saxons, the French, or the Germans, the Chinese can be considered a courageous people, except in the matter of passive endurance. They will endure torture, and even death, for motives which men of more pugnacious races would find insufficient—for example, *to conceal the hiding-place of stolen plunder.*"[10] I will have more to say about Russell in chapter 5, but for now I wish simply to indicate the family resemblance between his claim and Scott's narrative in order to show that the

[8]For a discussion of arguments about the legality and appropriateness of torture in Scott's time, see Elizabeth Hanson, "Torture and Truth in Renaissance England," *Representations* 34 (Spring 1991). For a history of torture, see Edward Peters, *Torture* (London, 1985), who argues that the connection between torture and the "inhuman" (and therefore the idea of human dignity and human rights) establishes an anthropological argument against torture. As I will suggest throughout the book, the European view of Chinese suffering occurs precisely at the intersection of the body as a site of human dignity and a series of anthropological arguments, whose historical contexts have a great deal to do with the development of a Western sense of self as modern.

[9]It is hard to believe, reading Scott's passage, that a human body could survive what the goldsmith survives, though anyone who reads about torture quickly finds out that the body lasts, in those circumstances, far longer than a reader of anecdotes might want it to, that in its strange and awful endurance the body itself conspires against the prisoner, becomes a weapon for the torturer rather than a protection for the victim. Mark Sussman, in an e-mail to me, responds to this note by writing: "This conspiracy between the body of the tortured and the torturer perhaps marks the disappearance of the object of torture—in this configuration the body is a weapon whose effectiveness rests in its ability to make itself a more effective weapon, to again be turned back on itself. So that there are only torturers, the tortured reduced to that inhuman status by their inability to inhabit their own matter; torture is the most profound homelessness."

[10]Bertrand Russell, *The Problem of China* (New York, 1922), 221 (emphasis mine).

"fact" of endurance, which we might initially have imagined as a referential feature of the anecdote, becomes from the perspective of this narratological history a "figure" or "trope" of endurance as well.

This is true also of the goldsmith's silence, which Greenblatt finds uncanny, nearly unimaginable, perhaps heroic (*LC*, 14). It is also active: the goldsmith does not simply fail to cry out, or even to cry; he attempts to bite off his own tongue. He dies without having uttered a word; his only moment of expression is a "gesture" that indicates that the ants in his wounds torment him "worse than we had done." The man's silence figures, as Greenblatt notes, the very act of torture it resists. The torturer's domination of the victim's body depends on its being made to cry out at will, on control over speech and silence. The "translation of pain into power is ultimately the transformation of body into voice," writes Elaine Scarry in *The Body in Pain.*[11] The inhumanity of torture as practice calls forth, in the voice, the very humanity of its victims. In this story, the goldsmith's silence suggests an inhuman strength, and the absence of his voice "justifies" the escalating inhumanity of Scott's behavior. That the goldsmith finally communicates only in response to pain caused by insects indicates, perhaps, the degree to which his silence remains outside the boundaries of the human.

And yet this silence too operates inside an anthropological system. In the nineteenth century suffering in silence becomes one of features of the Chinese most interesting and impressive to Western observers. This is Peter Parker, the American missionary doctor I discuss at length in chapter 3, describing, in 1845, a few of his patients' reactions to surgery performed without anesthesia: "The patient discovered great fortitude, coolly remarking on commencement of the first incision, 'it hurts, doctor'"; "The patient bore the operation with heroic fortitude, not seeming to notice the incisions"; "The patient bore the operation with great fortitude, not uttering a word."[12] The examples can be multiplied. But it is clear in any case that like his endurance, the goldsmith's silence is both a referential fact and a narrative trope, a mixed, anecdotal figure which by the time Greenblatt reads it has a history that extends well beyond the particularities of a single, seventeenth-century Chinese goldsmith. Rather than argue that one

[11]Elaine Scarry, *The Body in Pain: The Making and Unmaking of the World* (Oxford and New York, 1985), 42; further references in the text are cited as *BP.*

[12]These remarks are drawn from the "Report of the Medical Missionary Society in China" dated October 1845, from case reports prepared by Peter Parker. The citations appear on pages 4, 10, and 12, respectively.

trumps the other (insisting that the goldsmith really did endure silently, or, on the other hand, that this fact is just a fiction), which would suggest that the real is the enemy of fiction, it seems important to say that in this case the fictional fact sustains the referential one, that the two forms of facticity operate in collaboration to produce whatever in the passage makes someone attend to it.

One can see the work being done by the narrative facts—themselves connected to large-scale cultural stereotypes of the Chinese as insensitive to pain, stoic, and so on, all of which are discussed throughout the book—on Greenblatt himself by looking once again at his citational practice. The entire passage is cited below as Greenblatt gives it, but a look at both the Scott and Hakluyt editions of the text show that the sentences Greenblatt cites come from the middle of a longer paragraph. These lines precede the anecdote:

> The next day the Admiral took another of them, and sent him to me, who knew there was but one man with him: and therefore resolved with himself, not to confess any thing to us: he was found hid in a privy, and this was he that put the fire to our house, this was a goldsmith, and confessed to the Admiral, he had clipped many Ryals [the Dutch coinage then in use; clipping involves shaving precious metal off the edges of coins], and also coined some counterfeit: some things he confessed to him concerning our matter, but not much, the which the other had confessed before, but he would tell us nothing, [Greenblatt citation begins] Wherefore because of his sullenness, and that it was he that fired us, I thought I would burn him now a little, for we were now in the heat of our anger. (*ED*, F2; spelling modernized)

The narrative value of the goldsmith's silence must surely be considered in the context of his multiple confessions to the Admiral for crimes only tangentially related to the theft and fire, and in relation to Scott's supposition that it served a purpose, namely that the goldsmith knew that only one other man—who had been executed a day earlier—could implicate him in the crime.[13] His silence in the face of Scott's torture, like his confessions to the Admiral, can therefore be read, at

[13]The Hakluyt edition Greenblatt uses omits "and that it was he that fired us" from the final sentence of this citation; this diminishes the rhetorical effect created by the movement from "burn" to "fired" to "heat," in which the literal "burn" and the figurative "heat" make "fired" function literally and figuratively (that is, sylleptically), driving the synecdoche "us" before it. In the shortened version, Scott's torture appears even more brutish and self-indulgent than Scott's text makes it; this in turn increases the reality-effect of the text, which skews Greenblatt's reading of the passage, as I go on to argue.

least inside the terms of Scott's narrative, as a strategic gesture operating inside an economy of public justice. Given that Scott had at one point announced to a delegation of townspeople that he would not wrongfully shed the blood of an innocent man "for all the goods in the world," the goldsmith may well have been counting on the very principles of English justice that Scott later attempted to illustrate by releasing the man from Jortan to keep him from being killed (*ED*, E4).

The appearance, or should I say re-appearance, of the most shocking or heroic elements of Scott's story in nineteenth- and twentieth-century statements about Chinese people, taken together with a consideration of the larger context within which these sentences appear, alter the anecdote's referential force by suggesting that the narrative *as it appears in Greenblatt* depends at least partly on a literary history that precedes it. It also opens the more radical possibility that Scott's own experience of his torture of the goldsmith did not move unmodified through the "anecdotal" passage that leads from phenomenological experience to the mental experience of the real: that whatever he saw or heard was altered as it was processed into "experience" and "language" by historical forces, including the history of race, but also the history of storytelling, which formed the very ground of Scott's openness to the world. That Scott's sentences can be shown to belong to a narrative or experiential tradition—precisely to the tradition this book aims to elucidate—does not mean that this particular Chinese goldsmith was not heroically silent; nor does it diminish the fact of his felt pain. But it suggests that the referential weight of Scott's language may borrow something from a narrative tradition in which it participates.

The placement of this anecdote into a network, part of a general accumulation of such event-texts, aims to mine the anecdote's referential weight while recognizing the experience of such weight as itself already caught up in the projections of narrative. This neither to undercut the event's actuality, nor to suggest that the event itself is simply another fiction, but to recognize the ways that narrative expectations shape not only the "terrible sentences" but also the experience of reading them, or even of writing them. Or, to put it slightly differently: the goldsmith's relation to his pain might have been an event for the goldsmith; but for Scott, it was a culturally organized narrative. That the sentences he wrote to tell its story would emerge four centuries after the event as a "passage" and an "anecdote" that testify to reality beyond the fictionality of fiction suggests, despite the vast moral difference between Scott's relation to the torture and Greenblatt's, the historical power of these narrative tropes to generate cultural work. The challenge is how to read, recognizing that.

What one might say, to begin, is that two of the crucial, linked facts of Scott's passage, two of the facts that seem to speak the most violent possible intersection of imperialism and resistance to imperialism, namely torture and a corresponding silence/endurance, have come to be major features of the Western representation of Chinese people. As with Russell's claims about the "passive endurance" of the Chinese, these facts function at the level of stereotype and as a kind of rough sociology, in which a series of personal experiences produce a general theory of the race. I need not, at this late stage, spend time discussing the limitations of such an epistemological process. But what is worth remarking is that it operates on roughly the same epistemological model as the one Greenblatt proposes in his introduction: it depends, that is, on anecdotes. In text after text on China, a claim about the race or nation in general is sustained by an illustrative example, chosen precisely because the anecdote is the "literary form or genre that uniquely refers to the real," to cite Fineman again. Lydia Liu, writing about Arthur Smith's notorious *Chinese Characteristics*, refers to Smith's habit of using anecdotes to support general theories of "the Chinese" as part of a "powerful grammar of truth."[14] In this case, that same grammar operates in reverse: whereas for Smith the anecdote sustains the general theory, here the general theory legitimates the referentiality of the anecdote: of course the goldsmith would be silent, because the Chinese are notorious for their silence under torture.

The moving referential facts of the Chinese goldsmith's endurance and his silence are themselves, that is, already the product of a relation to anecdotality, whether in advance of the development of the stereotype or, more likely, in some collaboration with them. The anecdotal structure of these facts—which in each case come from anecdotes and become "theories" of the Chinese—thus operates from *inside* the passage that contains them. Whatever anecdote emerges from the collocation of these terrible sentences and this terrible event cannot therefore be understood as the origin of the referential scene it presents. Nor, vice versa, can any experience of that scene (and perhaps especially not Scott's) be understood simply as the origin of the sentences that pretend to document it, or the ones that make it an anecdote.[15]

[14] Lydia Liu, *Translingual Practice: Literature, National Culture, and Translated Modernity in China, 1900–1937* (Stanford, 1995), 56.

[15] This is not simply true in relation to the Chinese stereotype. One of the passage's more striking moments occurs when the goldsmith looks at the damage done to his body: "Then he, holding down his head, looked up on the wound." On one hand the implications of this as *event*—considered as an experiential moment—are devastating; one might say that the victim's self-regard presents him with the occasion to observe, as though from the outside, the decimation of his own body. On the other,

Rather than argue, however, that this internal imbrication with anecdotality delegitimizes Greenblatt's theorization of the form, I want to suggest that the complexity of this particular anecdote makes the theory Greenblatt develops in *Learning to Curse* even more illuminating than it is in its original elaboration. Whereas Greenblatt might be said to want to emphasize the degree to which anecdotes approach a reality untouched by other literary forms—their having "at once something of the literary and something that exceeds the literary, a narrative form and a pointed, referential access to what lies beyond or beneath that form"—my reading of this passage-become-anecdote suggests that whatever "lies beyond or beneath" literary form—that is, the world itself—can in its turn be said to possess "something of the *referential* and something that exceeds the *referential,* an event-ful form and a pointed, *literary* access to what lies beyond or beneath that form." Just as the anecdote points us to the referential beyond the literary, so does it point us to the literary beyond the referential; so does it suggest that whatever "beyond" one posits as the limit past which language games are unacceptable is itself constituted, in turn, by the possibility of the "beyond" that is literariness itself. And not necessarily because of some overarching theory of the inability of language to refer (though that, too), but because in this case the anecdote can clearly be shown to borrow the mode of expression of the real—and perhaps even of its perception—from literary figures that exist outside the "beyond" of the goldsmith's torture as event. In this sense, the anecdote's unique mixture of reality (the "beyond or beneath" of literary form) and literariness is the obverse of its unique mixture of the literary, as the beyond or beneath of the real, and the world as

---

consider the description of the 1757 execution of Damiens the regicide, which Foucault cites on the first pages of *Discipline and Punish,* and which serves as a model or precursor to the New Historicist anecdote: "After these tearings with the pincers, Damiens, who cried out profusely, though without swearing, *raised his head and looked at himself;* the same executioner dipped an iron spoon in the pot containing the boiling potion, which he poured liberally over the wound.... Despite all this pain, *he raised his head from time to time and looked at himself bodily....* The horses tugged hard, each pulling straight on a limb, each horse held by an executioner.... after several attempts, the direction of the horses had to be changed, thus: those at the arms were made to pull towards the head, those at the thighs towards the arms, which broke the arms at the joints. This was repeated several times without success. *He raised his head and looked at himself*" (*Discipline and Punish: The Birth of the Prison,* trans. Alan Sheridan [New York, 1979], 4 [emphases mine]. I am grateful to Christine Baumgarthuber for calling my attention to these sentences). Whether or not Damiens looked at himself, the fact that he is described as doing so three times in the space of a single page (the account is written by an officer of the watch) indicates the anecdotal importance of this gesture, which is taken to signify something so important it must be repeated three times. But what? And to what extent, we might wonder, did Damiens' behavior emerge from his own sense of what was expected of him?

such. To say this is not, I think, to engage in poststructuralist play about fiction and nonfiction. It is rather to observe that it is precisely *because* the anecdote "confounds" fiction and nonfiction, story and reference, that it acquires such a powerful epistemological force, providing Greenblatt with a rhetorical device around which to structure his introduction as well as a theoretical model and justification for the essays in *Learning to Curse*. A model with a force perhaps beyond, as I am suggesting here, what Greenblatt himself finds in it.

2. Pain's Language of Agency

The shockingly luminous quality of the events Scott describes—reading the passage feels like staring into the sun—comes in large part from its description of an act of torture and of the victim's implacable suffering. Torture is an act designed, at least in its self-justifications, to make its victims talk. Faced with the goldsmith's silence, Greenblatt asks, "is it the historian's task, after all this time, finally to compel him to speak?" (13). The question remarks the potential conjunction between Greenblatt's interpretive desire and Scott's torture of the goldsmith; it suggests that the historian's task is, like Scott's, though in another medium, to produce speech out of silence, meaning out of inscrutability.[16] Though this potentially devastating ethical comparison does not, rightly, detain

[16] I am not sure that in any case the passage can be interpreted to make the victim speak. Greenblatt confounds—unhelpfully, and with a bias toward the referential unjustified, I think, even by his claims regarding the anecdote's power—the literary text with the actual victim. One can describe and interpret the anecdote, and Greenblatt is doing so, as am I; in some sense the mere citation of the text allows it speech in a new time and for new tongues. One can also interrogate—a verb that has not come into the critical parlance for nothing—the terms under which such a passage could come to be written, as Greenblatt does in his introduction. But the goldsmith? What could or would he possibly have to say in or to the present? What could you want him to say? The slippage between the passage—which is *written*, after all—and the victim, the idea that one could make the latter speak through a reading of the former, does not to me suggest a respect for the victim's suffering in the real but rather an erasure of it. (To a very large extent the slippage depends on the metaphor of speech and the more general new historicist language of animation, of a critical waking of the dead [cf. Gallagher and Greenblatt 69, the closing of Greenblatt's "What is the History of Literature?" (*Critical Inquiry* 23.3 [1997]) or, indeed, the famous opening to Greenblatt's *Shakespearean Negotiations:* "I began with the desire to speak with the dead" (*Shakespearean Negotiations: The Circulation of Social Energy in Renaissance England* [Berkeley, 1989].)]). Jacques Derrida has written enough on the implications of metaphors of voice as breath and animation—see particularly the first section of *Of Grammatology*—for thinking about writing that I do not feel compelled to go through things here.

Greenblatt for long, it nonetheless indicates his awareness of the potential conjunction between the anecdote he cites and the process of literary criticism. In this sense, the anecdote presents us with a willing allegory of the act of interpretation.[17] Greenblatt's recognition of the metaphoric conjunction of interpretation and torture suggests once again that the anecdote's content interferes with the perception of its form, that whatever theory of the anecdote occurs here also acts as a theory of the act of interpretation that allows us to see the passage as an anecdote, or, for that matter, to read it at all. Whatever theory of the anecdote is emerging from this rereading of Scott's passage and Greenblatt's citation will not be able to argue that the theory of anecdote is exclusively a theory of narrative *form*. It is also a matter of interpretive *practice*.

We can continue further along the path suggested by this opening by attending specifically to the passage as a description of torture. It does not, one might begin by noting, describe the goldsmith's pain. Rather pain, when it appears, does so most clearly through the descriptions of the physical agents of torture, the screws and bullets and irons that cause the pain. Greenblatt insists pointedly on the reality of this pain, but an attention to its linguistic appearance suggests that whatever reality this pain obtains stems from descriptions that fail in any instance actually to describe it as pain.

The gap between the goldsmith's pain as the reader feels it and that pain itself, the degree to which Scott's sentences reproduce that pain without representing or being it, can be understood as a function of what Scarry calls pain's "language of agency."[18] Those who wish to speak of pain, Scarry writes, will often rely on metaphors that specify "an external agent of the pain, a weapon that is pictured as producing the pain," or that describe "bodily damage that is pictured as accompanying the pain. Thus a person may say, 'It feels as though a hammer is coming down on my spine,' even when there is no hammer" (*BP*, 15). Insofar as descriptions of physical or imaginary agents

> convey something of the felt-experience of pain to someone outside the sufferer's body, they both do so for the same reason: in neither case is the nail identical with the sentient experience of pain; and yet because it has

[17]Though with the following depressing result: that the goldsmith's uncanny silence, which finally testifies, in the *Exact Discourse*, to the diligence of Scott's efforts on behalf of the Company, can be said to represent in *Learning to Curse* the degree to which even the most recalcitrant silence will signify, in the hands of the right kind of interpreter, in a manner suited to the latter's needs.

[18]Greenblatt briefly cites Scarry in his introduction (*LC*, 14); I am extending that act of reference.

> shape, length, and color, because it either exists (in the first case) or can be pictured as existing (in the second case) at the external boundary of the body, it begins to externalize, objectify, and make sharable what is originally an interior and unsharable experience. (*BP*, 15–16)

Pain comes into language through metaphor. The instrument of pain (imaginary or real) articulates and objectifies "unsharable," nonlinguistic experience by producing a tangible image of its cause, and this tangible image in turn expresses metonymically the unspeakable effect that readers imagine it would create *on them.* The language of agency, then, produces a threefold process that moves pain first through metaphor (it is described in terms of a causal agent), then metonym (the agent's effect is deduced from its cause), and then identification (what kind of pain would that cause me?). What one "feels" at the end of such a process is, therefore, never the other's pain, but rather the constructed *fiction* of that pain. The complex act of generosity such empathy requires is also, therefore, a *literary* act produced through the movement of language in its relation to the real world that it both describes and fails to be.[19]

Because it occurs in language, this descriptive act is not without its pitfalls, which depend precisely on a confusion between the signifiers and signifieds in the production of pain. Scarry writes that "the mere appearance of the sign of a weapon in a spoken sentence, a written paragraph, or a visual image . . . does not mean that there has been any attempt to present pain and, on the contrary, often means that the nature of pain has just been pushed into deeper obscurity" (*BP*, 18). While one clearly sees the operation of this obscuring function almost everywhere in Scott's passage, with its relentless focus on the physical agents of pain, the irony of its operation—that pain often seems most visible

[19] Jean Améry makes a similar argument in relation to his own torture at the hands of the Nazis:

> It would be totally senseless to try and describe here the pain that was inflicted on me. Was it 'like a red-hot iron in my shoulders,' and was another 'like a dull wooden stake that had been driven into the back of my head'? One comparison would only stand for the other, and in the end we would be hoaxed by turn on the hopeless merry-go-round of figurative speech. The pain was what is was. Beyond that there is nothing to say. Qualities of feeling are as incomparable as they are indescribable. They mark the limit of the capacity of language to communicate. If someone wanted to impart his physical pain, he would be forced to inflict it and therefore become a torturer himself.

("Torture," *Art from the Ashes: A Holocaust Anthology*, ed. Lawrence L. Langer [New York, 1995] 130)

there where it is precisely not—also clarifies the importance of the only moment at which the goldsmith "speaks": "the emmets [ants] (which do greatly abound there) got into his wounds and tormented worse than we had done, as we might well see by his gesture." That this moment produces (in me, at least) far less sympathetic pain than much of the rest of the narrative shows how little the readerly experience of the goldsmith's pain actually has to do with his ability to communicate it. Instead, that pain appears most forcefully, becomes most real and objective, when it is metaphorized in the instruments of torture (which are themselves, let us not forget, metaphors made by the torturer). The screws and irons that the goldsmith never describes himself substantiate his pain in a way that his gesture cannot. Pain thus appears most forcefully to the reader not on the surface of the body but in the weapons that figure it most vividly, its nature—that is, its being as an unspeakable, unsharable referential fact that can only appear *otherwise*—obscured by the very objects that create it in the first place.

Insofar as the vast majority of descriptions of pain rely upon the language of agency, any testimony regarding the presence of pain will *necessarily* be anecdotal. To talk about pain is to be talking about the difference between language and reference; any claim that pain has occurred (even to the self) asserts its own truth only insofar as it tends to construct a compelling figure or narrative about the shape and feeling of the pain that objectifies that pain in language. While pain itself, then, bears no resemblance at all to the anecdote as Greenblatt theorizes it, any given sentence about pain may well be said to engage the same binocular look toward language and reality that characterizes the anecdote. Language about pain shares the anecdote's double bind: it is a detour from reality that leads to a powerful sense of the real. Any sentence about pain, one might say, "has at once something of the literary and something that exceeds the literary, a narrative form and a pointed, referential access to what lies beyond or beneath that form" (*LC*, 5). Pain's language of agency produces that referential access most successfully when the literary qualities of its expression are at their most compelling. And those qualities are at their most compelling when their metaphors most successfully confound the gap between language and the pain to which it refers.

The tendency to make felt pain a limit beyond which certain textualist modes of reading are not allowed can now be understood as a misrecognition of the fact that pain is precisely that thing that language can never access as such. Rather than think of pain as a limit for language, as that which finally proves language's impotence in relation to reality, think of pain as a limit of the real, as that experience or place from which the real births itself into language, apparently as a corpse.[20]

3. Anecdotal Theory

Scott's sentences do not, then, become just any anecdote. Let me pause to take stock of their various implications.

As I have been trying to show, the anecdote acquires the full weight of its significance for Greenblatt and for this chapter along four major lines, two more or less formal, two roughly thematic.

- Formal line number one: The passage acquires its status as anecdote from its appearance in Greenblatt's introduction. Its citation as a single uninterrupted block of text, the correspondence of that block with a classic narrative arc, and Greenblatt's role as an extradiegetic narrator combine to make it into the "interesting" single event that characterizes the anecdotal form.
- Formal line number two: The passage borrows two of its crucial features, silence and endurance, from the history of Chinese stereotypes, which themselves may well borrow from even older literary historical tendencies expressed in Stoic texts and in the quasiromances of the early Christian martyrs.[21] This borrowing, though it appears most visibly at the thematic level, must be understood as the articulation of a narrative or historical form whose emergence into anecdote operates within the basic epistemological structure of anecdotal racism—and which therefore participates in the production of the anecdote as micro-genre.[22]

[20] The reversal in the end amounts to more or less the same thing; if my version seems "new," it is because it attempts to undo a cliché that has too long opposed weak language to strong reality. Bemoaning the "failure" of pain to communicate itself (or to be communicated by language) is like being sad that a stone can't read. The tendency to articulate this kind of "failure" in the language of reproduction (as I do deliberately here, with "impotence" and "births") simply reproduces, in its own way, a fantasy of nonfailure connected to an anthropomorphized sense of the possible.

[21] On the "subversive agenda" articulated by the silent suffering of the Christian martyrs, of their endurance of pain and indeed their inviolability in relation to it, see Judith Perkins, *The Suffering Self: Pain and Narrative Representation in the Early Christian Era* (London, 1995), 104.

[22] It seems worth saying that "anecdote" operates in two separate but connected dimensions. In the case of racism, the anecdote functions *metonymically*, as evidence of a general theory of which it is a telling example; as a figure for how to do literary criticism, on the other hand, the anecdote operates as a *metaphor*, an allegory of critical form. I am grateful to Rebecca Walkowitz for suggesting this distinction to me.

- Thematic line number one: The anecdote's recounting of an episode of torture can be shown to interfere metaphorically with Greenblatt's sense of the task of the historian or literary critic. This allows him to produce an interpretation that makes the anecdote "speak" against poststructuralism and for the reality of the real. This interpretation can be read as an allegory of Scott's torture of the goldsmith, putting the critic and the torturer on the same rather than opposite sides.
- Thematic line number two: The anecdote's evocation of pain, or rather, its use of Scarry's "language of agency" to evoke pain (and thus its production of theme through form), appears to have a profound relationship to the very problem of language and reference that the anecdote as form had seemed initially to resolve. That is, although the anecdote of the goldsmith had seemed in Greenblatt's introduction to guarantee the presence of a tangible ground for historical literary criticism, the analysis of its pain-language threatened to expose that ground as the objectified linguistic remnant of an unapproachable real.

While the first of these lines might be said to apply to any theory of the anecdote in general—that it must be produced out of an undifferentiated or less-differentiated mass of language and experience in order to acquire the properties that will make it recognizable as an anecdote—the other three come out of a reading of the content of this anecdote in particular. Whatever methodological theory will be left over after this analysis, then, will have to be a theory of "the anecdote of the goldsmith" in particular rather than a theory of the anecdote in general, an intertwining of form, context, and content that does not promise much in the way of universal applicability. Given that being universally applicable is one of the things that theories are supposed to do, it hardly seems right to call what's left a theory at all.

Nonetheless it seems worth pressing on, if only to see how one might turn this remainder into something useful for the rest of the book. A theory of the anecdote in general and one of the goldsmith's anecdote in particular share a fundamental premise, namely that the anecdote is a privileged site of the relation between literariness and reality and that its special narrative and historical claims exert an interpretive pressure on the critics who read it. Whereas in Greenblatt's introduction this theory seemed to emerge exclusively from the anecdote's formal properties as Fineman described them, however, my reading of that same anecdote suggests that anecdotes are not born but made and that this becoming relies on the operations of anecdotal form and on the particular qualities, referents, and themes of its content. Rather than argue that an attention to the qualities of Greenblatt's anecdote undermines the theory he proposes, then, it seems most useful to revise the general theory as a particular theory: an "anecdotal theory," to borrow Jane Gallop's phrase,[23] in which the properties associated with this anecdote (functioning as an *example* of anecdotality in general) come to interfere with the properties of a theory that would stem from it, so that the theory that comes out of the reading finds itself limited by the particular act of reference that makes it possible to think itself as theory, the "exemplary" anecdote and the theory exerting a kind of mutual gravitational pull that keeps either one from falling too far toward the wells of absolute historical particularity, on one hand, or universal applicability, on the other. A theory of the goldsmith's anecdote remains anecdotal insofar as it depends on and draws from the particular circumstances of its emergence in Scott's *Exact Discourse*, Greenblatt's *Learning to Curse*, and in this chapter of this book. It is in this sense largely strategic, and therefore of limited use. But its utility emerges at least partially in the form of a self-reference: the production of the anecdotal theory itself has permitted these pages to organize through both anecdote and theory some of the book's major thematic problems, namely, the relations between reference, sympathy and the representation of suffering, and the degree to which any experience of those relations (in 1606, 1990, or 2009) interferes with, and is interfered with by, Europe's historical encounter with and production of China and Chineseness.

The major difference, finally, between the general theory of the anecdote as Greenblatt articulates it and the anecdotal theory of the anecdote as I have developed it here is that the latter restores the balance between the literary and the referential, which in Greenblatt's introduction had been powerfully skewed, despite the claims made for the anecdote's unique position between literariness and reality, toward the latter. "The existence or absence of a real world, real body, real pain," Greenblatt had written, "makes a difference" that any history or textual interpretation "worth doing" will have to speak to (15). But language too is

[23] See the introduction to *Anecdotal Theory*, in which Jane Gallop writes, "'Anecdote' and 'theory' carry diametrically opposed connotations: humorous vs. serious, short vs. grand, trivial vs. overarching, specific vs. general. Anecdotal theory would cut through these oppositions in order to produce theory with a better sense of humor, theorizing which honors the uncanny detail of lived experience" ([Durham, N.C, 2002], 2). This differs, especially with its emphasis on the trivial or humorous, from Greenblatt's use of the anecdote in *Learning to Curse*, but of course that difference depends on the thematic content of the anecdotes each author chooses.

real. Any historical or textual interpretation worth doing will remember and work through its particular modes of being, including its typologies (true, false), its genres (fiction, nonfiction, anecdote), its narrative-historical tropes (the silence and endurance of the Chinese), and its rhetorical or psychological figures (metaphor, metonym, identification). Greenblatt's extensive attention to the crime committed against the Chinese goldsmith takes his real body and real pain so seriously that it misses the degree to which its own theory of literary interpretation borrows from and depends on the linguistic qualities that make that body and pain "present" in Scott's sentences. Or, to put it rather more extravagantly: the presence of the real in Greenblatt's anecdote—which justifies the outrage he directs both at Scott and at the poststructuralist critics with whom he disagrees—derives its leverage from linguistic features (narrative tropes of Chinese pain, the experiential authority of the anecdote, the impossibility of speaking pain) operating inside the presence of presence, and which, rather than making that present present, simply indicate the degree to which the production of presence is subject to linguistic operations that are most successful when they obscure their own role in that production.

So it is that the literary experience of pain exists precisely at the nexus of a powerful, felt experience of the reality of another person's body and pain, on one hand, and the formal and thematic operations of the language that makes that pain viscerally present, on the other. That the former is so powerful as to produce an insistence that the scene of pain or torture cannot be the subject of certain kinds of reading (including poststructuralist ones) is a measure of the special hold pain has upon the contemporary imagination (and not, you will have observed, on Scott's). But as I have suggested, this insistence comes out of a forgetting—one encouraged by the sentences as literary and referential objects—to read the historical and narrative forms at work inside and around the text's sentences, and, therefore, inside or around the experience to which they refer. The sentences about the Chinese goldsmith anecdotalize this process by enacting its major mechanisms and figures in the referential space of its appearance in both Scott's text and Greenblatt's, reminding us that stories about Chinese suffering in particular have had a hold on European and American imaginations in the era of modernity, and inviting a set of questions that permit another necessary working through of the evidentiary status of experience.

That last phrase refers to Joan W. Scott's now-classic essay on "The Evidence of Experience." Speaking of the relationship between experience as an epistemological category and the work of antifoundationalist historians, Scott writes that "the evolution of 'experience' appears to solve a problem of explanation for professed anti-empiricists even as it reinstates a foundational ground" for their work.[24] My argument is that the anecdote's referential qualities allow Greenblatt to restore as the foundational ground for literary–historical criticism the "real bodies" and "real pain" that appear in the story of the goldsmith's torture, and that such a restoration of foundations ought to produce more philosophical suspicion, rather than less, when it allows its readers to feel good about being on the proper side of history, namely on the side of the goldsmith's body rather than that of Scott's language.

Greenblatt's transposition of the referential and literary qualities of Scott's sentences into another formal structure, namely that of the anecdote, opens up the question of literary and historical interpretation precisely there where Scott had tried, by calling his narrative an *Exact* discourse, to assert the seamless relation between language and reality. Greenblatt thus makes possible a meta-analysis designed to determine how each text generates from within itself a relationship between narratorial perception and the reality of its referential claims, a method that suggests that narrative form is the modality through which perception is, if not lived, then at least communicated.[25] Applying that idea to Greenblatt's own perception, citation, and renarration of Scott's sentences, and pairing it with a reading of the content of the sentences in question, I attempted to extend Greenblatt's thinking so as to produce a theorization of this mode of analysis that would recognize the degree to which its interpretive targets also functioned as sources. If the resulting theory of the goldsmith's anecdote—which is both a theory of interpretation and an illustration of the colluded operations of sympathy (including Greenblatt's sympathy), China, and the problems of the representationality of representation—is to survive beyond the arena of its own immediate applicability, it must prove useful in contexts beyond those of its own production.

Whether it can depends on your willingness to read the goldsmith's anecdote not simply as an example of a particular mode of reading, but also as a possible theory of reading in general. Such a theory, if true to its origins in anecdote, cannot, however, go on to suggest that any given theory can be made, with enough pressure on its examples, to seem anecdotal. Such a sweeping claim might be theoretical, but it would not be *anecdotally* so—that is, it could not

[24] *Critical Inquiry* 17 (Summer 1991), 781.

[25] I paraphrase Stuart Hall's insight that race is the modality in which class is lived. For a discussion of Hall's idea specifically within the context of the transnational movement of texts and people, see Paul Gilroy, *The Black Atlantic: Modernity and Double Consciousness* (Cambridge, 1993), 85.

be true to the anecdotally theorized work that has come out of this particular anecdote, the work that the reading of this particular anecdote has made possible. Rather, this particular theorization of the relation between fact and reality—a theorization of a relation that depends on a notion of anecdotality for its structure and intensity—must, unlike other theorizations of that same relation, ultimately return to its anecdotal origins in order to recognize its own beginnings in the encounter between literature and reference. If such a theorization can be useful to this book as it proceeds, it can be useful only insofar as it suggests that the evidentiary material that sustains any general or theoretical conclusion (be it anecdote or description, novel or poem, photograph, medical case study, or union pamphlet) must exert both formal and thematic pressures on the theory that it comes to sustain, so that ideas about anecdotes will express, however strongly or mildly, something of that anecdotal origin in their form, ideas about newspaper articles will owe something to the fact that they are about that particular form of mass production, claims about paintings or photographs will be responsible to the histories of those media, and to the longer histories of the image, and stories about torture will provoke an awareness of the figurative torture of interpretation, as we have seen. This in turn suggests that any forthcoming reading needs to pay a special attention to the manner in which its primary evidence emerges into its being as theme and form, that is, the ways in which reference articulates itself (or is articulated) within a generic framework that transforms it, or translates it, with the inevitable emendations, omissions, and additions, into something communicable. And it proposes, finally, that the book itself, considered as an articulation of methodology it pursues, will come in time to exert something of an effect on that methodology, and even that such a methodology might apply some pressure on whatever theory of the "book" (or of academic work) this book itself articulates. Though I am ultimately less likely than most to be able to read those particular effects, the neatness of this return, the fact that theoretical methodology of the book itself has been made to appear through a reading of the very material that organizes it as a single project, the fact that it has been produced through both a formal reading of the anecdote and a thematic reading of the crime of torture against a Chinese man, fills me with an immense, jubilant terror.

2 The Compassion Trade

Punishment, Costume, Sympathy, 1800–1801

> No interpretation pretends to be the description of a work, as one can speak of the description of an object or even of a consciousness, the work being an enigmatic appeal to understanding. Interpretation could perhaps be called the description of an understanding, but the term 'description' because of its intuitive and sensory overtones, would then have to be used with extreme caution; the term 'narration' would be highly preferable.
>
> —Paul de Man, *Blindness and Insight: Essays in the Rhetoric of Contemporary Criticism*

> The temporal gap between the literal and the allegorical meaning of a text is . . . the designated field of interpretive labor.
>
> –Shu-mei Shih, "Global Literature and the Technologies of Recognition," *PMLA* 119.1 (2004), 21

1. Costumes and Customs

Rather than spend the rest of the book searching for more goldsmith-style anecdotes upon which to work the analysis developed in the previous chapter, with the inevitable happy results, it seems crucial now to try to ignore or even violate the reading done so far by moving into a series of objects—some images, some texts—which, though they continue to demonstrate a fascination with the combined facts of sympathy and China, do so in rather different historical, literary, and mediatic forms. I would like, therefore, to turn from Stephen Greenblatt's introduction, whose long reach backward had put us at the turn of the seventeenth century, to examples that treat the relation between China and sympathetic exchange in a more recent and entirely different mode.

At the beginning of the nineteenth century, William Miller, a London publisher, printed a series of books on the "costume" of various national traditions, including Russia, Austria, Turkey, and, in a nice reminder that interest in the foreign and the unfamiliar had complex geographic boundaries in the early nineteenth century, Great Britain. The publisher's preface to *The Costume of Great Britain* summarizes the general epistemological and spectacular hopes of the series:

> By presenting to the eye a series of judiciously selected and well executed pictorial representations, forming striking portraits of single subject, accurately finished in the colours of the original, and aided by short descriptive essays, [these books] give more pleasing and definite ideas of the external character, style of dress, and peculiarity of occupation, than can be acquired by any other method, except actual personal observation.[1]

Imagined as the next best thing to personal observation, the volumes aimed to delight and instruct armchair travelers by giving them the visual material of culture and the interpretive means to decode it, working from the external character, dress, and occupational habits visible on the surface of these color images toward an entire field of cultural representation.

This cultural project, coupled with a strong preference for "striking portraits of a single subject," exerts a powerful influence on the formal structure and appearance of the two books in the series written by George Henry Mason. Though Mason had, as a lieutenant in Her Majesty's 36th Regiment based in southern India, spent several months convalescing in Canton in late 1789 and early 1790, almost nothing in either of his books gives any sense of his own experience there. The color plates function instead as instances or illustrations of general Chinese practices, as for instance in the caption to an illustration of a man playing a tambourine, which appeared in Mason's 1800 *The Costume of China:* "The Chinese have various instruments of the drum kind; but there is none which

[1] A full list of the volumes in the series appears in William Pyne's *The Costume of Great Britain: The Costume of Turkey, The Military Costume of Turkey, The Costume of Russia, The Costume of Austria, The Costume of Spain and Portugal, The Costume of Italy, The Costume of Rio Janeiro, And Its Neighborhood,* and *The Ancient Costume of Great Britain,* in addition to the two China volumes I discuss below (iii; the sentence cited above is from ii). The edition of Pyne that I cite is a 1989 reissue titled *British Costumes: An Illustrated Survey of Early Eighteenth-Century Dress in the British Isles* (Hertfordshire, 1989). All the volumes of the series were first published by William Miller of London. Their attempt to produce a singular national character out of a diverse group of images and habits expresses itself best in the fact that they all claim to give their readers the *Costume,* not costumes.

admits so much display of action and of antic as the tambourine, wherein they are not rivaled by any performers in Europe."[2] The spare description situates the tambourine inside a general economy of drum instruments. The accompanying picture likewise presents its readers with a scene completely devoid of context: a lone figure standing on a completely white background kicks backward to a tambourine he holds over his right shoulder, a shadow emerging from his right foot the singular and punctuating sign of a reality—a light source, a sun—outside his body. This is the Chinese manner of playing a tambourine, and no more: no visual sense of the world in which the tambourine is played, no sense of social space or of the particular context in which Mason might have seen a Chinese man playing a tambourine. The image is not, as the publisher's preface asserts, a portrait, which would imply that it registered some particular Chinese (or Austrian or Russian) person. Its claims to referential access depend on how the image and caption combine to illustrate rather than "portray" the person they describe, placing him or her inside a textual curiosity cabinet whose introduction to the culture, habits, and human economy of China doubles as an ethnographic manual. In this the image, and the book series more generally, is typical of the British in interest in collections of "types," which in volumes like "Street Cries of London" or "Costume of the Tirol," "were staples of English printmakers and publishers in this period," and "tell us something not only about late Georgian curiosity towards the world, but also about its urge to classify and categorise" (*CEW*, 45).

The particular set of choices organizing this kind of representationality can perhaps be clearest seen from the perspective of a counter-example: William

[2] *The Costume of China* (London, 1800). I am citing from an edition reprinted and intercalated with William Alexander's *The Costume of China* of 1805, in *Views of 18th Century China* (London, 1988), 58; further references in the text are cited as *CC*. A book titled *Costumes of China—Original Watercolours—1800*, containing the watercolors that appear in the published book, has recently been acquired by the Ashmolean Museum at the University of Oxford. It includes a publication proposal and newspaper article describing the book's initial costs (a total estimated outlay of £733, and a price of six guineas per unit, both quite high for the time), as well as a list of subscribers to its initial edition of 250 copies, which includes the names of "His Majesty's Library and the Dukes of York, Norfolk, Roxburgh and Northumberland and the Duchess of Devonshire," as well as two institutions: Christ Church College, Oxford, and the Manchester Library (Shelagh Vainker, "Costumes of China," *Orientations* 34.9 [Nov. 2003], 54.). Reprinted editions of *The Costume of China* from 1806, 1811, and 1821 exist at the Huntington Library in San Marino, Calif. In 1984, Craig Clunas had identified a volume given to the Victoria and Albert Museum in 1898 as the original for Mason's book, a claim that may have to be reevaluated in light of Vainker's work (*Chinese Export Watercolours* [London, 1984], 33–42; further citations in the text are cited as *CEW*).

Alexander's *The Costume of China*, published in 1805.[3] Like Mason, Alexander had spent time in China, working as the official draftsman of the important 1793 British embassy to China led by Lord George Macartney. Alexander's book thus functions simultaneously as a historical document and an ethnographic one.[4] The caption to his painting of "Three Vessels Lying at Harbor," for instance, opens with a paragraph on the construction of Chinese ships, but follows that general ethnographic information with a second paragraph that tells the reader that "The small vessel was hired for the service of the Embassy, and employed in transporting baggage" (48). Though the relative ordering of these pieces of information fits with the general thrust of the *Costume* series in which Mason's books were published, here the ethnographic work gives way to notes regarding particular Chinese people, places, or events associated with Alexander's own

[3] In 1825, Alexander also published a volume entitled *Picturesque Representations of the Dress and Manners of the Chinese*, which contains some of the same illustrations as his *Costume of China.* Notes to editions of *The Costume of the Russian Empire* and *The Costumes of Turkey* at the Huntington Library suggest that Alexander played an editorial role in selecting illustrations and writing captions for both of those volumes as well.

[4] Full eyewitness accounts of the 1793 embassy appear in Sir George Staunton's *An Authentic Account of an Embassy from the King of Great Britain to the Emperor of China* (Philadelphia, 1799), which was printed for Robert Campbell by John Bioren. See also Macartney's own *An Embassy to China; being the journal kept by Lord Macartney during his embassy to the Emperor Ch'ien-lung, 1793–1794* (London, 1962), which is edited with an introduction and notes by J. L. Cranmer-Byng. For readings of the 1793 embassy in the context of current theoretical arguments, and in relation to Macartney's infamous refusal to kowtow to the Chinese emperor, see James Hevia, *Cherishing Men From Afar: Qing Guest Ritual and the Macartney Embassy of 1793* (Durham, N.C., 1995), and chapters 2 and 3 of Lydia Liu's *The Clash of Empires: The Invention of China in Modern World Making* (Cambridge, 2005). As Staunton himself was to note in his translation of the Qing penal code, one of the major effects of the 1793 embassy in England was to undermine the largely positive vision of China promulgated by the Jesuit missionaries of the seventeenth century:

> The short residence in China of Lord Macartney's Embassy . . . was amply sufficient to discover that the superiority over other nations, in point of knowledge and virtue, which the Chinese have long been accustomed to assume to themselves, and which some of their European historians have too readily granted them, was in great measure fallacious; their knowledge was perceived to be defective in those points in which we have, in Europe, recently made the greatest progress

(*Ta Tsing Leu Lee; Being the Fundamental Laws, and a Selection from the Supplementary Statues, of the Penal Code of China* [London, 1810; Repub. Taipei, 1966] viii–ix, which was published by T. Cadell and W. Davies in London and by Ch'eng-Wen Publishing Co. in Taipei)

That said, Staunton goes on to suggest that had the members of the 1793 embassy spent more time in China, they would have discovered that much of what Chinese and Europeans think of each other "was to be imputed either to prejudice, or to misinformation; and that, upon the whole, it was not allowable to arrogate, on either side, any violent degree of moral or physical superiority" (ix–x).

experience as a traveler in China. In portraits of specific individuals, like the one of "Van–Ta–Zhin," for instance, Alexander shows us a figure whose presence in published narratives of the Embassy's failures meant that he could not be mistaken for just any Chinese person, even though his costume might signal for readers the general outfit of "A military Mandarine (or Nobleman) of China" (8).[5] Unlike the images in Mason's book, then, which functioned exclusively as "types," the paintings in Alexander's collection operate both historically and typologically, as representational encyclopedia and travel narrative; this is the difference between souvenir and collection, the difference between metonymy ("I was there") and metaphor.[6]

Though Alexander's book has the same title as Mason's, and even the same publisher, then, that only Mason's book appears in the "Costumes of Various Nations" series suggests that the representational difference between the two books registered in the moment of publication, even as the appearance of two separate books with the title *The Costume of China* within four years of each other testifies to the intensity of British cultural interest in China in this period, an interest sustained by the China trade in tea and porcelain, *chinoiserie* in architecture and furnishings, and philosophical and commercial debates about Chinese science, history, and writing.[7]

[5]That Alexander's *Costume* book features general ethnographic information at all may be understood as an effect of the form to which the book belongs; in Staunton's 1797 account of the 1793 embassy's voyage, Alexander's illustrations have, at least as far as the account itself is concerned, a completely documentary, historical effect. Some of the illustrations in Alexander's *The Costume of China*, like "Portrait of a Solider" or "A Sea Vessel Under Sail" are so generic as to approach the illustrative quality of the work done in Mason's *Costume*, but even there, the fact that Alexander himself painted the illustrations is enough to suggest the fact of a *particular* experience of China. It is worth noting, however, that some of the paintings Alexander did of China depend on his use or re-use of generic settings and figures. The Alexander paintings reproduced on pages 28–30 of Susan Legouix's *Image of China*, for instance, all feature the same crouching figure in slightly different contexts and poses (*Image of China: William Alexander* [London, 1980].).

[6]Susan Stewart:

> In contrast to the souvenir, the collection offers example rather than sample, metaphor rather than metonymy. The collection does not displace attention to the past; rather, the past is at the service of the collection, for whereas the souvenir lends authenticity to the past, the past lends authenticity to the collection.

(*On Longing: Narratives of the Miniature, the Gigantic, the Souvenir, the Collection* [Durham, N.C., 1993], 151)

[7]David Porter writes that the publication between 1615 and 1625 of the Jesuit Matteo Ricci's journals detailing his time in China "inaugurated a period of two centuries in European history where significant

Returning to the typological argument of Mason's books, one might begin to think their organization of the relationship between reference and representation as differing in several ways from either an "exact discourse" (recalling Edmund Scott's title for his account) or an "anecdote." Rather than make a claim to reference in particular, Mason's images and captions make claims to reference in general, suggesting that though this particular tambouriner, beggar, or tailor may not have existed as such, he or she illustrates the presence in China in general of musicians, beggars, and tailors, each of whom will more or less resemble this example. Mason's books are interesting, then, not simply as instantiations of particular illustrative scenes, but as collective documents that organize for their readers an entire typology of China, what Mason's preface to *The Costume of China* refers to as the "domestic and mechanical habits of an original and remote nation" (*CC*, 7).

Though the books never show particular Chinese people or events, what they do show allows them to deduce from the referential surface of the image the caption that will explain the image's exemplification of a general type. Considered inside the typological project of *The Costume of China* as a whole, the individual images might be said to function *like* anecdotes insofar as they enable the production of generality from particularity. In this sense of "anecdotal," the books' typological work, which grounds their large-scale production of a set of cultural truths, sustains itself by putting together image-caption pairs in which the image functions as an ersatz anecdote in its illustration of a possible particularity, while the caption urges that particular into generality, allowing the image to become the illustration of a general practice. If the epistemological structure of Mason's books resembles that of the anecdote, it is because, despite a series of major differences in the formal conventions of the books (encyclopedic and typological) and of the anecdote proper (small and individual), the books' overall project depends on its marshalling of individual openings onto reference—the images—that operate simultaneously as anecdotes and as illustrations. Even as the image anecdotally indicates the *possibility* of its represented content having been an event—the picture of some actual Chinese person's real behavior at some

developments in linguistics, theology, the arts, and economic thought were invariably refracted through an ever-expanding awareness of a rival civilization on the other side of the world" (*Ideographia: The Chinese Cipher in Early Modern Europe.* [Stanford, 2001], 242). The sense in which China was conceived as a rival to northern Europe in the nineteenth century (especially in England, France, and the Netherlands) must be understood as the crucial cultural subtext for a general interest in Chinese costume (even as that latter interest intersects with a European epistemological drive to categorize and represent the world to itself). As Porter notes, the nineteenth century saw a major rise in negative European attitudes toward China; Mason's books are in some sense on the cusp of this shift.

historical moment—it also claims to illustrate the general principle organized by the caption, for which the actual referential truth of one particular pose or another is of no serious consequence.

This movement between image-as-possible-anecdote and image-as-illustration can be arranged along a vector that organizes the image's epistemological relationship to the caption that accompanies it, with the anecdotal aspect of the image *preceding* the general claim the caption makes (the caption generates its description of general practice from the image-as-single-event), while its illustrative aspect *succeeds* that same claim in order to exemplify the authoritative general principle expressed in the caption. Seeing the anecdotal and the illustrative aspects inside each of these individual images suggests that Mason's books generate their epistemological power at least partly through a continuous formal oscillation between typology and instantiation, encyclopedia and (potential) event, in which the deductive making-visible of a law (Chinese tambouriners look like *this*) sustains itself via the simultaneous inductive presentation of an example (here is one representative Chinese tambouriner).

2. Exceptional Punishments

I have so far said little about these two books that could not have been said about any other book in the series; rather I have been trying to establish the performative and epistemological conventions within which Mason's work operated. But any theory of these conventions comes up hard against the fact that of the ten books in the series, only one did not have the word "costume" in its title: Mason's 1801 *The Punishments of China.*[8] Given the typological structure of the series as a whole, the title alone suggests that the fact of Chinese punishment was subsumable during the early nineteenth century under a general interest in costumes and customs (which tells us something about the meaning of "costume" operating here: "The custom and fashion of the time to which a scene or representation belongs; the manner, dress, arms, furniture, and other features proper to the time and locality in which the scene is laid."[9]). That it is the *only* volume in the series to operate under this larger definition of "costume," however, directs our attention

[8] *The Punishments of China, Illustrated by Twenty-Two Engravings: With Explanations in England and French* (London, 1801). I cite an unpaginated 1804 edition held at the Huntington Library in San Marino, California; further references in the text are cited as *PC.*

[9] *Oxford English Dictionary,* costume, n., 1.a.

to the historical divergence between eighteenth- and nineteenth-century European and Chinese punitive codes, largely around the issue of judicial punishment and torture. The growing European interest in "humane" modes of execution (of which the French use of the guillotine beginning in 1792 is one example), British objections to continental judicial torture dating back to the sixteenth century, and the radical changes in modes of public execution and imprisonment outlined by Michel Foucault in *Discipline and Punish,* were all expressions of the larger sympathetic shift around theories of the human and the humane that made impossible nineteenth-century state practices that had been commonplace across Europe only decades earlier.[10] By making punitive practice a feature of ethnographic knowledge, Mason's book expresses a generalized awareness of this shift. The fact that the ethnographic attention in the book series focuses solely on China is, however, an important early expression of the ecliptic cultural logic this book explores.

Within that context *Punishments* offers an instance of how the apparent violation of an established thematic structure can suggest the presence behind or underneath some apparently simple organizational principle (a series of books on national "costumes") of a far more complicated logic. In the Chinese case, "costume"—a "key sign and focus of ethnographic difference" in the colonial era—becomes a category far more complex and inclusive even than the "costumes" of the various other nations pictured in the series.[11] Rather than read

[10]Some measure of this change can be gathered from Victor Hugo's unfortunately precipitous announcement, in 1874, that "torture has ceased to exist." Edward Peters provides a useful summary of this transformation:

> In revision after revision from 1750 on, the provisions for torture in the criminal codes of Europe were rolled back, until by 1800 they were barely visible. Along with legislative revision, a large literature condemning torture on both legal and moral grounds grew up and was circulated widely. Its best-known example was Cesare Beccaria's immensely influential treatise *On Crimes and Punishments* of 1764. . . . Torture came to bear the brunt, and in many instances became the focal point, of much Enlightenment criticism of the *ancient régime*, and indeed of the legal and moral savagery and archaism of the early European world. (*Torture* [London, 1985], 74)

Ironically, of course, the European calls for the end of torture affected Europe almost exclusively, but did not stop Europeans abroad from institutionalizing torture as a mechanism of colonial control. Timothy Brook, Jérôme Bourgon, and Gregory Blue write that the British relied on the argument that Chinese natives only understood the use of force to introduce punishments banned in Britain to their colony in Hong Kong, for instance (*Death by a Thousand Cuts* [Cambridge, Mass., 2008], 256n50.).

[11]Nicholas B. Dirks, *Castes of Mind: Colonialism and the Making of Modern India* (Princeton, N.J, 2001), 92. Dirks is referring to ethnographic drawings, "pictures of 'typical' representatives of different

Fig 2.1 George Henry Mason and Pu Qua, *The Punishments of China*. "A Culprit before a Magistrate." Courtesy of The Huntington Library.

Punishments as the anomalous expression of British ethnography, however, in which it would emerge against the "conscious" structure of the book series as the return of its repressed ethnographic desire—instead of seeing the book as either the exception to a rule (in which case it might be safely ignored in a broader theorization of what the series means or does) or as the sole symptom of the series' logic (which would be to make it into the "unconscious" of the series to which it belongs)—I wish to take it as part of the literal surface of the logic of representation of which it takes part, as a member of the class that it helps to produce and which, in turn, is produced partially through and by its inclusion.

Punishments opens with a plate titled "A Culprit Before a Magistrate," reproduced in this text as figure 2.1, in which a man kneels in front of a desk, behind

groups, types, castes, and tribes" collected by Colin McKenzie in India in the early nineteenth century, but the mentality he describes is appropriate to a more general epistemological project intimately connected with imperialism. It is worth noting that Mason, who came to Canton in 1789 on doctor's orders to recuperate from an illness, was a "Major of Brigade to his Majesty's forces on the coast of Coromandel [the southeastern coast of the Indian peninsula]," and thus an intimate of the British colonial program (*Views of 18th Century China*, 6n1.).

which sits the magistrate, who is accompanied right and left by assistants (the prisoner is framed, like the magistrate, by two figures, who appear to be guards).

The second plate shows a man conveyed to prison, the third "A Culprit Conveyed to Trial," and the fourth, "An Offender Undergoing the Bastinade" (being beaten with a bamboo pole). From this point forward the book shows only punishments, which range in severity from the twisting of ears (Plate V) to the final image showing "The Manner of Beheading," which the caption says is "deemed in the highest degree ignominious" and therefore "only inflicted for crimes which are regarded by the Chinese government as the most prejudicial to society" (Plate XXII). Though the culprits and offenders in the various images are never visibly the same person, the book nonetheless can be seen to operate partly along the lines of a narrative structure—trial, imprisonment, punishment—that gives it the sense of a "beginning, middle, and end" that one might follow. Just where this narrative breaks down, at the moment when the punishments begin to succeed one another with no further sense of story, the ordering of the images and captions shifts to reflect a vertical hierarchy of punishment, a Dantean ladder of severity that offers the reader the pleasure of knowing that whatever comes next will be slightly more spectacular than what has just preceded it. Far more than *The Costume of China,* where the images succeed one another with no apparently discernible logic (a bricklayer, a carpenter, a mandarin in his summer dress), *Punishments* contextualizes its referential work inside economies of story and progress.

This exceptionalism must be read in relation to the book's own declared axis of typological selection. In the preface to *The Costume of China,* Mason acknowledged that many of his captions depended on information he had acquired from other writers on China, including Sir George Staunton (*CC,* 7). In *Punishments,* a year later, he also mentions his relation to those writers. But he went on to say:

> Various writers have mentioned other punishments, in addition to those represented in this publication, of a much severer nature, which have been inflicted by the Chinese upon criminals, convicted of regicide, parricide, rebellion, treason, or sedition; but drawings, or even verbal descriptions, of these would be committing an indecorous violence on the feelings, and inducing us to arraign the temperance and wisdom, so universally acknowledged in the government of China. (*PC* preface)

The Punishments of China thus begins with a statement of its own incompleteness, an acknowledgment that the narrative and typological structure that organizes it could be extended beyond "The Manner of Beheading" to punishments "of a much severer nature" that it will not show. While the book neither describes nor depicts the punishments, however, its invocation of the possibility of depiction—it could, remember, have said nothing about these absent illustrations—seems to respond both to a desire for comprehensiveness (shouldn't a book called *The Punishments of China* theoretically include *all* the punishments and not just a limited selection?) as well as the need to perform its own sense of decorum within a British context in which such pictures might do violence to feelings, and in which China's temperance ought to be "universally acknowledged."

This has complicated effects on the book's narrative organization. Its unrepresentability is, after all, not simply the unrepresentability of a limited text. Though in the costume book not everything of China is shown (and how could it be?), the representational claim there attempts to indicate a set of possibilities or limits from which one might deduce the unrepresented remainder: if a Chinese baker looks like this, and a butcher looks like that, well, then, the candlestick maker probably looks like something in between. So also with sailing ships and wheeled carts. But because *Punishments* explicitly locates the unrepresentable material in a "beyond" or "in addition to" the punishments it represents, it leaves the reader to imagine an unrepresentable outside to the typological circle traced by the book itself, as though the story were missing its ending, as though the axis of punishment extended infinitely beyond the book's limit, asymptote to some Platonically punitive sublime.

If the exceptionality of this moment is not to undermine the project of the series as a whole, it must be thought as a continuation of the typological work done there; imagine that Mason has written an encyclopedia whose final chapter consisted of a page announcing that the final chapter was missing, or produced a list that, *pace* Borges, who imagined this as an entry in a Chinese encyclopedia, includes as its final element "those not included in the classification."[12] That is, it must be considered within the broader framework of the books in which it appears as a gesture made within a larger economy of exposure and concealment, described explicitly, as it is here, as a salute to international or intercultural generosity and understanding.

[12] Jorge Luis Borges's Chinese encyclopedia lives on as one of the major initial figures of Michel Foucault's *The Order of Things*, and subsequently has come to figure a certain European relation to both China and modes of classification. For a longer discussion of the encyclopedia's role in the production of postwar French interest in China, see the introduction of Zhang Longxi's *Mighty Opposites: From Dichotomies to Differences in the Comparative Study of China* (Stanford, 1998).

The irony of that gesture stems from the fact that by declaring his respect for Chinese temperance—and therefore by tempering the complete picture of China's punishments—Mason opens the possibility that the Chinese are not that temperate after all. Saying you don't wish to judge someone implies that there is something there to be judged. Mason writes that to include images or descriptions of the severest punishments would be to "arraign the temperance and wisdom" acknowledged in the Chinese government. The French translation of "arraign" (the book appeared in a bilingual English and French edition) as *faire le procès*, to bring to trial, recalls the word's literal valence: the announcement that China is not on trial is an announcement that China is on trial. The book narrates a trial, and it is a trial, the content and the form approaching one another along the figural limit of the word "adjudication." The conclusion readers should draw from the book's captions and illustrations, Mason goes on to say, has to do not so much with their "novelty and information," but rather from the "sensation of security which they produce in those bosoms that heave upon a tract of the globe, where they are protected from being torn by lengthened agonies; where a person's innocence is not estimated by his mental or corporeal powers of enduring pain," and so on (*PC*, preface). *The Punishments of China*'s typological study of the Chinese judicial system (already vaguely mislabeled, then, as a list of "punishments," though certainly the book works that way as well) becomes at least in the preface not simply an illustration of the novelty of cultural otherness but also a cross-cultural judgment narrated as an allegory of the material it contains, a trial in which the most damning evidence is damning precisely because the text excludes it.

This alone gives a literary critic plenty to work with. But it turns out that the arrangements of Mason's books are even stranger, as is indicated by this extraordinary fact: in the caption to an image in Mason's *The Costume of China*, printed a year earlier than *Punishments*, one finds described precisely those punishments that Mason does not include in the later book! Below is the caption that accompanies "A Puppet-Show," which is reproduced as figure 2.2:

> A person mounted on a toll, and concealed as far as the ankles with a covering of blue calico, causes some very small puppets to perform a kind of play, the box at the top representing a stage. The little figures are made to move with much grace and decorum, on which account the Chinese puppet-show is rendered equally innocent as trifling, and may be presented without endangering the purity of the infant mind.
>
> The Chinese youth receive the earliest impressions of virtue and filial obedience; these precepts prevent their incurring the penalties prescribed

Fig 2.2 George Henry Mason and Pu Qua, *The Costume of China.* "A Puppet-Show." Courtesy of The Huntington Library.

> in the code of laws of that empire against such 'degenerate vipers'* as shall dare to violate any of those sacred ties which GOD and Nature have framed to attach them to the authors of their existence. The son, or grandson, of a Chinese, who is deficient in his duty towards his father or mother, grandfather, or grandmother, is condemned by the law to receive one hundred blows of a bamboo; if he gives them abusive language, he is strangled; if he lifts his hand against them, he is beheaded; and if he wounds or maims them, his flesh is torn from his bones with red-hot pincers, and he is cut into a thousand pieces. It is also conjectured that the stability and uniformity of the Chinese character—immutable for the known duration of four thousand years—it [sic] is supported solely by that progressive submission which rises, gradually, from the bosom of a family even to the throne.
>
> *See Shakespeare's *Lear.* (158)

The material from "if he wounds or maims them" forward, which describes the punishment now widely known (or imagined) as the "death by a thousand cuts," is exactly what becomes unrepresentable a year later, and becomes there the subject of Mason's claim that "Various writers" had discussed it. This unrepresentable punishment is known in Chinese as *lingchi chusi.* Timothy Brook, Jérôme Bourgon, and Gregory Blue describe it as a form of "tormented execution" involving the methodical cutting apart of the body of the convicted prisoner. As they show, *lingchi* became notorious not simply because it marked the extreme case of Chinese judicial punishment but also because its representations—particularly its photographic representations—coincided with an international political context that turned "China into a museum of all that Europe had left behind, a Pandora's box of leftover images" that helped give "the imperialist West the justification it sought to prove that it had to act in China."[13] In the early twentieth century, photographs of the last few *lingchi* executions circulated widely between China and Europe, all of them taken in a brief span of time between the development of convenient portable photography and the Qing government's banning of *lingchi* in 1905, as Brook et al. note. Mason's reference to the punishment in *The Costume of China* can be thought of as an early indicator of the West's eventual interest in it, as well as a reflection of the comparatively more positive cultural view of China held by most Europeans at the beginning of the nineteenth century.

Presumably it is the protected "infant mind" of the end of the first paragraph of the caption to "A Puppet-Show" that leads Mason metonymically into the "Chinese youth" of the second, though the general logic that would authorize that movement is hard to parse. The caption presents this information about Chinese judicial punishment in the context of a performance intended for the edification of children. The footnote to *King Lear* allows Mason to translate the show's pedagogical performance into an English context, where the phrase "degenerate viper," which Lear directs at Goneril, makes his betrayal explicitly generational.[14]

[13] Brook et al., 28. See their third chapter for a developmental history of *lingchi* in China; see 171–74 for a brief discussion of Mason's *Punishments.* I discuss the famous photograph of *lingchi* owned and reproduced by Georges Bataille at length in chapter 6; Brook et al. do so in chapter 8 of their book. On Chinese judicial torture more generally, see Bourgon, *Supplices chinois* (Brussels, 2007), and Antonio Dominguez Leiva and Muriel Détrie, *Le Supplice Oriental dans la littérature et les arts* (Neuilly-les-Dijon, 2005).

[14] The *King Lear* variorum shows no instances of "degenerate viper"; it is likely that Mason is citing Nahum Tate's revised and adapted version of the play, with which the eighteenth century was far more familiar than the original. Shakespeare's line is "Degenerate bastard! I'll not trouble thee" (I, iv); Tate rewrites this as: "Degenerate viper, I'll not stay with Thee" (*The History of King Lear,* in *Shakespeare Adaptations: The Tempest, The Mock Tempest, and King Lear,* ed. Montague Summers [Boston, 1922], 190.). That the original is "bastard" reinforces the sense that what is at stake is the failure of filiation to regenerate itself as filiality.

Lear's major plotline revolves around the legal structure of inheritance and the failure of children to refrain from becoming "degenerate vipers," or rather the failure of the legal force embodied in the king (or the generative life–force of the father) to keep them from doing so. The reference thus moves Mason from praise for the pedagogical mode of the Chinese puppet show, which protects innocent minds from dangerous ideas, to the indirect suggestion that the public apparatus of Chinese punishment performs a set of consequences for unfilial behavior designed to discourage future Gonerils and Regans.[15]

The Chinese puppet show thus stands in for both the modesty of one particular mode of public performance for children and for a correspondingly spectacular form of public punishment, each of them directed, in Mason's caption, toward the improvement of children, or rather, toward the location of children in a hierarchy of interpersonal engagement and pedagogical modesty (the "infant mind" must remain properly pure). Since the improvement of Chinese children connects directly, as Mason suggests, to the development of a more general filial piety that forms the bedrock of all Chinese social relations and indeed of all Chinese history, it makes sense that the puppet show's lone observer would be an adult. Though he cannot be, at least according to Mason's caption, the proper audience for a puppet show designed for children, his presence suggests the degree to which the importance of the education of the child in his or her role as child (relative to parents, grandparents, ancestors, or the emperor) remains a feature of the adult Chinese person. In the context of Mason's warmed-over Confucianism, the adult Chinese person, and through him, China itself, is as much the historical addressee of this particular performance as any child could be.

Rather than argue that the description of these punishments is somehow strangely mis-placed here from its proper location in the punishments book, or that Mason must have changed his mind about the decorousness of these descriptions between 1800 and 1801, I would like to suggest that the descriptions of "more severe" punishments are here dis-placed, in the Freudian sense of the term,[16] that is, that their presence here does not indicate a mistake but rather

[15]Remember that an insane Lear, in the farmhouse scene of Act III, does in fact put his two daughters on trial. In his madness, he asks that Regan be dissected for evidence of treachery: "Then let them anatomize Regan; see what breeds / about her heart. Is there any cause in nature that / makes these hard hearts?" (III, vi). But the trial, like the dissection (itself a kind of cutting into a thousand pieces), is imaginary, by contrast to the actually staged punishments of China, as Mason seems to be suggesting.

[16]In Freud's work, "condensation," "displacement," and "symbolization" are the three of major figures of dream work. Displacement has often been compared to metaphor, since both have to do

points toward the logic or organization that is proper to the books as they stand. The fact that the missing "beyond" of the *Punishments* book appears a year prior to its remarked absence in an entry on puppet shows must be understood *as part of rather than an exception* to the logic of the two books.[17]

What all this suggests for a broader understanding of the books' typological work in relation to Chinese judicial punishment is, beyond the general observation of the manner in which the texts combine to link punishment, performance, the status of adult and child, and the myth of Chinese immutability, fairly complicated. Following the trail to one more image-caption pair should, however, allow for at least a temporary summing up.

Late in *The Costume of China*, the reader comes across the picture of a man sitting on the ground, looking to his left with his legs out in front of him, knees bent upward, with tears in the fabric of his shirt. The plate, titled "A Lame Beggar," is reproduced in this text as figure 2.3.

Though the man in the image is not visibly crippled, the caption refers immediately to his lameness:

> Probably not born so, nor judicially afflicted with this calamity by Heaven in his maturer age; but caused by his own parents, who crippled him designedly, in order that he might become an extraordinary object of pity; this practice being reported (perhaps by Calumny, the genius of distortion) to be not very uncommon with the lowest order of Chinese.
>
> The unpleasant sensation which this object may at first excite will be materially dissipated by the consideration that all instances of natural deformity, be it of limb or feature, are so very rare among the populous nations of the eastern world, as to attract universal astonishment whenever they are presented to the view.
>
> It will be observed that the countenances of the four mendicants represented in this work are particularly characteristic.

---

with a carrying across of meaning from one place to another. Unlike metaphor, however, which tends to organize its displacements vertically from one realm of meaning to another (my love is a rose, for instance), "displacement" allows me here to suggest the degree to which this transfer occurs horizontally, within the text's own plane of self-understanding, rather than as a gesture to a completely incompatible (and therefore potentially unconscious) register of meaning.

[17] Such a reading gains comfort from the movement of the crucial cognate "decorum" from the caption to "A Puppet-Show" ("the little figures are made to move with much grace and *decorum*") to Mason's claim, in the 1801 preface, that to include the extreme descriptions "would be committing an *indecorous* violence on the feelings" of his readers.

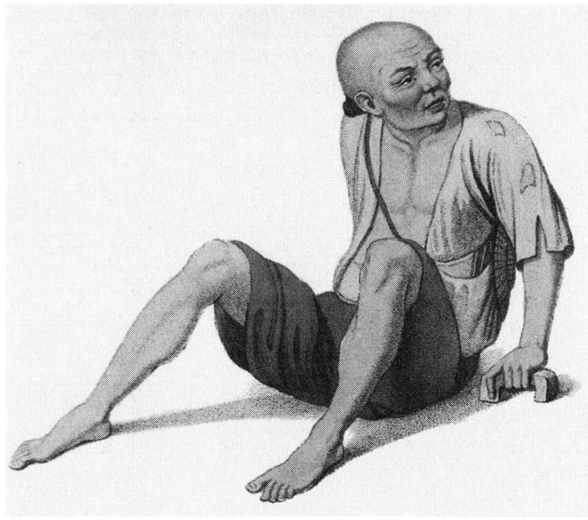

Fig 2.3 George Henry Mason and Pu Qua, *The Costume of China.* "A Lame Beggar." Courtesy of The Huntington Library.

> In the face of the Beggar with his Dog, misery and low artifice are apparent; in the aspect of the man with a Serpent, reluctance and self-disgust are visible; the features of the Beggar with a Monkey are expressive of softness supplicating compassion; and in the visage of this Cripple, pain and wretchedness are most forcibly delineated. (220)

Far more startling for me than the evocation of a sympathetic pain in relation to the image of a Chinese person is the typological intensity of the frame this caption establishes. The images of the four mendicants in the *The Costume of China* are "particularly characteristic," it argues, but the characteristicness has not so much to do with the variety of Chinese beggars as it does with the general typology of begging, divided here into a number of apparently universal aspects which find themselves expressed in these four images. At this point, more than anywhere else in Mason's two books, one feels an encyclopedic drive overpowering what one imagines as the images "themselves," that is, the images considered outside of the production (and reproduction) of ethnic typology that organizes them. In such a context, the redundancy in the phrase "*particularly* characteristic" suggests that the typicalness of the typical has been in play more than the text would like to admit.[18]

[18]The sudden and somewhat belated appearance of this explicitly typological frame, just two pages from the end of the *Costume* volume, is the only moment of its type in either book. It presents its reader with a map of the general program of the "Costumes of Various Nations" series, namely the

Considering the typological work done by "A Lame Beggar" in the context of the initially surprising appearance of the "more extreme" punishments in the *The Costume of China's* puppet show entry (rather than in the *Punishments* book itself, where one might have expected them), one might begin to say that the typological structure of Mason's work seems unusually connected to its presentation of judicial punishment and readerly sympathy, now finally visible along two major lines. First, the typological gap or failure of the *Punishments* book (1801), announced so clearly in its preface, seems to have been resolved in advance in *The Costume of China* (published a year earlier) inside a caption that explicitly connects the punishments deemed too indecorous for the second book to an explanation of the Confucian roots of Chinese filial piety, and remarks on the importance of public performances that reinforce them. And second, the general typological project of both books reaches its most "particularly characteristic" representations in a moment in which the reader's attention is drawn toward but then pushed away from a sympathetic identification with an apparently deliberate physical violence—the only moment in either book in which the reader is asked to notice the suffering of a particular person at all—that has been inflicted by parents on their child. The caption's reluctance to declare absolutely that this man has been crippled by his parents—you see it in the phrase "Probably not born so," the nod to Calumny and rumor, and the litotes of its assertion (the practice is "not very uncommon with the lowest order of Chinese")—suggest something of the rhetorical intensity that surrounds the claim it makes and, thus, something of its importance to the general work of these two books.

Let me draw some of these strands together. Though the violence done to the lame beggar depends in part on his family's poverty, the sheer fact of his being "crippled designedly" by his parents makes the juridical origin of that violence the same contract between parent and child that Mason reads, in the puppet show entry, as the legal foundation of all Chinese history and behavior (he is probably

---

encyclopedic characterization of a people for those who "wish to be informed respecting the individual manner, the external appearance, and the general character of different countries," as the publisher's preface to *British Costumes* has it (Pyne, ii). (It is precisely the movement from "individual manner" to "external appearance" to "general character" that defines the books' epistemological ambitions.) The caption to "A Lame Beggar," by reframing the three earlier pictures of mendicants as members of a group of four (which is not at all obvious—given the titles of the plates, the reader would be justified in not having connected the "Man With a Serpent" to the "Lame Beggar" at all) and suggesting that each member of that series represents one quarter of the sum total of mendicancy's aspects, expresses the representational and epistemological archetype of the entire costume-book project.

not, Mason says, "*judicially* afflicted with this calamity by Heaven"). That is, the logic whereby the parents cripple the child in order to make it economically productive depends on the assertion that its body is theirs to cripple, and thus on a sense that the ownership of a person's physical body has been subordinated to a larger filial structure in which the body belongs, even in its most intimate functionings, to someone located outside the "self" that nominally governs it.[19] The beggar's body thus testifies, thanks entirely to the caption that describes it, to the presence of the *same filial rules* Mason finds reinforced by the public performance of judicial punishments in China. The exclusion of the "more extreme" punishments from the *Punishments* book omits those punishments specifically reserved for high crimes against filiation; a year earlier, in *The Costume of China*, the question of filiation (and of cultural child-rearing more broadly) has organized itself around two forms of pedagogical performance: the verbal description of judicial punishments whose performative aspect expresses itself most vividly in the image of the adult watching the "Puppet–Show," and a singular, typologically extravagant instance of "pain and wretchedness . . . most forcibly delineated" on the body of a man whose pain and wretchedness the text attributes speculatively, hesitantly, with a nod to "the genius of distortion," to his deliberate crippling by his parents.

Is not, then, one might ask, the beggar's public begging, in which he becomes "an extra-ordinary object of pity," a kind of *performance* not simply of his own "crippled" body but of his submission to a set of social hierarchies that are the original cause and justification of that crippling? And is not, equally, his lameness a kind of *punishment of China* justified and enabled by the hierarchical mechanism

[19]This is not to suggest that in Europe or the Americas no limitations existed on bodily self-governance, since both slavery and the continued exploitation of women depended on just such a system (which functioned in both economic and juridical terms). For more on the relation between governance and bodies (including the body politic), see Steven Bruhm, "Aesthetics and Anesthetics at the Revolution," *Studies in Romanticism* 32.3 (Fall 1993). I wonder if what strikes Mason as remarkable in this caption—so remarkable that he has to communicate this rumor, even as he acknowledges it may not be true in general or in the case of *this* beggar—is that the violence is permanent and occurs across the parent-child barrier. Given shifting relationships to the notion of childhood in late eighteenth- and early nineteenth-century Europe, and the uneven distribution of those relationships across geography, race, gender, class, and individual, it is of course impossible to know. A book is waiting to be written on the ways in which an increased European attention to childhood, corresponding to a growing sense of the importance of an individual human being as life to be protected and cared for, interacted with the broader development of European imperialism and the West's ongoing interventions into other cultures in the name of the children of those cultures and of human rights in general. This book traces one aspect of the latter part of that historical complex.

of filial piety whose most public maintenance is done by the system of judicial violence Mason incompletely delineates?

3. English Writing, "Chinese" Pictures

The illustrations in Mason's two books, unlike those in Alexander's 1805 *The Costume of China,* were not done by their editor. Small captions beneath the paintings read "Pu Qua, Canton, Delin." In the preface to the *Costume* book, Mason writes that he "obtained correct drawings of the Chinese in their respective habits and occupations; the itinerant mechanics and handicraftsmen, in particular; fac-similes of which are exhibited on the subsequent pages. Not intended, originally, for public inspection, they are thus, at the insistence of some learned and ingenious friends, issued from his portfolio after ten years privacy" (7). Though the authenticity of the images is assured at the cultural level by virtue of their being painted by a Chinese person—and even more by Mason's insistence that they were designed to be private—they lose some of the indexical force of the portraits and landscapes in Alexander's *Costume* volume, each of which communicates, beyond the specificities of its content, the author's past presence at the site of portraiture. The difference between Alexander's portraits, or even the paintings in *The Costume of Great Britain,* all of which belong firmly to a European painterly tradition, and the background-less illustrations of Mason's two *China* volumes means that the paintings in Mason's books signified more than their simple referential content: they also exemplified some version of "Chinese painting."

But the paintings were not exactly Chinese, either. From the earliest days of the European China trade, China produced materials especially for export, generating porcelain patterns and even flavors of tea according to European demands and the specifications of expert tasters from the East India companies.[20] These products did not reflect, as their purchasers often assumed, Chinese aesthetic norms, but occupied instead a middle ground in which a set of aesthetic demands communicated

[20] On eighteenth-century anxieties about Chinese trade goods, especially porcelain, see Lydia Liu's "Robinson Crusoe's Earthenware Pot," and the third chapter of Porter's *Ideographia*; for a general overview of the China trade in artistic goods see Carl L. Crossman, *The China Trade: Export Paintings, Furniture, Silver and other Objects* (Princeton, N. J., 1972). As for tea, Jack Beecham writes that by 1785, the British East India Company was "buying and selling fifteen million pounds' weight of China tea per year," a figure that rose to thirty million pounds by 1830; at one time, he writes, "the tea tax provided a tenth of the British government's entire revenue" (*The Chinese Opium Wars* [London, 1975], 19, 29.).

through traders and marketing agents on both sides emerged through Chinese aesthetic and commercial practice for sale and exchange in Europe.[21] The China trade's production of goods for sale in Europe thus constitutes an early example of the figural work of a global economy in which trade goods functioned as cultural representations of their apparent origins, not only at the material level of the goods themselves (China is the land of tea and spices), but also as a series of representational surfaces on which were painted Chinese villages, people, and landscapes. After paper, porcelain may have been the eighteenth century's most common representational medium, one whose ambitions connected only marginally to the actual representational surface of China, but which nonetheless provided armchair travelers with a set of powerfully mediatized and mercantilized images of China itself.[22] That these images were from very early on produced in correspondence with the representational demands of European and American export brokers means that what they represented was never the authentic China it purported to be. As Craig Clunas writes, "Whatever the customer may have thought, he was not buying a piece of reportage, an accurate picture of the Chinese interior he was forbidden to penetrate. Nor was he buying a product of the Chinese imagination. Rather he was receiving his own preconceptions . . . reflected back at him by an artist whose sole concern was to please" (*CEW*, 25). The representational work done by porcelain (whose products were so often used to consume that other great Chinese product, tea, in a wonderful *mise-en-abyme*[23]) establishes a framework for understanding

[21] Margaret Jourdain and R. Soame Jenyns capture some of the combination of economic calculation and benevolent racism behind this trade by writing (in 1950) that "The Chinese took kindly to the imitation of models that came to them from foreign parts, and made 'expressly for Europeans articles adapted to their taste, and images in china, steatite and painted wood are made so cheaply among them that there might often be economy in getting them from China'" (*Chinese Export Art in the Eighteenth Century* [London, 1950], 13.). Their citation is from Evariste Régis Huc's 1854 *L'Empire Chinois.* The notion that Chinese people are good at imitating but not creating is a feature of anti-Chinese racism (some of it produced in China in the mode of self-critique) to this day.

[22] Armchair travelers, but also real travelers: consider in this context a sentence from John Bell's *A Journey From St. Petersburg to Pekin, 1719–22* (pub. 1763): "In the cliffs of the rocks you see little scattered cottages, with spots of cultivated ground, much resembling those romantick figures of landskips which are painted on the China-ware and other manufactures of this country. These are accounted fanciful by most Europeans, but are really natural" (117). The sentence indicates the presence of some common discourse in Europe, even in the early 1700s, about the possible representational truth of China-ware. But Bell's claim that the landscapes he sees "are really natural" also suggests the degree to which any particular experience of China could arrive in China already prepared to see certain kinds of vistas, to find them "natural" and therefore real.

[23] A pairing admirably condensed by Alexander Pope's *Rape of the Lock:* "From silver Spouts the grateful Liquors glide, / And *China's* earth receives the smoking Tyde" (3.109–110).

the meaning and value of Chinese export painting. Though watercolors were not especially valuable as commodities,[24] largely because the Chinese had no technological advantage in their manufacture, their production and trade operated along lines similar to that of the porcelain industry, with paintings produced to European standards by groups of artisans working under the direction of a master artist. The "high degree of division of labour in Chinese craft production generally, of which porcelain kilns at Jingdezhen were the most extreme example, . . . is hardly surprising, but it can hardly be over-emphasized," largely because it allows us to disconnect from European notions of genius and the single artist the commercial and mediatic context within which painters like Pu Qua operated (*CEW*, 73). Even the artist's name indicates the transnational context in which the paintings were produced: "Pu Qua" is not an actual Chinese name, but the product of a naming convention developed by Europeans in and around Canton, who tended to add the suffix "*qua*" to the names of Chinese merchants and painters.[25] In this sense, the "Pu Qua" written in alphabetic script at the bottom of the images in *Costume* and *Punishments* is another mark of the economic context from which the paintings emerged, and a lure likely to be read by British readers as a personal signature rather than a brand name.[26]

Clunas has found, in the Victoria & Albert Museum in London, a loose set of one hundred prints he believes to be the original images from which Mason drew the images for *The Costume of China*. Using watermarks, he has dated the collection to between 1780 and 1790, making it quite possible that this set of

[24] Jourdain and Jenyns describe the relative value of painting to such goods as silk embroidery, lacquered furniture, and porcelain: "In the case of paintings on glass and paper-hangings their brilliant colour and fantasy ensured a wide demand, but the art of China was measured by European standards. The realistic representation of birds and flowers was accepted from the late years of the seventeenth century. . . . But the representation of the human form was considered to be 'a high burlesque' and 'either hideous or ludicrous'" (15).

[25] The most famous person so suffixed was Howqua, or Wu Bingjian, the leading light of the Chinese merchant community in Canton. Craig Clunas finds no adequate explanation for the emergence of this suffix, which was represented in some paintings by "one of two characters pronounced *gua* which are otherwise meaningless and serve only to convey the sound." He concludes: "It seems likely that the *-qua* names whatever their origin (and they are seen already in early eighteenth-century documents) were simply a form of name somehow fixed to Chinese merchants and artists by Europeans and used only in intercourse with Europeans" (83).

[26] Pu Qua's status as an artist is reinforced on these pages by the work's dual "signatures." "Pu Qua, Canton, Delin.," and "Dadley: London, Sculpt" reflect a tradition in which an artist *delineavit* (has drawn) while an artisan *sculpsit* (engraved) the image. That said, Jourdain and Jenyns describe export watercolors in general as "never signed as they are the work of artisans" (31).

images was brought back by Mason from Canton.[27] For my purposes here, whether or not these images came back from China with Mason does not matter as much as the fact that they were sold as a set. Clunas's work on export watercolors shows that they were almost always sold in bound formats or loose sets that gathered together a variety of images (even images from different sources, in some cases), meaning that the images Mason "obtained" were likely purchased from one of several workshops catering to the foreign trade in watercolor depictions of China *as a set* designed to do the very representational work that they would perform in his *Costume* book of 1800. That is, the same European epistemological structure that made the book of types so popular in late Georgian England was the generating force behind the work of Pu Qua's studio and the production of this type of image generally, making Europe just as much an origin of the Pu Qua paintings as Pu Qua's studio itself. As Brook et al. remark, "Chinese watercolor artists quickly learned what would sell and happily allowed European aesthetic and moral tastes to determine what 'China' should look like—indeed, to determine what aspects of Chinese life should be judged visually appropriate or desirable."[28] From this perspective Mason's claim that the images were "Not intended, originally, for public inspection" can refer only to his state of mind when he purchased them.

As for the paintings' aesthetic qualities, a quick sense of their intermediacy can be gathered by comparing them to either the paintings in Alexander's costume book, or to any Chinese figure painting of the same era. In particular, the Chinese convention of showing distance by placing things higher in the frame seems—if one looks back at the opening image of *Punishments,* figure 2.1, above—to have been transformed through some hybridized mixture with European laws of perspective, even as the habit of a blank background retains something aesthetically Chinese. This mixed strategy, like that of much of Chinese export ware, "occupies a space which is neither wholly Chinese nor wholly European" (*CEW,* 11). If the nature of these compromises can "tell us a lot about how one culture saw the other in the age before photography"

[27] Though this is now possibly under dispute—see the discussion of Vainker's work in footnote 3. The paintings are on British paper. Paintings on "rice paper" (which does not come from rice but from pith, known in Chinese as *tongcao* [medulla Tetrapanacis]—see the discussion in Clunas 77–80) were also sold as export goods. Jourdain and Jenyns speculate that part of their attractiveness lay in its "velvet surface," which was "likely to appeal to the decorators of Cantonese enamel and porcelain" (31). But the appeal of *surface* may have functioned in Europe as well, perhaps as a part of a kind of phenomenologics of Chineseness whose major attribute was to be simultaneously smooth, opaque, and reflective.

[28] Brook et al., 25.

(*CEW*, 11), it is because the intersection between a set of representational demands and the practices that met them indicate, through the sheer materiality of the representational objects themselves, both the commercial power exerted by the European China trade in the eighteenth and nineteenth centuries, and, by virtue of the representational struggles around the objects as they appear in Mason's books, something of the problem of "translation" across aesthetic and epistemological categories that characterizes every cross-cultural relationship.[29]

What all this suggests is that the illustrations that accompany Mason's two books depend only partially on his control of the representations they give. This is true not simply because he himself did not paint them, or because he seems at least on one occasion unable to direct (or to recall his directions for) what the images represent at all,[30] but largely because the manner of representation was incompatible with contemporary habits of European portrait painting. The typological work Pu Qua's paintings do, then, depends at least partly on the kind of image they are, especially when it comes to the total absence of contextual background; in Alexander's book or in Pyne's *British Costumes,* the figures in the foreground have their referential force sustained at least partly by the landscaped backgrounds in which they occur, above all when those backgrounds feature other, smaller figures that place the foregrounded subject in a social and anthropological context. The difference between the images in Mason's books and those of the rest of the series means that in *Punishments* and *The Costume of China,* the epistemological vacillation between caption and illustration, already present in the other books, can be understood as an effect generated not solely by the book's form (its pairing of images and explanations) but also by its mode of production, with Mason struggling to put into words his own interpretation of an image that emerges from a different aesthetic and cultural context than his own, and with which he sometimes—as in the instance of the "Lame Beggar"—appears to be in conflict. At the same time, each of Pu Qua's paintings functions, no matter how much it resists its caption, or how much it emerges from the commercial demands of a European aesthetic, as an instance of Chinese art. It thus commu-

[29]Indeed, Vainker refers to a list of expenses to the publisher, William Miller, which includes a payment to Thomas Stodhart for "correcting five drawings" in the collection. The published drawings "in many cases show more shading and modelling than the originals," which leads Vainker to suggest that the printed versions have "undergone two stages of Westernisation," the first when they were made by Pu Qua's workshop, the second when they were corrected by Stodhart (53).

[30]Mason comments on the illustration for Plate XVIII of *Punishments* that "This plate appears to represent a section of the cage described in Plate XV," which hints at the degree to which his captions were always interpretive.

nicates at the formal level some notion of cultural "costume" or custom regardless of what specifically it shows.[31]

A reading of the relationship between caption and image in Mason's two books will therefore have to account for the books' hybrid provenance, the degree to which their representational material speaks to the difference between its two intertwined sources, and to the difference between the mode of production of the paintings in Canton and the mode of production of the books in London, a difference captured nicely by Mason's elision of the distinction between his role as customer or tourist in the Chinese context and the degree to which the books establish him as a patron in a European one. These differences seem very much behind the interpretive struggle of the captions to respond to images which, though their origin very much lies in Mason's Europe, nonetheless appear at times to yield only reluctantly to his interpretation (or, worse, yield the "wrong" interpretation).

It would be fun to read this interaction between English writing and Chinese pictures as an allegory of the eighteenth century's struggle over the proper hierarchy of alphabet and ideogram, in which Chinese writing first seemed (in Leibniz, for instance) to offer up a model for divine script before becoming one more piece of evidence for Chinese stagnation.[32] But such a reading makes the books too exclusively the site of a binary cultural battleground, too much a reprise of the old imperialist agon, and falls too quickly into the longstanding theoretical lure of distinguishing images sharply from texts, when in fact "there are no 'purely' visual or verbal arts."[33] It thus fails to recognize the degree to which Pu Qua's paintings do not emerge from some authentically Chinese space outside the world of

[31] Such a "custom" would likely have registered for most of Mason's readers as "primitive," as this summary of the state of Chinese painting, published in John Barrow's 1804 *Travels in China*, suggests: "With regard to painting, [the Chinese] can be considered in no other light than as miserable daubers, being unable to pencil out a correct outline of many objects, to give body to the same by the application of proper lights and shadows, and to lay on the nice shades of colour, so as to resemble the tints of nature" (Clunas, *CEW*, 96). Barrow's use of "no other light" in relation to his complaint about "the proper application of lights and shadows" is another neat *mise-en-abyme*, in which the representational figure he uses to describe his portrayal of the Chinese is also the literal representational practice he says they cannot master.

[32] For particular instances of this struggle, see Haun Saussy's *Great Walls of Discourse and Other Adventures in Cultural China* (Cambridge, 2002), Zhang Longxi's *The Tao and the Logos: Literary Hermeneutics, East and West* (Durham, N.C., 1992), and Liu's *The Clash of Empires*, among many others. The most exciting recent theorization of Western concepts of the ideograph appears in Christopher Bush's *Ideographic Modernism*, forthcoming 2011.

[33] W. J. T. Mitchell, *Picture Theory* (Chicago, 1994), 5.

European mercantilism, but actually testify—as does Mason's career as a soldier in a British regiment in India—to the forms of interaction that come from inside the historical context to which Pu Qua belonged, in which his desire to produce images that would sell well to Western visitors meant that he had, perhaps, a richer and more developed sense of what Mason "wanted" from his pictures than did Mason himself.[34] And it fails to recognize that whatever produces the images in Mason's book does so in terms of a series of complex interactions with the accompanying texts and paratexts (and in which those texts themselves "'incorporate' pictorial practices."[35]). Pu Qua's participation in the narrative and referential complexity of these two books, then, does not so much dislocate a smooth and established trajectory as re–dislocate the already swollen hinges of their jointure, allowing us to read on the surface of the text more of the formal, historical, and interpretive problems whose scars it already bears. "Pu Qua," in this sense, is both *a* name for the difference the text produces in the mode of its own self-production as a material object and *the* name of a particular historical person whose actual participation in the production of *Punishments* can be read as both a cause of its complex written relation to its own images—and as an effect of the global history necessary to create it in the first place.

4. The Compassion Trade

It remains then to explain the particular eventfulness of the narrative–logical trajectory that moves from the preface to *Punishments* to the images of the "Lame

[34]Writing in 1810, Staunton suggested that the watercolors were historically inaccurate, saying of the illustrations in Mason's book that "the fancy of the painter has given, in some instances, a representation of cruelties, and of barbarous executions, which it would be very erroneous to suppose have a place in the ordinary course of justice, although something of such a nature may, no doubt, have been practiced heretofore under some tyrannical and sanguinary Emperors; and even perhaps in the present age, upon some particular and extraordinary circumstances" (*Ta Tsing* xxvi–xxvii). In general, Staunton in his preface is interested in presenting the Chinese penal code as rational in relation to the Chinese situation; where "the laws have not in any considerable degree, the active concurrence, either of a sense of honor, or of a sense of religion," it makes sense that they should include a wide range of possible punishments, including severe ones (xxvii). Staunton's relatively moderated (though clearly culturally particular) take on the Chinese penal code is very much aware of its taking place in relation to a set of developing cultural stereotypes about Chinese cruelty, of which Mason's book was only one instance; that Staunton's side "lost" the debate can be judged from the wide and ongoing presence of the stereotype.

[35]Mitchell, 4.

Beggar" and the "Puppet-Show" published in *The Costume of China,* now considered as an act within a broader framework of knowledge-production, mediatic representation, and commercial exchange that includes the relation between caption and image, Mason and Pu Qua, England and China.[36] In calling that trajectory "eventful," I wish to suggest the degree to which it escapes, or seems to escape, the convention that organizes the books as a whole.[37] And by "event," I mean, in turn, that which remains inside the convention even as it escapes it, allowing it to be thought of as a form of "surprise" outside the parameters of the convention itself, and as a possibility whose production outside the convention's own self-regarding optic constitutes part of its ontological framework.[38] The event is what breaks the surface of the convention, makes it differ from itself, even as it continues to gain its significance from the convention that is its ground.

That the sequence that carries us from the 1801 preface to "A Puppet-Show" to "A Lame Beggar" escapes in several important ways the formal and thematic conventions established by these two books and by the series to which they belong is by now, I hope, quite clear. That this escape is very much a patent feature of the book's own self-regard (as exemplified by the 1801 preface), that the escape is at once concealed by the texts, which do not address it directly, and also placed by

[36] The history of "caption," which shares a Latin root with "capture," is instructive: the OED gives usage examples from the seventeenth, eighteenth, and nineteenth centuries in which "caption" functions as a legal term meaning "Arrest or apprehension by judicial process" (capture, n., 1.b.). This suggests that the words' adjudication of their images figures already at the level of their range of possible meanings the judicial process that the books illustrate, as well as the one they perform.

[37] I paraphrase and cite Gayatri Spivak's phrase, "the event is what escapes the performative convention" ("'The Slightness of My Endeavor': An Interview with Gayatri Chakravorty Spivak." *Comparative Literature* 57:3 [Summer 2005], 264). Giorgio Agamben notes an etymological connection between "escape" and "exception" that operates in this reading insofar as what "escapes" the conventions of Mason's texts does so partly by virtue of its visible exceptionalism (only one book with *Punishments* in the title; only one moment of meta-typological intensity; only one instance of open sympathy). As Agamben writes, "the exception is situated in a symmetrical position with respect to the example, with which it forms a system. Exception and example constitute the two modes by which a set tries to found and maintain its own coherence" (*Homo Sacer: Sovereign Power and Bare Life,* trans. Daniel Heller-Roazen [Stanford, 1998], 21). But while "the example is excluded from the set insofar as it belongs to it, the exception is included in the normal case precisely because it does not belong to it" (22)—that is, the exception must be included in the system as an indicator of nonbelonging. In this sense, it belongs, of course, to the set in which it functions as the mark of nonbelonging.

[38] Alain Badiou: what "composes an event is always extracted from a situation, always related back to a singular multiplicity, to its state, to the language connected to it, etc. In fact, if we want to avoid lapsing into an obscurantist theory of creation *ex nihilo,* we must accept that an event is nothing but a part of a given situation, nothing but a *fragment of being*" (*Theoretical Writings* [New York, 2004], 97).

those texts into the open, like Poe's famous letter, is also, it seems to me, indisputable. This concealing and unconcealing makes the sequence an event.

The sequence is punctuated by the moment at which the caption to "A Lame Beggar" recognizes the possibility of the reader's sympathetic relationship to the image—the only time in either of Mason's books that a caption explicitly acknowledges the reader's potential relation to the "pain and wretchedness" of the things it depicts. "The unpleasant sensation which this object may at first excite," Mason writes, "will be materially dissipated by the consideration that all instances of natural deformity, be it of limb or feature, are so very rare among the populous nations of the eastern world, as to attract universal astonishment whenever they are presented to the view" (*CC*, 220). Your English "unpleasant sensation" is a Chinese person's "universal astonishment,"[39] a form of sympathy that makes sense only in a world where we have completely forgotten the appearance of this figure in a typology of Chinese workers produced for European consumption. The difference between sensation and astonishment marks the difference between an interiorized consideration of the lame beggar as a body in pain and a socio-cultural reading in which one simply notes the presence of something from the far end of the bell curve. The caption resists the sympathetic reaction in the name of an ethnographic expertise that runs in two different directions: first it suggests, however hesitantly, that this man has been crippled by design, and second, it asserts that since *natural* crippling is exceedingly rare in the East, the reader should not be overly concerned about this particular instance of it. *The Costume of China*'s most typologically archetypical description thus comes at exactly the moment at which it feels obliged to defend against the reader's reaction to its images as though they were unmediated representations by insisting both on the likelihood of the man's being crippled on purpose and on the sociocultural "fact" that there aren't that many crippled people in China anyway. Neither of these facts can exactly be drawn into the picture. The caption therefore corrects an apprehension of the image as the portrait of a particular sufferer by returning the image to its typological status in relation to the entire book series.[40]

[39] My reading of "unpleasant sensation" as the index of a potential sympathetic pain depends on the fact that the end of the caption declares that "in the visage of this Cripple, pain and wretchedness are most forcibly delineated" (*CC*, 220). The "Beggar with a Monkey," the same caption says, expresses "softness supplicating compassion"—another index of the text's sense that the images are *asking for* (supplicating) a certain kind of sympathetic attention. The actual caption to the "Beggar with a Monkey," incidentally, says nothing whatsoever about compassion or sympathy (*CC*, 166).

[40] If Clunas is right that the images at the Victoria & Albert Museum are the ones Mason used for his *Costume* book, then the real typological scandal is this: among the one hundred images in the set

The caption's attempt to reduce the reader's sympathy can now be returned to the preface of the *Punishments* book published a year later. At preface's end, Mason directs the reader's regard to the equivalent "punishments of England," which he judges to be effected "in a manner the most instantaneous and least sanguinary that a compassionate people could adopt; and whose natural intrepidity is farther manifested by this attention to the pangs of suffering humanity" (preface).[41] That last clause can be read to refer to the English attention to the pangs of English criminals, manifested in the relatively compassionate and bloodless execution by hanging. But "attention to the pangs of suffering humanity" is also the emotional mode of the book itself, whose attention to Chinese punishments which themselves do not exhibit an attention to suffering exercises a prosthetic compassion toward Chinese "culprits" and "miscreants," and a commensurate critique of Chinese judges and magistrates, its judicial system, and its civilization.[42]

What remains to be thought, then, is the social situation that allowed this hesitant arrangement of typology and sympathy to emerge, and which halts the transformation of the one into the other by the judicious application of anthropological knowledge about China itself: the well-known temperance of the Chinese government and the statistical rarity of "natural deformity" come into play in order to stop the slide of typology into sympathy, of knowledge into identification. In both cases knowledge about China appears at precisely the moment at which the books threaten to become akin to the literature of sympathy with which any Englishman of the period would have been intimately familiar. The eventfulness of this sequence thus points towards a social and indeed epistemological situation in which the twin drives of knowledge and sympathy hang in one another's balance.

Now we must recall the immediate historical context for the sudden surge of interest in things Chinese in early nineteenth century England, for which the Macartney Embassy of 1793 was a crucial catalyst. No European relation to China in this era—especially no relation in a Britain inundated with Chinese export goods, organized around new cultural and behavioral spaces and rituals that integrated

---

are forty that the book does not reproduce, and among these, astonishingly, is *another* image of a beggar—a fifth one (the image is reproduced in Clunas, 39).

[41] It's not the case, as Pericles Lewis reminds me, that one cannot have sympathy for a type—think of sentimental fiction, or Oxfam ads, media in which the type rather than the individual constitutes the major generic site of sympathy.

[42] That the framing of this moment is implicitly Christian should not come as a surprise. "Suffering humanity" is a stock phrase that describes both an attribute of Christ (he expresses and displays, on the cross, his own suffering humanity) as well as humankind more generally in a wide variety of Christian sources.

recognizably Chinese material into everyday life (tea time, for instance; or the Chinese garden)—occurred outside the framework of worries about international trade. Throughout the eighteenth century, Chinese demand for silver, largely a product of the Qing economy's remonetization, dominated its trade with the rest of the world. The resulting flow of silver bullion to China—Andre Gunder Frank estimates that between 1600 and 1800 China purchased as much as *half* of the world's total production, much of it carried by Europeans from their New World mines—created a great deal of mercantilist anxiety throughout Europe (mercantilists, you will recall, held that the state's supply of capital in the form of bullion was the direct expression of its international strength). This anxiety expressed itself in legislation requiring the British East India Company to have homegrown manufactures account for at least ten percent of its trade, a requirement largely met throughout the eighteenth century by cooking the books.[43] The rectification of the trade deficit had been one of the major goals of Lord Macartney's notoriously unsuccessful 1793 embassy. Macartney's samples of England's most technologically advanced products, which he hoped would convince the Chinese to trade, were met, however, with disdain, the Qianlong emperor famously writing to Macartney that "We have never valued ingenious articles, nor do we have the slightest need of your country's manufactures."[44]

Considered in relation to this context—which was, let us not forget, the immediate context for the publication of Staunton's account of the 1793 embassy, which Mason consulted, as well as Alexander's 1805 *Costume of China* volume—the "attention to the pangs of suffering humanity" Mason praises in his English

[43] Andre Gunder Frank, *ReOrient: Global Economy in the Asian Age* (Berkeley, 1998). The gap between the Chinese and European economies can be measured by the fact that between 1660 to 1720, "precious metals made up on average 87 percent of VOC [Dutch East India Company] imports into Asia"; as for the British East India Company, it "had to resort to over- and under-invoicing" in order to comply, at least on paper, with the demand that it export British products (Frank 74). Descriptions of the general economic situation in the late eighteenth and early nineteenth centuries appear in the early chapters of Hunt Janin, *The India-China Opium Trade in the Nineteenth Century* (Jefferson, N.C., 1999) and Jack Beeching, *The Chinese Opium Wars* (London, 1975). For a corrective to Frank's Sinocentric world system, see Kenneth Pomeranz, *The Great Divergence: China, Europe, and the Making of the Modern World Economy* (Princeton, N.J, 2000). Adam Smith discusses the China trade, and particularly its relation to silver, at length in *The Wealth of Nations* (New York, 2000), esp. 237–38.

[44] Cited in Joanna Waley-Cohen, *The Sextants of Beijing: Global Currents in Chinese History* (New York, 2000), 92. As Waley-Cohen argues, this position, read by the British as an outlandish declaration of cultural arrogance, should be understood as an exercise of caution justified by, among other things, late eighteenth-century massacres of Chinese expatriates by Europeans in the Philippines, Batavia, and Taiwan (93). Frank gives a slightly different translation of Qianlong's letter: "I set no value on objects strange or ingenious, and we have no use for your country's manufactures" (273).

readers might be thought of as a gesture inside an international economy of sympathy, a sympathy whose anthropological and geographic extension to the world beyond Europe was only then on the verge of occurring. That a difference between English and Chinese sympathy in relation to judicial punishment was already the subject of some kind of cultural discourse is testified to, of course, by the sheer appearance of this book in the costume series, and by Pu Qua's sense that a set of portrayals of Chinese punishments would sell to European buyers (meanwhile, where were the Chinese books designed to produce compassion in relation to the suffering English?).[45] But here I am also opening the possibility that the idea of sympathy itself, as one self-conscious justification for the publication of such books, ought to be thought in relation to the politics of international trade as a kind of affective and cultural surplus, as though compassion itself were a good whose excess in the British Isles would allow it to be sent, along with British silver, to the Far East. Rey Chow has made a similar argument about twentieth-century debates around human rights, noting that in the 1980s and early 1990s discussions about the release of Chinese political prisoners almost always took place as part of business negotiations involving US companies' desires to invest in the Chinese economy.[46] I will have more to say about this later on, but for now, in this context, consider this site of intersection between English trade and the growing sense of the importance of sympathy in defining the nature of human beings and their social relations: the opening sentences of the first chapter of Adam Smith's *Theory of Moral Sentiments:*

> How selfish soever man may be supposed, there are evidently some principles in his nature, which interest him in the fortune of others, and render their happiness necessary to him, though he derives nothing from it except the pleasure of seeing it. Of this kind is pity or compassion, the emotion which we feel for the misery of others, when we either see it, or are made to conceive it in a very lively manner. That we often derive sorrow from the sorrow of others, is a matter of fact too obvious to require any

[45] A lengthier and better-informed comparison between the two legal systems in this era comes with the publication in 1810 of Staunton's translation of the Qing legal code. In the translator's preface Staunton writes that though there "are certainly many points upon which these laws are altogether indefensible. We shall look in vain, for instance, for those excellent principles of the English law, by which every man is presumed innocent until he is proved guilty; and no man required to criminate himself.... But it will scarcely escape observation, that there are other parts of the [Chinese] code which, in a considerable degree, compensate these and similar defects, are altogether of a different complexion, and are perhaps not unworthy of imitation" (xxiv).

[46] See the introduction to *The Protestant Ethnic & the Spirit of Capitalism* (New York, 2002).

> instances to prove it; for this sentiment, like all the other original passions of human nature, is by no means confined to the virtuous and humane, though they perhaps may feel it with the most exquisite sensibility. The greatest ruffian, the most hardened violator of the laws of society, is not altogether without it. (9)

Smith would go on to publish the great critique of British mercantilism in his 1776 *The Wealth of Nations,* and the conjunction between the two books allows us to see how closely the theorization of sympathy as the source of humanness and of morals more generally *could* dovetail, and did so in Smith's body of work, with a theory of human behavior organized around labor and exchange.[47] This congruity allows me to suggest that the sympathetic drive articulated in Mason's preface to *Punishments* appears in much larger European philosophical context in which the idea of sympathy as a fundamental aspect of the human is inextricably intertwined with theories having to do with the development of such global (and globalizing) concepts as "Western civilization" or "political economy," two forms whose practical workings out spent a great deal of energy thinking about and around the China trade. Because, considered as the subject of exchange, sympathy functions like a gift—it can be given without the consent of the person one feels compassionate toward—it would have been in 1801 the only tradable commodity that English people could force China to accept from them.

Compared to the *The Costume of China's* aggressive dismissal of sympathy in relation to the lame beggar,[48] the economics of compassion articulated

[47]The movement from "sympathy" in *Moral Sentiments* to self-interest (in *The Wealth of Nations*) has often been read as the product of a major change in Smith's philosophy, producing an apparent paradox generally referred to as the "Adam Smith problem." In their introduction to *The Theory of Moral Sentiments,* D. D. Raphael and A.L. Macfie dismiss the idea that the works conflict, citing material from the sixth edition of *Moral Sentiments* (published in 1790) that refers specifically to its having fulfilled the promise of *The Wealth of Nations* (20–25) and noting that the original material for both books was likely worked out at roughly the same time as part of Smith's first lectures at the University of Glasgow in the early 1750s. Alexander Broadie compares the production of mutual sympathy in Smith's *Theory of Moral Sentiments* to the process of "truck, barter, and exchange" he describes in *The Wealth of Nations* in "Sympathy and the Impartial Spectator," *The Cambridge Companion to Adam Smith,* ed. Knud Haakonssen (Cambridge, 2006).

[48]On the second page of *Moral Sentiments,* Smith, in arguing for the universality of sympathetic identification, connects it successively to judicial execution and to begging: "The mob, when they are gazing at a dancer on a slack rope, naturally writhe and twist and balance their own bodies, as they seem him do .... Persons of delicate fibres and a weak constitution of body complain, that in looking on the sores and ulcers which are exposed by beggars in the streets, they are apt to feel an itching or uneasy sensation in the correspondent part of their own bodies" (9). That the major narrative event of Mason's two books passes through this same pairing suggests, if nothing else, that in the context of

in the preface to *Punishments* feels strange and self-contradictory indeed. But the elliptical sequence whereby Mason's books tie modest decorum to critical judgment, violent judicial punishments to a children's puppet show, antisympathetic typology to a compassionate attention to suffering—not to mention caption to image, a pairing that expresses formally the historico-commercial relationship between Mason and Pu Qua—must be thought of as elliptical *and* as a sequence, a single string raveled into a single knot.

The sequence, with all its apparent contradictions, opens itself to a literal reading *as* contradictory insofar as it records an oscillation between two profoundly incompatible forms of interest: first, the typological–ethnographic desire of the entire costume series, the desire to know and to organize that knowledge so as to make sense of the world; and second, the desire to attend specifically to the customs of a culture that generate sympathetic pain and a gratitude for the gift of Englishness, that is, the desire to generate in relation to another culture perceived as powerful and strange a cultural power of one's own.[49] The incompatibility between these two forms comes from the fact that the epistemological desire of the book project depends on a relatively neutral cultural position in relation to otherness, whereas the wish to produce sympathy leads of necessity to a negative judgment on the question of China's temperance and wisdom, and abets, tellingly, the myth of historical stasis that would, later in the nineteenth century, justify (in most cases after the fact) the punitive drive to shake China up through trade, modernization, and warfare. That the preface so openly announces its wish to respect that temperance in the same sentence that implicitly "arraigns" China for lacking it can now be seen as the stuttering expression of this dialectic, the single and most open moment of the logic of this event, its narrative beginning—where we first saw and began reading the problem of the text—and its logical "ending," its closure, all at once.

Only by grasping the internal logic of Mason's books as a form of coherence, as a total expression of their ideological and literary positions, can we also place the movement they generate between texts, between sympathy and its negation, between cruelty and its abnegation, within the more general framework of

---

thinking sympathetically such a thematic passage can be unfolded *naturally*, that is, without announcing a special or unusual conjunction.

[49] For foreigners in China at the end of the eighteenth century the desire to learn more about China took place in relation to a Chinese government that was explicitly uninterested in letting foreigners know much about China. In the preface to the *Costume* book of 1800, Mason remarks on the "very circumscribed limits which are marked out for foreigners at Canton" and tells the story of an attempted expedition into the city that resulted in the temporary arrest of one of his company and the group's return to the part of the city reserved for foreign traders (6).

material exchange to which they also belong. The "total" Mason, or Mason's books as a "total" event, belongs properly to all of its dimensions—to the modalities of literariness that open themselves to close reading, to the modalities of ekphrasis that open relations between picture and word, to the modalities of form that arrange its typologies, to the system of international exchange that allowed Mason to purchase Pu Qua's pictures, and led Pu Qua to paint them, and to the historical developments that link the rise of the culture of sympathy to this particular moment in England's trade relations with China. Only within this totality do contradictions express and illuminate the system to which they belong, and which they represent *as a totality* over and against any particular motive, conscious or unconscious, Mason might have had for writing what he did, or William Miller for publishing it. Only insofar as they do this, and do it within the frame of this particular reading, do they speak, also, to the social situation of their era. What they show is, quite simply, the ways in which sympathy emerged alongside, and through, the dual facts of material and political economic exchange, and the degree to which a *compensatory* relationship between the economic and the sympathetic could appear well before its conscious apprehension as a tool of international political relations, and the ways in which deeply modern structures of knowledge like the typological volume were themselves articulations of that relationship.

One might think of the "literary," unrealistic (literally preposterous) logic whereby the Mason texts indicate this situation as a formal gesture that reverses the structure of the anecdote as Joel Fineman defines it. If in theorizing the anecdote's referential opening to history, Fineman had to read and foreground reference against the predominantly literary appearance of anecdotal form, here one might say that I have had to foreground the literary aspects of these texts in order to overcome the rhetorical and formal weight of their call to reference, to typological actuality. Whereas in Greenblatt the attention to the goldsmith's "real body" and "real pain" might be said to occur, however, in the mode of resistance to the violence of imperialism, in Mason's text the sympathetic gesture that emerges "against" the will of the text (and at the same time very much "for" it) must be understood as part and parcel of a burgeoning representational violence, in which the distribution of national forms of sympathy, particularly as connected to forms of judicial punishment, would become part of the cultural justification for European and American interventions (whether through trade, diplomacy, foreign aid, or warfare) in countries that were not able to express a compelling counter-narrative to humanist sympathy (or were not able to back up their own national story, whatever it was, with military or cultural power that might have permitted open resistance).[50] The history of human rights in the twentieth century is, as I suggested in the introduction, an etiological cousin to the sympathy that these two books both conceal and express through (both because of and despite) the contortions of their form. The shadow cast by that cousinage flickers, today, amidst dreams of a total global convergence.

[50]To be clear: no representation happens without some violence; this argument is historical, not moral.

3 The Chinese Body in Pain

American Missionary Medical Care, 1838–1852

They were like poetry but they were only sentences to learn the spelling from.

—James Joyce, *Portrait of the Artist as a Young Man*

Aesthetics is born as a discourse of the body.

—Terry Eagleton, *The Ideology of the Aesthetic*

I closed the previous chapter by suggesting that the sympathetic exchange generated by the interaction between the reader of Mason's books and the people it represented had to be thought within the more literal exchange of goods between England and China, and could therefore be conceived as a kind of aggressive affective response—a structure of feeling, to borrow Raymond Williams' term—in which British impotence at the level of the material good was assuaged by Chinese impotence at the level of the emotional one.

The interchange between sympathetic and economic exchange captured so neatly by the figure of Balzac's mandarin must stretch a bit to cover the figural and historical range that connects George Henry Mason's two books on China to the diplomatic failure of the Macartney Embassy that preceded it. But it takes only a little imagination to see how an amplified figure binding Europe's sympathetic impulse to its relation to the Chinese economy can bring a good deal of the nineteenth-century relations between East and West under its umbrella. Only four decades after the publication of Mason's *The Punishments of China,* tensions around trade and diplomatic recognition, coupled with internal pressures on

China's Qing dynasty rulers, would lead directly to the two Opium Wars fought between Britain and China (1839–42 and 1856–60; the French fought alongside the British in the second war). The wars' major underlying cause lay in the confrontation of Chinese legal and economic sovereignty and Western trading interests. The Chinese government's refusal to accept anything other than silver in payment for its goods, so clearly established by Qianlong's response to Macartney, continued to aggravate its Western trading partners, who cast about, as Macartney himself had, for goods that the Chinese would want enough to pay silver for. Beginning in the late 1700s, the British East India Company, using poppies grown in India, began to sell opium to Chinese merchants in exchange for silver coin and bullion, a major step in redressing the imbalance that had defined China's trading relation to the rest of the world for the previous two hundred years. The trade in opium, at about seventy-five tons a year in 1773 (the year the East India Company acquired its fifty-year monopoly on the opium trade), grew to 1,400 tons annually by the late 1830s, becoming "the largest commerce of its time in any single commodity, anywhere in the world."[1] The wars themselves were the result of the clash produced by the Qing government's attempts to halt the opium trade and British resistance to doing so.[2] Among other things the "unequal treaties" signed between the victorious Western powers and the Chinese government at the end of these wars had the effect of opening up China to foreign travel, trade, and missionary work; as a result, the British gained the land that became Hong Kong, a number of Chinese cities became official "treaty ports" (until 1842 the only site for legal trade between China and the West had been the foreign concession area of Canton), and Christians were granted full civil rights, including the right to evangelize and own property. The negotiation of these treaties thus brought together in an especially real way the relation between sympathetic and capitalist exchange

[1] Jack Beeching, *The Chinese Opium Wars* (London, 1975), 39. The financial estimate comes from Edward Gulick, who places the value of the opium traded annually in China in the 1830s at $15 million (*Peter Parker and the Opening of China* [Cambridge, 1973], 81.).

[2] The actual incidents leading up to both wars were marred by cultural misunderstandings on both sides. But they simply provided an occasion for what was in effect an armed heist; one of the results of the Convention of Peking, signed in 1860, was to legalize the opium trade. For a basic though somewhat dated history of the wars, see Beeching; on trade, see Hunt Janin, *The India-China Opium Trade in the Nineteenth Century* (Jefferson, N.C., 1999); for a scholarly reading of the issues at stake, see the first section of James Hevia, *English Lessons: The Pedagogy of Imperialism in Nineteenth-Century China* (Durham, N.C, 2003); on Hevia, see Haun Saussy, "China and the World: The Tale of a Topos," *Modern Language Quarterly* 68:2 (June 2007).

(and their mutual intertwining with military power); indeed, the very question of how an explicitly Christian compassion might be extended into China's interior was part and parcel of the negotiations whereby Britain and France forced open Chinese markets and treaty ports to Western goods.[3]

1. Market Penetration

Within a historical context there is always room for cultural analysis, since, first, the particularities of any given moment will outline for us the possible shapes of the general and the real, and since, second, those shapes reveal the apparent exceptions, the statistical outliers, the conscious or unconscious forms of resistance to history whose apprehension within the frameworks of the possible grants history the truth of its lovely, protean complexities. In pursuit of those complexities, and of the remainders or exceptions within them, the rest of this chapter focuses on one particularly benevolent expression of the interaction between sympathetic and economic exchange in China: the life and work of the first director of a Western missionary hospital there, Peter Parker. In the twenty years between his founding of the Ophthalmic Infirmary in Canton and his 1855 resignation from the hospital, Parker and his colleagues treated some fifty thousand patients for all manner of injury, illness, and disease, from cataracts to leprosy, hernias to gunshot wounds, developing such a reputation that sufferers traveled hundreds of miles from China's interior to obtain medical care there.[4]

[3]This emphasis on the real-world role China played in the cultural imagination of China should not be taken to diminish the importance of figuration and language, even within things as real as wars. Important parts of the Opium War treaty negotiations involved debate over the use and translation of particular Chinese words (which were therefore also taken as one of the war's "causes"). See Lydia Liu's *The Clash of Empires: The Invention of China in Modern World Making* (Cambridge, 2005) for a lengthy and provocative analysis of the debates over the English translation of the Chinese *yi*; see also Hevia's *English Lessons.*

[4]For much of the biographical material on Peter Parker I am relying on Edward V. Gulick's *Peter Parker and the Opening of China* (Cambridge, 1973); further citations in the text are cited as *PP.* The name of Parker's hospital reflected a set of medical ambitions derived at least partly from the difference between Chinese and Western medicine at the time; diseases of the eye, particularly cataracts, were prevalent in China partly because Chinese medicine did not have methods for treating them. The hospital's Chinese name appeared on a sign over the hospital entrance: *Pu Ai Yi Yuan,* or "Hospital of Universal Love," which reflected Parker's sense of the different work his hospital was doing for its Chinese and Anglophone audiences. Stephen Rachman observes that allowing the choice of ophthalmology corresponds to the biblical injunction to restore sight to the blind, a reference by way of the hospital's English name that would have been lost on Chinese audiences ("*Memento Morbi:* Lam Qua's

Parker also trained several Chinese students in Western medicine, traveled to the United States and Europe to raise funds for his group of medical missionaries, and served, from 1852 to 1857, in a number of official diplomatic capacities for the U.S. government. Though gaps in Parker's medical records and the absence of testimony from his patients make it difficult to establish the full range of his impact on the people he treated and the community in which he lived, it is certainly fair to say that in his lifetime he was the most visible face of Western medicine in China, both for the Chinese he treated and for the many Americans and Europeans who heard about, admired, and contributed to his work.[5]

Parker's legacy to the present lies in a surprisingly large amount of representational objects and textual forms—among them letters, journals, poems, sermons, and medical case studies, line drawings of medical symptoms and, most notoriously, oil portraits of his patients—most of which can be found today in the Parker archive at the Harvey Cushing/John Hay Whitney Medical Library of the Yale University Medical School. Considered as a whole collection, these documents constitute a significant historical effect of the new, sympathetic "cognitive style" promoted by the rapid expansion of capitalist markets, a style driven, as Thomas L. Haskell has argued, by a radically amplified sense of moral distance and a concomitant expansion of the geographic field in which Europeans and Americans felt like they could intervene.[6] Though Britons might well feel that the

Paintings, Peter Parker's Patients." *Literature and Medicine* 23.1 [Spring 2004], 142.). Further citations of Rachman in the text are cited as *MM.*

[5]Gulick notes that Parker generally did not record his medical failures; given that most patients returned home shortly after treatment and had no further contact with Parker, the long-term effects of his care cannot be evaluated.

[6]Haskell originally made these arguments in two essays on "Capitalism and the Origins of Humanitarian Sensibility," which are reprinted, along with responses to his work by David Brion Davis and John Ashworth, in *The Antislavery Debate: Capitalism and Abolitionism*, ed. Thomas Bender (Berkeley, 1992). I find Haskell's remarks on the origins of sympathy convincing and useful because they avoid imagining the relation between sympathy and capital as an act of willed ideological complicity, a ruse played by the bourgeoisie on the working classes. It is clear that the expansion of compassion in various ways helped sustain the exploitations of capitalism and coexisted with a great deal of European violence against others both at home and abroad (as Davis puts it in the case of abolition, "the growing power of antislavery in early industrial Britain was at least partly a function of the fit between antislavery ideology and the interests of an emergent capitalist class" [Bender, 308]). This chapter, like much of the book, is in the position of arguing for the truth of this historical case without then arguing that the expansion of sympathy was therefore in any simple way morally "wrong" or *simply* a conscious tool of European and American elites. Like the scholars working on the antislavery movement, none of whom regrets the end of slavery, I am trying to show the moral complexity of a particular history. Insofar as my analysis favors explanations of Haskell's type—which he understands as Weberian, and I read within a more Foucauldian framework—it does so in order to

suffering Chinese patient was "far off," Parker wrote in a 1841 fundraising letter to a Scottish admirer, if those of "undoubted benevolence, yet of *contracted* views, but inform themselves of the extent and condition of the whole world," they would "expand their sympathies wide as the wants of men, and put forth exertions commensurate with their abilities and opportunities of blessing a world."[7] The entire Parker archive testifies to the essentially planetary scope of this sympathy. Its objects are the direct product of the new fluidities of capital—for which "money is as easily given to be expended on the one side of the world as the other," as Parker wrote—that allowed Parker and the other medical missionaries he worked with to put this newly expanded compassion into active practice.[8]

All this expansive compassion was staged, throughout Parker's writings and indeed in the pamphlets and documents announcing his founding, with T.R. Colledge and E.C. Bridgman, of the Medical Missionary Society in China in 1836, through a series of remarkably explicit references to the medical practice these young men intended to undertake. China's "fevers are as burning—insanity as raving—leprosy as polluting—blindness as great—its cancer and stone as painful, and gout as excruciating," Parker told the readers of his fundraising letter, "as they would be, if only the Mersey or the British Channel separated them from the skill and charity that could relieve them."[9] Such an assertion of equal pain allowed Parker to direct his claims about the need for sympathy toward a potent universalism. Operating at the level of the species, Parker's call to recognize the Chinese sufferer's pain as equal required his donors to recognize that sufferer as a fellow human being. The legitimacy of that recognition thus relied on the ways that a universally vulnerable human body could overcome, both literally and figuratively, the barriers that geography or culture posed to international exchange.

---

trace the history of a range of thinkable possibilities that define an era (Foucault) and to suggest that systems of behavior and belief relatively disconnected from each other might nonetheless sustain one another by establishing a set of general principles from which one or the other system might be justified or sustained (Weber).

[7] *Statements Respecting Hospitals in China Preceded by a Letter to John Abercrombie, M.D., V.P.R.S.E.* (Glasgow, 1842), 7.

[8] In the rhetoric of this argument we see how changes in technologies of travel and capital flow were crucial supports for the expansion of moral distance sympathy required; the difference between the stranger at the doorstep and the one on the other side of the world was effectively erased by the presence of those who, like Parker, were willing to travel from one to the other in order to go to the latter's aid.

[9] Peter Parker, *Statements Respecting Hospitals in China*, 7.

But there was more to the medical missionary project than a simple corporeal universalism. It was in fact precisely the body's universal qualities that would allow Parker and his colleagues to circumvent the cultural and political barriers that kept them from evangelizing to the Chinese. The Chinese government's resistance to Western trade and travel could not easily be extended, after all, to the interior of Chinese bodies. "Exclusive as China is, in all her systems," Parker and his friends wrote, "she cannot exclude disease, nor shut her people up from the desire of relief." Like Mason's descriptions of the Chinese prisoners, in which a sense of outrage directed at the Chinese government for its cruelty was turned to a recognition of the uniquely British attention to the pangs of a universally "suffering humanity," Parker, Colledge, and Bridgman's emphasis on the shared humanity (and frailty) of their Chinese patients allowed them to circumvent the government that would keep them isolated from Western influence. Though we should beware of taking too seriously the puffery inherent in fundraising letters, it is clear enough that for the Medical Missionary Society, the body's universal vulnerability to suffering allowed it to function, essentially, as an evangelical and sociological Trojan horse—or, as Parker, Colledge, and Bridgman had it at one point, as China's "only open door."[10]

We are accustomed to recognizing universalism of this type as the projected philosophical substructure of an aggressive Western imperialism. Within its historical context, however, the position that argued for the equivalence of English and Chinese fevers was a comparatively progressive one. Nineteenth-century American hierarchies of physical sensitivity to pain operated along scales involving race, class, gender, and experience in more or less the directions one would expect: the famous nineteenth-century American neurologist S. Weir Mitchell once wrote that "in our process of being civilized, we have won, I suspect, intensified capacity to suffer. The savage does not feel pain as we do."[11] Parker's faith in the Chinese desire for relief from pain, coupled with his assertion of the equality of suffering, put him, against Mitchell and other less clever racists, on the side of those who tended to deduce from their arguments about the universal equality of pain "important implications for the actual

[10] T. R. Colledge, Peter Parker, and E.C. Bridgman, *Suggestions for the Formation of a Medical Missionary Society offered to the consideration of all Christian Nations, more especially to the kindred nations of England and the United States of America* (Canton, 1836), 9.

[11] Cited in David Morris, *The Culture of Pain* (Berkeley, 1991), 39. S. Weir Mitchell, incidentally, treated Charlotte Perkins Gilman, whose *The Yellow Wallpaper* was intended specifically as a rebuke to his methods.

treatment of human beings," including theories of universal human rights, of the type toward which we see Parker slouching in his fundraising letter.[12]

Even as it produced a sense of the potential equality of cultural claims to compassionate relief, however, Parker's discussion of medicine and shared pain also sustained quite explicitly a discourse about cultural transformation tied to the kind of epistemological project that would help the West better understand China, trade with it, and evangelize it. Records of the treatment of the Chinese, noted an early Medical Missionary Society address, "will in time be curious and instructive documents, and such as will enable us to glance at the penetralia of domestic and social life in China, which we now can only read of, or view at a distance, from the very outskirts of the country."[13]

Leaving aside the classically masculine progression that would lead Westerners from China's "outskirts" to its "penetralia," I wish instead to concentrate on the latter term, whose explicitly medical connotations once again link the specific material project of the missionary hospital to the larger political and economic context in which it occurred. Because the major difference between Western and Chinese medicine in this era was that Chinese doctors did not do surgery (and in general avoided cutting into the body at all), the desire to glance at China's penetralia unites the missionaries' epistemological interest with the defining difference between Western and Chinese medical practice. A willingness to open up the body, to surgically manipulate its parts and mysteries, held the key to Parker's ability to cure conditions for which Chinese doctors had no ready solution. For Parker and his colleagues to imagine that their medical practice would take them into China's penetralia thus linked medical practice to ethnography, the former not only allegorizing the latter (as one might cheerfully expect from this sort of literary criticism), but literally making it possible, the opening of Chinese bodies not only *resembling* the opening of Chinese cultural life to the West, but *inaugurating* it.[14]

[12]Martin Pernick, *A Calculus of Suffering: Pain, Professionalism, and Anesthesia in Nineteenth-Century America.* (New York, 1985), 166.

[13]T. R. Colledge, Peter Parker, and E.C. Bridgman. "Medical Missionary Society in China address" *Signed by T.R. Colledge, Peter Parker, and E.C. Bridgman, with minutes and proceedings* (Canton, 1838), 15.

[14]A second example: through the medical missions, the doctors wrote, "Everything about [Chinese] domestic history, ways of thinking, social feelings, nay the very penetralia of their hearts and dwellings, are brought under contemplation" (*The first and second reports of the Medical Missionary Society in China, with minutes of proceedings, hospital reports, &c.* [Macao, 1841], 8.). Here again, the proximity of Chinese "hearts" to Chinese "penetralia" suggests how tightly knit were the metaphors

By the time of Parker's invocation of the problem of moral distance in his 1841 fundraising letter, then, his own experience in China had already prepared him to imagine that missionary medicine could resolve this problem in two different ways. First, it could bridge the distance between Westerners and the Chinese by taking advantage of the universal fact of pain and the desire for relief, producing or even forcing an occasion for interaction that would overcome any reluctance to engage in cross-cultural exchange. Second, the actions taking place in the neutral meeting ground of the operating theater would decrease distance by giving the Chinese a favorable impression of these benevolent Westerners and allowing the Westerners in turn to understand the lives of the Chinese—this latter providing, as Parker, Colledge, and Bridgman suggested to their potential donors, substantial benefits outside the field of medicine. As the missionaries cut apart, sewed together, and otherwise repaired their wounded patients, as they spent nights at the bedsides of those with whom they shared no common language, as they urged them to praise the God who had brought them to the Ophthalmic Infirmary rather than the doctors whose hands had rifled their flesh, they attempted to suture these Chinese strangers to a moral and cultural world that would profoundly change their relationship to their bodies, to suffering, and to the imaginary geographies of the planet.

Indeed a sense of the planetary organism's increased, recursive awareness of every part of its surface was crucial to the philosophical work that imagined the very possibility of a "cosmopolitan law," as Immanuel Kant wrote in 1795, figuring that awareness specifically as an extension of *feeling:* "intercourse . . . which has been everywhere steadily increasing between the nations of the earth, has now extended so enormously that a violation of right in one part of the world is felt all over it (*an allen gefühlt wird*)." That such a position encoded Western superiority in a universal and disinterested rationality was presumably part of its appeal, though in Kant's case, it was also turned toward an attempt to protect non-Europeans from European imperialism.[15] Likewise, for Parker, the willingness to recognize foreign bodies as no different from familiar ones was a gesture turned very much back toward the project of sympathy itself, since it was because the

that bound together the general project for which Parker was soliciting funds in his 1841 fundraising letter.

[15] Kant, *Perpetual Peace: A Philosophic Essay,* trans. M. Campbell Smith (London, 1917), 142. In the preceding paragraphs Kant discussed the violations of the right of hospitality perpetrated by European imperialists in Africa and the Americas and praised China and Japan for "wisely" refusing Europeans entry to their shores.

Chinese were like us in body that we might, in time, convince them to be like us in spirit. Throughout Parker's life and work this evangelical and cultural project was inextricably tied to the specifically medical contours of the work in which he engaged, both because of the metaphorical importance of penetralia, and because, as he, Colledge, and Bridgman wrote, "purity and disinterestedness of motive are more clearly evinced" in medical care than in any other arena of life.[16] That the Medical Missionary Society's views were hardly disinterested, given their evangelical ambitions, need not detain us long. Rather, I wish to draw attention to the way that medicine became for these men the public and highly visible site of a universal, benevolent neutrality, even as its practice enacted the kinds of penetration and transformation that were typical of the larger projects of both soft and hard imperialisms that sustained them.

2. Face, Tumor, Style

Physical pain feels like an encounter with the world's irreducible ontological being. No one can tell you that something of yours hurts when it doesn't, or doesn't hurt when it does. The idea that someone else could adjudicate the value of one's pain tends to produce a real sense of outrage, just as the plaints of those who suffer from pains we deem minor or irrelevant can seem like the most extravagant whine. Physical pain, one might say, functions as the final frontier of culture, the last refuge of the actual and the real. And this is why imagining pain as the product of culture strikes most people, reflexively, as a dangerous gesture: it threatens to remove from the individual subject the right to determine and shape the public meaning of what seems to be his or her most private experience and, in the process, encourages a kind of decadent cultural disregard for the subject's right to make truth claims about itself. This is why Stephen Greenblatt can insist that any criticism that fails to attend to the bare reality of the goldsmith's pain, or which imagines it simply as a fictional effect, ignores with an almost total irresponsibility the raw stuff of reality, or confuses the latter with some linguistic game.

The last three decades have seen a tremendous growth in historical and sociological treatments of pain, ranging from case studies to local and global histories, descriptions of particularly significant events in the cultural experience

[16]Medical Missionary Society in China address," 13.

and value of pain (the discovery of chemical anesthetics, for instance) to millennia-long histories of pain's medical treatment that think shifts in its normativity, its relation to theories of the body, the state, and of the divine. Such treatments almost inevitably begin their cultural and historical analyses with a discussion of pain's intense reality, since this is in some important sense the first anthropological fact about pain: that it shares with rocks and other hard places an uncannily doubled relation to the cultural and the real.[17] "While pain appears at one moment as an unmediated and unmistakable fact, the next moment it seems produced by a dialectic interaction of biological and social processes," write the editors of one recent collection on chronic pain. The remark captures perfectly the awkward matrix by which pain appears, from moment to moment, or sometimes even inside a single moment, to be the product of radically disparate kinds of causes, and directs us to attend to the *nature* of pain as precisely that which preserves, even when it acts so visibly inside the field of culture—and indeed calls out for a cultural field in which it might acquire public recognition and care—some irrevocable grasp on a nature that precedes it.[18]

Lest a sense of pain's cultural complexity be understood as a purely contemporary knowledge whose apprehension was unavailable to our benighted forebears, we should recognize that nineteenth-century imperialists understood this just as well as we do—even if they did not have the good taste to theorize it. As Talal Asad has noted, Western interventions in the colonies frequently attempted to manage local relations to physical pain, retaining (and finding valuable) kinds of suffering deemed necessary for the transformation of local conditions to modernity (the destruction of cultures, of autochthonous familial structures, and the like), while attempting to eradicate through violence or pedagogical remediation those forms of suffering deemed barbaric, irresponsible or gratuitous in relation to the project of modernization. Because, as Asad writes, pain "is . . . a way of constituting the epistemological status of the body," such attempts

[17] See for instance David Morris and Martin Pernick; Arthur Kleinman, *Social Origins of Distress and Disease: Depression, Neurasthenia, and Pain in Modern China* (New Haven, 1986) and *The Illness Narratives: Suffering, Healing, and the Human Condition* (New York, 1988), among many other works; on narratives of pain, Arthur Frank, *The Wounded Storyteller: Body, Illness, and Ethics* (Chicago, 1997), Cheryl Mattingly, *Healing Dramas and Clinical Plots: The Narrative Structure of Experience* (Cambridge, 1998), and Roseleyne Rey, *The History of Pain,* trans. Louise Elliott Wallace, J. A. Cadden, and S. W. Cadden (Cambridge, 1998).

[18] Arthur Kleinman, Paul Brodwin, Byron J. Good, and Mary-Jo DelVecchio Good, "Introduction," in *Pain as Human Experience: An Anthropological Perspective* (Berkeley, 1992), 8.

to transform the nature of physical pain carried with them profound implications for a variety of cultural practices (among them various forms of bodily transformation or "mutilation," religious rituals, or such practices as *sati* or cannibalism) that themselves articulated large-scale social relations, reinforced cultural norms, and located the body in a social world.[19]

As it collects and negotiates the pain and suffering of those on whom Parker worked, the Parker archive formalizes an encounter with a nearly cavernous epistemological otherness centered on a differential experience of physical pain. The paintings, boxes, and case studies that make up the Parker collection seem in their recording of this otherness to preserve some measure of the preternatural reality of the past. As I shall suggest, the record established by the paintings, case studies, and other objects collected in his archive at the medical library at Yale indicate the historical possibility of a relation to Chinese suffering that escapes or betrays the pressing possibilities of national-economic allegory we saw in the work of George Henry Mason, or the intensely realistic ontology of pain elaborated in Greenblatt's reading of the torture of the Chinese goldsmith. Pressing the quotidian experience of Parker's operations against the historical and formal contexts in which they emerged, this chapter reads the chronicle of Chinese pain that appears in the Parker archive as the expression of an entire *style* of representation that organizes—or seems to organize—a relationship between the cultural and the real.

3. The Lam Qua Portraits

Six years after opening his hospital in the foreign concession area along the Pearl River in Canton, Parker, having left China because of the first Opium War, traveled to the United States and Europe in order to raise funds for his missionary work. While in London, Parker had occasion to visit Guy's Hospital, where he met with several doctors and visited the institution's medical displays. Touring the hospital as a guest, he came upon several oil paintings of Chinese patients exhibiting extraordinarily large external tumors. He described the encounter in his personal journal:

> Found a collection of my patients in the Museum. Copies of the original. But no one suspected they had been operated on. I as a stranger asked who

[19] Talal Asad, *Formations of the Secular: Christianity, Islam, Modernity* (Stanford, 2003), 92.

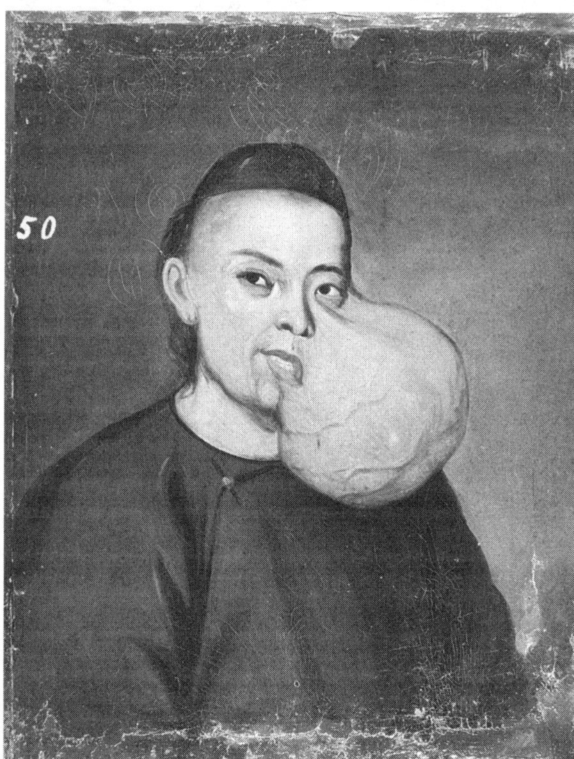

Fig 3.1 Parker collection, no. 50. Courtesy of Yale University, Harvey Cushing/John Hay Whitney Medical Library.

> operated. 'Not operated upon etc . . . ' was the reply. 'Yes, they have, all of them & with success,' I informed them. Much interest was expressed in learning the history of the etc.[20]

The moment must have been a fairly triumphant one. The paintings—painted by the Cantonese artist Lam Qua at Parker's request during the years following the hospital's founding in 1835—had apparently been exhibited at Guy's as illustrations of medical curiosities, pictures of people with external tumors of a size then completely unknown in the West. By revealing that these were paintings of his patients, and, what's more, by announcing that he had removed the tumors, Parker impressed his British colleagues with his surgical skill and medical expertise ("Much interest was expressed in learning the history," as he writes) and turned the subjects of the portraits from unfortunates into patients, a shift in role that would have lent much support to Parker's arguments about the

[20] Gulick, 105.

ease with which Britons could participate in alleviating the suffering of the Chinese.[21]

The portraits Parker had come across at Guy's were part of a larger collection of at least 114 pictures, showing some eighty of Parker's patients, painted by Lam Qua (Guan Qiaochang) in the years between 1836 and 1852.[22] The fact that we know Lam Qua's real name marks already a major difference between his status in Canton and that of the watercolorist Pu Qua, whose name appears on the pages of Mason's *Punishments* book. By the mid-1830s, it was possible for a painter working in the Western style, as Lam Qua did, to acquire an international reputation and to have that reputation make his studio one of the mandatory stops on any new visitor's tour of Canton. From a three-story building located near the factory district, Lam Qua and his numerous assistants produced singular portraits of wealthy merchants in the English grand manner of Sir Thomas Lawrence or Sir William Beechey, and they also generated business through the rapid production of souvenir images of Canton, "combining factory models of production with the romantic notion of the autonomous individual artist," much as Pu Qua had done three decades earlier (*MM*, 140).[23]

[21]The episode is nonetheless bizarre. How could Parker not have known that copies of the paintings, which he had had made in Canton between 1836 and 1840, were at Guy's Hospital? Or rather, how could the paintings have gotten to Guy's without Parker's help? In his memoir of his years as a medical missionary, Parker's colleague William Lockhart asserts that Parker "presented a set of [portraits] to the Museum of Guy's Hospital" (*The Medical Missionary in China: A Narrative of Twenty Years' Experience* [London, 1861], 171.). But if Parker presented the portraits himself, he could only have done so on the same 1841 trip during which he claims to have "found" them there, in which case his anecdote of discovery makes no sense. That said, if he didn't bring the paintings from Canton with him, then how did they get to Guy's at all? According to Sander Gilman, the portraits "were used by Parker on his trip to England as well as in the United States to illustrate his presentation of his case studies to such groups as the Boston Medical Society in order to raise funds for his missionary work" ("Lam Qua and the Development of a Westernized Medical Iconography in China," *Medical History* 30 [1986], 62.). Again, this makes little sense in light of Parker's story about coming across the paintings in Guy's. So either the paintings traveled to Guy's without Parker's knowledge, which would contradict Lockhart's testimony and Gilman's essay, or the story Parker puts down in his journal is misleading.

[22]Today, eighty-six of these portraits are at the Harvey Cushing/John Hay Whitney Medical Library at Yale University Medical School. Twenty-three remain at the Gordon Museum at Guy's Hospital. Gulick writes that the only other portrait is at Boston's Countway Library, but in a recent essay Rachman writes that four other paintings (which Gulick seems not to have known about) belong to Cornell University, and another is at the Peabody Essex Museum in Salem, Mass. (156n2; Sander Gilman has written of *five* portraits at Cornell [61n9]). I refer to individual portraits by their catalog number in the Yale system.

[23]Some of Lam Qua's best known sitters "included Chi Ying, the signatory of the Treaty of Nanking [which ended the first Opium War], Commissioner Lin (Lin Chong), who was 'responsible

The respect paid Lam Qua did not indicate in any simple way the triumph of a colonial education, the mark of the civilizability of the Chinese or the production in Canton of a colonial demimonde of sinified Westerners and Westernized Chinese. The quality of his work provoked as much anxiety as it did admiration, as his eventual fallout with his teacher George Chinnery suggests.[24] Recalling the more general Western contempt for Chinese visual art, which especially in the case of the representation of people "was considered to be 'a high burlesque' and 'either hideous or ludicrous,'" allows us to see how Lam Qua's skill in portraiture could constitute a threat to the idea of irreducible cultural difference that would have sustained a general sense of Western superiority in the mid-nineteenth century.[25] Given that on at least one occasion a Lam Qua painting was mistaken

---

for the onset of the Opium War,' as well as Peter Parker, Sir Henry Pottinger, and numerous other Western and Chinese dignitaries" (Larissa Heinrich, "Handmaids to the Gospel: Lam Qua's Medical Portraiture," in *Tokens of Exchange: The Problem of Translation in Global Circulations,* ed. Lydia Liu [Durham, N.C., 1999], 243); his work was shown at the Royal Academy in London in 1835, and appeared in exhibitions in the U.S. and France in the 1840s and 1850s. For more historical background on Lam Qua, see Carl Crossman, *The China Trade: Export Paintings, Furniture, Silver and other Objects* (Princeton, N.J., 1972), 25–39, and Heinrich, 242–44; see also Heinrich's *The Afterlife of Images: Translating the Pathological Body between China and the West* (Durham, N.C., 2008), whose second chapter is a version of the essay I cite here. Craig Clunas also discusses Lam Qua briefly in *Chinese Export Watercolors* (London, 1984). The differences between Lam Qua's place in the historical record and that of Pu Qua, who sold watercolors to George Henry Mason, indicates as much about the dramatic changes in the interactions and communications between Canton and the West as it does about the relative difference in each painter's ability to produce high art in the Western style. By the mid–nineteenth-century China could be a career for more kinds of men (but only men) than just merchants and sailors, a truth attested to by the residence in Macao and Canton from 1825 to 1852 of the English artist George Chinnery, whose portraits and landscapes of southern China and its business and diplomatic elites constitute a crucial visual record of the experience of Western expatriates in Canton during this period. That—at least according to some reports—Lam Qua got his start as painter by studying with Chinnery (after starting as his brush-cleaner) indicates that the "commerce" between the Western and Chinese communities in Canton included fields of activity and behavior not linked exclusively to the trade in export goods, and that some members the foreign "community" of southern China were by the 1830s actively or passively transferring their culture to the Chinese who worked for or with them.

[24]The details on this relationship are sketchy. Crossman seems quite sure that Lam Qua studied with Chinnery, Rachman and Heinrich less so. Crossman, citing the French traveler "Old Nick" (Paul Émile Daurand Forgues) attributes the conflict between the two men to Chinnery's claim that Lam Qua was a "wretchedly bad painter whose sole merit comes from having stolen from him some models and some methods," and the fact that Lam Qua could undercut Chinnery's prices for portraits, thereby costing him business (26). In these two complaints—that the Chinese entrepreneur is an imitator who relies on "secrets" stolen from the West and that labor costs allow him to undercut his Western competitors—one finds the classic form of a debate that continues to this day.

[25]Margaret Jourdain and R. Soame Jenyns, *Chinese Export Art in the Eighteenth Century* (London, 1950), 15.

for work by the British artist Thomas Sully suggests that commentators who insisted that Lam Qua "could never entirely eliminate his Chinese mannerisms" in his portraits were asserting the impossibility of bridging a cultural gap that looked already to have been fairly well bridged.[26]

The paintings Lam Qua did of Parker's patients constitute the most important single body of his work. Often grotesque, startlingly strange and otherworldly, the portrayals of human bodies and their enormous, motley tumors force into shocking visibility the boundaries that separate subjects from objects, the living from the necrotic, the human from the inhuman. What makes the paintings unusual in relation to the other work of their place and era has not to do simply with those tumors, however, nor solely with the fact that the people in the portraits are poor or sick—the Pu Qua watercolors, after all, featured criminals, beggars, and manual laborers of all kinds—but rather that these poor and relatively anonymous people were painted in a style and a medium normally reserved for a different class of person entirely. Lam Qua's portraits thus stood outside not only the conventional ambit of the China trade in visual art, which favored portrait paintings of powerful merchants and officials, landscapes of the Canton waterfront, or collections of Chinese types of the sort drawn by Pu Qua, but also of the normative conventions of pictorial representation as they existed in the mid-nineteenth century. Their cultural and representational work takes place within in an economic and aesthetic context in which they were deeply anomalous.

Before attending to the particular ways in which these portraits collectively represent Chinese pain, I want to spend some time looking at the features of their mimetic and historical appearance. Already in the overview of Lam Qua's place in the global market for fine art we see how the compositional expertise the portraits displayed granted them a representational legitimacy (and access to "truth") that Pu Qua's watercolors never had, a difference measured by the fact that Lam Qua's portraits did not require lengthy captions to explain them. Lam Qua's painterly expertise lies at the core of what Roland Barthes might call his "reality-effect,"

[26]Heinrich, 244. Crossman's chapter on Lam Qua suggests that the portrait of Wu Bingjian (Howqua) in the Museum of American China Trade was originally believed to have been done by an Englishman; Heinrich is my source for the Sully anecdote. The cultural difference between "English" and "Chinese" styles did not simply stem from Western prejudice, but was actually put into commodity form by Lam Qua's studio. Sander Gilman cites William Fane de Salis, who commented that in 1848 a "painting in 'English' style was worth £10 and was 'fashioned with good drawing and perspective'" while a "Chinese painting" was worth £8 "because it was 'out of all drawing proportion and perspective'" (61).

namely the degree to which his portraits by virtue of their sheer formal quality allow their mimetic scenes easily to refer to the realm of truth.[27]

That such a reality-effect could produce a more or less mistaken reading of the paintings does not interfere with its efficacy as an effect. As Parker's experience at Guy's suggests, the images lent themselves equally well to two very different interpretations: they could be understood both as evidence of the work of medical missionary practice—in which case they functioned as the "before" images of a sequence created by Western intervention—and as evidence of "the way things are" in China, home of the medical monstrosity, in which case they encoded not so much a process as a fixed temporal fact about the nature of Chinese life. Though the latter of these readings was historically wrong in relation to the portraits' actual production by Lam Qua at Parker's behest, it was representationally "right" in the sense that it was a legitimate reading of the what the portraits showed and how they showed it, a correct apprehension of the reality-effect that the portraits generated through their mastery of the English grand style. What follows begins with a consideration of how the portraits work in the historically correct reading—the one Parker intended—before considering how they mean in the throes of the more single-mindedly synchronic context in which they signified at Guy's before Parker's corrective. Around these two readings, which reveal the paintings' mimetic relation to *time* and to *realism*, respectively, appears the context in which their representation of suffering will ultimately be read and understood.

Because the paintings show patients prior to the tumors' removal, the people represented in the portraits are captured at a very particular moment in their lives—the moment at which their physical bodies are about to stop looking like the portraits that captured them. The disjunction present in the vast majority of portraits lay therefore between the "person" represented and the tumor he or she bore; these are portraits of beings whose most salient representational fact has, shortly after the portraits were made, been removed from their bodies. The "return" whereby the body, following the operation, becomes or re-becomes a self without a tumor establishes itself forcefully in the viewer's imagination, which grapples therefore with an oscillating awareness of the particular life *with* the tumor that must have pre-existed the moment of portrayal and the life *without* it that succeeded it. The portraits—which, it bears repeating, show a class of person who has only rarely in human history been painted in this way—are thus poised

[27] Roland Barthes, "The Reality Effect," in *The Rustle of Language*, trans. Richard Howard (Berkeley, 1989).

Fig 3.2 Parker collection, no. 67. This patient was never operated on, and later died. Courtesy of Yale University, Harvey Cushing/John Hay Whitney Medical Library.

on the boundary between life and death. Each of them shows a being whose body will never again be worth representing with oil on canvas, and which thus appears at the vanishing point of its own cultural and mediatic presence.

The uncanny quality of the tumor as each painting's *raison d'être* and disappearing horizon recomposes the effects of the portraits as a representational medium. In portraits of cultural elites, the private sitting transforms itself through oil and canvas into a public object designed to assert the relation between the private person and the community to which he or she belongs, the portrait thereby functioning primarily as the public assertion of private being, evidence that the sitter's private person mattered enough in the public sphere to be permanently and painstakingly recorded. But the sitters in the Lam Qua paintings cannot be said to have had "private" lives, at least not in relation to the world inhabited by Parker, Lam Qua, and other Canton elites, largely because any such privacy could only be established in relation to a public life to which they had never had any access. The patients' compositional presence might therefore be said to represent the impossibility of the very relation a portrait conventionally aimed to capture. Or

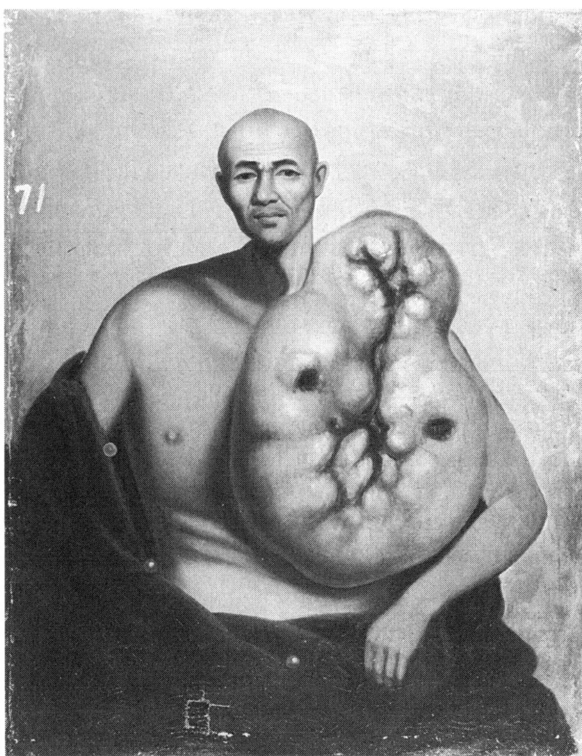

Fig 3.3 The tumor as viol. Parker collection, no. 71. Woo Kinshing, age 49. Courtesy of Yale University, Harvey Cushing/John Hay Whitney Medical Library.

rather, the "public" life that the portraits established for the sitters emerged solely from the fact of the portraits themselves, which in turn owed their existence to the presence of tumors whose future absence their function it was to record. This is why in many cases the name of the sitter is not recorded on the portraits at all. For a Canton merchant a Lam Qua portrait might have been said to instantiate in material and representational form the public fact of his private life, a gesture that made the public visibility of the private the coin with which posterity's regard could be purchased. But for Parker's patients, the operation functioned in reverse: the portraits instantiated in material form the private fact of the patients' public lives, capturing their visibility as public figures immediately prior to its disappearance. In the unlikely event that one of these patients would see his or her own portrait after its making, the best he or she could hope to say was not, "That is me," but "That *was* me (and is me no longer)."[28]

[28]It is perhaps for this reason that the entire collection includes only one before-and-after sequence, in which the healed patient makes a reappearance following the amputation of his arm. Heinrich reads the difference between the two portraits as a narration of the healing benefits of

We see how such an analysis operates at the level of the individual patient whose presumably tumor-free life after surgery goes unrecorded by either the portraits or Parker's case notes. But it functions just as well in relation to the history of human health in China. The reason these patients had such large tumors was that Chinese doctors did not perform surgery. Benign external tumors that in the United States or England would have been removed early, after only a short period of growth, were allowed in China to grow for years. The Lam Qua paintings thus record more than the disappearance of particular tumors; they also record the disappearance of such tumors in general, as the spread of Western surgical techniques presaged a future in which no tumor would be allowed to grow to the kind of size that would permit it to be portrayed, as the tumors so often are in the portraits, as a kind of functional extension of the body and the landscape in which it appears. The portraits record, then, not only the disappearing representational horizon of the individual patients, but also the vanishing medical horizon of a certain experience of the body—an experience that though it depended on a rather precise set of differences between Chinese and Western medicine of the mid-nineteenth century nonetheless must have looked to Western audiences like the fossil remnant of an atavistic, uncanny past associated with the Chinese nation.[29] It is in this sense that the tumors record and preserve the double experience of time: the lived, individual time required for them grow on any given body and the imaginary temporal extension of

---

Western medicine on their subject, Po Ashing. Though this exceptional portrait might be said to undermine the general principles I am laying out in this chapter, its presence makes sense once we consider that Po Ashing was, as far as Parker knew (and as he noted with some pride) China's first surgical amputee. While the second portrait might therefore be said to represent the felicitous "after" in which Po Ashing's tumor has been removed, it is also a painting of the amputation itself. The sequence's "interest" in Po Ashing as a person—which might by virtue of its before-after structure seem to extend from representation to narrative—must therefore be understood both as a single sequence of two paintings, and as two separate paintings indicating two separate medical conditions, the tumor and the amputation. His tumor gone, Po Ashing becomes worthy of a portrait a second time by virtue of his amputation, which allows him once again to cross the representational barrier and have his privacy made public.

[29] As both Gilman and Heinrich have argued, the collection of portraits tends to produce a slippery metonomy between nation and disease, so that the Chinese patients confirm for the Western viewer a "double stigma—first, the sign of pathology, and second, the sign of barbarism" that extends beyond the particularity of the individual to become a feature of China imagined as "the *cause and source* itself of the spectacular illnesses" the portraits show (Gilman, 65; Heinrich, 255). Though Chinese and English fevers might burn equally, the shores of the Thames or the Charles had no sufferers equivalent to those living in the Pearl River Delta, and that difference, though it might encourage an increase in sympathetic obligation, did China's national standing no favors.

their future disappearance. While the former indicated a history of nearly unimaginable pain suffered and endured, the latter pointed toward a time of pain eradicated and defeated. The movement from the first time to the second is the final and somewhat monotonous subject of all of the portraits, considered from the historical perspective to which Parker's influence assigns them.

Under such a perspective, the portraits' fundamental task was to record the *narrative* of Parker's surgical interventions in China, to mark a temporal "before" whose subsequent "after" affirmed missionary medicine's benevolent possibilities. But as Parker's encounter with the portraits at Guy's Hospital suggests, such a diachronic reading could easily disappear behind the dramatic visual impact of the portraits themselves. For someone who did not know their history, the portraits instead captured some facts about the state of China and—more dramatically, given the intensity with which any portrait aims to address the subjective person of its sitter—an instance of pain *being* suffered and endured, a suspended moment of anguish whose intensity, measured by the size of the tumor and our identification with the object of its attachment, threatens to extend infinitely the moment of pain the portrait shows, unfurling it to all the temporal and subjective corners of the sitter's life. Though such a perspective on the portraits would miss what, for Parker, they were most fundamentally "about," most scholarly interpretations of the portraits' work have adopted just such a synchronic point of view, allowing the internal dynamics of the portraits' composition to affect what we know about their originally intended purpose. Indeed, a complete picture of the portraits' meaning must recognize the way they generate at least partly through the actual history of their circulation two seemingly incompatible interpretations of their representational work: Parker's diachronic one, under which the portraits testified to the before and after of his missionary labor, and a more synchronic vision, which emerges from some combination of the visual shock provoked by their contents, and the compositional work of the image that has arranged them.[30]

[30] For an instance of the latter reading in a historical context closer to Parker's own, consider this unsigned 1845 review of twenty-eight Lam Qua portraits appearing at the Society for Medical Improvement in Boston: "These monstrous growths are very serious things to our fellow-creatures of the Celestial empire. But they are so out of all reasonable proportions, and sprout up in such strange shapes and places—and China is so far off, and a China man is so much an abstraction to our minds—and the almond-shaped eyes, the pigtail, the brown-sherry complexion and the Oriental environments of the sufferers, so blind us to the naked fact of the existence of an unsightly or devouring malady, that we cannot help looking at them with a little twitching about the *levator anguli oris*, which if not inhuman is at least highly unbecoming." If the tumors were comical—the *levator anguli oris* muscle is

The synchronic structure of the Lam Qua paintings has been admirably analyzed by Stephen Rachman, who argues that the images' energy relies on a powerful formal movement between two differing aesthetic modes, "likeness" and "representation," that apply unequally to the major representational objects captured on the canvas. Rachman cites one of Parker's very few mentions of Lam Qua, which appears in the case notes of a patient named Lew Akin: "I am indebted to Lam Qua, who has taken an admirable likeness of the little girl and a good representation of the tumor." Parker, Rachman writes, was probably using "*likeness* in the old, conventional sense as a term of resemblance appropriate to portraiture (of persons), and *representation* as a term of resemblance appropriate to objects, a usage connoting graphic realism—likeness for people, representation for things" (*MM*, 145).[31] As Rachman goes on to show, the tension in many of the collection's paintings between tumor and person figures "two ways of seeing," one in which the viewer attends to individual facial features and the "broader categories of the normative human, the male or female, the old or young, beautiful or plain, or perhaps the ethnic/racial category of the Chinese," the other in which the eye "observes objects by type or classification, be it medical or some other system" (*MM*, 146). Rachman goes on to generate from this observation an extensive reading of the portrait of Parker's patient Leäng Yen, who seems to be deliberately hiding her face behind a hand surrounded by a massive, purpled tumor. Withholding her likeness even as she proffers her

responsible for the lateral movement of the mouth—it was because the "far off," abstracted qualities of China and the Chinese "blinded" the viewer to the images' historical provenance; they become funny precisely because they are removed from history. What is remarkable in this account is how this historical removal is accomplished through the narrative catalog of the discrete and specific racial, cultural, and geographic characteristics of the Chinese—their color of their complexion, their shape of their eyes, the Manchu queue, and so forth. The removal of the Chinese from the realm of sympathy occurs because they are "far off," but this removal actually generates an awareness of the reviewer's *own* inhumanity, which however quickly dismissed suggests that the paintings generated for this reviewer at least enough of an identification with the Chinese as to require him to dismiss it. Hence the uncanny and slightly inhuman laughter, whose description in terms of muscular action feels as monstrous as the tumors. The review appeared in the May 21, 1845, issue of the *Boston Medical and Surgical Journal* (32.16), and is cited in Lawrence Weschler, *Mr. Wilson's Cabinet of Wonder* (New York, 1995), 140. Weschler cites speculation that the author of the review was Oliver Wendell Holmes.

[31] As Gilman has shown, this double regard has something to do with a significant shift in early nineteenth-century medical illustration from schematic to mimetic representation, coupled with the belief that since diseases were patient-specific, the "image of the identifiable patient as the bearer of a specific pathology" was the most effective illustration of any given disease (63). Gilman goes on to write that by the mid-1800s, the idea of the patient as a specific bearer of disease had been replaced, at least in the case of tumors, by an emphasis on cellular pathology, leading to the disappearance of the patient in medical illustration, who was "replaced by the emblem of the disease, the tumor" (65).

representation, refusing the cultural generosity of Lam Qua's act of portraiture, the immortality of canvas, Leäng Yen reveals the underlying motivations of the entire portrait series (she could not have shown her face and withheld the tumor) and gains for herself some marginal control over her representational fate.[32]

The tension organizing likeness and representation in the Leäng Yen portrait appears elsewhere in the collection of paintings, where it tends to operate on two levels at once. On one hand, the paintings frequently double on their aesthetic surface the tumors they show with features of the patients' bodies. In one portrait, a woman's pendant earrings mirror the tumor that hangs from her neck; in another, a young girl's gangrenous feet are placed parallel to her mother's bound ones; in yet another, a man carries his tumor like a viol; and in the landscapes, "compositional dynamics and structure . . . construct implicit metaphorical relationships among the pathology, the human body, and the environment."[33] In these cases, the movement between representation and likeness operates at the level of the paintings' composition, with the tumors' astonishing singularity integrated into the visual space of the paintings, made comprehensible within the aesthetic field by the logic of their repetition. The *representational* properties of the tumors—their shape, color, or location—thus find themselves doubled as the paintings remark their *likeness* to some other feature of the visual field in which they appear.

The relation between likeness and representation established in the compositional structure of these images, like the relation between past and future time established by the paintings' implied narrative, develops an interpretive armature for the Lam Qua paintings through the production of a dialectical relationship between two of its features. These two general interpretive strategies, the compositional–synchronic and the narrative–diachronic, form at the meta-

[32] Rachman reads this gesture against Leäng Yen's behavior over the course of her medical treatment, during which she repeatedly refuses to trust or be grateful to Parker for his care. Rachman's reading suggests the presence within the collection of moments at which the general Western reception of the paintings can be undone by an attention to the details of a particular artwork and its relation to the case study that describes its patient. By moving back and forth between the written material of the case study—of which Parker is of course still the origin—and the representational field of the painting, including what it captures of the sitter's willingness to be painted at all, Rachman generates individual and historical difference inside the Parker archive. Although the paintings may, following Gilman and especially Heinrich, be said to domesticate the Chinese people they show by making them the uncanny allegory of China's diseased body politic, a sustained attention to a single painting can, Rachman suggests, show meaning operating outside the framework of Western cultural and scientific superiority.

[33] Heinrich, 256.

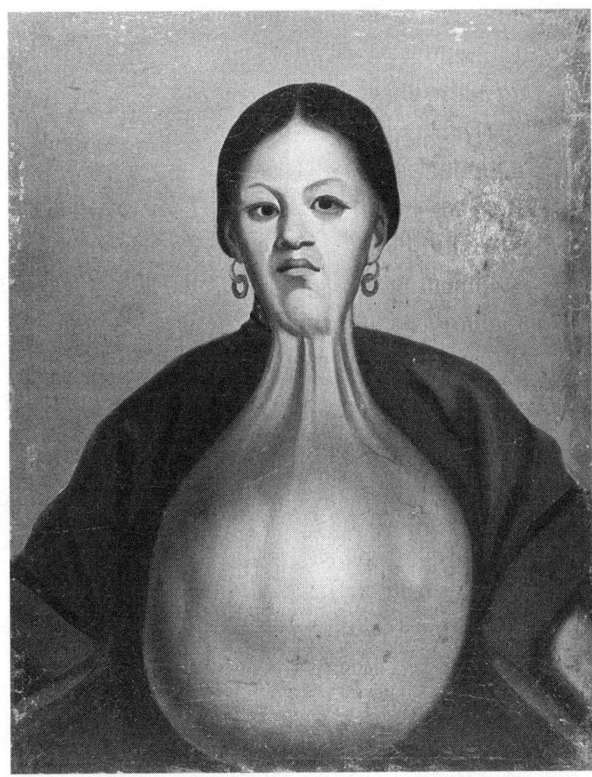

Fig 3.4 The pendant earrings. Parker collection, unnumbered. Yang She, age 20. Courtesy of Yale University, Harvey Cushing/John Hay Whitney Medical Library.

critical level a dialectic of their own, in which the paintings move, as indeed they have in historical fact, between interpretations focused on their relation to the medical missionary project and their relation to the generic history of painterly form. Neither of these interpretations seems bound to get the upper hand. They belong to different conceptual fields; and the full range of the paintings' meaning operates in the space between those fields, which it therefore includes.

But all this interpretation leaves behind what the paintings actually show, or would show, if they were portraits and not historical documents on missionary medicine, or purely formal expressions of a relation between likeness and image. The most striking thing about the portraits *as portraits* is that the people who appear in the paintings do not in any way "express" their pain. Their absolutely stoic, uncannily undisturbed faces look out from the paintings as though daring the viewer to mention the tumor that accompanies them.

To return to the language of representation and likeness, we can begin to think about this representational situation by noticing that it emerges from the ways in

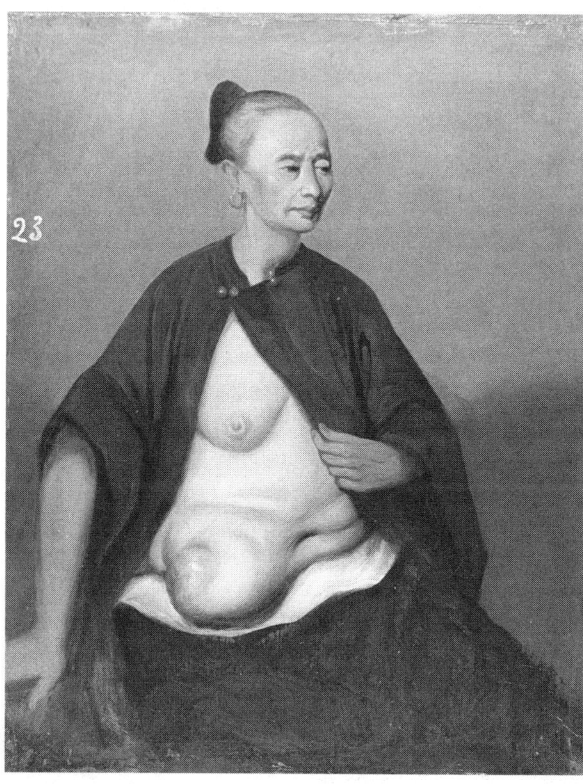

Fig 3.5 The tumor and/as breast. Parker collection, no. 23. Courtesy of Yale University, Harvey Cushing/John Hay Whitney Medical Library.

which any given sitter's likeness represents, or fails to represent, a subjective awareness of the tumor that the paintings represent as part of his or her body. The dialectic of representation and likeness, so driven in the case of the paintings' compositional structure to establish a relation between the tumor and its landscape, seems to founder at precisely the moment at which it would seem most necessary: there where it would indicate to us the relation between the person and the thing, there where the person who is the paintings' putative subject could express some *subjective* relation to the object growing on and out of his or her body. The overall effect of this absence or indifference is to make the subject's experience of the tumor disappear, and thus to suggest that Parker's patients bore their tumors with remarkable stoicism. But this stoicism has the curious effect of divorcing what one might call the objective representation of pain—its evidence, its "representation"—from the subjective one that would locate that pain in the living and active consciousness of a human body—its likeness. Seen from this angle the relationship between pain's representation and its likeness, its objective dimension and its subjective one, will recall the entire dialectical structure established by pain's twining of the ontological and the cultural. Pain's tie to the pure reality of being, its demand that we cry that reality out to the world and have it recognized in the space of culture, here seems subject to a representational short circuit, in which the transition that would take us from objective evidence of pain (the tumors) to their subjective expression (in faces) does not take place.

Larissa Heinrich's response to that short circuit has been to attribute the patients' apparent stoicism to the demands of the English grand style.[34] A reasonable explanation. But it cannot account for the appearance of that same disjunction between objective and subjective pain elsewhere in the Parker archive, most notably as a feature of the Medical Missionary Society's surgical case reports, whose written form owed little to the strictures of painterly styles familiar to Lam Qua. Heinrich supplements her mention of the English grand manner with the speculation that paintings also communicated "the vision of the Chinese patient that Parker wanted to communicate to his Western audience, the vision that Parker himself had of what it meant to be Chinese and to suffer from what seemed inconceivably horrible pathologies" (251). This is closer to what I will suggest, though I will not be making Parker the exclusive intending agent of the representational material in either the paintings or the case reports. Instead, as I shall suggest in what follows, the division between subjective and objective pain that appears in both the portraits and the case studies intervenes philosophically *inside* the dialectic of pain that constituted Parker's major cultural context for understanding his Chinese patients, where it exposes the limits of that context in ways so radical that Parker can only barely register them.

In returning the paintings to the larger context of the archive, I follow the dictates of their own history of circulation. Though the portraits strike us today as by far the most spectacular emblems of Parker's life work, they were not historically the major form through which Parker's contemporaries received word of the labors of the medical missionaries. That word came rather through Parker's surgical case studies, which were included among a variety of budgetary and administrative information in the series of quarterly reports on the state of the Medical Missionary Society, which also were regularly reprinted in the *Chinese Repository* (Canton's expatriate news organ) and distributed in the United States. It was the case studies, far more than the paintings, that were the source of

[34] Heinrich calls the "unexpected lack of emotion" the subjects show "perhaps the single most striking feature of the paintings as a body," and ascribes this lack to the general stoicism of the English grand style, in which "trappings of identity were projected out onto the attire and setting in which the subject was placed," as well as to shifts in the habits of Western medical illustration (250).

Parker's international reputation and of information on the state of Chinese life and medical care—they were, in fact, the very "instructive documents" that the medical missionaries had imagined their society would provide.[35]

In the years leading up to the discovery of chemical anesthetics in 1846, as you will see in the citations below, Parker recorded with relentless attention his patients' reactions to the pain of surgery.

> During the operation to amputate Leäng Yen's arm: "The patient after her decision was fully formed contemned [sic] the idea of pain, and at the moment of sawing the bone inquired when that part of the process would take place." (*First and second*, 60)
>
> "Twelve patients with [hare-lips] have been received, and in several instances in one week from the operation the patient has been quite cured. The fortitude of these little children has been very noticeable, they appearing, often through the whole operation, almost insensible to pain." ("First report," 9)
>
> Case no. 1675, on Leang Ashing, aged 27, for removal of facial tumor: "During the incisions through the integuments and the dissecting out of the tumor he did not move a muscle, change a feature of his countenance, or draw one long breath, so that apprehensions were even entertained that he was insensible; but if spoken to he answered deliberately and correctly." ("Fourth quarterly report," 4)
>
> Woo She (case no. 4016), for the removal of a cancerous breast: "Her fortitude exceeded all that I have yet witnessed. She scarcely uttered a groan during the extirpation, and before she was removed from the table, clasped her hands and, with an unaffected smile, cordially thanked the gentlemen who assisted on the occasion." ("Seventh quarterly report," 8)

[35] Parker's reputation traveled mainly through written descriptions of his medical work; the paintings, as a number of commentators note, were rarely shown in public. (A proposed exhibition of the paintings in the 1970s was canceled [see Peter Josyph, "The Missionary Doctor and the Chinese Painter," *MD* (August 1992), 6.]; Rachmann writes that the paintings were "rarely seen by the public or by scholars" [156n2].) The case reports were by contrast widely reprinted, appearing in public letters like the one Parker wrote to John Abercrombie, in the published annual minutes of the Medical Missionary Society and in the *Chinese Repository*, a monthly magazine edited by Bridgman, which was the main source of news about China's foreign missionary community both in China and abroad. Like the paintings, the case studies functioned as both testaments to Parker's surgical work and as ethnographic documents that taught readers about the people and diseases of China.

Case no. 4903, Choo Yihleäng, a shoemaker, for removal of a tumor on the right side of his neck: "During the operation the patient was perfectly collected, and did not utter a groan: spoke with natural voice when spoken to, and repeatedly requested the operater might not be alarmed." ("Eighth quarterly report," 11)

Yáng Káng, 35, facial tumor: "The patient discovered great fortitude, coolly remarking on commencement of the first incision, 'it hurts, doctor.'" (*Report of the MMS for 1844*, 4)

"The patient bore the operation with heroic fortitude, not seeming to notice the incisions, and remarked shortly after, that he had not suffered much." (*Report of the MMS for 1844*, 10)

For amputation of the arm of Kwo Síhái: "The amputation was speedily performed, and the patient sustained the shock remarkably well, considering his loss of blood, and the time that had elapsed. He spoke in a natural voice the moment after." (*Report of the MMS for 1844*, 17)

Like the paintings, these case studies present a Chinese relation to pain defined by the representation of a startling and quasi-heroic stoicism. And like the paintings, they generate that stoicism by presenting a startling disjunction between tumor and person, representation and likeness. The patient's "natural" voices, like the expressionless faces of the portraits, communicate again and again the act of nontranslation (the nonact of translation?) whereby the objective evidence of pain does not appear in the subjective response to it.[36]

Recalling Elaine Scarry's analysis of the representational structure through which pain tends to move into language, we might say that what is at stake in these descriptions is the relation between perception and mimesis, between the objective visual evidence of pain and its subjective expression. This distinction exposes the difference between what Scarry calls pain's

[36]Heinrich is extrapolating, I think, when she refers to Parker's "fixation with—and awe of—what he perceived as a peculiarly Chinese ability to cope with extreme pain" (251). Nowhere in the case reports does Parker actually comment on how he feels about the Chinese "ability to cope with extreme pain"; nowhere, in fact, does he even seem to notice that he keeps noticing the Chinese reaction to pain, or suggest that he considers this to be a Chinese "ability." The peculiar disjunction between Parker's description of individual relations to pain and his nonreflection on it will ground much of my analysis below.

"language of agency" whose origin is a literal or metaphorical wound—a description of a surgery, the picture of a tumor—and the subjective expression of pain whose origin is not the wound as such but rather the subjective experience that the wound causes. In narrative terms, the difference between these two is like the difference between description and narration, the one an unmotivated recitation of facts whose model is a totally objective realism of the type later attempted by the French new novel, the other a guided and intentional tour whose presumed mimetic telos is the intention of a narrating or narrated subject.

In general, one might say that the language of pain operates in the gap between these two representational modes. Any given cultural relationship to pain governs the representational work that translates from one side of the gap to the other, establishing the rules for both the content and the form of pain-language that determine, for instance, how loudly it is appropriate to react to a hangnail, what forms of speech count as suitable expressions of grief, and so on. Such protocols establish a relationship between what one might call the descriptive "evidence" of pain—the visible or invisible wound—and the narrative "expression" of it, in which legitimate expressions earn the subject the right to have his or her pain recognized, tended to, sympathized with, and the like, and illegitimate ones are written off as complaints or not recognized at all.[37]

Any given expression of pain is thus not simply a single representation, but an act that insofar as it is a representation expresses the general cultural *aesthetic* that determines it. Such an aesthetic does not just determine the appropriate cultural content of any given expression of pain; rather it organizes an entire field of relationships between what one might call the "public" evidence of pain and its subjective expressions. The wound's metonymic work, which appears in its physical appearance, the content of a description, or in the case of psychic pain, in the reporting of an acknowledged fact (a death in the family), produces a kind of cultural baseline against which the subjective representation of pain can be evaluated. This movement between perceptual evidence of pain on one hand and its subjective representation on the other is what I am calling pain's cultural aesthetic: the set of codes that organizes the movement from description to narration, from the presence of pain established through the virtual objectivity

[37] Unsurprisingly, differences in this context will array themselves unequally according to social structures like race, class, and gender; and in the case of pain especially, also, in relation to age.

of a cultural norm to the narration of a relation to that pain—"It hurts, doctor"—that comes from a singular subjective perspective.[38] Parker's reports on his patients' reactions to surgical pain are not simply, then, records of a set of medical facts, or even evidence for cultural differences in the experience of pain. Because the subjective representation of pain necessarily involves the figural transfer of interior to exterior, intention to expression, the patients (as "characters" in the reports) can be said to be expressing a representational *style* that the reports' narrating subject simultaneously registers and does not recognize as such.

As a style for reacting to pain, the attitude Parker's patients express can be most simply described by the fact that it splits the "pain" that Parker recognizes merely by looking at the tissue damage he sees—that is, pain's purely descriptive or "realistic" evidence—from the subjective narrations of face and voice that Parker expects to reflect that damage. From the perspective of an aesthetic that expects and encourages the mimetic transfer from inside to outside, the style Parker's patients embody registers most intensely as an *absence* or a failure to represent, as the words "expressionless" (to describe the faces) and "natural" (to describe the voices) suggest. Parker's descriptions of these patients thus continually registers the absence of an artificial—that is, human-made or subjective—representational gesture that would carry the physical damage done by his surgery into the realm of expression, that would, in other words, and very much like Parker himself, encode the objective details before him with some degree of narration or character. The most remarkable thing about Parker's frequent observation about this absence or failure is that he himself never seems to notice it. He never, that is, turns his observations regarding specific patients into a general theory of the Chinese relation to suffering and, indeed, would insist in his 1841 fundraising letter—despite having recorded evidence that suggested precisely the opposite—that, Chinese gouts and English ones being equally painful, the Chinese suffered just as the English did.

In using "style" to mean something other than a literary style, I wish to insist both on the strict representational qualities of what the patients do in Parker's case reports and to grant the word "style" an expanded set of meanings that

[38] These rules govern mimetic form as well as its content. Parker's mention of the man who says that "It hurts, doctor," is telling: Yáng Káng's phrase bears reporting in the case study because of the surprising divergence between the information produced by its content and the insouciant coolness of its "coolly" delivered form. The phrase calls attention to itself as a representation of pain that does not call formal attention to itself as a representation of pain.

include "attitude, stance, posture, and consciousness."[39] I would like to recognize, in other words, that modes of being are expressive enactments of the subjective and cultural forces behind human activity. By suggesting that Parker's Chinese patients express a style, I mean, therefore, to find in moments of profound bodily crisis something other than a "raw" or "natural" reaction to the pain of the body as reality's barest fact, and thus to open once again the possibility that even pain is, despite the dominating contemporary sense of its deep and unquestionable realness, the product of a set of representational and cultural codes that govern precisely how that realness establishes itself in the real and, thus, the relation between subjective and objective reality.

Doing so allows contemporary readers to recognize these Chinese patients as something other than the abused representamens of Lam Qua's portraits or Parker's case reports. Though of course those portraits and reports constitute the only access anyone today can have to Parker's patients, it nonetheless seems worth trying to acknowledge the patients' status as "makers" of a relation to pain rather than reading them exclusively as the hapless objects of an aesthetic apparatus (portrait painting) or nonfictional genre (the medical case study). I say this not to make some well-meaning claim about restoring the subaltern to speech, but rather to recognize the historical fact that these patients seem to have affected Parker's case studies beyond what he as their controlling subject was capable of perceiving in them.

Parker's patients did not, of course, conceive of themselves as the producers of a style; nor did Parker ever indicate his conscious apprehension of their doing so. Nonetheless, the fact that he so frequently reports on his patients' natural voices suggests that something in their reactions to surgery spoke to him an important cultural difference in the experience of pain, a difference that he found it necessary repeatedly to describe. As far as lived experience is concerned, the visitors at Canton's Ophthalmic Hospital surely felt their pain enough; people came to the hospital because they wanted to be cured, not because they wanted to demonstrate for the famous doctor the legendary stoicism of the Chinese, or to exhibit for academic readers of the coming centuries some new ideology of the anesthetic. In thinking about the patients as generating, however unconsciously, something that Parker (also unconsciously) perceived and described in ways that can in this present be perceived and described as a representational style, I wish

[39] Rebecca Walkowitz, *Cosmopolitan Style: Modernism Beyond the Nation* (New York, 2006), 2. On the philosophical grounds for a far broader analytic sense of style than most literary critics use, see chapter 2 of Nelson Goodman, *Ways of Worldmaking* (Indianapolis, 1978).

simply to suggest that they belong—just as Parker and Lam Qua do—to the general historical tradition that ties sympathy to China in which every subject of this book, from Adam Smith to George Mason to Peter Handke, also takes part.

Some measure of the importance of this representational mode comes if we look at what happens to Parker's surgical reports after the introduction of chemical anesthetics. In the 1848 report on the activities of the Ophthalmic Hospital, Parker notes that he had "through the politeness of D. N. Spooner, Esq., . . . received from Boston the apparatus of C. Jackson, the *author* of this discovery, and a good supply of sulphuric Ether, with a letter from the latter gentleman explaining particularly his mode of procedure."[40] Parker tested the procedure on a farmer (case no. 25,870): "In forty-three seconds, the muscles of his arm suddenly relaxed and he ceased simultaneously to inhale the ether, and in a state of insensibility he was laid back upon the table his head still being elevated. . . . [he] had no recollection of the incisions during the operation." Parker reported several other cases in which anesthesia was used in the fifteenth and sixteenth reports, which cover the years 1848 to 1851, though he seems to have switched from sulphuric ether to chloroform in 1849.[41]

This development produces what social scientists call a "natural experiment," an occasion to test the hypothesis that one of the major features of the case studies (and the Lam Qua paintings) is their representation of the Chinese patients' relation to pain, their representation of a "style" of representation in which the perceptual marks of pain do not translate into the mimetic surfaces—the faces and voices—that conventionally represent pain by moving it from fact to experience. The following are reports from operations in which Parker used chemical anesthesia:

> "After inhaling the vapor three minutes, though able to return an intelligent answer to questions put to him, the tumor was quickly extirpated without sensibility either to the *knife* in making the incisions and dissection, or the *needle* in applying the sutures."

[40] *Minutes of the Annual Meeting of the Medical Missionary Society in China; And Fifteenth Report of its Ophthalmic Hospital at Canton for the years 1848 and 1849* (Canton, 1848), 13. Parker's attribution of the invention of anesthesia to Charles Jackson was, though he may not have known it, a highly controversial statement. By 1849, the U.S. Congress had taken up the question of who invented the procedure (the other major contender was William Morton), though it never resolved the issue. Jackson died in an insane asylum; Morton died a pauper.

[41] *Fifteenth Report*, 13–14.

"the stone was extracted, the patient being under the influence of chloroform. As he revived, he asked when the incision was to be made, and was answered by showing him the calculus."

"During the operation she seemed as if in a quiet sleep, and remained so some minutes after the arteries were tied and the sutures applied, when on being spoken to, she awoke, and the natural expression returning to her countenance, she glanced her eyes downwards, and with a smile remarked, 'I do not see the tumor!' "[42]

The story-form of the last two citations became a staple of the surgical report in the era immediately after the invention of anesthesia: an operation is performed, and the patient awakes to ask when the thing is going to start.[43] It is not surprising that this structure would reappear in the Chinese context. What is remarkable, however, is that these reports so closely resemble the ones Parker made regarding his patients in the years *before* anesthesia's discovery. Consider particularly the case of Leäng Yen, who had her right arm amputated above the elbow: "The patient . . . at the moment of sawing the bone inquired when that part of the process would take place." Here a patient whose arm is being sawed off *without anesthesia* asks the very question that became the classic trope of the anesthesia success story. The narrative structure that functions in the first instance as testimony to the remarkable fortitude of the Chinese becomes in the second proof of the miracle of chloroform.

It would perhaps be too much to suggest on this evidence that one of the effects of anesthesia in Parker's practice was to erase the visible appearance of the representational style Parker's patients so expressed in the years before anesthesia. But it would be less ridiculous to assert that the growing use of anesthetics was in the process in the mid-nineteenth century of removing the subject from the operating table, of turning the surgical procedure from a confrontation between two people into an encounter between a professional and a thing. Once a patient

[42] *Minutes of the Annual Meeting of the Medical Missionary Society in China; And Fourteenth Report of its Ophthalmic Hospital at Canton for the years 1848 and 1849*, 12; *Minutes of the Annual Meeting of the Medical Missionary Society in China; And Fifteenth Report of its Ophthalmic Hospital at Canton for the years 1848 and 1849*, 17; and *Minutes of Two Annual Meetings of the Medical Missionary Society in China; Including the Sixteenth Report of its Ophthalmic Hospital at Canton for the years 1850 and 1851*, 21–22.

[43] See for instance the material in Julie M. Fenster, *Ether Day: The Strange Tale of America's Greatest Medical Discovery and the Haunted Men Who Made It* (New York, 2001).

was anesthetized, his or her personal or cultural relation to surgical pain became irrelevant to the surgeon's experience of the operation—indeed, it became less than irrelevant; it disappeared. The "natural expression" on the countenance of one of Parker's patients following anesthesia exhibits neither her cultural relation to pain nor some chosen representational organization of body and self, tumor and person. It indicates quite simply the effects of anesthesia, which in removing the patient from consciousness also removed the body from a "natural," that is, a living, self (and so Parker at one point refers to a patient "reviving" from anesthetic sleep). It is telling that the reconciliation of the body and the self indicating by the patient's "natural expression" is described by Parker as a "return."

One way to think about the change in Parker's case reports, then, is to consider it an indication of a more general anesthetic shift that defines modern medicine's relation to the surgical patient, who becomes under anesthesia merely a body-thing, a representation with no likeness. Given that the aesthetic, representational dimension of the language and cultural experience of pain depends on the presence of a subject who brings the represented "inside" of felt pain "outside" into the communal world, then, one might say that the pain of surgery under anesthesia, because it is not experienced by a controlling subject, ceases to be representable.

But this does not explain why the language in which Parker described his operations remained unmodified by the enormous representational change that anesthesia made. It is tempting, because of the historical scope of the idea, to claim that the Chinese patients functioned as the proleptic anticipation of life after anesthesia. A reading along these lines would suggest that in the experience of performing surgery on his patients, the cultural differences that separated Parker from the Chinese essentially functioned as a kind of advance warning, the Chinese bodies he dealt with thereby becoming figures of an anesthetized modernity defined by the triumph over pain, or, more dystopically, by the total death of human feeling. I will have more to say about the relation between an anesthetizing modernity and the aesthetics of Chinese suffering in chapter 6. For now, however, I wish to propose that the strange nondifference tying Parker's pre-anesthetic descriptions of Chinese pain to his post-anesthetic ones marks, by way of the negation of difference, the most profoundly "unrealistic" moment of the Parker archive, a moment when the putatively objective, descriptive language of his reports conceals a difference that it nonetheless leaves out in the open. This moment of blindness to the stylistic register in which his patients' relation to pain functions thus doubles, or allegorizes, the very stylistic structure (of description that does not "narrate") that it does not, or cannot, notice.[44]

It is, finally, by suggesting that the relation to pain these patients express in Parker's prose is also as a style, a style that his work obsessively represents but does not recognize, that I can in turn propose that the case studies constitute not simply a set of representations in the mixed genre of medical case report (focused on representations of disease and surgeries) and character study (focused on the patients' "likenesses"), but also an allegory of representationality itself.[45] In this last role, the patients' style—a style whose major aesthetic feature is the non-translation of inside to outside, perception to mimesis, and thus the refusal of Parker's assumptions about the proper representational relationship between

[44]The word "skeuomorph" names an aspect of an object's design that mimics an important feature of one of its cultural predecessors, as for instance when light bulbs shaped like candle flames are used in chandeliers, or when a computer operating system organizes its zeroes and ones into "files" and "folders." Skeuomorphs are, as Nicholas Gessler has suggested, profoundly metaphorical, and the metaphors they encode aim to provide users with information that will help accustom them to a new technology ("Skeuomorphs and Cultural Algorithms," http://www.sscnet.ucla.edu/geog/gessler/cv-pubs/98skeuo.htm [accessed November 25, 2008]). By producing this information on the surface of the new object itself, rather than in, say, a user's manual, skeuomorphs materially indicate a cultural and technological lineage within which a new object can be experienced and understood. If Parker's use of the language of fortitude after 1848 is skeuomorphic, it is so because in retaining the descriptive features of the language he used before anesthesia, it encodes the novel experience of the anesthetized patient within a history of relationships to pain *to which it may in fact not belong.* That is, even though from my perspective the relation between Parker's patients and their pain, considered as a question of representational style, changes radically before and after anesthesia, Parker may have preserved the descriptive language he used in the pre-anesthetic cases because it had established in advance a representational framework within which he could understand what anesthesia did. In this sense, of course, it is actually the case that the Chinese patients functioned for him as the proleptic vision of life after anesthesia. But they did not do so because Parker anticipated in seeing their reactions to pain the development of a world in which chemical anesthesia was widespread, but rather because when it came time to describe that new world and its effects on his operating table, he borrowed a descriptive language with which he was already comfortable to do so. Though Parker never gives any indication of this fact anywhere in the case reports, it may in fact be the case that for him the arrival of anesthesia was intimately connected at some conscious level with a relation to his Chinese patients' relation to pain. The sheer retention of the language of fortitude suggests that this was so. But this does not tell us anything about the representational style that can be discerned in the pre-1848 case studies; it simply tells us that for Parker (and perhaps for the readers of his case studies over the years) the skeuomorphic qualities of the language he retained allowed patient behavior under anesthesia to be understood through an intellectual and linguistic matrix that borrowed from the patient-behavior to which he was already accustomed.

[45]For an essay that connects the development of the genre of medical case study to the development of a more general "humanitarian narrative" driven by its "reliance on detail as the sign of truth," and which includes the modern novel, see Thomas Laqueur, "Bodies, Details, and the Humanitarian Narrative," *The New Cultural History,* ed. Lynn Hunt (Berkeley, 1989), 177.

pain and subjectivity—opens up inside the generic conventions of Parker's case reports the possibility of telling a different *kind* of story about pain than any one that Parker could conceive. A reading of Parker's case studies that finds there the presence of a representational style that seems to present the opening gambit in the now-classic story about Chinese insensitivity to pain can thus, with a small shift in perspective, be seen simultaneously to produce the possibility of an actively generated representational style whose very assumptions about the proper relationship between pain and subjectivity imply a wholesale rejection of an aesthetic model predicated on the opposition between inside and outside, experience and expression. Such a violation of the classic codes of Western aesthetics could perhaps be described as an a-aesthetic, not a refusal but simply an absence of the aesthesis that represents representation as the movement from presence to mimesis.

Through the conjunction of their undermining of a conventional mode of representation, and through their belonging to one, Parker's patients figure the larger historical work of the perception of Chinese pain, and so ravel the themes of the book as a whole. They do so, following this reading, by representing for us the apparent possibility of nonrepresentation, of an "epistemological status of the body," to use Asad's phrase, that does not return us to the kind of representational relation that we (or Parker) expect to see when we think of the relation between pain and language. If one imagines this nonrepresentation, this a- or nonaesthetic, as the "resistance" of the patients themselves, one can slide fairly easily into a conclusion of the type made popular by work done in the wake of theories of postcolonial hybridity, in which any resistance to interpretation (or to representation) is recognized as the deflection of an aggressive imperialist mimesis. Such a reading has the unfortunate effect, however, of minimizing the very resistance it finds, since in making the resistance to representation a subjective gesture, it returns it to the very field of representation it had abandoned, the nonaesthetic now "representing" (in a political as well as a mimetic sense) the subaltern's subject position and his or her agency in relation to it. It seems crucial therefore to resist such a return, allowing the non-style I have identified here to exist without subjective attribution, a gesture that permits it to retain much of its strangeness and indeed to enact at the level of *this* interpretation the very thing that makes this nonstyle so interesting in its own historical context, namely the "refusal" (which is not a refusal, but an absence or a negation, a nothing not opposed to a something) to cross the mimetic line that carries us so comfortably from description to narration, objectivity to subjectivity.

It seems better then to attribute all this work to the archive as such, personifying the collection of documents and not the actual people involved, while remaining aware of the ways in which the archive does and does not resemble a human being. And here one might remark that the most important singular feature of the representational structure the archive shows us lies in the seemingly paradoxical confrontation of the fact of its incessant recording of the nonaesthetic scene (all those paintings and case reports) without ever becoming capable of registering or commenting on the thing that it so obsessively records. As though the fact of nonmimesis were the psychological or historical blind spot of the archive as such, the symptom to which it was doomed to return again and again without ever being able to recognize it. If the archive *were* a person, it might resolve this trauma—a sort of primal scene of its own nonexistence, of the negation of the fact of recording and representation on which it relies—on the psychiatrist's couch, where over the course of a series of expensive conversations it would discover that it had been relentlessly fleeing toward the theoretical site of its own disappearance, a problem it would eventually appear to resolve by having an affair with its analyst.

As for us, it may make more sense to attribute the blind spot to the historical complex that bound Parker to his patients, and both these to Lam Qua, and think of it as a moment in which the encounter with a profound epistemological and mimetic otherness was simultaneously registered and ignored. Both the registration and the ignoring tell us something about what was happening at that instant: the registration of this difference draws our attention to the assumption, present in Parker just as much as in the more recent work of Scarry, that pain is inextricably bound up with a certain kind of representation, particularly representation of a type that links subject to object, culture to ontology, in an unshakeable and necessary dialectic. When that dialectic does not appear, we feel as though were are in the presence of the alien, the inhuman: which may explain why Parker, so devoted to thinking Chinese humanity as equal to his own, could simply not *discuss* at a metadescriptive level the very thing his case studies kept describing. Its capture in the archive, which registers with an indifferent precision the being-there-ness of this troubling difference inside the real, owes something to the indexical logic of the photograph. In detective stories, the inadvertent clue, arrested unconsciously in the background of the image that indexes the real beyond all human intention, tends to resolve with an impeccable neatness the mysteries of plot and action. Less true here. But if the Parker archive does clue us into something, it is the possibility that the kind of sympathetic exchange required by the enormous shift in Western "cognitive style," so caught up in the Chinese case with the history of economic exchange, relied strongly on a relation to *representational* exchange focused on the objective appearance and subjective narration of pain. As the book progresses, and especially beginning in chapter 5, I will cleave more closely to the trail indicated by this clue, drawing out through discussions of representation and mimesis this interesting third dimension of the history of modern sympathy, a dimension which I will ultimately argue indicates the limits of our contemporary thinking about pain and representation, and shows how fully our understanding of pain's ontological dialectic belongs—even when it seems to exceed it—to the discourse of sympathy and China from which it has emerged here.

4. The Calculi of Suffering

It is difficult to pinpoint the moment at which a cultural stereotype acquires enough mass to snowball down the historical hill under its own power, generating through its tumbling the amount of anecdotal "evidence" needed to qualify it as a scientific fact. If one could locate such a moment in the history of Chinese insensitivity to pain—particularly in the language of Chinese insensitivity to personal pain, rather than the stereotype of indifference to others—it would lie somewhere just beyond Parker's records of his time in China, which would relate to it as weather to an avalanche, indirectly. Both Heinrich and Gilman have made compelling claims about the effects Parker's case studies and the Lam Qua paintings must have had on the audiences that saw them, about the ways in which they reproduced the general language of primitivity and barbarism that governed imperialist racism. But their analyses cannot extend to Parker himself; though he paid for the paintings and wrote the case studies, it remains utterly unclear what he himself thought he was doing thereby, or whether he believed any conclusions about China should be drawn from his life's work. Parker's continuous writing about his own activities never moves from description to narration, one might say, never makes a connection between what he did and what it meant, either to him or to some larger history, just as, barring a few moments of religious crisis during his years of theological study at Yale, he almost never discussed his own interior life.[46]

[46]As Gulick, his biographer, puts it, "No great subtlety is evident in Parker's self-analysis, but we do find abundant commitment and dynamism" (12). Even Parker's letters to his family from Canton bury their emotional content under the strictures of reportorial neutrality; a letter dated April 2, 1867,

This failure to plumb his own motivations or to discuss the meaning and value of his Chinese experience produces in the entire Parker archive a strange blankness on the subject of his person. That blankness contrasts sharply with the profoundly readable surfaces of the paintings or the case reports, or even the abject weirdness of the archive's strangest objects, a few boxes of urinary calculi—kidney stones—which in all cases signify loquaciously, encoding and figuring the historical conditions from which they emerged and the people whose bodies they metonymize, synecdochize, and otherwise represent. It is precisely this contrast that makes the archive so compelling, since the archival materials' complex jabber seems to be the exact thing that Parker himself—though he registered it, wrote it down, paid for it to be painted, or collected it in boxes—never really responded to.

In this subjectively neutral relation to the objects and writings he collected, the Parker archive also develops what one might call a style, in the sense of a recognizable stance or attitude, that does not differ much from the one Parker's patients produced in their representations of pain. Just as "it hurts, doctor" registered the physical presence of pain at the level of content without translating that same presence into the voice's tonal form, Parker's archival collection registers his life's experiential content—operations performed, patients seen, stones removed—without ever giving that content anything but its most "natural," that is, its blankest and most "objective" form and expression. From this perspective, the archive itself, considered as Parker's life's work, restages the relationship to pain that seemed to fascinate him in the case studies, so that the material he collected testifies as much as anything could to the nineteenth century's "obsession with pain" without ever bringing the material or perceptual evidence of that obsession over into the subjective or historical foreground, or suggesting, except implicitly, that it was worth collecting at all.[47]

What the archive does explicitly say, however, it says by virtue of its presence at Yale, where the sheer material accumulation of words and objects it contains testifies as much as any porcelain cup or lacquered fan to its imbrication in a process of international exchange. That exchange participated only obliquely in the major forms of international trade that dominated the American encounter

---

for instance, opens with a full page explaining how many letters Parker has written to his family without receiving a reply, followed by this sentence: "I do not complain very much, but mention the facts."

[47] James Turner, *Reckoning with the Beast: Animals, Pain, and Humanity in the Victorian Mind* (Baltimore, 1980), 80.

with China in this era, its marginality measured by the fact that though Lam Qua's portraits of Canton elites hang in several East Coast museums, his paintings of Parker's patients are almost all owned by university libraries. But the collection's status as an object of cross-cultural exchange should not for all that be ignored. It was, after all, in the narrative codification of a hypothetical financial transaction between a penniless European and a nameless Chinese mandarin that the entire cognitive structure undergirding Parker's Medical Missionary Society was most economically disseminated and thought. The Parker archive does not, to be sure, contain any sort of Chinese fortune, but the information and the representations Parker collected are in fact the material return for Parker's saving the lives of any number of Chinese patients (some of them actual mandarins)—as he, Colledge and Bridgman had predicted when they declared that the case books he kept would "in time be curious and instructive documents, and such as will enable to glance at the penetralia of domestic and social life in China."

In this context, perhaps the archive's most representative objects are the forty kidney stones collected in yellowing plastic boxes and stored, like the Lam Qua paintings, in the library's basement. These dumb accretions of calcium, magnesium, and phosphate, at least one of which Parker cut from a corpse, are the material testaments to the economy of Chinese death and Western fortune that constituted the philosophical and practical ground of Parker's twenty years in Canton.[48] Like paintings or the case studies, these quite literal "penetralia" of Chinese life bind objective pain—the largest of the stones measures seven inches around—to a total negation of subjectivity, since in the case of the stones the possibility of subjective narration has been completely evacuated from the material surface of the object, whose "naturalness" indicates profound bodily suffering but does not express it. Though these calculi do not in any way document the military violence of the wars that made possible Parker's continued

[48]In the Sixteenth Report of the MMS, Parker writes of a patient who died of complications produced by his stone that "with some difficulty the consent of his relatives was obtained to extract the stone, which, considering the prejudice of the Chinese against anything like an autopsy, may be regarded as a triumph" (11). Parker tells another story in which his request to pay a family to acquire the corpse of a former patient for dissection is refused (see Heinrich, 265–66); Leäng Yen at one point demands that Parker pay her for the right to operate, which Parker does not do (see Rachman, 150). The paintings were the result of a similar negotiation: Parker's memory of Lam Qua's claim "that as there is no charge for 'cutting' [surgery], he can make none for painting," also figures objects whose most profound mode of visibility has to do with their representational work as the subjects of barter and the bearers of economic value. As Rachman notes, the claim must be read in the context of Parker's having noted in 1851 that he had paid Lam Qua twenty-five dollars for "paintings of tumors" (143). The "no charge" line appears on the first page of Josyph, and on Rachman 142.

work at the Ophthalmic Hospital, their mere presence at Yale collocates the history of the best aspects of West's humanitarian narrative with the economically motivated violence that made that narrative's expansion possible; they would not be in a box at the library, after all, had the Opium Wars not kept Chinese territory "open" to Western missionaries; and yet they would surely have killed at least some of their sufferers, had that opening not taken place.

By the end of the nineteenth century, the calculus that balanced Chinese lives against Western money would be taken up in a far more literal and cruder form, as American politicians and labor organizers, borrowing from the general language of Chinese indifference to pain that Parker's archive at its dumbest level represents, used that indifference to justify physical and legal violence against immigrant workers in California. To see that violence as another iteration of the equation between Western financial success and the death of someone Chinese is to recognize the hypothetical murder of the Chinese mandarin and even Parker's box of urinary calculi as the outmoded effects of a less competitive age. How such an iterability might be calculated, and the story of the representational and cultural work that produced it, is the subject of the next chapter.

4 Chinese Bodies, Chinese Futures

The "Coolie" in Late Nineteenth-Century America

A map of the world that does not include Utopia is not worth even glancing at, for it leaves out the one country at which Humanity is always landing. And when Humanity lands there, it looks out, and, seeing a better country, sets sail.

—Oscar Wilde, *Plays, Prose: Writings and Poems*

1. The Chinese Invasion

We ended chapter 3 with a vision of a box of kidney stones, whose mute witness to the transpacific exchange that makes possible their appearance on the cover of this book I took as an allegory for the silence of the archives to which they belong. The representational play in those stones—like the representational play in the Lam Qua paintings, which allowed for the remarkable story of their "rediscovery" by Peter Parker at Guy's Hospital in London—belongs at least partly to the distance that separates their current state from their origins. Whatever disgust or sympathy they generate decays, like the half-life of some strange animal isotope, with the passage of time and space, so that they can come safely and harmlessly to rest in a library basement.

Though they did not know it, the migration of those stones from Canton to Yale University in mid-century was the material precursor to the far more complex movement of living beings out of China in the second half of the nineteenth century. Most of these migrants and sojourners ended up in the New World, working in plantations in Hawai'i or Cuba, in the guano mines of Peru, or in the mines and on the railroads of the American West, and serving as the fantasized replacements for the forms of labor lost in Europe's, and eventually the United States', turn away from legalized slavery.

By the middle of the nineteenth century, the connection between California, Asia, and a particular form of human labor began to emerge as a commonplace of American political and cultural life. As Moon-Ho Jung has remarked, 1848 is the year in which the word "cooly," used since the sixteenth century to refer to Indian and Chinese laborers, moved "from the appendix to the main body of Noah Webster's American dictionary," this at the very moment at which "coolies," owing partly to the rise of abolitionism, were becoming "indentured laborers in high demand across the world, particularly in the tropical colonies of the Caribbean."[1] When Daniel Webster claimed, in remarks regarding whether California should join the union as a slave or a free state that immediately preceded the Compromise of 1850, that slavery was impossible in the American West because "California and New Mexico are Asiatic, in their formation and scenery," the connection he asserted between Asiatic geography and the future of American labor emblematized far better than he could have known at the time the dilemmas that would make the coolie such a controversial figure only twenty years later.[2]

The national discussion regarding Chinese labor went through a number of stages over the latter half of the nineteenth century. Before the Civil War, pro- and anti-slavery writers alike condemned the coolie trade, arguing either that it

[1] Moon-Ho Jung, "Outlawing 'Coolies': Race, Nation, and Empire in the Age of Emancipation," *American Quarterly* 57, no. 3 (2005), 679. See also Jung, *Coolies and Cane: Race, Labor, and Sugar in the Age of Emancipation* (Baltimore, 2006).

[2] Daniel Webster, "The Constitution and the Union" (otherwise known as the Seventh of March Oration) *Congressional Globe*, 31st Cong., 1st sess., Appendix, 280–81. Webster's speech laid much of the ideological groundwork for the Compromise of 1850, which allowed California to enter the Union as a free state, divided the New Mexico territory from Texas, and substantially strengthened laws governing the capture and return of fugitive slaves. But Webster was by no means the first American to bring the American landscape, Asia, and the natural forms of labor together in a geographic imaginary. Haun Saussy, in "The First Chinese Americans (?)," cites a pamphlet encouraging the settlement of Carolina written by Jean-Pierre Purry in 1733, which claims that "the great article whereby one is sure of prospering and making a fortune [in Purrysburg], without much work or expenditure, is the planting of a sufficient quantity of white mulberry trees to raise SILKWORMS: for there is perhaps no country in the world where these trees grow so well, or where the silk is as beautiful, as in Carolina" (*Ex/Change* 14 [October 2005]. Also available online at http://www.cityu.edu.hk/ccs/Newsletter/newsletter14/Contribution2.htm).

resembled in all its particulars the African slave trade (it included an equally harrowing middle passage[3]), or in some cases that it was substantially worse, and thus it demonstrated the benevolence of the American slave system.[4] In 1852, Chinese laborers embarked for San Francisco aboard the American sailing ship the *Robert Browne* mutinied against their American officers and crew, causing an international diplomatic scandal (mediated in Canton by the U.S. *chargé d'affaires* there, none other than Peter Parker) and drawing attention to the violence and exploitation surrounding the trade in Chinese workers.[5] When in February 1862, in the middle of the Civil War, Abraham Lincoln signed "An Act to Prohibit the 'Coolie Trade' by American Citizens in American Vessels," his fortification of the ideological bona fides of the Northern position on the trade in human beings also confirmed a national consensus on coolie labor.

That consensus did not last long. Despite widespread portrayals of Chinese people as animals, pagans, insects, and savages (about which more later) the prospect of cheap labor was compelling enough to cause the formation of the

[3]Coolie" vessels were known as "floating hells"; Robert Schwendinger gives mortality rates of around 30 percent for two voyages from China to Peru in the early 1850s and cites an estimate that only a third of Chinese laborers who made it to Peru lived to complete their five-year term of service (*Ocean of Bitter Dreams: Maritime Relations Between China and the United States, 1850–1915* [Tucson, 1988] 23, 27.). His third and fourth chapters deal extensively with American involvement in the trade in Chinese workers in the pre–Civil War period.

[4]"No inferior race of men can exist in these United States without becoming subordinate to the will of the Anglo-Americans," wrote antislavery activist Hinton Helper in 1855, while worrying that "the copper of the Pacific [would become] as great a subject of discord and dissension as the ebony of the Atlantic" (cited in Alexander Saxton, *The Indispensable Enemy: Labor and the Anti-Chinese Movement in California* [Berkeley, 1995], 19.). And J. D. B. De Bow used the iniquities and violence perpetrated on Chinese workers to cast a softer light on the American alternative. De Bow, writes Moon-Ho Jung, considered the new human trade in the Caribbean to demonstrate "the moral superiority of the U.S. South and the dire consequences of interfering in the racial order. The 'human conduct' of American slaveholders, he argued, 'preserved' human life and the four million American slaves deserved to be spared 'the risk of being exposed to evils' characteristic of other plantations societies" (692).

[5]When the ship and its Chinese workers were recovered (some workers were killed in the mutiny, some committed suicide, and others escaped), they were returned to Canton, and Parker arranged for a court of inquiry to consider the case. Though Parker's inquiry resulted in seventeen prisoners being sent to Chinese authorities for trial, the Chinese commissioners found all seventeen not guilty and released them. Diplomatic missives ensued, with no change to the final situation, and an angry Parker finally wrote to the commissioners to say that in the future "the United States will execute their own laws in cases of piracy occurring on the high seas," warning that if the United States succeeded in capturing any of the former passengers on the *Robert Browne*, they would be "tried and punished by the United States as an example for the future" (Schwendinger, 44). By the late 1850s, however, Parker had become a major advocate for the abolition of the trade in Chinese workers; see Schwendinger, 56–57.

American Emigrant Company in Hartford, Connecticut, in 1863 in order to acquire Chinese "miners, mechanics (including workers in iron and steel of every class), weavers, and agricultural, rail-road and other laborers... in any numbers, and at a reasonable cost."[6] Six years later, Cornelius Koopmanschap's offer, made to several hundred delegates at the nation's first convention on Chinese labor, "to import thousands of laborers from China for one hundred dollars a head," Andrew Gyory writes, "triggered a chain reaction of interest in importing Chinese workers" including orders for workers from railroad owners in Tennessee and manufacturers from Ohio and Missouri.[7]

For our purposes here the particularity of various American positions on indentured labor from Asia matter less than the series of connections such positions generated and reproduced. The alleged *character* of Asian labor—or rather, the characterization of a certain form of labor as Asian—sustained the prosecution of Chinese immigrants throughout the late nineteenth century, and, as Jung notes, "rationalized U.S. expansion abroad, from China and Cuba in the 1850s to the Philippines in the 1890s."[8] In so doing, the association between China, labor, and the western United States established a historical legacy for thinking about the Asiatic racial character that has persisted through the twentieth century and into our own.

I wish therefore to concentrate on the ways that the linked set of associations—California, Asia or the Asiatic character, and labor—consistently produced a discourse about the physical body of the Chinese worker and its relation to physical suffering. This discourse borrowed from "expert" testimony about China produced by American and British missionaries and was sustained in the related fields of history and economics by theories of "Oriental despotism" and the "Asiatic mode of production," which following their initial articulations on the continent began to appear in American newspapers in this period.[9] The major field of its expression was the battle against Chinese immigration during the latter half of the nineteenth century. This battle's most explicit framework—the threat of "degraded" labor—was consistently synecdochized in the body of a faceless

[6] Cited in Andrew Gyory, *Closing the Gate: Race, Politics, and the Chinese Exclusion Act* (Chapel Hill, N.C., 1998), 19.

[7] Gyory, 31, 33–34.

[8] Jung, "Outlawing 'Coolies,'" 698.

[9] Karl Marx, for instance, published a series of articles on the Asiatic Mode of Production in the *New York Daily Tribune* in 1853, as Perry Anderson notes in his survey of the history of the idea (*Lineages of the Absolutist State* [London, 1974], 475.).

Chinese worker whose physical body, understood as an outgrowth of his racial and cultural heritage, became the implacable source of the threat he posed to the American worker (and indeed, to the United States in general). Figured as enduring, impervious to physical pain, and mechanical or slavish in its relation to freedom, pleasure, and a volitional relation to history, this body spoke to Americans—or rather, was spoken, ventriloquistically, *by* them—most insistently of the possibility of a future that promised to rewrite the relationship between suffering and human being.

2. The Machine Body

A 1902 American Federation of Labor (AFL) pamphlet designed to encourage the permanent extension of the Chinese Exclusion Act—whose passage in 1882 had radically restricted immigration from China, and inaugurated an era of race-based immigration policy that persisted in law until the mid-1960s—opens with a review of the Chinese worker's place in California history. Acknowledging the presence of Chinese laborers in the state when it was "more or less a great mining camp" and they caused "no alarm or discomfort" to white America, the pamphlet nonetheless argues that "pro-Chinese sentimentalists" who suggest that "without Chinese labor the Pacific States would not have advanced as rapidly as they have done" need to rethink that claim in light of a reply by a "well-known California physician": "advancement with an incubus like the Chinese is like the growth of a child with a malignant tumor upon his back. At the time of manhood death comes of the malignity."[10] The comparison of the Chinese to an incubus captures the combination of sexuality without reproduction and effort without progress that the Asiatic stereotype represented in 1902. That the Chinese were parasites on the social body of the nation, stunting its natural growth, stripping it of nutrients, and providing no benefits in return, was the subject of countless complaints. Twenty years earlier, James Whitney had written that presence of Chinese workers shut California off "from the legitimate elements of growth which would have made her, in all the essentials of material and moral prosperity, tenfold stronger than she is to-day. Chinese labor has operated not only to prevent, but to destroy, the normal development of the State, and to thrown [sic] upon the people

[10]Samuel Gompers, *Some Reasons for Chinese Exclusion. Meat Versus Rice: American Manhood Against Asiatic Coolieism. Which Shall Survive?* (Washington, D.C., 1902), 5. Further references are cited in this text as AFL.

unwonted burdens."[11] The AFL's nameless physician drew on this same the framework of growth, parasitism, and development to declare the Chinese a cancer.

The AFL pamphlet concatenates almost perfectly a longer history of representations in which major shifts in the industrial landscape and class relations were displaced, metonymically, onto Chinese immigration in general, which in turn was represented by a series of anonymous Chinese bodies portrayed as ideally suited to new, slavish forms of labor. This was partly an effect of the different kinds of work done by white and Chinese workers, as the latter were excluded from skilled labor by organizations of craftsmen attempting to protect their economic status.[12] But the effect of that difference was to tie Chinese workers ever closer to the idea of a proletarianized future, so that larger, ungraspable processes of capitalist development were given a coherent and easily understood form in the synecdoche of "the Chinese coolie," a figure which in turn became a metaphor for all Chinese people and indeed for Asian history in general.[13] Like an incubus or, indeed, a tumor, the "coolie" was understood as a life-form whose parasitical existence depended on the gradual hollowing out of the host that sustained it.[14] The problem was not that the Chinese did not "generate," but rather that their labor produced a growth inimical to the health of the country as a whole, largely because it rerouted the flow of capital around the European worker.

By working for cheaper than the white man would (or could—as we shall see), the "coolie" also came to signify the "increasing transnationalization of labor markets," Colleen Lye writes, representing both the "biological impossibility" and the "numerical abstraction" that was at the heart of industrial labor: the Chinese

[11] James Whitney, *The Chinese and the Chinese Question* (New York, 1888), 116.

[12] White workers who competed directly with the Chinese, Alexander Saxton writes, "were for the most part those who were no longer capable (if they ever had been) of bidding for jobs against skilled white tradesmen" (264).

[13] On this topic, see Robert G. Lee, *Orientals: Asian Americans in Popular Culture* (Philadelphia, 1999).

[14] Parker, cutting into his Chinese patients' bodies, had marveled at the complexity and size of the vascular systems their tumors built to sustain themselves. Though the AFL's desire to excise the Chinese tumor on California's body resembles in many ways the more literal project taken up by Parker's hospital work, the difference in the nationalities of the afflicted suggest that the force of the tumors in Parker's paintings did indeed bleed over into the idea of China they portrayed. As though the mere fact of *having* enormous tumors were enough to suggest, also, that China or the Chinese were *like* them—a metonymic effect Larissa Heinrich and Sander Gilman both ascribe to the Lam Qua portraits.

"coolie" was a person, but also a machine.[15] It was this latter quality that allowed the "coolie" to metaphorize both the *process* of industrial production and its *product,* as though the numberless faceless and identical Chinese workers had simply been stamped out on a production line like so many millions of pins.

If the coolie's body seemed naturally suited to the rigors of industrialization, then, it was because it was itself the imaginary product of an industrial process, and because it was a product produced—or so it seemed—to work in the kind of factory that produced it. It would be hard to underestimate the obsessive insistence with which this fact was apprehended and narrated as a *biological* feature of the Chinese worker, most neatly summarized as an ability to endure low levels of constant pain. The coolie's "endurance" was endlessly repeated, explained, and raged against in the nineteenth century literature, where it was consistently understood as the racial substructure that enabled the Chinese worker to accept wages far lower than his Irish or German counterparts. "You cannot work a man who must have beef and bread, and would prefer beef, alongside of a man who can live on rice," James G. Blaine told the U.S. Senate in 1879. "In all such conflicts, and in all such struggles, the result is not to bring up the man who lives on rice to the beef-and-bread standard, but it is to bring down the beef-and-bread man to the rice standard." Cited on the last page of the same AFL pamphlet that began by comparing the Chinese to a tumor, this sentence generated the document's nutritionally focused title, "*Some Reasons for Chinese Exclusion. Meat versus Rice: American Manhood against Asiatic Coolieism. Which Shall Survive?,*" even as it gave Feuerbach's gastronomic thesis, "*Der Mensch ist, was er ißt*" ("Man is what he eats"), first published in 1850, an unexpectedly racial form.[16]

More broadly, the coolie's ability to endure small levels of pain or consume only the meagerest food and lodging represented an almost inhuman adaptation to contemporary forms of modern work. "As concerns ability for labor," wrote James Whitney, "they are generally considered as possessed of a great endurance rather than of great bodily strength. It was calculated that, of those employed in

[15]Colleen Lye, *America's Asia: Racial Form and American Literature, 1893–1945* (Princeton, N.J., 2005), 57.

[16]The phrase appeared in a review of the chemist Jakob Moleschott's *Lehre der Nahrungsmittel.* A portion of Feuerbach's review that suggests that the differentiation between meat and rice, manhood and slavery was already a part of mid-century thinking about nutrition: "A man who enjoys only a vegetable diet is a vegetating being, is incapable of action" (cited in Melvin Cherno, "Feuerbach's 'Man Is What He Eats': A Rectification," *Journal of the History of Ideas* 24, no. 3 [1963], 401.). The Chinese preference for rice appears, in this context, easily assimilable to a sense of the Chinese as frozen in history, or as willing slaves, in contrast to revolutionary, self-defending, progressive Europeans.

the construction of the Pacific Railway, it required five Chinese laborers to do the work of four of those of our own country."[17] Likewise Henry George, in the *New York Tribune* in 1869: "They take less earth at a spadeful than an Irishman. But in a day's work take up more spadefuls."[18] It is George's second sentence that reveals the threat endurance posed to European labor. In a new economy defined by mass production, individual strength was giving way to the ability to suffer light burdens repetitively. "It should be kept in mind that . . . the value of physical strength, pure and simple, has been diminishing for more than two hundred years," Whitney wrote. "What gunpowder and arms of precision have done to degrade the value of physical prowess in war, improvements in implements and machinery have done to debase the value of physical strength in the arts and industries, and the Chinaman is equal to all the demands, whether of peace or war, of civilized or barbaric existence" (64).[19] Hence the image on the frontispiece of the AFL's pamphlet in 1902, "The American Gulliver and the Chinese Lilliputians" (figure 4.1 below), which shows a white laborer pinned to the ground by banners reading "cheap labor," "heathen competition," and "starvation wages" as an endless stream of tiny Chinese workers flows toward and over him. The threatened triumph of the coolie promised a victory of quantity over quality, of consistent small efforts over heroic large ones, of the faceless horde over the individual, and of mass production over unalienated, organic labor. This is why the Chinese are so often compared to insects, and why "the white laborer who would compete with them . . . must, like them, abdicate his individuality."[20]

[17] Whitney, *The Chinese Question*, 64.

[18] Cited in H. J. West, *The Chinese Invasion; Revealing the Habits, Manners, and Customs of the Chinese, Political, Social and Religious, on the Pacific Coast, Coming in contact with the free and enlightened citizens of America . . . containing careful selections from The San Francisco Press* (San Francisco, 1873), 28.

[19] As for Henry George, he continued: "The tendency of modern production is to a greater and greater subdivision of labor—to confine the operative to one part of the process, and to require of him close attention and manual dexterity, rather than knowledge, judgment, and skill. It is in this qualities that the Chinese excel" (West, 28).

[20] AFL, 19. On insects: "Silent and persistent as the white ants that destroy the strongest timbers while the householder sleeps, they go further and further" (Whitney, *Chinese Question*, 137); Rudyard Kipling, cited in the AFL pamphlet: "There are three races who can work, but there is only one that can swarm" (10). The AFL pamphlet also refers to a "hive of 450,000,000 Chinese," and Arthur Smith in his notorious *Chinese Characteristics* discusses "the enormous aggregation of the population in huge hives" (17) (Arthur Smith, *Chinese Characteristics* [Norwalk, Conn., 2003], 187 [further references are cited in this text as *CC*]). The Rev. E. Trumbull Lee was one of many to refer to the Chinese as "locusts"; see Rev. E. Trumbull Lee, "Anti-Chinese: Coolie Question Discussed by a Portland Pastor,"

Fig 4.1 "The American Gulliver and the Chinese Lilliputians." Frontispiece of *Some Reasons for Chinese Exclusion. Meat Versus Rice: American Manhood Against Asiatic Coolieism. Which Shall Survive?* (1901). Courtesy of The Huntington Library.

At home, the Chinese also undermined the American future by refusing to consume like Americans. More than simply an ability to live in conditions impossible for white workers, Chinese nonconsumption was conceived as an active refusal to return wages to the American economy that made them possible. The AFL report again: "The home market should grow with the population. But the Chinese, living on the most meager food, having no families to support, inured to deprivation, and hoarding their wages for use in their native land, whither they invariably return, cannot in any sense be regarded as consumers. Their earnings do not circulate [another vascular metaphor], nor are they reinvested—contrary to those economic laws which make the for the prosperity of nations."[21] The Chinese simply "do not, will not, and cannot take up the burdens of American citizenship" (AFL, 35).

originally in Portland Daily News, February 13, 1886; also available online at http://www.ohs.org/education/focus_on_oregon_history/APH-Document-Lee-Article-1886.cfm.

[21] This case was made with special force in the AFL pamphlet because its anti-Chinese position competed with the pro-Chinese, pro-business arguments that saw the generous treatment of Chinese immigrants as a way of helping U.S. companies gain traction in overseas Chinese markets. John Eperjesi has shown how the American Asiatic Association, founded in 1898, used its journal to spread the idea that

The movement between "will not" and "cannot" in that last sentence indicates the degree to which the alleged behavior of Chinese immigrants, which tended to begin from voluntarist arguments, tended to end with biological ones. An "absence of nerves," remarkable "staying qualities," and a "capacity to wait without complaint and to bear with calm endurance," were all features of Chinese people in general described by the American missionary Arthur Smith in his 1894 *Chinese Characteristics*, the most widely read American work on China in the late nineteenth and early twentieth centuries.[22] "If he is a handicraftsman he will stand in one place from dewy morn till dusky eve," Smith wrote, "and do it every day without any variation in the monotony, and apparently with no special consciousness that there is any monotony to be varied" (*CC*, 92). The phrase "no special consciousness" brings together, in a manner typical of the new sociological thinking of this period, the voluntarist and biological aspects of social life. Rather than suggest that the Chinese worker feels monotony like the American, but simply deals with it better, Smith imagines that the Chinese worker does not experience monotony or repetition in the first place. Framed as a lack of consciousness of what to Smith must have seemed a well-nigh objective state of affairs, the Chinese difference—if difference, of course, there was—came to rest on a theory of culture that imagined the body as the natural outgrowth of a set of circumstances that shaped the parameters of will, of suffering, and even of sensory awareness.

That such a difference expressed itself in the apparently objective idiom of the human body reminds us that the body is always also a phenomenological lens. The scale of our experience is objectively and subjectively anthropomorphic,

---

"the future of this Republic is bound up with its prestige on the Pacific Ocean" and dreamed of the economic plenitude that would follow the sale of widgets to millions of widgetless Chinese. Eperjesi ultimately sees in the association's work an attempt to "stabilize a terrain of [economic] crisis by giving capital a clear vision of the future. The idea that the China market provided the solution to crisis," he writes, "was nowhere given in advance by the needs of capital" ("The American Asiatic Association and the Imperialist Imaginary of the American Pacific," *boundary 2* 28:1 [2001], 218.). See also Eperjesi, *The Imperialist Imaginary: Visions of Asia and the Pacific in American Culture* (Lebanon, N.H., 2004). For a discussion of the ways in which this racialized take on labor circulated in relation to the development of models of the ideal consumer in early twentieth-century United States culture, see chapter three of Grace Kyungwon Hong, *The Ruptures of American Capital: Women of Color Feminism and the Culture of Immigrant Labor* (Minneapolis, 2006).

[22] Lydia Liu writes in her introduction to Smith that his book was only replaced as an authority on China by Pearl S. Buck's *The Good Earth* (1931), and cites a 1925 survey that ranks *Chinese Characteristics* first on a list of the most important Western works on China. Among its many translations were several in Chinese and Japanese, which Liu discusses at length in *Translingual Practice: Literature, National Culture, and Translated Modernity—China, 1900–1937* (Stanford, 1995).

objectively in the sense that we cannot grasp or make meaning otherwise than through bodies, and subjectively because in each case the body through which meanings are grasped or made is so particular: we all speak from *a* body (one of many), but also from the specific physical being of *our* body (unlike, we feel, anyone else's). What Smith's racism required, and what indeed was being recognized in the new sociology and anthropology of the turn of the century, was a theory in which the phenomenological apparatus of any given body, far from being either universal (the same for everyone) or individual (and totally relative), was the dictate of a cultural or racial system that preceded it.[23] Such an ontology of the body would suggest, as did Smith, that the realities of everyday experience were in fact secondary to some other (racial, cultural) feature of existence through which undifferentiated human bodies came to be Chinese, Irish, German, Italian, or African, and, with only a few exceptions, stayed that way for life.

For Smith (as for the AFL pamphlet), then, the body was the field upon which cultural difference exercised its power, the raw material whose form expressed most nakedly the racial logic or cultural identity that determined its relation to pain, monotony, labor, nutrition, consumption, pleasure, and morality. If, as Smith argued, "we must take account of the fact that in China breathing seems to be optional," it was not only because doing so allowed us to determine our proper relation to the Chinese, but because the Chinese person's optional breathing was also the expression of the nature of the Chinese body, which in turn told us something about the nature of the Chinese race and Chinese culture (94). Once established, of course, the indisputable fact of this Chinese nature sustained an endless series of conclusions that reinforced the stereotype, which is why the claims about Chinese bodies appear so repetitively throughout anti-Chinese discourse (without for all that becoming too "monotonous"). The AFL pamphlet, for instance, includes a statistical table demonstrating the Chinese disregard of San Francisco's "Cubic Air Ordinance." Enter a Chinatown dwelling, the accompanying text suggests, and you will find persons who had they not been disturbed "would have slept in the dense and poisonous atmosphere until morning, proof against the baneful effects of the carbonic-acid gas generated by human defiance of chemical laws and proof against all the zymotic poisons that would be fatal to a people of any other race in an hour of such surroundings" (AFL, 22).[24] Framed by the logic of his impossibility, the Chinese worker's failure to consume reveals itself

[23] On the relation between the postwar sociology of the Chicago School and Asian America, see Henry Yu, *Thinking Orientals: Migration, Contact, and Exoticism in Modern America* (New York, 2002).

[24] The pamphlet is citing the "Report of the Special Committee of the Board of Supervisors of the City and County of San Francisco, appointed to investigate and report upon Chinatown, July 1885."

not as an act of unpleasant privation undertaken by someone too poor to rent a bigger place or buy beef stew, but as the natural outgrowth of the biological cage that hosts him. The Chinese subject could no more awaken to his own privation or boredom than an animal could to human language.[25]

In framing Chinese exclusion as a choice between "American manhood" and "Asiatic coolieism," the AFL pamphlet voiced a common concern among anti-Chinese activists: that the gradual replacement of workers of European descent by Chinese ones would result in the "Chinafication" of American life. The final fear was that we (Americans) would all become coolies. Though writer after writer was willing to insist that at the individual level such a transformation was improbable—that, as Blaine suggested, you simply *can't* feed a man on rice if he needs beef—the battle against Chinese exclusion was nonetheless understood as a more general battle against modernization itself, and indeed against the new forms of human consciousness demanded by the age. Hence Smith: "To the Anglo-Saxon race, at least, it seems a matter of course that those who live in an age of steam and of electricity must necessarily be in a different condition, as to their nerves, from those who lived in the old slow days of sailing-packets and of mail-coaches. Ours is an age of extreme activity. It is an age of rush . . . The effect of overworking our nerves shows itself not mainly in such affectations as 'fiddler's cramp,' 'telegrapher's cramp,' 'writer's cramp,' and the like, but in a general tension" (*CC*, 90–91). Though Smith wants to dissociate the "general tension" of a nervous modernity from the job-specific illnesses he refers to, it is nonetheless telling that each of these "cramps" is a repetitive stress injury caused by the replication of small, individually insignificant gestures, as though the general tension of the times were the result not of any single,

[25] Reading Smith from the perspective of Martin Heidegger's meditation on boredom reveals the importance of the Chinese ability to endure monotony. For Heidegger, "Dasein is simply an animal that has learned to become bored; it has awakened *from* its own captivation [by the world] *to* its own captivation. This awakening of the living being to its own being-captivated, this anxious and resolute opening to the not-open, is the human" (cited in Giogio Agamben, *The Open: Man and Animal,* trans. Kevin Attell [Stanford, 2004], 70.). Being human is to have the capacity to be bored; hence the Chinese acceptance of the monotonous puts them on the other side of the dividing line, with the animals. It is for these reasons that anti-Chinese activists often insisted—echoing the hopes of the manufacturers entranced by Koopmanschap's proposals to import Chinese workers—that the Chinese could not be trusted to unionize, that they lacked the fellow-feeling and political will necessary to strike. Such claims were nonsense, as Chinese workers struck on a number of occasions, both on their own and as part of "mainstream" strikes. See Gyory for a description of the cigar makers' strike of 1877; he cites the *Labor Standard* which remarks that "in joining the strike, the Chinese 'showed themselves capable of *real* civilization" (98). The notion that Asian workers, because of Confucianism, are generally more pliable than European ones persists to this day; see Manuel Castells, *The Rise of the Network Society,* 2nd ed. (Oxford, 2000), 193.

significant event or crisis but of the daily, unceasing, worrisome, and morbid reiterations of the new modern life—itself simply an allegory of work on the industrial production line. Only a page later, Smith marvels at the Chinese worker's ability to "write all day like an automaton" (*CC*, 92).

So it was that the Chinese body could figure the West's potentially "Chinese" future, as though somewhere in the particular embodied qualities of the Chinese—which included, as Yellow Perilist discourse made clear throughout the period, the fact of their sheer number—lay the obscured and secret fulcrum of the future to come. Angle the lever one way, and you got the return to mass slavery and oligarchic despotism presaged by Chinese labor in the United States. Push the burden from the other side, as optimists and missionaries dreamed, and it was the Chinese who would be transformed, ushering in an age of universal Christian sympathy.

This latter, much-desired shift would not come easily, Smith thought. The "character and conscience" that had taken the West a thousand years to develop could not just "be suddenly taken up by the Chinese for their own, and set in operation, like a Krupp gun from Essen, mounted and ready to be discharged" (*CC*, 329). This separation of character (painstakingly built up) and the mass-produced good (the *prêt-à-tirer)* reinforced the very division that separated his individualized Westerners from his undifferentiated Chinese, labor defined by individuated strength and willpower from its slavish, mechanical, imitative Oriental counterpart. The terms of Smith's withholding indicate how dearly the West aimed to sell the final proof of civilization abroad.

Though the comparison between culture and the Krupp gun distinguishes the former's artisanal mode from the latter's mass production, the fact that the latter is also a weapon recalls Whitney's anxieties about what "gunpowder and arms of precision have done to degrade the value of physical prowess in war," *degrade* being the privileged term for describing what Chinese labor would do to white labor in the United States. The military framing of these two metaphors hint at an underlying anxiety that Whitney, at least, was willing to make explicit: "China is stronger on the Pacific Coast in men capable of bearing arms than ourselves, and . . . she can transport ten warriors from the middle of the kingdom to San Francisco at less expense than the United States can convey a single soldier and his knapsack from Chicago to the Coast; . . . she can send vessels with stronger armor and heavier guns to breach the walls of Alcatraz than we could provide for defense, and could send them in a shorter time."[26] Whitney thus clarifies the stakes of "the Chinese question"

[26] Whitney, 195.

by literalizing the threat of a Chinese future in martial terms. It would be foolish to say that this military angle—present also, though less directly, in Smith's comparison between culture and a Krupp gun[27]—reveals the final truth about anti-Chinese agitation on America's West Coast, which would then turn out to have been about national warmongering all along. But it makes sense to understand the articulation, however metaphorical, of a Chinese military threat as yet another dimension of larger concerns about the Chinese "invasion" of the United States through immigration and the generally "Asiatic" quality of the Western landscape, that is, as expressions of anxiety about European sovereignty over the American territory, and, more pressingly, about the sovereignty of an idealized, monocultural, and artisanal past over a multiracial, mass-produced future embedded in both the body of the Chinese worker and the very landscape of the nation.

3. That Dystopian Feeling

It should not therefore surprise anyone that a good number of late nineteenth-century Americans took it upon themselves to write stories that imagined the invasion of the United States by an army of the Chinese. Such stories tended to be organized around the prospect of a horde of numberless, faceless Chinese pouring over American borders and bludgeoning a valiant nation into submission by degrees: more or less the plot of Pierton W. Dooner's *Last Days of the Republic* (1880), Robert Woltor's *A Short and Truthful History of the Taking of Oregon and California by the Chinese in the Year A.D. 1899* (1882), and a number of short stories published in the *Overland Monthly.* Borrowing from the larger cultural discourse that imagined the coolie as marked by a capacity for enduring the suffering of either boredom or physical pain, these stories featured Chinese armies indifferent to their own casualties and characterized by, as Woltor put it,

[27] Lest these metaphors be understood simply as metaphors, however, let us return to the vehicle of their meaning. Following the outbreak of the Taiping Rebellion in China in 1851, China became a ready customer for Western military equipment. The successes of the "Ever-Victorious Army," led by foreign officers including Charles "Chinese" Gordon, prompted such enthusiasm for Western weaponry, Joanna Waley-Cohen writes, that they "converted Li Hongzhang, the man who was to play a leading role in Chinese politics and international affairs from the late 1860s until his death in 1901, to active enthusiasm for foreign firepower and its technology . . . Under Li's auspices China became such a good client of Krupp, the German weapons manufacturer, *that Alfred Krupp hung a picture of Li over above his bed.*" (*The Sextants of Beijing: Global Currents in Chinese History* (New York, 1999), 184–85; emphasis mine). In 1896, Li toured the United States, where, among other things, he encouraged Congress to relax immigration restrictions on Chinese workers.

"a stoic indifference to pain, which makes them fearless to deeds of blood, and a certain coolness in moments of excitement and danger, when calmness is invaluable."[28] These stories leavened American defeat with tales of Chinese cowardice, cruelty, and poor character, pitting the venality of the invaders against an American populace too trusting of foreigners, which they punctuated here and there with a doomed, authentic hero whose efforts clarified the need for a breed of American ideologically and militarily equipped to resist future foreign invasion. Successful books in this genre thus reinscribed the logic of individual, craft labor in the body of their heroic protagonists, clarifying once again the value of manual labor over factory work, manhood over coolieism, and—looking ahead to another military conflict between Asia and the West—Rambos over Rimbauds.

The rest of this chapter examines a book which, though it belonged to the genre, did none of those things, a book that was by most common measures of literary success an abject failure. The reading I pursue does not redeem the book, nor does it find in its collocation of character and event some perfect mirror of its time, or the secret key to the ideological apparatus of its era. It reads it, instead, within the relatively banal framework of its failure—because even its failures are in no way spectacular or impressive. And it finds there an opening onto possibility, a tangential take on the historical framework within which the nineteenth century thought the "Chinese problem," that was, if nothing else, a possibility inherent in the social. Whether such a possibility constituted a minority opinion in the society of its time, or whether in fact the novel or its author intended in any way to communicate the relationship to China, to sympathy, and to the future of modernity that I will argue that it does communicate, makes little difference here. What matters is that the novel—Arthur Vinton's 1890 *Looking Further Backward*—imagined, bravely or unknowingly, a form of sympathetic and material exchange in which the entire problematic with which we have been concerned so far resolves itself, not without significant violence, into an open and actionable future for the citizens of both the United States and China. In this future the forms of *material exchange* presaged by the rise of transnational markets for factory labor and the rise of industrial production are resolved not through Chinese exclusion—as the United States government did in its anti-immigration act of 1882—but through their inclusion in a new transpacific polity.

[28]Robert Woltor, *A Short and Truthful History of the Taking of California and Oregon by the Chinese in the Year A.D. 1899* (San Francisco, 1882), 77; Pierton W. Dooner, *Last Days of the Republic* (San Francisco, 1880). William F. Wu discusses these novels, as well as the *Overland Monthly* short stories, in *The Yellow Peril: Chinese Americans in American Fiction 1850–1940* (Hamden, Conn., 1982).

What were the more successful models of anti-Chinese fiction from which Vinton's *Looking Further Backward* could have borrowed? Certainly the market for paranoid invasion science fiction was robust in the 1890s: Ignatius Donnelly's *Caesar's Column*, published a year after *Looking Further Backward* and featuring a successful American worker's revolt (set in 1988) against an Orientalized, cosmopolitan oligarchy, sold 60,000 copies in its first year alone (and appeared in German translation three years later).[29] And M.P. Shiel's short stories, collected in 1898's *The Yellow Danger*, were reissued in the United States following their success in Britain, their readers thrilling to tales of hand-to-hand combat and violent torture.[30] Whatever pride of place *Looking Further Backward* has in the

[29] Ignatius Donnelly, *Caesar's Column: A Story of the Twentieth Century* (Cambridge, 1960). The book was originally published in Chicago, a factor which may be partially explained by (or help to explain) its far more transnational outlook—though the oligarchy is "Asiatic" in form, the novel's enemy is a generalized world culture that derives not from military invasion but from the progress of monopoly capitalism. For more on Donnelly, see Lye, 63–72, and Saxton, 283–84. It was not until the early twentieth century that English-language writers began to worry explicitly about a military invasion coming from Japan, presumably for reasons having largely to do with the changing positions of the two major East Asian nations, codified most clearly in the Japanese victory against Russia (1905) and the fall of the Chinese Qing regime in 1911. A united Asian front including Japan, China, and India attacks the West is in H. G. Wells' *The War in the Air* (1907); Richard Thompson discusses a series of articles written by U.S. Congressman Richmond P. Hobson (in *Cosmopolitan* magazine!) under the title "If War Should Come," which was "the most detailed prognostication of the course of a Japanese-American war that had been offered up to that time" (The Yellow Peril, 1890-1924," Ph.D. diss., U. of Wisconsin, 1957, 427–34 passim). Or, consider Marsden Manson's *The Yellow Peril in Action: A Possible Chapter in History* (San Francisco, 1907), in which the combined might of the Chinese army and the Japanese navy erases the United States' presence in the Pacific and demands, as part of the peace treaty, that the U.S. Constitution be amended to grant aliens equal rights of citizenship. Like Hobson's articles in *Cosmopolitan*, Manson's fictional account of the war (which he set in 1910) aimed at least partially to educate Americans in the commercial and military value of the Pacific Ocean and the United States' presence there (in Guam, Hawaii, the Philippines, and the West Coast ports). To that end, it included a fold-out map illustrating the United States' "masterly position" between the world's three great oceans (18). Jack London's "The Unparalleled Invasion," which appeared in *The Strength of the Strong* (New York, 1914), imagines a China modernized with Japanese help taking over the world through sheer demographics until its population is annihilated by a race-anxious Western coalition using germ warfare.

[30] M. P. Shiel, *The Yellow Danger* (London, 1888); republished in the United States and England with an additional subtitle as *The Yellow Danger: Or, What Might Happen if the Division of the Chinese Empire Should Estrange All European Countries* (London and New York, 1899). I am grateful to R. John Williams for drawing this novel to my attention. Williams's dissertation brilliantly connects several Chinese invasion novels of this era to the later ties, in the modernist work of Ezra Pound, between technology and China. For longer discussions of fantasy and science fiction featuring the Chinese, particular the notorious villains Fu Manchu and Ming the Merciless, see William F. Wu, Sheng-Mei Ma, *The Deathly Embrace: Orientalism and Asian American Identity* (Minneapolis, 2000) and Robert G. Lee, *Orientals: Asian Americans in Popular Culture* (Philadelphia, 1999); on Chinese invasion science

pantheon of paranoid, anti-Chinese American science fiction must lie, therefore, in the fact that it neither followed the models that preceded, nor inspired the works that followed it, in the fact, that is, that its imagination of the future was so uncompelling as to allow it—along with Vinton's literary career more generally—to disappear without leaving much of a mark on even that small subsection of American literary history to which it belongs.

Vinton's failure to pick up on the stock formulae of anti-Chinese science fiction may be at least partially explained by his location within the United States. Unlike Dooner's *Last Days of the Republic* or Woltor's *A Short and Truthful History of the Taking of Oregon and California,* both of which were published in San Francisco and surely found there a white reading audience well acquainted with the coolie stereotype and attuned to anxieties about Chinese labor, Vinton's novel was published in Albany, New York, presumably by virtue of Vinton's many connections in that state, where he worked as a lawyer and, after retiring in 1884, became the assistant editor of the *North American Review.* The Northeast was not immune to the pressures of Chinese labor—an attempt to bring seventy-five Chinese workers to break a strike at a shoe factory in North Adams, Massachusetts, in 1870 produced an outcry that spread across the Northeast and Midwest, a mass meeting involving three to four thousand people, and widespread coverage in local newspapers.[31] But the issues most pressing to the writers of classically anti-Chinese science fiction in California did not weigh as heavily there.

Most crucially, however, the intellectual and social context in which Vinton's book appeared, and to which his novel directly responds, involved the politico-economic furor instigated by Edward Bellamy's 1888 utopian novel, *Looking Backward, 2000–1887.* In the years after its publication, *Looking Backward,* "the single most influential narrative utopia of the nineteenth century" and the third-best-selling American fiction of its age (behind *Uncle Tom's Cabin* and *Ben-Hur*) inspired political movements, socialist salons, and ambitious revolutionaries throughout the United States and Europe and prompted widespread public discussion about disparities in wealth and living conditions, which were felt by so many to be on the verge of destroying the dream of the Republic.[32]

fiction of the 1990s, see Eric Hayot, "Chineseness: A Prehistory of Its Future," in *Sinographies: Writing China,* eds. Eric Hayot, Haun Saussy, and Steven G. Yao (Minneapolis, 2007).

[31] For more on the North Adams strike, see Gyory, *Closing the Gate,* chapter 3 and Robert Lee, *Orientals* 55–56.

[32] Philip E. Wegner, *Imaginary Communities: Utopia, the Nation, and the Spatial Histories of Modernity* (Berkeley, 2002), 62.

The novel tells the story of Julian West, a Bostonian who falls into a deep hypnotic sleep in 1888, and wakes up 112 years later to a new world. In the Boston of the year 2000, the entire population has been united under the banner of an economic and political system called "Nationalism," and the American Gilded Age is no more than a historical nightmare from which the residents of the new twenty-first century are delighted to have awoken. Nationalism, West discovers in a series of conversations with Dr. Leete, the man in whose basement he comes to, is a social system organized around the full state regulation of the economy and a general devotion to the common good. Under Nationalism, all citizens enjoy equal access to the fruits of their collective labor, drawing on communal stores and dining halls and benefiting from a credit system designed to deter hoarding and profligacy.[33] Each person works in a job best suited to his or her particular set of interests and skills, and the nation as a whole is governed by a committee of people whose election comes as a result of their success in the workforce. What's more, the wealth produced by such a system allows all of Nationalism's subjects to live as well as the wealthiest members of West's nineteenth-century Boston.[34]

Vinton's *Looking Further Backward* was just one of several novels and pamphlets to piggyback on the ideological ferment created by Bellamy's bold vision of a United States—and indeed a planet—unburdened by the class divisions and exploitations of the Gilded Age. Such fictions took part in the late-century struggle to represent (and control) the American future of industrial capitalism and the kind of labor it required, particularly as it affected the relation between individual work and concepts of production and consumption. Bellamy's success, as well as the parodies and responses that followed, indicate the degree to which this struggle mattered to the public culture of its time.

[33] Women were considered an "allied" rather than co-equal force with men in Bellamy's utopian future, though the very fact of their inclusion in the structure of the national political economy was enough to draw praise from some contemporary feminists. For a revisionary critique of what she calls Bellamy's "vaunted feminism," see Sylvia Strauss, "Gender, Class, and Race in Utopia," in Daphne Patai, ed., *Looking Backward, 1988–1888: Essays on Edward Bellamy* (Amherst, 1988).

[34] Tacked on to all the discussion of Nationalism is a fairly improbable love story, which serves as the novel's plot. In it, Julian West ends up marrying Leete's daughter, who in an astonishing coincidence turns out to be the granddaughter of Julian's 1887 fiancée. This logic of amorous substitution provides, as Jonathan Auerbach has noted, an affective validation of "Bellamy's entire project of systematically yet invisibly bureaucratizing traditional ideologies of nationhood" ("'The Nation Organized': Utopian Impotence in Edward Bellamy's *Looking Backward*." *American Literary History* 6.1 [Spring 1994], 37.).

Set in 2023, twenty-three years after West's miraculous awakening, Vinton's novel presents the total collapse of the Bellamy's American utopia. In his preface, Vinton declares his admiration for Bellamy's elucidation of the social problems of the late 1880s, but goes on to say that *Looking Further Backward* will "point out wherein the Bellamy Nationalism would prove disastrously weak": on the subject of national defense (6). The results of that weakness appear from the novel's title page, which declares that is merely the transcript of lectures given to the freshman class at Boston's Shawmut College—the very place where Julian West had, in Bellamy's novel, wound up as a professor of history—by a Chinese man, Won Lung Li. Over the course of these lectures, Li lays out for his students the events of the preceding twenty-three years: the United States' fall into ideological complacency and self-satisfaction, its failure to police its borders against "emigrants from the slums of other nations," and, most of all, its willingness "to abandon every thing"—everything, that is, that made the nation great—"for the sake of an idea."[35] In 2020, a Chinese nation threatened by the worldwide spread of Nationalism, and strong enough to fight back, invades the United States. By the time Li delivers his lectures, the Chinese army controls 70 percent of U.S. territory, leaving only the Upper Midwest in the hands of resistance fighters led by West's son Leete. West himself has been killed in action, and Li leavens his lectures with frequent excerpts from the former's diaries, which allow him to recount recent history from a nineteenth century, pre-Nationalist point of view with which he himself is forcefully aligned.

Scholarship has largely read Vinton's novel as a work of American dystopian literature, or as one of several responses to Bellamy, and has paid little attention to the Chinese context (other than to remark, as Jean Pfaelzer does, the genre's predictable alignment with nativist racism).[36] The book becomes more interesting in that context, because the very idea of imagining the future as "Chinese" literalizes so compellingly the economic concerns articulated in the anti-Chinese immigration debates and, in fact, turns them into aspects of literary form. In other words, what we have here is Marxist Literary Criticism 101: in a culture

[35]Arthur Vinton, *Looking Further Backward, Being a Series of Lectures Delivered to the Freshman Class at Shawmut College, by Professor Won Lung Li* (Albany, N.Y., 1890), 31. Further references are cited in the text as *LFB*.

[36]Williams is the only scholar I know who thinks of Vinton in an Asian American context. Wegner discusses Vinton as a respondent to Bellamy, and Jean Pfaelzer locates him in an American dystopian tradition, though neither addresses the novel for more than a couple pages (Pfaelzer, "Parody and Satire in American Dystopian Fiction of the Nineteenth Century" *Science-Fiction Studies* 7.1 [March 1980]).

in which China's status as a threat to national and economic integrity and indeed to the possibility of an American future is routinely discussed in terms of an "invasion," we get a novel whose major formal feature is a relation to the future, in which an actual Chinese invasion poses a threat to American national and economic integrity. Beginning with this gives us a major guide on how to read *Looking Further Backward,* whose most significant events operate largely at formal levels and whose imagination of its own future—the future, that is, of the novel's present—comes up against a profound mimetic impasse: although the novel does a very good job of imagining the future *until* 2023, it can only gesture, and then only vaguely, at the future beyond it.

But I am getting ahead of myself. Before coming to the ways in which *Looking Further Backward* moves past the anthropomorphic bottleneck created by anti-Chinese discourse of the late 1800s, let us at least look at the novel. It is characterized, as a novel, by a very strong tendency toward paralepsis, that is, toward the production in one formal arena of the overall narrative of the "solution" or resolution proper to a problem created in another formal space. This tendency appears most clearly in three places: first, in the novel's many reversals of the Asiatic stereotype, which consistently displace and defamiliarize contemporary cultural formations by shifting their national origin or moral value, retaining the stereotype's *terms* but inverting its *logic;* second, in the fact that the novel generates the *characterological* progress of its protagonist—Won Lung Li—exclusively in *narratorial* terms, so that the movement between two types of storytelling becomes the only site in which Li can be said to develop any "character" at all. Third, the novel's startling resolution of major *political* questions occurs inside the field of *grammar,* so that the entire problematic of civic and political life gets resolved not in the diegetic arena (through something like a description of the new Chinese-Americans responding happily to their situation), but rather by a pronominal switch whose field of reference reaches beyond the diegesis. Together these three reversals constitute the novel's total structure of feeling, the framework within which the novel does the work of all science fictions: imagining futurity as an effect of the present.

First, then, the stereotype: the novel's Chinese are "men of high breeding and great intellectual attainments," West writes in his diary, whose "polished manners and skill in conversation . . . would have made them charming hosts, under different circumstances" (144). And they have "tender and sympathetic hearts," Li tells his students, shedding "many tears over the suffering of the captive nation" (176). By contrast, the Americans are mechanical, robotic, and sheep-like. Li speaks of a general "loss of individualism" (28), and writes that "under

Nationalism men had become mere routinists" (93). West notes the "mechanical" obedience of the Americans to the orders of the occupying army, blaming it on a "destruction of individualism" (72–73), and writes that "under the Nationalistic system each man's duty was so exactly defined, that to go beyond its limits was treason, and though men had not yet been by it degraded into absolute machines" (109–10). Even modified by a "not yet," West's "degraded" ties Vinton's critique of Nationalism most explicitly to the labor politics of the 1890s, referring simultaneously to the general threat posed to individual labor by factory work and to the specific threat of degradation posed by the Chinese worker as a proxy for industrial modernization.

These reversals, which are largely focused on personal character, align themselves with some significant historical reversals as well: the conquered American population is sorted and then subjected to a reverse middle passage fully comparable to the one endured by Chinese laborers or African slaves. Though many died of death and disease en route, Li reminds his students, those who reached foreign shores were not much better off: "sold at private sale and public auction as laborers to whosoever would hire them, they became practically slaves. The mortality among them is frightful to contemplate, but we may well doubt if those who died were not more fortunate than those whose existence continued for a longer term of years" (86). Meanwhile, steamer ships coming from China repopulate the American coasts, so that by 2023 between one-third and half of the population of any American state is Chinese.[37]

This reversal of the terms and logic of racial stereotype lays the ground for the more complex dislocations that operate in the novel's character and address. Consider the second of the novel's major paralepses: that the emplotment of its major character is nowhere directly addressed, but instead appears purely as a result of his alterations in narrative style. This occurs because Li devotes substantial portions of his lectures to reading from the diaries of Julian and Leete West; these diaries, though diegetically subordinate to Li's voice, nonetheless occupy an increasingly central role as the novel progresses.

[37] By retaining the diction of contemporary American discourse about China, but inverting its historical and stereotypical form, Vinton enacts one of the classic gestures of dystopian or satirical fiction, one whose most perfect articulation comes in a film like *The Planet of the Apes* (itself, of course, an allegory of the civil rights movement). The novel's predictability in this field, however, must be understood at least partly as a necessity of its genre: we need to think of the genre of dystopian fiction as differing from science fiction not in its commitment to defamiliarization, but in the way that it tends to produce defamiliarization via pure *reversal* (which helps explain why dystopian fiction is generally uninteresting).

Why does this matter? Consider the differences between these two citations, the first from Li, the second from West's son, Leete:

> No idea that they were to be deported had entered the heads of the drafted men on the Common when they were formed in lines and the roll of their names was called; but when the armorers of the war vessels appeared and carts containing chains and shackles were driven up, something of the truth became apparent. The lines wavered, then broke into disorder, and the attempt of the armorers to manacle those nearest to them, resulted in a rush that drove them back. Some such resistance was expected by the Chinese commanders, and the Common had been surrounded by a strong cordon of troops. These now advanced with fixed bayonets until the rioters were huddled in a disorganized, indignant, and terrified mass at one end of the Common. The bolder spirits among the Americans wrenched off the branches of the trees, and using them as clubs endeavored by a sudden rush to break through the ranks of the military. It was at this point that the word "fire" was given, and a murderous discharge was poured into the mass of unarmed, helpless rioters. (101–02)

> She gave me a very graphic account of poor Jack Storiot's death. He was one of those who had been assembled on the Common for deportation, and one of the first whom it had been attempted to manacle. We all knew Jack's high spirit and impetuosity, and I have no doubt that this insult of the Chinese threw him into a great passion. He was one of the first to attack the Chinese and fell most horribly mutilated. Margaretta told me that one of the papers had published a list of those who had been killed or wounded in this horrible massacre. The paper had been suppressed by the Chinese as soon as it appeared, but the Nesmyth's had fortunately been able to secure a copy, and this she now brought to me. As I read over the list of names I saw many that I knew; fortunately my intimate friends had not been there, but Tom Hammond, Lafayette Brett, Babcock Tyler and Will Peckham were among the killed, and Aleck Warner, Charlie Bell and several other old school friends were among the wounded. It was an awful thing. I spoke of it that evening to Commissioner Hi and he told me that no one could regret it more than the Chinese did. It was one of the terrible results of war, to be excused only by its necessity. "We have hearts," he said, "but we must do our duty." (153–54)

The same event described from two perspectives: the first contains no names, no individual characterizations, no dialogue, and conceals its activity under a string of passive constructions (four in the first sentence alone) of which the most crucial appear in the final sentence, when the word "fire" is "given" and the discharge is "poured," in each case by no one in particular, into the bodies of the rioters. The second is framed as dialogue and includes another one (Margaretta gives Leete the account, Leete talks to Commissioner Hi), and contains an individual characterization of one of the rioters, particular names and details, an emotional reaction to the situation ("It was an awful thing"), and a discussion of its value. Most importantly, Leete's discussion of the newspaper list of those killed, in drawing attention to the spread of information, shows how the story one tells about an event depend on its circulation and distribution inside a social field. Li's lecture, on the other hand, takes that social field for granted—or rather, it *constitutes* the dominant social field within which the narrative circulates (like the Chinese in 2020, it suppresses the names of those involved).

If one allows the difference between these two descriptions of the Boston massacre to stand in for the more general difference between the mode of narration that appears in Li's lectures and the one that organizes the diaries, one sees how the novel organizes itself around two different types of narration, each of which is associated with a particular type of narrator (a Chinese professor, two members of the American resistance), a particular temporality (2023 or 2020), and a formal relationship to novelistic discourse (diegesis vs. metadiegesis).[38] The former is self-consciously aligned with an emphasis on historical causality largely disconnected from individual actors, and communicates narrative information in general statements characterized by passive or expletive constructions ("There was, however, much suffering among those whose flight had exhausted their credit cards" [124].). The latter relies on forms of emplotment and character that much more closely resemble those of the traditional novel.

One way to think about *Looking Further Backward*, then, is as the product of a formal conflict between two modes of storytelling. The first is primarily indicative; the second is primarily mimetic. The first "tells"; the second "shows." Because the novel begins and ends with Li's voice, and because he reads the diary sections aloud, these two modes are arranged in a diegetic hierarchy. And yet the hierarchy established by the purely formal positioning of the narrative modes in the novel is undermined by the fact of the novel's increasing

[38] All this doubled by the reference to the actual Boston massacre of 1770, at which only five people died, the end of American independence thus recapitulating its beginning.

commitment to the metadiegetic diaries, which practically overwhelm the lectures by the end of the book. All in all, more than half of the total volume of Li's fourteen lectures (that is, roughly 100 pages of a 179-page novel) is given over to the West's journals, including fully two-thirds of the lectures in the book's second half (about 69 of the last 100 pages).

This formal conflict is the product of actions happening inside the story, rather than the result of decisions made by the "novel." Li chooses to read the diaries to his class; Li fills in his relatively bloodless narration of the Boston massacre with details about Leete's friend Jack and the suppression of the news by the Chinese; nearly two-thirds of Li's lectures ventriloquize two members of the American resistance. From this perspective we can reimagine the novel as the story of a year in the life of its Chinese lecturer. In such a reading, the conflict between narrative modes is Li's personal struggle with two competing modes of narration, the first his expressed and conscious preference, the second his unconscious, expressive one.[39] The narrative space (measured in pages) the novel accords to each of these two narrative modes indicates, then, both a formal conflict and the effect of the development of Li's character over the course of the book. Narrative style is, indeed, the only line along which Li's character can be said to develop at all.[40]

If the narrative mode that gradually takes over the novel is explicitly marked as both representational and American, then Li's increasingly citational lectures must be understood at least partly as personal accommodations of an American style that does not—at least at the novel's opening—seem to be his preferred

[39] From a psychoanalytic perspective, one might argue that Won Lung Li's ever-lengthening citations of the diaries tell the story of a Chinese scholar of history at Shawmut College so caught up in an Oedipal relationship with his predecessor that he gradually gives over his own narrational space to him at the cost of losing his own voice. As West himself notes at one point, the typically Chinese respect for ancestors seemed to provoke in the Chinese he met an increased admiration as he was, thanks to the miracle of hypnotic sleep, something like 150 years old: "Ancestors and the men of antiquity had been so long objects of veneration in the Celestial Empire, that I, who had been a contemporary of their progenitors seemed in their opinion to be entitled to the same respect that they entertained for those progenitors. They listened to me, therefore, as if the accumulated wisdom of two centuries spoke in my words" (143). Here the novel offers a clue as to Li's interest in West by making it signify both in terms of a local Oedipal relationship (revolving around the chair of history at Shawmut) and a cultural one.

[40] My reading of the ways in which characters and narrative modes "compete" for space within the limited framework of the novel owes a great deal to the work of Alex Woloch, who in *The One vs. the Many* (Princeton, N.J., 2003) develops a narratological practice that analyzes the distribution of "character-space" within a global "character-system," and reads this formal structure as a crucial feature of the novel's historical development as a genre.

narrative mode. His description of the "Chinafication" of the United States (176) is thus matched by an "Americanification" of his own speech, a gradual slide from lectures that indicate history to diaries that privilege limited, individual experience over a structural explanation of "causes" and their "results" (17).[41] From this perspective, the novel is "about" not only the Chinese invasion of the United States but also an individual intercultural experience in which a member of the invading culture transforms himself (or is transformed) by narrating the history of the invasion to which he belongs. Rather than a monodirectional tale of invasion and conversion, then, the novel represents the mutual (and largely unconscious) imbrication of the colonizer with the colonized, the Chinese with the American, and the immediate present with the recent past. Though the terms of that imbrication are hardly equal—at novel's end, Li remains a history professor, while West has been killed in combat—they nonetheless complicate a sense of the novel's temporal structure. Li's narratological shifts consistently recall us to the present tense of the novel's narration, so that the novel's *discourse* (how it tells) continuously shadows its more spectacular *story* (what it tells), in effect establishing another story-field within the novel's diegetic frame.

This structure, which turns Li into far more than a narratological amanuensis, lays down the field of comprehensibility for the novel's third major formal disruption. This one has to do with the relationship between citizenship and grammar and involves a shift in Li's politics of address, which can now be read as a crucial event inside the discourse-story the novel represents. Consider the first sentence of Li's first lecture to the Shawmut College freshmen: "I come before you as a stranger. I am born of a race that the race you are born of has for centuries been trained to think of as an inferior race" (10).

This "you" serves a double function. Motivated internally by the students to whom Li speaks, it also addresses the novel's 1890 readership. In fact, the "you" makes more sense as a reference to nineteenth-century readers, since by 2023, the students at Shawmut would have had three years to unlearn the idea of Chinese racial inferiority and adjust to the fact that half the population of Boston was of Chinese origin. Li's "you," retained throughout the novel, thus continually

[41] Not that there is anything especially American about representation, or Chinese about lecturing. Within the internal narrative economy of the novel, the transformation it narrates moves from the United States to China at the political level, while moving from China to the United States at the narrative one.

implicates the 1890 reader in a system of racial prejudice that the story's progress severely tests. Though it is perhaps not fair to say that the novel is narrated in the second person, the relentless appearance of the second-person plural, by confusing the novel's real addressees with its fictional ones, subjects its readers to a pedagogical mode of address that subordinates them to, and separates them from, the text's primary narrative voice.

All this changes in the final lecture. Li opens the discussion by noting that "it is with regret that I cease to quote from Professor West's diary," before announcing that "what I have to say to you to-day, in this, the closing lecture of your freshman year, will be expressed to you in my own words" (177). Given what I have described as the conflict between narrative modes, Li's claim about his "own words" appears to be the final salvo in a formal war, a bold recapturing of his voice and a declaration of his independence from West's political position and storytelling style. The pages that follow occur entirely in Li's preferred indicative mode and give a brief sketch of the course of the Chinese takeover of the United States, distinguishing sharply between the second person and the first: "At the time that I speak to *you*, the Nationalists are hemmed in on all sides, save on the frozen north, from communication with outside nations. The front line of *our* armies forms a semi-circle stretching from Montreal south along the western base of the Alleghenies to the Ohio . . ." (186–87; emphases mine).

And then we come to the novel's final two paragraphs:

> Let us now, in closing, consider hastily the benefits which the invasion of the Chinese has brought to us.
>
> We are no longer a defenseless people, ready to be subjugated by the first armed nation that attacks. Our material prosperity was never greater. Our soil supports a greater population than it did before. Chinese frugality has replaced the wasteful lavishness that prevailed in private life under the Nationalistic government. Woman no longer competes with man, but has become as the Gods intended she should be, the handmaiden of male humanity. What was good in Nationalism we have retained. What was bad we have discarded and replaced by what is better. Under Nationalism, individualism was reduced to a minimum; with us to-day it is honored and given every chance to develop. (187–88)[42]

[42] In her discussion of the Vinton novel, Pfaelzer writes that "the story ends with a passage from Julian's diary: he realizes that the Chinese have gained control of all but a small area of the mid-western

The first "us" is rhetorical. The second one, at the end of the first sentence, arguably refers only to the Chinese. Beginning with the "we" of the second paragraph, however, Li's pronouns point unmistakably to the United States' new population, conceiving himself and the students for the first time as members of a single group. The grammatical unity supposes a political one; the transformation of Li's first person singular into the plural thus signals the possibility of a new political subjectivity whose form of government is neither purely Chinese nor purely Nationalist, but a mixture of both.

Because, as I've suggested, Li's continual use of "you" determines much of the novel's fictional relationship to its doubled audience (students and reader), the shift to "we" signals more than a simple call to patriotism. It invites the reader, within the formal terms already privileged by the novel, to take on the burden of a *truly* utopian, quasisocialist citizenship in which the positive aspects of Bellamyian Nationalism—mainly the end of class warfare and the abolition of the gap between rich and poor—are retained and leavened with a good dose of individualism (and, not incidentally, of sexism).[43] Never represented, only indicated, the biracial, bicultural utopia to which Li refers in the novel's final paragraphs appears most visibly in the formal shift from "you" to "we," where the novel's narrator and its audience, separated since the beginning of the novel, are finally drawn together.

The awkward balance of these two emotional modes, which together comprise the novel's total structure of feeling, parallels the position of Vinton's novel within the larger discourse on China of his time. For nineteenth century progressives and union activists, the mechanization of labor proceeded *through* its "Chinafication," with American individualism (and its beefy manhood) under attack by forms of factory work especially suited to Chinese bodies and their biological impossibilities. In Vinton, however, it is the Chinese who save the misguided American socialists from themselves: Bellamy's utopian distribution of the burden of labor produces precisely the kind of mechanized, docile population that

states, and he knows that 'it's just a matter of time before they close in'" (68). Pfaelzer must be referring to a different edition of the book, though none exists that I know of. My edition ends as I describe it above. A version of the phrase Pfaelzer cites appears in Li's final lecture, not West's diary, and is given in my edition as "It is but a question of time when we close in upon the last remnant of the Nationalists" (187).

[43] Indeed the transnational, transracial "we" here, spoken to an audience of presumably male college students, gains much from its exclusion of women (now "handmaidens of male humanity") from the labor force and the classroom, something that men of every race and nation can apparently agree on.

union activists feared would result from widespread proletarianization in the first place. This is at some level not surprising; "the enemies of Utopia sooner or later turn out to be the enemies of socialism."[44] But Vinton's detournenment of the Chinese position in American racial politics did more than discredit socialism; by so obviously reversing the rhetorical function of the Chinese, *Looking Further Backward* revealed how malleable the Chinese were as a figure for American futurity. And in turning them to this particular use—in imagining them, that is, as the historical preservers of individualism—Vinton also made the Chinese the best Americans of all: cultured, civilized, capable of ordering a massacre and of weeping at its unhappy results, the novel's Chinese figure a relation to modernity that is simultaneously sympathetic and productive, compassionate and mercenary. The novel thus turns the idea of Chinese stasis and stagnation, so common a part of the nineteenth-century stereotype, into a beneficial trait. It is precisely by not changing that China returns to the West—if only through the barrel of a gun—the values the latter left behind in its progressive, future-oriented and suspiciously European fervor for ideas.

Having spent the novel's first 178 pages feeling badly about the American setbacks, or identifying with West's frustrated attempts to prompt the machine-like Nationalists to react appropriately to invasion, what did Vinton's readers think of this seemingly belated attempt to turn history's lemons into lemonade? If, as Raymond Williams has suggested, novels are useful because they can establish in advance of politics a "structure of feeling" that provides readers with an emotional and/or experiential framework through which to grasp material transformations in their worlds—if, that is, novels express, sometimes unconsciously, new apprehensions of the present into which they emerge—then whatever emotional work Vinton's novel does belongs to a complex structure of feeling indeed.[45] For such a structure must include, if it is to be complete, both the generally dystopian, bleak events of most of the novel, with all their startling inversions and threats about the military weaknesses of socialism, and the final two paragraphs, which promise a militarily robust, individually-oriented,

[44]Fredric Jameson, "Of Islands and Trenches: Neutralization and the Production of Utopian Discourse," *Diacritics* 7, no. 2 (1977), 3.

[45]Williams defines a "structure of feeling" as "a social experience still *in process*, often indeed not yet recognized as social but taken to be private, idiosyncratic, and isolating," and as "a cultural hypothesis" about the nature of a social present still in the process of emerging (*Marxism and Literature* [Oxford, 1977], 132–33.).

quasi-utopian America that differs from the United States of 1890 in having become at least partly socialist: Nationalism with Chinese characteristics. What the novel gives readers to grasp, that is, is an emotional complex that recognizes the limitations of the present—Vinton writes in the preface that "the existence of great private fortunes is a menace to the welfare of the State" (6)—and then punishes readers for believing in Bellamy's utopian resolution to those limitations by forcing them through the emotionally difficult loss of his Nationalist solution. The suffering of the novel's Americans, like the frustration of the Wests at the mechanically slow response of the Nationalists to invasion, is intended to make the reader suffer as well: in fact, one might say that the novel's argument against Bellamy occurs largely on the basis of the emotional evidence provided by the identificatory suffering it causes. That the novel finally offers the reader a happy ending suggests that it aims to force the reader to pass *through* that suffering into a contented and sympathetic recognition of its necessity. The reader's final emotional position resembles that of the Chinese officers who weep over the massacre in Boston: the suffering they witness, though terrible, speeds the production of an ameliorated, post-Bellamyian socialism that protects individualism and remains strong on national defense. Becoming the interpellated subject of Vinton's utopia requires a recognition of the importance of bearing without *political* complaint the suffering required to produce it.

4. Learning to Lose

In forcing the American reader to endure transformative suffering, by redeeming that suffering through the literary mechanism of the Chinese army, the novel *encodes* but does not *represent* the relationship between endurance and labor that drove the nineteenth-century Asiatic stereotype. The coolie is, in fact, never seen in the novel—only in the least embodied, most moral-philosophical ways does the question of a "Chinese" relation to suffering appear in *Looking Further Backward* at all (in Li's descriptions of the weeping officers, for instance). But suffering occurs—displaced, as with the novel's narrative or its political union, into another register—onto the bodies of the Americans enslaved and killed by the Chinese. And their suffering is the result of the United States' adoption of a form of labor designed to *eliminate* suffering from labor: it is because the Americans implement Bellamyite Nationalism that they eventually must be killed in Boston and New York or sold into slavery abroad.

Though the idea that suffering is part of life is nothing new, the ideological shape of the argument made in the United States in the late nineteenth century allows us to see this recognition in Vinton as part of the larger historical process whereby the modern relation to suffering was articulated and framed. Recalling now Talal Asad's claim that the West's "humanizing the world" created colonial subjects with appropriately modern relations to suffering and sympathy, and thus to the difference between wasteful and necessary pain, I wish to suggest here that Vinton's novel allows us to extend Asad's analysis to Europe and the United States as well. The humanization of the world and the recognition of the values of "necessary" suffering were values that had to be communicated to (and indeed imposed on) the national populations who were presumably the source of their philosophical origin. For it is clearly the message of *Looking Further Backward* that certain kinds of suffering must be endured and that the violent necessity of even something like a middle passage might, with enough perspective, be accepted as a regrettable side effect of the production of a freer world. If the novel has a structure of feeling, it is one that establishes through the manipulations of its formal and thematic properties the "truth" of this new system, in which the suffering of slavery and murder become the price of a politico-economic structure that accommodates the necessities of modern labor while retaining a respect for individualism. The fact that the novel never portrays the results of its utopian program—the only hint of its presence comes in Li's final paragraphs—suggests how difficult it must have been to actually imagine. This imaginary future functions, unrepresented, more as the novel's dream than as its fulfilled wish; indeed, one of the ironies of the novel is that the entire invasion has to happen, and Li must go through an elaborate ballet around narrative form, only to get to the point where such a system can be *referred* to, if not exactly imagined into being.

This imaginative impasse illustrates the limits of the novel's compromise with "Asiatic form," this latter understood as the relation between monotony, labor, and capital embodied in the "coolie" figure. Rather than seek to undo the losses caused by industrialized modernity, and thus attempt to preserve in fiction the purer, whiter, more Jacksonian America to which industrialism was opposed, Vinton's narrative attempts to think the possibility of a future defined by the combination of Chineseness and labor, a future it imagines as the permanent structure of modern life. The loss that such a future constitutes produces the "happy" ending that makes the novel's emotional structure so weird, since the resolution of the problems of industrial capitalism can only occur through the suffering caused by the novel's refusal, having made the Chinese a *deus ex machina* of American history, to relegate them back to the historical margins where they "belonged." In this, the novel is quite different than Jack London's "The Unparalleled Invasion," where the rise of China produces world unity and a decision to wipe out all the Chinese. For Vinton, by contrast, the American landscape, insofar as it is also the landscape of modernity, is now and will continue to be "Asiatic" in "formation and scenery," because the very nature of the world has in fact become "Asiatic" as well.

Rather than leading, as it does in the more dystopian narratives of Chinese invasion, to a deadening automatization of the American people and the end of "freedom," the novel's "Chinafication" of the United States is thus the *cost* of freedom's purchase. In this sense the political warfare of the novel functions as an allegory for the economic situation to which "China" generally referred in the late nineteenth century (just as any literal Chinese "invasion" metaphorizes the Chinese immigration to which "invasion" referred figuratively in the first place). Buried in the novel's acceptance of a political domination by the Chinese is thus an insight about the nature of capitalism and the globalization of the labor market that has historically been difficult to come to terms with, namely the notion that the production of transnational networks of labor and trade undermines the isolability and independence of the nation-state.[46] Vinton's abandonment of the political concept of the United States is essentially the mark of that recognition, though the novel is at its most utopian when it suggests that American individualism could, unlike the nation-state, be retained in the future Chinese colony.

What happens, in this future, to the Chinese "coolie"? The crucial figure in so much of the discourse about China and the American future makes no appearance in Vinton's novel at all. Here one might say, as Walter Benjamin did of the masses in the oeuvre of Charles Baudelaire, that Vinton's "most important subjects are hardly ever encountered in descriptive form."[47] The coolie's "absence" from the novel functions as a determining negative space, an ideological black hole around which the novel revolves and from which it cannot escape.

[46] In *Membranes: Metaphors of Invasion in Nineteenth-Century Literature, Science, and Politics,* Laura Otis shows how the discovery of the cell and the development of vaccines for contagious diseases prompted anxious imperialists to frame control of national borders in a variety of organic metaphors, particularly ones organized around the possibility that viruses pass into the body by "passing" as its legitimate citizens (Baltimore, 1999).

[47] Some Motifs in Baudelaire," in *Charles Baudelaire, a Lyric Poet in the Age of High Capitalism* (London, 1983), 122.

Vinton's Chinese resemble Julian West more than they do the American Nationalists; in many ways, they are simply the ghosts of the good nineteenth century haunting the United States into remembering its forgotten values. Only in the presence of his major feature—the ability to suffer, to endure without complaint the cost of an "Asiatic" modernity—do we see the shadow presence of the coolie in this novel. By novel's end, everyone still living must accept this cost, and the reader is enjoined to imagine himself (via the interpellating "you" of Li's final words) as yet another citizen of the novel's new Chinese America. This is the emotional task Li proposes at the end of the novel: that the reader should give up on the hierarchies of cultural or racial superiority that sustained anti-Chinese discourse in the nineteenth century—and that helped make it such a useful figure for the economic problems it represented—as the price of imagining modernity's post-Nationalist, and post-nationalist, future: that readers, in short, learn to be *like* coolies (in their relation to suffering and self-directed sympathy) so that they wouldn't have to *become* them.

While during the eras of George Henry Mason and Peter Parker the Euro-American experience of Chineseness at home dealt mostly with transnationalism in the form of the circulation of Chinese things—abetted by the travels of Western people who inaugurated the trade in them—the American late nineteenth century is where the West confronts for the first time the large-scale circulation of Chinese *people*. The stakes were accordingly raised, as the economic threat posed by Chinese labor threatened with an immediacy unavailable to a box of tea or a theory of sympathy the integrity of an experience and way of life that most American and British writers identified as the West's exclusive civilizational province (think of Arthur Smith on the Krupp gun). Ironically, of course, one "solution" to this ideological problem involved—as it did, perhaps, in Mason, and as it does so often in racial discourse, conceiving of people as "things."[48] But a particular kind of things: the issue with Chinese workers was not that they were inhuman *as such* but rather that their humanity itself was inhumane, not only in its indifference to the suffering of others (by then an old story) but in its willingness to take its *own* suffering for granted; the Chinese, that is, were *like* animals but were not animals, which is why so much time had to be spent insisting that they were *like* them.

[48] My thoughts here are very much influenced by a recent essay by Christopher Bush, "The Ethnicity of Things in America's Lacquered Age," *Representations* 99 (Summer 2007).

Into this scene, whose outlines are by now well known, Vinton's novel came and went. The complex play of commensurability and incommensurability *Looking Further Backward* organizes around the anti-Chinese discourse it knew does not make it "ahead" of its time in any sense; it is, rather, completely of its time without for all that being identical with it. The coolie's biologically impossible body threatened a future in which modernity had to be "endured" rather than fought off—and, thus, a future in which the condition of the coolie's suffering body was to become the condition of all bodies everywhere. By moving the problem of that suffering into the affective register, Vinton purchased the utopia engendered by the conflagration of modernity at the price of an enduring loss, one whose suffering was the very condition of the possibility of a future without coolie labor. And although the fact that *Looking Further Backward* generates this return of suffering through the Chinese army shows how close it was to the imaginary of the late nineteenth-century United States, that it was the Americans who suffered most from the narration shows how far Vinton was willing to go to think the terms of the system that tied the American future to China without, like so many others, eliminating one of those terms through legal or physical violence. Still, the novel's violence is at least partly genocidal. It thus apprehends how deeply the Western perception of Chinese suffering had to do with the possibility of genocidal transformation, though not, as Vinton is practically alone in imagining, of the Chinese as a race, but of the very possibility of an organic human subjectivity disconnected from the suffering of alienated labor. This does not invalidate the idea of an ontological link between Chineseness and suffering, but reconfirms it, though in a more global and self-directed register.

6. The Anthropomorphic Aperture

Connecting the history of Asiatic form explicitly to the anxieties faced by mainstream American culture about both exoticism and technology shows how the Asian body in America has always been (seen as) a doubled or doubly mediated figure, forced to bear on its surface the mutually intermediating concepts of racial otherness and industrial modernization. In the American context, that body's figural duplicity has most often been marked by the convention of calling it "inscrutable," suggesting that its exterior surface conceals an unavailable internal meaning. Indeed one might think of all the ink spilled on explaining the Chinese in the late nineteenth century as an attempt simultaneously to undo and preserve that inscrutability, the project of explaining its mysteries raveled with the pleasure of reveling in its irreducible strangeness.

That this inscrutability revealed itself again and again in the faces, manners, and speech of particular Chinese bodies suggests that the duplicity of the Chinese as an ideological figure (signaling simultaneously past and future, racial primitivism and modernization, suffering and a possible end to suffering via indifference) was best made intelligible by giving it an anthropomorphic form. To be in the presence of an Asiatic figure, and, by extension, to be in the presence of an Asiatic body already layered over with this figure as stereotype, meant for many Americans feeling threatened by the visible duplicity of an embodied, human sign. Or, to be in the presence of the visible duplicity of an embodied, human sign was to be in the presence, by definition, of something Asiatic: past and future, animal and superman.

Though the claim that the Chinese were "inscrutable" attributes this uncertainty to the subjective surfaces of the Chinese face (inexpressive) or language (impenetrable), it may be truer to say that the representational uncertainty provoked by the Chinese resided with the encounter with a form of racial and cultural otherness that posed (or was made to pose) so insistently the complex, multifaceted questions of labor, or globalization, and of modernization. Arthur Smith, for instance, refers early on in *Chinese Characteristics* to "a wood-cut representing an oak tree, in the outlines of which the observer is invited to detect a profile of Napoleon on the island of St. Helena, standing with bowed head and folded arms. Protracted contemplation frequently fails to discover any such profile, and it would seem that there must be some mistake, but when once it is clearly pointed out, it is impossible to look at the picture and not see Napoleon too. In like manner, many things are to be seen in China which do not at first appear, and many of them once seen are never forgotten" (*CC*, 11–12). Like the image of Napoleon and the oak tree, the Chinese surface was representationally ambiguous, presenting now this face, now that one, leaving the American observer with the sense that there might always be *another* picture in the picture. If the surface exterior of the Asiatic was, as Colleen Lye suggests, "modernization rendered visible,"[49] it was because the Asiatic body represented to (white) America the newly created subject of modern technology and modern labor, born to endure processes occurring on scales extreme enough to exceed the measure of "humanity" itself, making it impossible to see all aspects of the world picture at the same

[49] Lye, *America's Asia*, 94.

time. So the complex and multiple *truth* of the Chinese as a figure, the degree to which it united in a single object the contradictions of the American experience of its modern future, became the *falsehood* attributed to the Chinese as people, as though the multiple representational functions the Chinese figure was made to bear in white America could only be perceived as an anthropomorphized cascade of masks and misrepresentations that concealed some withheld inner kernel.

Perhaps because American ideas about the Chinese so insistently returned to the question of bodies, to the physical ability to endure the conditions of modern life and modern labor without complaint (for example, the ability to survive on a near-starvation diet), work in Asian American Studies has consistently thought of race as located most fundamentally in a set of human minds and human bodies. Lye argues, to the contrary, that the structures that make the Asiatic a figure for (and index of) globalizing labor markets suggest that race is not a human concept but an economic one, that the "form" governing its representation and even its phenomenological experience owes more to the movements of capital than to the white perception of racial otherness. Considered within the framework of this discussion, the lesson might be, pushing Lye's insight one step further, that the *body* itself is not an anthropomorphic object, at the same time that it is the original and least distorted of all anthropomorphisms—the only anthropomorphic object, one might say, that is completely *like* itself. The experience of the Chinese as duplicitous is a recognition—and rejection, given the negative connotations of "duplicitous"—of this complex and frequently unwelcome truth, of the ways in which bodies, in becoming vehicles of historical and economic meaning, leave behind their status as the naked, fleshy apertures of some purer and more apparently original form of being. (Pheng Cheah: "Humanity and all its capacities are . . . product-effects generated by forces that precede and exceed the *anthropos*."[50])

Lye's forceful de-anthropomorphization of the concept of race in the American context thus leads us to a broader theory of the disappointments of what one might call anthropomorphic desire, that is, of the disappointments produced by the awareness that an originary fantasy of the body's personal and human simplicity can only be thought in relation to such larger and more inhuman concepts as transnationalism, diaspora, globalization, or the history of the means of production. Utopian fiction has long been one of the means by which humans

[50] Pheng Cheah, *Inhuman Conditions: On Cosmopolitanism and Human Rights* (Cambridge, Mass., 2007), 10.

have reconciled these two seemingly incommensurable modes of historical time (which Fredric Jameson has called the "lived" and the "geologic").[51] In *Looking Further Backward,* we see how Vinton's transformation and universalization of the coolie's embodied suffering into an affective and future-oriented register is only possible because of the novel's grasp of the malleability of the coolie's anthropomorphic form, so that Vinton's imaginary future retains the conceptual and ideological kernel of the coolie (the unity of modernity and suffering) while shedding its physical husk and—more or less—its racial and cultural specificity.

But the unceasing repetition of fantasies about the coolie's body, which have in our time given way to larger-scale anxieties about the low cost of Chinese labor (understood not as a racial feature but as an economic one) and about the physically dangerous and abusive working conditions in Chinese factories (here "racial" form still echoes), remind us that the other side of our recognition of the body's nonanthropomorphism is its relentless return to the anthropomorphic, that is, to a sense of the body as the most basic and truest idiom of individual experience and historical interpretation. It is tempting to describe the relation between these two concepts of the body as dialectical, the movement between the body as phenomenological base and the body as cultural superstructure thus defining one major organizing framework of Western thought since, say, the intellectual revolutions produced by Hegel or Marx.

This would require, however, ceding the very premise of the argument, because such a dialectic would imagine that the "original" and fully self-sufficient body were not, like the body that figures modes of production, itself already a *figure* for something, namely, for the lack or absence of distorting figuration.[52] The opposition is not between the nonfigural and the figural, but between a figure of nonfiguration and a figure that wears its figuration openly. Into this lopsided dialectic—for it turns out that both its thesis and antithesis are, finally, on the same side—strides the "Chinese body," whose duplicity encoded the anathematic awareness that the honest and open body it fails to *be* is in fact the one it most accurately *represents.* And likewise, crucially, as regards the coolie's relation to pain: in Vinton's novel, what is the transformation of the racially specific experience of physical suffering into a generalized one, after all, but the extension of an experience belonging to a single type of body to the entire realm of human being?

[51] "Actually Existing Marxism," *Polygraph,* 6–7 (1993): 170–95.

[52] Here we see that in being a figure for the lack of figuration, the "human" or "original" body effectively represents to us the ideal of a "genuinely" real body that could never exist.

Carried from the "inside" of the Chinese figure to a universal "outside," from physiology to affect, suffering's travels figure the movement from an inscrutable inner life oriented around a mystery of otherness to the expression of a coherent logic of national self-defense that recognizes that some forms of pain are the cost of an "individual" human future liberated from the yawning threat of the human machine.

Placed in the open, the experience of suffering reveals itself as the fundamental condition of Vinton's utopian modernity, while the Chinese, stripped of their private racial relation to pain, become as "American" as anyone else in the diegesis—which is why it doesn't matter that the Chinese army creates a hybrid nation full of immigrants. When Julian West—whose last name had signaled in Bellamy's *Looking Backward* the replacement of the nineteenth century's frontier of space to the twenty-first century's frontier of time—dies in the battle of Lake Erie in Vinton's novel, the nineteenth century dies with him. And Won Lung Li becomes the end of history's "last man," narrating to a captive audience the grammatical accommodation with sympathy which, in externalizing pain's Asiatic form, makes that form the condition of a universal modernity whose idiom is the transpacific.[53]

[53] Francis Fukuyama's *The End of History and the Last Man* (New York, 1992), drawing on a particularly Kojèvian Hegel, produced another version of a relation to universal modernity, three years after the fall of the Berlin Wall. Fukuyama's argument that "a uniform horizon of economic production possibilities" "guarantees an increasing homogenization of all human societies, regardless of their historical origins or cultural inheritances," resembles in a number of ways the universalism Vinton imagined a century earlier, though in a more positive mode (xiv).

5 Bertrand Russell's Chinese Eyes; or, Modernism's Double Vision

---

When an event is considered at close quarters, at the moment when it is lived through, everything seems subject to chance: one man's ambition, some lucky encounter, some local circumstance or other appears to have been decisive. But chance happenings offset each other, and facts in their multiplicity coalesce and show up a certain way of taking a stand in relation to the human situation, reveal in fact an *event* which has its definite outline and about which we can talk.

—Merleau-Ponty, *Phenomenology of Perception*

Anyone who rifles through the boxes of miscellaneous material that are part of the Peter Parker collection at the Yale University Medical Library will find preserved—in the fifth series of the first box—a pair of letters. The exchange, dated April 1935, occurred between Secretary of the University Carl Lohmann and Milton C. Winternitz, then in his last year as dean of the university's medical school. It opens with a note from Lohmann:

April 9, 1935

Dear Dean Winternitz:

Among other things which accompanied the Canton Hospital-Cadbury-Peter Parker correspondence was the enclosed Chinese document.

> Thinking that it was an expression of high sentiments expressed by some Oriental savant for our beloved University, I asked Professor Asakawa to take a hasty skedaddle through it.[1] It turns out to be the request of a druggist, one Kwang Wan Lung Hing, that somebody pay some attention to an unpaid bill. I patronize our local druggist as I am constantly reminded to do by placards in the street cars. I regret that I am not the one addressed. Maybe it is yours.
>
> Sincerely yours,
>
> C.A.L.

Winternitz responded in a similarly playful mood the following day:

> Dear Carl:
>
> During the past few months I have reached the point where I can no longer understand bills which are submitted in good old Anglo-Saxon. How would you expect me to interpret a Chinese manuscript? I thought it was a new form of art after the fashion of Gertrude Stein's poetry, so I guess I was further off than you were. Be this as it may, the document is an exquisite one.
>
> Sincerely,
>
> M.C. Winternitz, M.D.

The letters' humor results from the movement from high to low. In Lohmann's letter, what begins as a "document" and "expression of high sentiments" turns out to be, following a linguistic "skedaddle," simply a druggist's request for payment. Winternitz, likewise amused, repeats Lohmann's differentiation between low bill and high manuscript, playing with the idea of Chinese writing as a mark of high civilizational history and the ordinariness of commerce. The reference to Stein I will say more about in a moment, but for now direct your attention to Winternitz's final line, which returns the bill to a "high" position by referring to it not only as a "document"—the term Lohmann uses in his first sentence—but as an

[1] Asakawa Kan'ichi, an historian and political scientist who began teaching history at Yale University in 1907 (he was simultaneously curator of the Asian collections in the library).

"exquisite document." The "Be this as it may" that introduces this characterization announces the turn away from humor and back to seriousness, and so insists that despite the fact that this piece of paper is a bill, it is "exquisite" simply because it is written in Chinese. That the druggist's bill remains, even after its function has been recognized, an "exquisite" document, that its movement from "manuscript" to invoice does not disturb, finally, the exquisiteness of its presence as visual image, indicates once again how powerfully Chinese writing has operated in the Western imagination of the past few centuries.[2]

Some measure of that power finds its way into Winternitz's mention of Gertrude Stein. The reference is topical: Stein had been on a triumphant lecture tour of the United States since 1934. She was the most famous literary figure of the moment, a celebrity whose dinner party remarks were reported in the gossip pages and whose talks drew audiences of hundreds of curious and eager listeners. Stein's literary signature, the repetitive and elliptical style popularized by the phrase "a rose is a rose is a rose," became the much-imitated subject of newspaper columnists and other writers around the country.[3] That Winternitz could joke that a document written in a foreign language struck him as "after the fashion of Gertrude Stein's poetry" reflected both the widespread popularity of Stein's work and the ways in which the deliberate obscurities of her style had come to figure a general idea of what a "new form of art" could be in 1930s America.

Whatever inexact resemblance brought together Stein's style and Chinese writing for Winternitz can be placed within the broader question of China's relation to Anglo-American modernism, a relation that owed much to the well-known work done by modernist poets to translate Chinese philosophy and poetry and to claim them for their own aesthetic and intellectual heritage; the publication of Ezra Pound's translations of Chinese poetry in *Cathay* in 1915 and of

[2] Those operations are the subject of a great deal of critical work. A classic example of the critique of the fetish of Chinese writing that also fetishizes Chinese writing is Jacques Derrida's *Of Grammatology*, but Derrida is already going back to G. W. Leibniz, whose dream of a pure language briefly and hopefully made Chinese its avatar. Rey Chow has a summary and critique of Derrida's claims about Chinese writing in chapter 2 of *The Protestant Ethnic & the Spirit of Capitalism* (New York, 2002). See also Haun Saussy, *Great Walls of Discourse and Other Adventures in Cultural China* (Cambridge, 2002).

[3] Following the surprise press conference convened as Stein's ship came into New York harbor on October 24, 1934, for instance, headlines in the New York papers included "Gerty Gerty Stein Stein Is Back Home Home Back," "Gertrude Stein Barges In With a Stein Song to Stein," and "Gertrude Stein, Stein is Back Back, and It's Still All Black, Black" (Janet Hobhouse, *Everybody Who Was Anybody: A Biography of Gertrude Stein* [New York, 1975], 177). A presentation at Princeton by Heather O'Donnell directed my attention to this habit. As for a specific Yale connection, on November 4, Stein attended the Yale–Dartmouth football game with Alfred Harcourt.

Amy Lowell's in the collections of imagist poetry published in the latter half of that decade suggested that modernism's difficult language and rejection of conventions of meter and rhyme owed something to the far East. By the time Winternitz could joke that a druggist's bill written in Chinese had appeared to be a new art form in Stein's distinctive style, the idea that some connection existed between China and new modes of writing deviating ever farther from common sense forms of reference and meaning had already been expressed by many of the modernists themselves. In this context, his joke about the resemblance between a Chinese druggist's bill and Stein-like art, however much it depended on a culturally distorted notion of the meaning of Chinese writing as "exquisite," makes a fairly reasonable connection.

That connection's value for understanding modernism has been the subject of much critical work in the last decade. Scholars like Robert Kern, Zhaoming Qian, and Steven G. Yao, among many others, have sought to grasp the consequences of the modernists' appeal to China for the meaning and history of modernism as a literary and cultural movement whose origins have conventionally been thought of as purely Western.[4] The fate of that critical work within the modernist studies has been mixed: evidence of China's importance to modernism's early history has only occasionally influenced narratives of modernism's origins in European industrialization, philosophy, and aesthetics. For someone interested in undermining the integrity of the national or supranational categories that tend to drive literary work, the slightness of this influence has been a bit frustrating. It suggests that too much scholarship on modernism remains caught in a monolingual, monocultural narrative in which the effect of a variety of transnational "outsides" can only be an interesting or informative sidelight to the real work of understanding what Anglo-American modernism of the early twentieth century was and what it can mean today.[5] As I will go on to suggest in the remainder of this

[4]Robert Kern, *Orientalism, Modernism, and the American Poem* (Cambridge, 1996); Zhaoming Qian, *Orientalism and Modernism: The Legacy of China in Pound and Williams* (Durham, N.C., 1995); Steven G. Yao, *Translation and the Languages of Modernism: Gender, Politics, Language* (New York, 2002). See also Mary Paterson Cheadle, *Ezra Pound's Confucian Translations* (Ann Arbor, 1997); Huang Guiyou, *Whitmanism, Imagism, and Modernism in China and America* (Cranbury, N.J., 1997); and Yunte Huang, *Transpacific Displacement: Ethnography, Translation, and Intertextual Travel in Twentieth-Century American Literature* (Berkeley, 2002).

[5]If I am being precise by adding adjectives to "modernism," it is because I am trying to avoid using "modernism" in general to mean "Anglo-American modernism between 1914 and 1922," or some other restricted phrase. This in order to resist the Anglocentrism of the standard narrative as it applies to geography, language, and time. Any discussion of a particular modernism is also, of course, a discussion of the meaning of modernism in general; though this is not the place explicitly to make the

chapter, the solution to nationally limited approaches to modernism is not to place some other nation at modernism's center but rather to recognize the limitations of originality, to see that the influences—even the apparently internal ones—on the development of such an aesthetic and cultural mode as modernism must be thought outside the boundaries of a single language, a single historical moment, or a single national formation.

More so than the other chapters of this book, then, this chapter intervenes in a local and specific critical field. It describes some features of the current state of scholarship in Anglo-American modernism and the critical habits I see there, and to elaborate a possible alternative to those habits. Because the crucial analytic turn within the broader discussion will rely on a single modernist perception of a Chinese relation to physical pain, the chapter takes its place in this book as an *example* (and not an elaboration) of the potential critical value of the historical work I have pursued so far. Remembering the attention I have given in previous chapters to the fact of mediatic or typological forms (anecdotes, books of types, medical case reports, science fictions), it seems worth saying that as example, this example will also serve as a figure for one of the book's most vital metacritical tasks, namely the expression of a methodology that can understand the historical and cultural work of China in the West outside of conventional notions of influence, authenticity, and origin.

1. What a Line Does

> Quickly, as if she were recalled by something over there, she turned to her canvas. There it was—her picture. Yes, with all its greens and blues, its lines running up and across, its attempt at something. It would be hung in the attics, she thought; it would be destroyed. But what did that matter? she asked herself, taking up her brush again. She looked at the steps; they were empty; she looked at her canvas; it was blurred. With a sudden intensity, as if she saw it clear for a second, she drew a line there, in the centre. It was

---

argument, my preference rests with a far more geographically and temporally open version of the general category, of the type elaborated in the recent work of Susan Stanford Friedman. See, for instance, her "Periodizing Modernism: Postcolonial Modernities and the Space/Time Borders of Modernist Studies," *Modernism/Modernity* 13.3 (Sept 2006). See also Eric Hayot, "Modernisms' Chinas: Introduction," *Modern Chinese Literature and Culture* 18.1 (Spring 2006).

> done; it was finished. Yes, she thought, laying down her brush in extreme fatigue, I have had my vision.[6]

The charm of imaginary art, like that of imaginary artists, lies in its unimaginability; whatever it does, however it produces and organizes an aesthetic world internal to the novelistic or poetic space in which it appears, in the end justifies itself directly in proportion to the audience's inability to evaluate it on terms other than its own. Lily Briscoe finds her central line, draws it, declares her canvas done, her vision had: the novel ends. The conjunction of that metafictional ending and Lily's line guarantees, more than any mental picture of her painting, the authority and legitimacy of her judgment. And the vectoring together of these two separate worlds—one the coastal Britain of Virginia Woolf's *To the Lighthouse*, the other the landscape of a particular reading—invites just like any metafiction a consideration of their interaction as ideas, a productive, pleasant confusion between the "I" and the "vision" that belong properly to Lily in one context but might, in another, be said to be properties of VirginiaWoolf, whose vision also announces its closure in the blankness of the page below these, the final lines of Woolf's novel. Whatever aesthetic is articulated here doubles itself in the coincidence of closure, referring to Lily's world and to Woolf's all at once.

The coincidences that produce an immediately compelling connection between Lily Briscoe and Virginia Woolf have made Lily a central figure in the history of Bloomsbury modernism. Two recent books in modernist studies reinforce such a reading, testifying to the generative force of Woolf's novel and to the ongoing struggle to define and understand modernism, a literary movement that has seemed in recent years to approach the present more and more closely instead of receding, as it should, into its proper historical moment.

Both books—Anne Banfield's *The Phantom Table*, and Patricia Laurence's *Lily Briscoe's Chinese Eyes*—attempt through historical and cultural analysis of Woolf and her circle to describe the origin of modernist style and to find explanations for the monumental formal shifts that defined the movement.[7] The origins they find are, however, quite different, and it is their difference I wish to explore in this

[6]Virginia Woolf, *To the Lighthouse* (San Diego, 1981), 207; further references in the text are cited as *TTL*.

[7]Anne Banfield, *The Phantom Table: Woolf, Fry, Russell, and the Epistemology of Modernism* (Cambridge, 2000); further references in the text are cited as *PT*; Patricia Laurence, *Lily Briscoe's Chinese Eyes: Bloomsbury, Modernism, and China* (Columbia, S.C., 2003); further references in the text are cited as *LB*.

chapter, with a sense that it expresses something about the current shape of modernist studies. In what follows, I begin by reviewing the argument of both books, showing how each of them manages to put similar textual facts to radically dissimilar uses. This review leads to a sticking point, a moment at which the difference in the historical claims about Bloomsbury's origins separate the two analyses. At that moment, the chapter will diverge, producing a close reading of the life of one major Bloomsbury figure, Bertrand Russell. That Russell happened to observe, in 1922, that one of the major faults of the Chinese people was their callous disregard of the suffering of others will allow the major themes of the book to coincide with the discussion of modernism. This conjunction will generate not only a new reading of the "origins" of one important strain of Anglo-American modernism but also a way of thinking modernism comparatively—as simultaneously inside and outside an internationalist frame that includes China, sympathy, and the literary experience of a total planetary indifference to human pain.

Banfield's *The Phantom Table* borrows its title from Andrew Ramsay's explanation to Lily about what kind of philosophy his father does: "Subject and object and the nature of reality," he says. "Think of a kitchen table . . . when you're not there" (*PT*, 23).[8] That Mr. Ramsay is a philosopher of the unseen kitchen table is not, Banfield argues, a coincidence. Rather, this fact places Mr. Ramsay (and, by extension, Lily, Mrs. Ramsay, all of *To the Lighthouse*) squarely within the frame of the most important currents in English philosophical thought of the late nineteenth and early twentieth centuries. The major figures discussed are Woolf's father, Leslie Stephen; the Cambridge philosophers G. E. Moore, Russell, and Ludwig Wittgenstein; and the aesthetic theorist Roger Fry, each of whom played a major role in creating an atmosphere in which Woolf and the rest of Bloomsbury could move from the problem of a kitchen table to a broad theory of subjects, objects, and sensations.

Among the philosophers, it was Russell, Banfield argues, who exerted the greatest influence on Bloomsbury's modernism; though other studies have relegated him to the sidelines and given pride of place to Wittgenstein, *The Phantom Table* shows that Bloomsbury cannot be thought seriously without Russell's work.[9] The core of Russell's Realism, Banfield argues, lies in his theory of

[8] Lily Briscoe refers to a "phantom kitchen table" later on that same page.

[9] Ludwig Wittgenstein's reception today surely has a great deal to do with the degree to which his writing functions so well alongside poststructuralist theory; Marjorie Perloff's claim that such readings

"sensibilia," his name for sense-data unperceived by any particular subject. "In Russell's conception, in some sense the private world is already there, like an empty room or chair, to receive the subject and in that sense independent of it, imposing a skeletal framework on his point of view" (*PT,* 73). When a person walks into a room and stands between two other people already there, Russell wrote, "a third world, intermediate between the two previous worlds, begins to be perceived" (*PT,* 73). The subject is thus at the center of a "here" and a "now," but any given center or perspective is subjectively neutral, simply an effect of relations in space and the potential reception of sense-data. The result, Banfield says, "is a theory of knowledge with at its center the strange notion of a subjectless subjectivity," a subject more like a photographic plate than a "person" (*PT,* 70).

Whether or not such a theory accurately describes the world is not the point; Banfield aims instead to explain a particular theory of knowledge and demonstrate its relation to modernism. "The debate about modernism stands in need of a new formulation," she writes, "which takes into account its revolutionary conception of the objects of sensation, at once physical and subjective" (xi). This is where Woolf comes in. Banfield's argument is not simply that Woolf wrote *about* this new conception of objects (in which case, the mention of a phantom table would do the trick), but rather that she wrote *through* it, that her fictions not only refer to a Russellian epistemology, but articulate it, manipulate it, and revise it. Russell's "here" and "now" become, for instance, Woolf's well-known "moment," a local time "not simply equivalent to the present" (*PT,* 118). Grasped as the center from which perception recedes to a misty circumference, the Woolfian moment makes the here-ness and now-ness of the present explicit, holding it still in a collocation not yet subjected to time or memory. When no human subject exists to observe the moment, as in the second section of *To the Lighthouse,* "Time Passes," the novel's "nows" lose their connection to public time, so that the "nights *now* are full of wind and destruction," and

require significant distortions is compelling but outside the scope of this chapter (see *Wittgenstein's Ladder: Poetic Language and the Strangeness of the Ordinary* [Chicago, 1996], 11–15 passim.). Banfield argues that, at least as far as Bloomsbury is concerned, Wittgenstein's arrival in Cambridge (and especially his work after the *Tractatus)* comes too late to be significant in the rethinking of subject-object relations: "We can thus take the rise of Wittgenstein's influence as a kind of cut-off point for the philosophical background of Bloomsbury" (*PT,* 9). Later, Banfield writes that it "would not be necessary to insist on Russell's importance if the subsequent course of British philosophy, marked by the influence of the later Wittgenstein and relegating Russell's epistemology to the philosophical past, did not minimize it" (41).

"*Now,* day after day, light turned," and someone asks, "What power could *now* prevent the fertility, the insensibility of nature?" (*TTL,* 128, 129, 138; emphases mine). In each case, the "now" indicates the possibility of a perspective unmoored from a subject; the fact that these perspectives can be described means that they in some vital way *exist.* They guarantee the real, and in a godless universe that fact forces a confrontation with the limitations of the subject, with the end of life.

All this leads, in the second half of *The Phantom Table,* to a rethinking of Woolf's aesthetics, worked through Cambridge epistemology and Roger Fry on Cézanne. It is here that Lily Briscoe assumes a major importance, her painting figuring not only the opening onto a Russellian theory of the world but also, by novel's end, a major revision of that theory that privileges aesthetic form over the immediate experience of sense-data. In the novel's first section, Banfield remarks, Lily "begins in the Impressionist manner," facing the Ramsays' house and painting some version of what she sees (*PT,* 288). Though, as she tells William Bankes, the picture "is not of them," that the mother and child she paints might become instead a patch of color, the picture nonetheless depends on the here and now of its painting, and it registers the sense-data of its moment: Russell, more or less unreconstructed (42). But in the novel's third section, with Mrs. Ramsay dead and Mr. Ramsay and the others off to the lighthouse at last, Lily paints her picture from memory. Her "solution is the 'discovery' in the accidental arrangement [of] a form," says Banfield (289); as someone comes into the drawing room, sits down, and casts "an odd-shaped triangular shadow over the step," Lily subordinates representational imagination to geometric figure, sense-data to structure (201). "Lily's completed painting is a Post-Impressionist one" (Banfield, 289).

Banfield's conclusion is worth reviewing in full

> So Mr. Ramsay's logical philosophy, found wanting in "The Window" [the novel's first section], becomes the philosophical "backbone" of Woolf's artist's art. "If I were painting myself I should have to find some—rod, shall I say—something that would stand for the conception," Woolf writes; "one is living all the time in relation to certain background rods or conceptions," she continues. Lily's painting, unable to bring back the living Mrs. Ramsay, attempts no "pale reflex"; it "transforms" the vision of which she was part, uniting lighthouse and window by applying . . . the aesthetic of the central division to *To the Lighthouse*'s own composition. (289)

Crucial to the composition of the picture (which doubles for Banfield, as it does in the novel, for the compositional practice of the novel itself), is Lily's central line, the line Thomas Matro calls "a literal version of the 'central line' that Fry uses in *Vision and Design* to explain his aesthetic" (*PT,* 286). For Banfield, Lily's "vision" functions not as a single viewpoint, but as a series of moments, a "vision composed of fragments, yet ultimately achieving a strange, contingent unity—contingent on the very having occurredness of these moments, shaped by an uncompromising refusal to turn away from the consequences of this series of givens which constitute a life, a history, a novel" (*PT,* 388). The vision is, then, not only an arrangement of moments but also a mode of resistance. What it resists is, perhaps, what has made Woolf's modernism less compelling to some than that of Eliot or Pound, namely the production of reality as a mode of (ideological, religious, sexual) desire.[10] Like Cézanne's "eyeless vision of plastic color," made into a figure for the age by Roger Fry, Lily's painting is a geometric apprehension of a collection of possible (not necessarily human) perspectives. They are "given," as Banfield suggests (388). But they are not given to anyone in particular.

"Eyeless": In *The Phantom Table,* the word first appears in reference to Cézanne and post-Impressionism (258), is later opposed to "common-sense" vision (266), at one point describes the "world of logical forms in whose net the empirical is caught" (363), before coming to rest on the final page in the "vision of plastic color" given by Cézanne. By then, it has become a figure for the imaginary English painter as much as for the real French one; Lily's eyeless vision of the central line closes out her painting, the novel, and Banfield's book. Lily does, of course, have eyes, but because the quest to "describe the world seen without a self" aims to produce a vision unbeholden to any single subject's vision, those eyes must, in the aesthetic produced by the intersection of Russell and Bloomsbury, subordinate themselves to the possibility of their own nonexistence.[11]

What should one make, then, of the fact that Lily's eyes are described in the novel, five times, as *Chinese?* "Lily's picture! Mrs. Ramsay smiled. With her little Chinese eyes and her puckered-up face, she would never marry; one could not take her painting very seriously" (*TTL,* 17); "'And now,' she said, thinking that Lily's charm was her Chinese eyes, aslant in her white, puckered little face, but it

[10]Banfield: "The Bloomsbury aesthetic is like other modern aesthetics in its religious reference, although without the reference to institutionalized belief, as with Joyce or Eliot. . . . What remained of a religion emptied of belief was the emotion" (359).

[11]The world seen without a self" is voiced by Woolf at the end of *The Waves,* and cited by Banfield as the invocation for the "project of a language of sensibilia" (297).

would take a clever man to see it" (*TTL*, 26); "But, she thought, screwing up her Chinese eyes . . . " (*TTL*, 91); "in her little grey dress with her little puckered face and her little Chinese eyes" (*TTL*, 104); "she stood screwing up her little Chinese eyes in her small puckered face" (*TTL*, 157).[12]

This is where Patricia Laurence comes in. *Lily Briscoe's Chinese Eyes* produces an archaeology of Lily's vision that locates its origins not in Russellian epistemology, but in the intellectual, aesthetic, and personal contacts between Bloomsbury and China. These range from Julian Bell's visit to China in 1935 to a series of relationships between figures marginal or central to Bloomsbury and Chinese intellectuals and writers (E.M. Forster with Xiao Qian, G.L. Dickinson and Fry with Xu Zhimo, and the sixteen-month correspondence between Woolf and Ling Shuhua);[13] they include also the general aesthetic availability of Chinese art (the subject of essays and lectures by Fry) and Chinese kitsch (in the catalogs of the Liberty department stores); translations of Chinese poetry by Arthur Waley, Pound, and others; and the journalistic coverage of the Boxer Rebellion (1895–1900) and the fall of the Qing dynasty (1911).

The circumstantial case is, then, compelling; hard to imagine that the word "Chinese," as Woolf applies it to Lily's eyes in *To the Lighthouse*, did not signal more than just a physical shape. For Laurence, the Chinese eyes are a synecdoche for an entire ethos of investigation, of cross-cultural influence, and of literary hybridity explicitly differentiated from a pernicious Orientalism:

> Lily's "Chinese eyes" suggest not the Empire's foraging glance toward the distant lands of China and India for trade and gain, but the new aesthetic voyaging in the East during the modernist period. . . . Lily's embodiment of "Chinese eyes"—Woolf's brilliant cultural, political, and aesthetic

[12]It is worth noting that three of these references make Mrs. Ramsay the source for the characterization (in free indirect discourse on p. 17, direct psycho-narration on p. 26; the description on p. 104 is also part of a long piece of free indirect discourse). The other two (on pp. 91 and 157) both appear in sections that feature free indirect discourse through Lily herself; only in the first of the two is Mrs. Ramsay diegetically present to focalize the observation. In part three of the novel, Lily's eyes are never referred to as Chinese; by then, Mrs. Ramsay is dead. The care with which the adjective "Chinese" is distributed ought to make readers equally careful about ascribing the adjective to Woolf or pressing too hard on its meaning. The amount of narrative and philosophic pressure put on Lily's eyes throughout the novel, however, makes an account of their "Chinese" character necessary.

[13]Julian Bell, Woolf's nephew, had an affair with Ling Shuhua during his time in China. The affair is discussed extensively in Laurence's book; it is also the subject of a novelized account by Hong Ying, who has been sued for defamation by Ling's descendants. For a reading of the Ling-Woolf correspondence within the optic of Orientalism and feminism, see Shu-mei Shih, *The Lure of the Modern: Writing Modernism in Semicolonial China, 1917–1937* (Berkeley, 2001), 215–21.

> stroke—suggests . . . not only the incorporation of the Chinese aesthetic into the 'English' artist, but also European modernism's, and now, our own questioning of our cultural and aesthetic place or "universality." (10)[14]

This is, in any case, the project. As ambitious as Banfield in her attempt to revise some of the core features of our contemporary understanding of modernism, Laurence aims to transform a single or local modernism into "interrupted modernisms, multiple modernisms, migratory modernisms, or an evolving international modernism" (359).

Just as Banfield reads Lily's central line within the context of a Russell-influenced post-Impressionism, Laurence reads the line as an extension of Bloomsbury's experience of China. The Chinese, Laurence argues, "have been preoccupied with the calligraphic line in painting for centuries" (352).[15] For Woolf, Laurence says, the Chinese emphasis on "line" (at the expense of, say, perspectival verisimilitude) must have signified as a mark of geometric abstraction, a uniting of artistic practice (the fingers on the brush, the wrist just so) and aesthetic form. And so, in the last lines of *To the Lighthouse,* as Lily has had her vision, "the relationships," Laurence writes, "are suddenly clear in the placement of this line. Woolf's unwitting vocabulary of 'rhythm,' 'line,' 'stroke,' and 'pause' to describe Lily's process and her own not only captures modernism but also Chinese traces: the lines and strokes of the calligraphic brush that creates a

[14] The distinction between Empire's "foraging glance" and a "new aesthetic voyaging" that is presumably less imperialist aims to absolve Woolf of the potential association with Orientalism. But to believe that Orientalism requires an explicitly "foraging" epistemological form requires a profound misunderstanding of the nature of Orientalism, which is a mode of writing and knowing that does not need explicitly to imagine itself as connected to the imperial project. As an *ideological* form Orientalism must be understood as more than simply a kind of "taking sides" for or against imperialism. It is the cultural structure within which knowledge emerged during a specific historical period and within a limited geographic and cultural framework (which was itself internally complex on the question of "sides" and of cross-cultural influence).

[15] Whether anyone can really say that as large a group of people as the Chinese (over centuries) has been singly preoccupied with a single feature of the aesthetic, whether the word "line" here manages to denote simultaneously something culturally Chinese and something culturally English, what the terms of a "preoccupation" would be, are all important questions and go to the heart of the longstanding debate (or "problem," as far as the West is concerned) around the issue of (a) Chinese aesthetic(s) (The first question being, is there one? And the second being, is there more than one?). Comparison with a sentence like "the Europeans have been preoccupied with representational perspective in painting for centuries" shows how Laurence's characterization might be simultaneously vaguely right but wrong in many of its particulars. For more on the debate around China and aesthetics, see Haun Saussy, *The Problem of a Chinese Aesthetic* (Stanford, 1993), and Zhang Longxi, *Allegoresis: Reading Canonical Literature East and West* (Ithaca, N.Y., 2005).

continuum from words to paintings" (*LB*, 387).[16] The coincidences between terms like "rhythm" and "line" and the ones writers and critics like Fry were using to describe Chinese paintings or describe Chinese aesthetic values suggest almost inexorably, at the end of a few hundred pages of literary history and archival research, that something "Chinese" is happening here.[17]

The difficulty of figuring out what that "Chinese" thing is, or how Chinese it might be—even whether one ought, as some critics have suggested, to rethink the entire apparatus of Anglo-American modernism through the Chinese lens[18]—can be measured by the ease with which the words that justify Laurence's reading of Lily's line appear in Banfield's *The Phantom Table* as symptoms of a completely different explanation:

> The same mathematical knowledge which sustains Mrs. Ramsay undergirds Lily's painting, whose "*pauses*" and "*strokes*" formed a "*rhythmical* movement": "all were related"; "she scored her canvas with brown running nervous lines which had no sooner settled there than they enclosed . . . a space." . . . Lily's solution—"something to the right, something to the left, and the whole is held together"—again resembles Russell's "observed complex fact," where "this patch of red is to the left of that patch of blue." (*PT*, 286; emphases mine)

In this example, the critical method, as in Laurence, depends on extensive (and convincing) citational juxtaposition undergirded by the historical fact of physical or literary contact; reading Woolf after Banfield, one feels quite simply that something Russellian is happening here.

How Russellian, how Cambridge-philosophical, post-Impressionist; how Chinese? At one point in *Lily Briscoe's Chinese Eyes* Laurence writes, "What the West

[16]What Laurence means by "unwitting" is, I think, one of the crucial questions here: it seems to mark the limits of her scholarship, which cannot directly prove what Woolf was thinking as she wrote of Lily's rhythms and pauses.

[17]Woolf, Laurence notes, assigned "Chinese eyes" to at least two other people: Mrs. Dalloway's daughter, Elizabeth, and John Donne (*LB*, 346). In those cases, the "something" that happens is, it is fair to say, less clear, probably because neither figure in Woolf's work goes on to articulate what are taken to be Woolf's own aesthetic principles and values.

[18]Zhaoming Qian, for instance, makes this argument at length in *Orientalism and Modernism* and elsewhere.

learns then from the Chinese 'codes' of perception and aesthetics is the dissolution of the boundary between the visual and verbal and the subject and the object" (384). But what one might say in response to Laurence is that there is at least one other major competing explanation for how Bloomsbury learns about the "dissolution of the boundary between the visual and the verbal and the subject and the object," namely Banfield's. The encounter between these two books, Banfield's on one hand and Laurence's on the other, presents scholars of Bloomsbury modernism with two quite different, and differently compelling, derivations of modernist aesthetics.

The confrontation between these two books stages one of the more interesting divides in contemporary scholarship on modernism, namely the one between a philosophical, epistemological approach and a cultural, internationalist one. It is not remarkable that *The Phantom Table*, for which Lily's eyes constitute such a major trope, makes no hay of the fact that Mrs. Ramsay describes them as Chinese; no more remarkable, that is, than that Laurence deals only cursorily with the entire apparatus of Cambridge philosophy, despite her interest in the Chinese modifications of Western aesthetic subjectivity. What we've got here is, as the prison boss said, a failure to communicate. The immediate solution is presumably for more people to read both books. But the real issue has to do with the nature of Anglo-American modernism itself, or rather the contemporary critical sense of its nature: Is it, following Banfield, an aesthetic movement primarily defined by a new philosophical experience of the "objects of sensation," a line connected most immediately in the modernist moment to figures like Henri Bergson, the Cambridge philosophers, and the phenomenologies of Edmund Husserl and others?[19] Or is it, instead, the product of a quasi-postcolonial shift in geopolitical experience, a turn Eastward or Southward (or inward to Easts and Souths already present in the West) in search of modes of resistance to industrial capitalism or a tired Romanticism, fired in the crucible of its

[19] A critical tradition that ends with *The Phantom Table* easily includes such recent works as Sanford Schwartz's *The Matrix of Modernism* (Princeton, N.J., 1985), Jon Erickson's *The Fate of the Object* (Ann Arbor, 1995), and Douglas Mao's *Solid Objects: Modernism and the Test of Production* (Princeton, N.J., 1998). As I understand this trajectory, it differs in important ways from the recent emphasis in literary and cultural criticism on material culture, perhaps best embodied on the literary side by Bill Brown's work on "things" (see for instance "Thing Theory," *Critical Inquiry* 28 [2001].). Where the subject-object line depends for its weight on philosophy, work in material culture grounds itself in the comparative lightness of the physical artifact. For a take on Chinese material culture in the context of British modernism see Judith Green, "'A New Orientation of Ideas': Collecting and the Taste for Early Chinese Ceramics in England 1921–36" in *Collecting Chinese Art: Interpretation and Display*, ed. Stacey Pierson (London, 2000).

frequent recourse to translation, primitivism, and appropriation?[20] There is of course no need to decide between these two Anglo-American modernisms (or to imagine that they are the only two available), but the limitations of what any one person can study make it difficult for scholarship to consider modernism's philosophical heritage and its intercultural, translational one without privileging one of them over the other, usually by assigning one of them a prior existence in which the other merely intervenes.[21]

Lily Briscoe's central line can in the right hands bend toward modernisms both philosophical and Chinese. The trajectory that links Lily's painting to the novel, her character to Woolf's, her aesthetic to Fry's, and her epistemology to modernism's, unites an enormous amount of intellectual material. Only in the assignment of all that material to a single origin, the move to Cambridge or the move to China, does the line divide, separating two modernisms and two trends in modernist scholarship. This dilemma can be resolved not by choosing one track over the other but by abandoning the singularly original structure that any such choice requires.

The scholarly divide illustrated by the differences between these two books is not simply an issue for scholars of Anglo-American literature. What is at stake is nothing less than the question of modernism itself, of the possibility of thinking modernism globally or internationally, without conceiving of modernism as something that spreads across the world from a single European origin (Eliot's *Waste Land,* Flaubert's *Madame Bovary,* Joyce's *Ulysses*) to a variety of other countries, which in turn produce local modernisms defined by a combination of their imitation of the aesthetic or philosophical principles of modernism "proper" and the local conditions under which they appeared. Such a theory of modernism will never be able to open itself to the possibility that modernism

[20] *Lily Briscoe's Chinese Eyes* in such a context bookends a tradition whose recent work includes Marianna Torgovnick's *Gone Primitive: Savage Intellects, Modern Lives* (Chicago, 1990), Michael North's *The Dialect of Modernism: Race, Language, and Twentieth-Century Literature* (New York, 1994), and, in the Chinese context, the work of Robert Kern and Steven G. Yao.

[21] In the American context, the epistemological and cultural explanations for modernism have an easier time coming together, most visibly in the Harlem Renaissance or, closer to home in this context, the Imagist movement, which explicitly marketed itself as a new mode of perception (and hence a model for a new relation between subjects and objects), at least initially, through the examples of Greek (in the case of H.D.) and Chinese (Ezra Pound, Amy Lowell). What this suggests is that the "modernism" Banfield and Laurence wish to revise may *already* be local, particular, and therefore in some sense "international" (that is, it is British modernism at stake here, Bloomsbury modernism most specifically); what we have may not be a problem in the scholarship of modernism but a problem in the scholarship of modernisms.

could not only be *imitated* but *defined* by these transformations and, thus, will remain trapped in a chauvinism that is both Eurocentric and temporally limited (Eurocentric *because* temporally limited). In such a schema, the emergence of a "Chinese" modernism (or a Japanese, Hungarian, or Latin American one) can only be understood as the belated (and often diluted) expression of the authentic original.

It seems to me that two possible directions will allow us to escape the trap of mapping the great historical canard of capitalist progress (in which the rest of the world is simply a primitive and undeveloped version of the West) onto literary history. First, it ought to be possible to do work that suggests that at the so-called origin of European modernism, the foreign has already inserted itself: that is, in other words, that what has been for a long time conceived of as an aesthetic movement whose concerns were purely European can be shown to have at its core features that draw from other cultures. The impact of African art on Picasso and other modernist artists is well known. Here the project is to turn the fact of cross-cultural influence (from South to North, and East to West) into a kind of "common sense" of modernist studies globally. Second, it ought to be possible to reconceive a definition of modernism itself that would not simply generalize the traits of the two or three "original" modernist texts of the early twentieth century, but would consider the entire global cultural output that has occurred under the name "modernism," which would permit an understanding of "modernism" from a much larger historical and cultural perspective. In such a schema, the various "other" national modernisms would find a place not as derivative products of an origin but rather as full partners in a literary movement that *continues to evolve.* It may turn out that when the great history of modernism is written its most "central" works will not turn out to be those of its apparent European origins but those of its strongest and most compelling moments elsewhere; it is possible, for instance, to consider much of the avant-garde performance and visual art being produced in China and elsewhere today as an ongoing testimony to the relevance of modernist "values" largely conceived.

The point, then, would be that all modernism is partly local, partly defined by local characteristics and local histories. But also that the local is in turn defined by a relation to the global—in fact you can't know what the "local" is except in relation to some global world that the local is not. The "local" makes itself local through a *relation to* travel, trade, and cultural flow, just like the global does; it's simply a different relation. Everyone knows this, and yet when it comes to modernist scholarship in Anglo-American studies, such a perspective is too frequently forgotten, or, when it is remembered, it is remembered at the expense of philosophy, as though cultural particularity and philosophy were mutually exclusive. I have suggested that what divides Banfield from Laurence is precisely this difference: that Banfield's book cannot attend well to the cultural and international possibilities latent in Woolf's work and that Laurence cannot attend well to the philosophical ones. What is needed is a kind of double vision. This chapter attempts to provide one, illustrating the general principles contained in these last few paragraphs by way of an intense attention to and close rereading of the philosophical and literary material that Banfield and Laurence address.

2. Bertrand Russell's Chinese Eyes

Imagine a novel. Its hero is the philosopher Bertrand Russell. In the time the novel is written, everyone has heard of him; with Einstein, he may be the most famous intellectual in the world.

The novel begins in 1920, with a trip Russell makes to Russia, a trip he expects to allow him a richer sense of the limitations of industrial capitalism; the Bolsheviks, he feels, will offer a serious alternative to the economic and political models of the West.

Instead, Russia turns out to be a "continually increasing nightmare."[22] In addition to a growing sense that "the average working man feels himself the slave of the Government," as Russell writes in a book he publishes later that year, the trip is marred by an unpleasant, difficult boat trip down the River Volga, during which his friend Clifford Allen becomes extremely sick.[23] Russell notes the event in his journal:

> One of us lies at death's door, fighting a grim battle with weakness and terror and the indifference of the strong, assailed day and night by the sounds of loud-voiced love-making and trivial laughter. And all around us lies a great silence, strong as Death, unfathomable as the heavens. It seems that none have leisure to hear the silence, yet it calls to me so insistently

[22] Bertrand Russell, *The Autobiography of Bertrand Russell: 1914–1944*, vol. 2 (Boston, 1968), 141.

[23] Bertrand Russell, *The Problem of China* (New York, 1922), 60. Further references in the text are cited as *PC*.

that I grow deaf to the harangues of propagandists and the endless information of the well-informed.[24]

The silence "strong as Death" that Russell hears connects him to a world beyond politics. As he listens, called to silence by the illness of his friend and the indifference of the loud-voiced around them, he grows "deaf" to the Bolshevik propaganda he has come to Russia to hear. A year later, Russell will write that it "was on the Volga, in the summer of 1920, that I first realized how profound is the disease in our Western mentality, which the Bolsheviks are attempting to force on an essentially Asiatic population, just as Japan and the West are doing in China" (*PC*, 12).

Readers of this imaginary novel will begin to recognize, in the appearance of the metaphor of "disease" in this last sentence, sustained by the reference to the Volga, Allen's actual sickness and the great figural silence of Death it calls forth, a leakage between the body and the body politic, the insistent drip of a metaphor of illness and health, in Russell's language. Years later his biographer Ray Monk will write: "It was as if, travelling through the vast Russian countryside on a steamboat along the Volga, he underwent another conversion experience, another sudden realisation, this time of the sickness of Western civilization" (*BR*, 581).

The metaphor of illness and disease will return throughout Russell's descriptions of China. There, in late 1920, he seems determined to resist this violence, this disease, on behalf of the Chinese. In early letters home, he describes Europeans he sees as though they were "carriers of some deadly affliction" (*BR*, 593). The ones he sees in Shanghai "almost all look villainous and ill"; in Changsha, he says, "The Europeans have a few factories, a few banks, a few missions and a hospital—the whole gamut of damaging and repairing body and soul by western methods."[25] And, in a letter he pens to an American businessman, Russell connects Western capitalism to a willful and deliberate violence and indifference to the pain of others: "comfortable plutocrats of other countries consider every inhabitant of a communist country deserving of death by slow torture. When operations have to be performed, it is impossible to obtain anaesthetics, because capitalists are of the opinion that the anguish endured is deserved by those who

[24] Ray Monk, *Bertrand Russell: The Spirit of Solitude* (London, 1996), 580. Further references in the text are cited as *BR*.

[25] Russell, *Autobiography*, 197, 199. These two citations appear together in Monk's description of Russell's trip, contextualized there as here in terms of a larger metaphor of disease and illness (*BR*, 592–93). Monk foregrounds that metaphor throughout his descriptions of Russell's trips to Russia and China, and I am grateful to him for calling my attention to it in Russell's language and work.

threaten to make them less rich."[26] The visit to China thus takes place under the shadow of disease and illness, metaphorical and actual.

But Russell may have found in China a cure for the those fatal afflictions: "Apart from the influence of Europeans," he writes, "China makes the impression of what Europe would have become if the eighteenth century had gone on till now without industrialism or the French revolution."[27] No industrialization, no French revolution: here the facts of an other history provide—relying, of course, on the old story of Chinese historical stasis—an "Asiatic" alternative to the "Western mentality" being imposed globally by Europe, Japan, and the Bolsheviks.

In the throes of this discovery, much Chinese violence can be forgiven. Writing to a friend in February 1921, our hero says:

> I have no home on this planet—China comes nearer to one than any other place I know, because the people are not ferocious. It is true that the soldiers occasionally run amok,[28] sack a town and bayonet all who do not instantly deliver up their whole wealth. But this is such a trivial matter compared to what is done by "civilized" nations that it seems not to count. 20 million people are starving in the provinces near here, and the Chinese do nothing to relieve them. But they are better than we are, because the famine is not caused deliberately by them, whereas we deliberately cause famines for the pleasure of gloating over dying children.[29]

[26] Bertrand Russell, *The Selected Letters of Bertrand Russell: The Public Years, 1914–1970*, ed. Nicholas Griffin, (London, 2001), 220–21.

[27] Russell, *Autobiography*, 199.

[28] The etymology of the word "amok" gives this complaint a strange twist: first found in English as a translation of the Portuguese *amouco*, it originates in the Malay word *amoq*, meaning "engaging furiously in battle, attacking with desperate resolution, rushing in a state of frenzy to the commission of indiscriminate murder . . . Applied to any animal in a state of vicious rage" (*Oxford English Dictionary*, amok, a. and adv.). The term's return East to describe Chinese soldiers offers another example of the recursive nature of the history of Western imperialism, as the word borrowed from Malay to describe what seemed to Westerners a particular cultural type of behavior (from the *Voyages* of Captain Cook: "To run amock is to get drunk with opium . . . to sally forth from the house, kill the person or persons supposed to have injured the Amock, and any other person that attempts to impede his passage") makes its way to Portuguese, then English and England, and then back to China to describe behavior which it therefore implicitly identifies as "Asian." The *OED* gives another instantiation of this recursiveness, turned to quite a different cultural valence, from Thoreau's *Walden*: "I might have run 'amok' against society, but I preferred that society should run 'amok' against me." I first heard about the etymology of "amok" from Paul Kramer, who spoke of it while giving a paper at Cornell University in summer 2003. But see also Sanjay Krishnan, "Reading Globalization from the Margin: The Case of Abdullah Munshi," *Representations* 99 (Summer 2007).

[29] Russell, *Selected Letters*, 223–24.

Readers familiar with the history of the West's Chinese dreamers will hear in this apologia echoes of Matteo Ricci, Edgar Snow, or Philippe Sollers. The novelist, they will say, has done some homework.

But the story cannot go on forever like this. A few weeks after writing that letter, our hero will become sick; feverish, delirious, he almost dies. So it is that the metaphor of disease and illness Russell carries with him to China becomes realized in his own body. He does not, in the middle of the illness or afterward, following a long and strenuous recovery, recognize the irony. It nonetheless produces a temporary change in his opinion of China. Writing to a friend in June, he says: "This place seems cruel to Europeans. When one is robust it is full of charm, but in bad health it is terrifying." And his partner Dora Black, in a letter to her mother, reports that "People here are horribly callous about relief. They leave their neighbours severely alone, even when they are dying... [They] just remain placidly indifferent" (*BR*, 602).

The tables, as they say, have turned. And in the last days of our hero's convalescence, Dora, who has cared for him all through his illness, visits her doctor to inquire about the fact that she has missed her period. Diagnosis: pregnancy. The child Russell has longed for will finally be his. The couple pack their bags and head back to England. Life usurps death, the West replaces China, the dream is over.

But we are not quite done with the story; or rather, there is an afterword.[30] At home, Russell writes a book, *The Problem of China*. It is full of praise for Chinese history, its culture, its intellectual integrity. "[O]n the balance, I think the

[30] Things are even more complicated in fact than in my imaginary novel. In late March, having gotten wind of Russell's illness, a newspaper in Japan reported that he had died. The news spread quickly around the world, producing emotional reactions ranging from sadness to disbelief; on the latter front Monk reports that Russell's brother Frank told English journalists that "dying in Peking... was not the sort of thing his brother would do without letting him know" (600). One missionary paper, remembering Russell's vitriolic critiques of organized religion, noted the event with a single sentence: "Missionaries may be pardoned for heaving a sigh of relief at the news of Mr. Bertrand Russell's death," an anecdote Russell recounts with some pleasure in his *Autobiography*: "I fear they would have heaved a sigh of a different sort when they found that I was not dead after all" (vol. 2, 189). Indeed, he seems to have gotten a great deal of pleasure from the misunderstanding. In a letter to Ottoline Morrell in May, he wrote:

> "I have realized one ambition which I almost despaired of, I have read an obituary notice of myself. In Japan I was reported dead, and the *Japan Chronicle* had a long article on me. My illness has not changed me in the slightest, in fact it has made hardly more impression than a bad toothache. I have missed much by not dying here, as the Chinese were going to have given me a terrific funeral in Central Park, and then buried me in an island in the Western

Chinese one of the best nations I have come across, and am prepared to draw up a graver indictment against every one of the great powers" (220). Nonetheless its author will with reluctance offer a list of three Chinese "defects": avarice, cowardice, and callousness.[31]

On the subject of callousness, Russell has this to say: "Famines in China can be permanently cured only by better methods of agriculture combined with emigration or birth-control on a large scale. Educated Chinese realize this, and it makes them indifferent to efforts to keep the present victims alive. A great deal of Chinese callousness has a similar explanation, and is due to perception of the vastness of the problems involved" (221–22). So far so good; echoes of the letter from February 1921. The text continues:

> But there remains a residue which cannot be so explained. If a dog is run over by an automobile and seriously hurt, nine out of ten passers-by will stop to laugh at the poor brute's howls. The spectacle of suffering does not of itself rouse any sympathetic pain in the average Chinaman; in fact, he seems to find it mildly agreeable.[32] Their history, and their penal code before the revolution of 1911, show that they are by no means destitute of the impulse of active cruelty; but of this I did not myself come across any instances. And it must be said that active cruelty is practised by all the great nations, to an extent concealed from us only by our hypocrisy. (221–22)

It is important to understand the context within which Russell locates the "residue" of Chinese callousness. On the one side, he attributes as much as possible of what might *appear* to Westerners to be callousness to the distribution of arable land and population; the indifference of the Chinese intelligentsia to structural famine, he argues, must be grasped as a function of an inability to solve

---

> Lake, where the greatest poets and emperors lived, died, and were buried. Probably I should have become a God. What an opportunity missed!"

(*Selected Letters*, 226).

[31] The request for such a list comes, crucially, from an "eminent Chinese writer." As Lydia Liu has suggested, the narration of this fact consolidates "the author's own knowledge about the other even as the subjectivity of the anonymous other is consumed in the process of appropriation" (*Translingual Practice: Literature, National Culture, and Translated Modernity in China, 1900–1937* [Stanford, 1995], 46.). Liu follows this observation with an extensive discussion of the history of Russell's *Problem of China* as it was received in China. Shu-mei Shih also discusses this moment in Russell in *The Lure of the Modern* (23–24).

[32] Interesting to consider this in light of the American missionary's reaction to reports of Russell's death, which the missionary seems to have found mildly agreeable (see n.30).

the problems that underlie it. And on the other side, Russell distinguishes this "residue" from the "active cruelty" that he locates broadly in Chinese "history" and more narrowly in the Chinese penal code prior to 1911, both forms of cruelty Russell acknowledges to be practiced by all nations in any case. The particular experience of the relation between China and pain comes, then, not from a description of torture, violence, or structural indifference, each of which Russell excuses or excises from consideration. The residue, he writes, "cannot be . . . explained": the average Chinese person finds the spectacle of suffering mildly agreeable.

Faced with a set of cultural differences—an apparent indifference to famine, a penal code invested in judicial torture—Russell places them within a framework that allows them to be understood as contingent rather than genetic, as functions of particular circumstances rather than expressions of some deep-set Chinese national character (in the first case, geographic ones, in the second, the general tendency of nation-states toward "active cruelty"). Though the Chinese react this way to famine, though they have been actively cruel, these facts do not themselves justify an argument for Chinese callousness. English readers should understand them instead as expected responses to a set of historical facts. Other human beings, other great nations, would in the same situation believe roughly what the Chinese do, behave roughly as they behave. But the residue "that cannot be so explained" remains outside the economy of historical causality.

In the imaginary novel, Russell's claim regarding the failure of the "spectacle of suffering" to rouse in Chinese people any "sympathetic pain" echoes Dora's complaint that people "remain placidly indifferent" to their neighbors' suffering, each claim caught up in a network of associations that revolve around the presence of disease, illness, and indifference to pain ("whereas we deliberately cause famines for the pleasure of gloating over dying children"). A reading of this narrative as narrative rather than as history foregrounds the presence of illness and pain as figures, allowing for an appreciation of the text's high-wire structuralism, the mode whereby it organizes its categories, reverses them, moves them from nation to body, body to nation, East to West, and back again. The novel, one might say, not only represents the Western experience of China as a site of resistance to modernity, but also the degree to which any individual experience of that Chinese dream will inevitably—and perhaps always at the moment when it is most invested in its own "fairness" and most on the "side" of China itself—take up and work through the history of a Western-imagined "China" and the topos of an Orientalism whose broad outlines have become visible since the late 1970s.

That Russell manages to explain so much about Chinese torture and indifference so rationally marks him as a far more culturally sensitive reader of China than many of his predecessors, even as his discovery of the limits of his explanations on the grounds of a low-grade sadism ("he seems to find it mildly agreeable") repeats an all-too-familiar cliché. But, in an imaginary novel, the cliché proves itself to be simultaneously individually discovered and narratively predictable, so that Russell comes to his story about the dog in the street not only as the latest Westerner to remark this Chinese indifference to the pain of others, but also as a character whose friend fell ill on the Volga, who almost died in Beijing, whose partner in the dawn after a dark hour finds in her own body a surprising, fecund germination. Though his relation to China exemplifies once again the structure of Orientalism that exceeds Russell and is in some sense indifferent to him, it also belongs uniquely to Russell, to the vagaries of his letters, his body, his political essays; in short, to his person.

That pairing—the historical relationship to China on the one hand, the personal one on the other—comes in an imaginary novel on Russell and China to take the place of a biographical conclusion that might have to choose between them: rather than forcing a decision that, say, that Russell is just another Orientalist, or that he isn't, here the novel produces instead a sense both of the inevitability of Russell's position and of the astonishing coincidences necessary to produce it.

If I have been reading Russell's life as a novel, then, it is because the word "novel" allows for a reading of coincidence and figure that in "real life" will inevitably seem outlandish, extravagant, precisely because it could have, in real life, happened another way, or because the details chosen to make the story must proceed by excluding the many other details that do not fit. That's why one person can generate any number of biographies, whereas a character is generated by the story even as it appears to generate it: Vronsky's horse breaks its back not because it has a weak spine but because the story needs the back to break.[33] Whereas Russell gets sick in Beijing, but he could have, we think, just as easily stayed well. The advantage of reading the experience novelistically, with all the

[33] Woolf, reviewing a biography of Christina Rossetti:

"Here is the past and all its inhabitants miraculously sealed as in a magic tank; all we have to do is to look and to listen and to listen and to look and soon the little figures—for they are rather under life size—will begin to move and to speak, and as they move we shall arrange them in all sorts of patterns of which they were ignorant, for they thought when they were alive that they go where they liked; and as they speak we shall read into their

small distortions that requires, is that it turns coincidence into inevitability, and thus permits a reading of what were probably in the experiential moments a series of disconnected and jumbled facts as something more like a story. And the advantage of that, in turn, is that it allows one to produce around the body of Russell not simply a particular representation of Chinese indifference—the moment when Russell decides to explain the residual callousness that counts as one of the faults of the Chinese—but rather a narrative in which the character named "Russell" finds itself implicated not simply as a neutral observer (that is, as a public intellectual making a set of political claims about geopolitical China) but also as a body, as a trajectory, as a narratological object: What if, I am asking, the coincidences of Russell's life come to tell a story—a story unobserved by anyone—that figures not simply a moment in the history of the Western perception of Chinese indifference but also, in philosophical terms, a relationship to the history of a particular English modernism?

3. Pain and Cambridge Philosophy

Russell's observation about Chinese indifference is a classic example of its genre, and it should be understood as an instance of the general historical line this book has traced so far. It also belongs to the relatively more local genre of books on the Chinese character exemplified by Arthur Smith's *Chinese Characteristics.* Just like Smith's book, Russell's *The Problem of China* found itself rapidly translated and reprinted in China by scholars attempting to think the relation between national character and modernity. Russell's chapter on the Chinese character appeared in the *Dongfang zazhi* [Eastern miscellany] in 1922, and Lydia Liu cites a note from its translator Yuzhi, who wrote that "the question of the Chinese *guomin xing* [national character] is one that fascinates us more than anything else."[34] The implications of the debate on national character for Chinese intellectuals' relations to modernism and modernity, brilliantly elaborated by Liu, remain outside the scope of the chapter, but I refer to them here to note that the Anglo-American

---

> sayings all kinds of meanings which never struck them, for they believed when they were alive that they said straight off whatever came into their heads. But once you are in a biography all is different."

(cited in Hermione Lee, *Virginia Woolf* [New York, 1999], 8–9).

[34] Liu, *Translingual Practice*, 47.

context is only one of the many situations in which Russell's work must be thought, and that, as for "modernism" itself, it is by no means decided in advance that the Anglo-American context must be considered the "original" or primary context within which Russell's trip to China generates its theoretical and historical meaning.[35]

Within this general context, however, it is possible to further refine the discussion of pain so as to make explicit and direct the connection between Russell's observations on the Chinese character and the philosophical work on subjects and objects that became such a crucial feature of Bloomsbury modernism. And here it turns out that pain's relation to subjectivity is a major theme in the work of Russell's student, Wittgenstein, whose revisions and rejections of Russell's theories of subject and object biographers have made responsible for Russell's turn away from philosophy (this already in the mid-1910s) and toward politics, a turn that would lead directly to the trips to Russia and China.

"Only I can know whether I am really in pain; another person can only surmise it," Wittgenstein would write.[36] He meant that pain is a private fact: I can assert my pain to another, groan more or less convincingly, exhibit a wound that would cause most people pain, but none of these guarantees my pain in any public realm. To move pain into language, to speak of pain, is already to cross the boundary between my individual consciousness and the world, to assert inside a particular set of public rules the fact of my own experience.

Wittgenstein introduces "pain" as he ponders the relation between language and reference:

> How do words *refer* to sensations?—There doesn't seem to be any problem here; don't we talk about sensations every day, and give them names? But how is the connexion between the name and the thing named set up? This

[35] David Der-Wei Wang's work on the relationship between violence, history, and representation in twentieth-century Chinese fiction, for instance, adumbrates an entire dimension of the experience and representation of violence that opens up the question of the moral and historical dimensions in the Chinese context of such apparently "universal" features of literary language as "realism" and *aporia* (see the discussion of Shen Congwen on 25–27). As Wang points out in the introduction, even apparently universal paradigms for the relationship between violence and representation in Western criticism borrow extensively from the "local" histories within which they occur (as for instance Adorno on the Holocaust; see 4–5) (Wang, *The Monster That Is History: History, Violence, and Fictional Writing in Twentieth-Century China* [Berkeley, 2004].).

[36] Wittgenstein, *Philosophical Investigations*. 3d ed., trans. G.E.M. Anscombe (Oxford, 2001), §246. Citations from *Philosophical Investigations* refer to the passage number, not a page number, and appear in the text as *PI*.

> question is the same as: how does a human being learn the meaning of the names of sensations?—of the word "pain" for example. Here is one possibility: words are connected with the primitive, the natural, expressions of the sensation and used in their place. A child has hurt himself and he cries; and then adults talk to him and teach him exclamations and, later, sentences. They teach the child new pain-behaviour.
>
> "So you are saying that the word 'pain' really means crying?"—On the contrary: the verbal expression of pain replaces crying and does not describe it. (*PI*, §244)

Wittgenstein describes the relation between language and pain as neither exactly denotative (the word "pain" does not "point" in any clear way to pain) nor precisely nominative ("pain" is not simply a conventional sound for "the experience of pain").[37] If the verbal expression of pain "replaces" crying, as Wittgenstein argues, it is because "pain" neither names the experience of pain nor points to it, but rather means, effectively, "what I mean when I cry." Sensation *as such* remains private, and only becomes speakable—but never *as itself*—upon entry into language. Wittgenstein: "The essential thing about private experience is really not that each person possesses his own exemplar, but that nobody knows whether other people also have *this* or something else" (§272). "Pain" cannot be said to describe or to mean; it is, rather, *used:* "You learned the *concept* 'pain' when you learned language" (§383).

Russell's story of the dog in the street is a story about pain, about the recognition and expression of pain, and about reactions to that recognition. Inasmuch as it responds to pain, the story is an artifact of the type described by Elaine Scarry, a verbal or material object that manifests the experience of pain, or attempts to make the inanimate structure of the planet responsive to the human condition of pain. As Scarry writes: "A material or verbal artefact is not an alive, sentient, percipient creature, and thus can neither itself experience discomfort nor recognize discomfort in others. But though it cannot be sentiently aware of pain, it is in the essential fact of itself the objectification of *that awareness;* itself incapable of the act of perceiving, its design, its structure, *is* the *structure of a perception.*"[38] The structure of a perception: in the same way that a bandage objectifies—makes into an object—a subjectless perception of wounds and

[37] Later in *Philosophical Investigations*, Wittgenstein writes: "So it may look as if what we were doing were Nominalism. Nominalists make the mistake of interpreting all words as *names*, and so of not really describing their use, but only, so to speak, giving a paper draft on such a description" (§383).

[38] Scarry, 289.

wounding, a story that tells of pain objectifies, puts into the ink on the page its own acknowledgment of the *state of pain* it perceives, or even, as seems to be the case with Russell, the presence of a sympathetic pain that reacts to the fact of the pain it observes.

If a dog is run over by an automobile and seriously hurt, nine out of ten passers-by will stop to laugh at the poor brute's howls. Considered in the terms of a Russellian theory of sensibilia, the scene presents four possible "subjective" perspectives: that of the dog, that of the passers-by who laugh, of the single passer-by who doesn't, and of its observer. Only one of these might be said, in this narrative, to be properly "occupied": the observer, who hears the dog's howls, sees the passers-by and their reactions, and frames these within a syntax that makes the former the cause of the latter, reads howling as pain and laughter as pleasure ("he seems to find it mildly agreeable"). The method of narration is uncomplicatedly realist, epistemologically sure-footed. One feels a long way from Lily's portrait from memory, from the post-Impressionist privileging of geometry over representation, from the eyeless possibilities of an encounter with something like the subject's future death.

Considered in terms of its perception of pain, however, the story acquires a more complex geometry. Draw a line from the dog to the laughing passers-by, to indicate their relation, and another from the passers-by to the observer, because their laughter is effectively what he reports on. Another line must go from the dog to the observer, as it is his being touched by the "brute's howls" that produces his evaluation of the dog's pain. And modify that line, in turn, by the line that connects the dog to the passers-by, because the whole reason for telling this story lies in perceived difference between the Chinese reaction and the Western one, between the two different attitudes toward the fact of the dog's pain. What the observer observes, in this sense, includes the dog's pain, the Chinese reaction to that pain, his *own* reaction to that pain, and the difference between them, which makes the fact of the reaction *visible* as such. The observer occupies, then, not one but two perspectives, one in the immediate moment of a visceral experience and the other in a more evaluative (later?) experience that includes the initial experience of the scene. One more line, then, between the observer of the first perspective and the one of the second. This is not so much eyelessness as the multiplication of eyes, a slow but surefooted generation of modernism inside the realistic, and an arrangement of perspectives that contrasts obscure forms of oral signification—laughter, howling—with the epistemological surefootedness of an observer who *thinks he knows exactly what he sees.* This assuredness renders the observer narratologically invisible, or permits him to imagine himself as such. (The narrator "adds nothing," Lacan remarks; and

Derrida replies: "As if one had to add something to intervene in a scene."[39]) Whatever visibility remains will be clearest to readers of the imaginary novel: the narrative of Chinese indifference recapitulates and allegorizes Russell's personal experience in China, his own sense of its "cruelty." What the observer sees without knowing it is the possibility of his own meaningless suffering and death.[40]

The story of the dog on the street thus reproduces and anticipates both the basic questions of Cambridge philosophy in the modernist period and some of its major tropes: the occupation of perspectives, a more general telemetry of vision and experience, to be sure, but also the sense of "pain" as a particularly fertile site for the investigation of relations between subjects, the relationship between language and humanity, and so forth. That all this happens in a Chinese context, within the frame of an explicit attempt to experience and narrate large-scale cultural difference (remember Russell's initial motivations for going to China, his sense that it could offer civilizational resistance to Western industrialism) allows the question of subjects, objects, and the nature of human reality to take a final turn. Because if "pity . . . is a form of conviction that someone else is in pain," and "pain" itself depends on a human entry into language (both these ideas from Wittgenstein, produced as part of a lifelong supercession of Russell's own arguments about sensibilia), then indifference or laughter in relation to the pain of others indicates a failure to recognize those others as human. That is, the Chinese do not recognize Russell in his illness in the way in which he recognizes himself; they do not recognize the dog in the way in which Russell recognizes the dog: as subjects.

The story of the dog thus at first appears to be largely cultural: Russell seems to be explaining to a British audience the difference between "us" and the Chinese, a difference he defines as residual to rational explanation and elaborates

[39] Jacques Derrida, *La carte postale: de Socrate à Freud et au-delà* (Paris, 1980), 457.

[40] To put a slightly finer point on this, and to locate its philosophical force once again in the precise material context with which I am dealing here, consider the following narrative, which appears in Marc Riboud's *The Three Banners of China* (New York, 1966):

> "One day I was walking in Liu Li-chang, a mean street in the old quarter of Peking which is always crowded. A man of over fifty, no doubt a worker, was returning home on his ancient bicycle. He was pedalling [*sic*] slowly and with difficulty. All of a sudden his front fork broke and he fell face down on the road. The men and women walking along this narrow street neither turned back nor stopped; they simply moved to avoid him. Nobody helped the old man. He got up on his own, his mouth covered with blood. Such indifference was the hallmark of the old China. If there had been a youngster there, perhaps he would have followed the example of Lei Feng, learned at school. Perhaps not." (135)

with an example. But for Russell, as for Wittgenstein and as for moral philosophers like Adam Smith, indifference to pain is not just a randomly chosen example of human behavior, but, rather, a central fact of what makes human beings human. What looks like a simple story about cultural difference turns out, seen from this angle, to depend on a complex network of recognitions and failed recognitions, each of which goes to the heart of whether Chinese callousness can in the end define the Chinese as inhuman(e), and on a epistemological history whose privileged trope makes this particular example especially telling. The primacy of pain and pity to the modern conception of self and subject makes the encounter with a different relation to pain still inside the scope of the human effectively unimaginable: indifference to pain is not subject to negotiation. That feeling depends not just on epistemology, not just on culture: it requires both.

In Banfield's reading of *To the Lighthouse,* the encounter with indifference indicates time, not culture.[41] It is not just that the things are indifferent to people, but also the reverse; lost in attics or libraries, buried and misremembered, hidden, forgotten, the things and the people go on with their lives as behind them a mountain of people and things gather themselves briefly together in the arms of the angel of history, then disappear under clouds of newer debris. Russell, attempting to explain why we think the table we saw yesterday is the same table we see today, calls the joining together of multiple possible temporal perspectives a "biography."[42] Though the word conjures life, the table's biography—like the person's—is a "life" constituted not in the presence of a metaphysical subject but merely in the presence of *possible* observation: like sensibilia, biographies do not have to be observed to exist. "The result," Banfield says, "is not so much a loss of reality, but a redefinition of it that only increases the conviction of its mind-independence" (*PT,* 101). And in this mind-independence, the individual biography, the life of a person or a thing, matters little in comparison to the vast indifference of time, the multiplicity of perspectives from which any one, any one thing, is not, cannot, or never will be seen, located, and differentiated: from which its pain will never produce a recognition. It is the ill, lying recumbent, Woolf once wrote, "who

[41] Ramsay "learns not a moral lesson but a law of time, the self's inevitable end amidst the indifference of things." The "self" Banfield refers to is large, and includes not only the human subject but also the work of art and the work of philosophy (*PT,* 351).

[42] Banfield writes: "Presumably the public table itself would have a biography, since it persists over time, just as the person, Scott or Bismarck, would be a 'public neutral object' with spatial continuity, known by description" (100).

know what, after all, Nature is at no pains to conceal—that she in the end will conquer; heat will leave the world; stiff with frost we shall cease to drag ourselves about the fields; ice will lie thick upon factory and engine; the sun will go out."[43]

Nature's indifference, like the universe's, refers humanity to the "big" death of galactic time. Russell's meeting with indifference in China is an encounter with the "little" death of life times, the famines and the soldiers running amok and his own illness, but all of this crucially mediated through a sense that this indifference depends on culture, not ontology. The indifference Black and Russell report experiencing—an indifference marked by the failures of others to see them as they would like to have been seen, to occupy the points of view from which their suffering would have mattered—is not universal. It is "Chinese." Insofar as the recognition of someone's pain can, in an indifferent world, mark a moment of perception—insofar as the material artifact, a table or a chair, reflects the "structure of a perception" of pain that outlasts the moment of perception (and is in the long run completely indifferent to the particularity of it)—the moment of what Wittgenstein calls "pity" reflects a brushing against death, large or small, an awareness of time's indifference. But also a willingness to remark that indifference, to heal its wound, to produce something like a publicly available testament to the perception of indifference and pain. At least, let us say, in the modern: if the Chinese seem to Russell indifferent to the pain of others, it is perhaps because of a different kind of eyelessness, one that even in the occupation of a perspective that can see pain remains indifferent to it (or finds it "slightly agreeable"). This too is cultural; I say so not to condemn Russell for his limitations but because those limitations define the rules of the language game whereby indifference, pain, and China can come to metonymize modernism.

I am talking about the structure of a perception.

4. The Chineseness of Suffering

In 1926, some five years after Russell's trip, a year before *To the Lighthouse,* Virginia Woolf published in the *New Criterion* an essay titled "On Being Ill." In illness, she writes, the "make-believe" of ordinary intercourse comes to a halt.

[43] VirginiaWoolf, "On Being Ill," *The Essays of Virginia Woolf* vol. 4, ed. Andrew McNellie (London, 1994), 322. Jean-François Lyotard makes the fact of the sun's eventual fade the signature ground of human reality in the contemporary world in his introduction to *The Inhuman: Reflections on Time,* trans. Geoffrey Bennington and Rachel Bowlby (New York, 1993).

Though while healthy we serve in "the army of the upright," joined in the great human struggle to move forward, holding hands, to improve and to share, to cultivate and teach, in illness "we go alone." "That illusion of a world so shaped that it echoes every groan, of human beings so tied together by common needs and fears that a twitch at one wrist jerks another, where however strange your experience other people have had it too, where however far you travel in your own mind someone has been there before you—is all an illusion. We do not know our own souls, let alone the souls of others."[44]

The byways of the self's "virgin forest," though offering little consolation as regards an incipient human loneliness, nonetheless have some advantages. In illness, Woolf writes, no one can sustain the attention required by history or narrative fiction. But a line or two of poetry, broken off in the name of other tastes, "sudden, fitful, intense," can lead to an unexpected blooming:

> In illness words seem to possess a mystic quality. We grasp what is beyond their surface meaning, gather instinctively this, that, and the other—a sound, a colour, here a stress, there a pause—which the poet, knowing words to be meagre in comparison with ideas, has strewn about his page to evoke, when collected, a state of mind which neither words can express nor the reason explain. . . . Foreigners, to whom the tongue is strange, have us at a disadvantage. The Chinese must know the sound of *Antony and Cleopatra* better than we do.[45]

Hearing sounds divorced from sense, as though prior, then, to language, the ill become, like Lily Briscoe, modernists, singing earless lines in the houses of the mind. Relative to an "us"—and only relative to us, though the choice of example matters—the Chinese (all foreigners) are in a state of permanent illness; the dumbshow of an English Shakespeare speaks to them of unoccupied perspectives, of a world without subjects, without language, in which sounds register merely on some autochthonic recording machine. Or, in reverse: illness makes "us" Chinese, the self-estrangement it provides akin to a geographic displacement, an interior foreignness that grants a privileged awareness of the properties of linguistic form (and, thus, to the classic structure of modernist aesthetics). Language's foreignness—a howl, a bark of laughter, or the bar-bar of a foreign tongue—enters the body like a poison, or an angel, through the ear.

[44] Woolf, "On Being Ill," 320–21.
[45] Woolf, "On Being Ill," 324–25.

Is this coincidence—yet another conjunction of the Chinese, pain, the unoccupied perspective of an inhuman episteme, and a fairly standard modernist aesthetic of estrangement, each of these intertwined enough with the others to make untangling quixotic—just a coincidence?[46] I wish to end this chapter by suggesting that the answer to that question is no, that this series of conjunctions and coincidences, this improbable network of metonymic connections between China, philosophy, humanity, illness, and pain, means something beyond the fiction I have proposed. This is what the word "overdetermination" is for: to allow us to see how biographical action can be the effect of an ideological discourse, despite the best individual will of its participants.

What this discourse tells us about modernism is that any attempt to simply compare modernisms from two or more national locations will fail if it does not understand that every philosophical and literary modernism is itself subject to an internal, undermining comparative action, in which the "foreign" always and in advance inhabits the "native" national paradigm. The story I have told about Russell intends to suggest that his relation to China was not simply an external feature of the history of Orientalism, nor simply that his experience of China and Chinese pain were shaped by his relation to philosophy, but rather that the categories through which Russell thought—the categories that allowed him to ask the fundamental philosophical questions of perception, of language, and of the nature of the human—were themselves already affected by some relation to Chineseness. That the relation to Chineseness was itself equally affected, and in advance, by the philosophical categories that it helped shape I take as the paradoxical but necessary corollary to this first idea.[47]

[46] On at least one other occasion, Woolf connects China to bodies and pain. In an essay called "The Chinese Shoe," written in memory of Lady Henry Somerset, she laments the degree to which the "natural desire" of Somerset's "lively and courageous nature" was stunted by those around her, "until we feel that the old Chinese custom of fitting the foot to the shoe was charitable compared with the mid-Victorian practice of fitting the woman to the system" ("The Chinese Shoe," in *The Essays of Virginia Woolf* vol. 3, ed. Andrew McNeillie [London, 1994], 390.).

[47] I have left aside here two references to Elizabeth's "Chinese eyes" in Woolf's *Mrs. Dalloway* and one to her "oriental bearing" (*Mrs. Dalloway* [San Diego, 1981], 123, 135, 131), as well as to a moment in that novel in which China becomes the measure of the nearly immeasurable boundaries of the British imperium: "when the sentence was finished something had happened. Something so trifling in single instances that no mathematical instrument, though capable of transmitting shocks in China, could register the vibration; yet in its fullness rather formidable and in its common appeal emotional; for in all the hat shops and tailors' shops strangers looked at each other and thought of the dead; of the flag; of Empire" (18). For an analysis of this passage, see Christopher Bush's *Ideographic Modernism* (Forthcoming 2011).

I am not arguing, therefore, that Russell's thought was originally or essentially "Chinese." That some aspect of his thought included China is, it seems to me, simply true, and was generally true for anyone living in England during that era. The difficulty comes in moving from a claim about "China" as a feature of the cultural and individual experience of the Bloomsbury group to one that says, as Laurence does, that without China Bloomsbury would be unthinkable. Banfield's work demonstrates the incompleteness of such a story. The problem is not with Laurence's work as such—or rather not with the particular claims she or Banfield make for the importance of the issues they discuss to the ferment of modernism. The problem is that the bar for relevance has been set too high, encouraging scholars to turn complex historical claims about literary form (because modernists thought about China sometimes, the modernism they created owes something to China) into simple but impossible causal ones (without China modernists would not have thought of modernism at all). Given that the latter claim will not convince anyone, what results is a critical world in which competing claims from "outside" the standard cultural context that organizes literary critical work (usually the nation-state; sometimes a continent or region) can never acquire the critical force of those claims that emerge from "inside" the standard context, because the totalities of the latter will never overturn the totalities of the former. It isn't that they should; it's that they can't, and that expecting them to is one of the ways in which Anglo-American modernist studies implicitly justifies its monoculturalism and monolingualism. The genius of Said's *Orientalism* was to make visible the degree to which the apparent "outside" had been "inside" for a very long time: he did not simply reverse the origins, relocating them from West to East; he undermined the whole structure of Europe's sovereign originality.

Perhaps Lily's line—like the lines of the two approaches to modernism captured in *The Phantom Table* and *Lily Briscoe's Chinese Eyes*—ought to be considered outside the parameters of Euclidean geometry. If, as Banfield argues, the line moves past realistic representation into modernist formality, if it hints at perspectives unoccupied by human eyes, then there is no reason for it to obey the Newtonian conveniences of everyday life. It might be said, then, not so much to bifurcate (which gives us, once again, two approaches) as to stretch, to allow parallels to cross, to bend according to historically and geographically local centers of gravity. Following such a line, we would not study—to put the question into its most traditional formulation—the "encounter" *between* Orientalism and modernism, but rather work the interpenetration of those two categories prior to a generalized awareness of them as categories, understanding that each of them depends, in some way, on the apprehension of the other in advance, just as the

West's philosophical fascination with pain lays the groundwork for Russell's personal encounter with China, and the reverse. There are no single origins. A scholarship that pursued such a course would be able to affirm that formal line in all its remarkable complexity: Lily Briscoe's Chinese yes. But don't lay down those brushes yet.

5. The Hypothetical Mandarin (Reprise)

In *Everybody's Autobiography,* written shortly after her return to Europe from her American tour, Gertrude Stein remarked that many people had thought it was funny when, in her opera *Four Saints in Three Acts,* "they asked Saint Therese what would she do if by touching a button she could kill three thousand Chinamen and the chorus said Saint Therese not interested." But Saint Therese was interested in building convents, not killing Chinese people, Stein writes; the hypothetical had nothing to do with the kinds of concrete practicalities with which Saint Therese concerned herself. Stein goes on to recall the first time she heard the hypothetical of the Chinese mandarin from the philosopher Hutchins Hapgood. Hapgood "liked to think of the number of angels on the point of a needle . . . and . . . always complained of me that I had too good a time for anybody who was so virtuous." One day, frustrated by Stein's "virtue," Hapgood asked her a "test question. Would I if I could by pushing a button would I kill five thousand Chinamen if I could save my brother from anything. Well I was very fond of my brother and I could completely imagine his suffering and I replied that five thousand Chinamen were something I could not imagine and so it was not interesting."[48]

In Stein's resistance to the idealized stupidity of the dilemma appears the possibility of a response to the figuration of Chinese people as objects in a "test question" for European virtue which, by saying neither yes nor no, refuses the premise of the hypothetical as hypothetical. Such a refusal speaks most immediately to Stein's pragmatic commitment to things over ideas, and to the hard-

[48] Gertrude Stein, *Everybody's Autobiography* (New York, 1971), 89–90. *Four Saints in Three Acts* was first staged on Broadway in February 1934, shortly before Stein set off on her book tour and only a year before the Lohmann-Winternitz exchange at Yale. The difference between Saint Therese's line, in which she is not interested in killing Chinese because she has better things to do, and Stein's, in which she is not interested because she cannot imagine "five thousand Chinamen," once again shows how the relation to the hypothetical opens always in two directions: the first toward an economy of costs (including opportunity costs), the second inside an economy of representation (including the transfer between reference and the sympathetic imagination).

edged, pellucid qualities of her thought. But, it also suggests how the generally recognized modernist investment in China elaborated in so much recent scholarly work might be *directly* connected to the hypothetical mandarin that figures the larger ambitions of this book.

The seemingly coincidental reappearance of the mandarin in Stein's prose, the ease with which the dean of Yale's medical school could imagine her writing as "Chinese," indicates, finally, how seriously one might take Russell's casual reproduction of the stereotype of Chinese indifference to the suffering of others. Here, as elsewhere, the evidentiary relationship between that reproduction and Russell's philosophical impact on Woolf's modernism generates the problem of the example-effect, which has to do not so much with the "failure" of China or Chineseness to assert themselves at the "heart" or "core" of philosophy, but rather with the ways in which China's appearance in and around philosophical cores (whether of modernism or of human rights) functions as a kind of disappearing appearance. What difference, then, made to the nexus of sensibilia and modernism by Lily's "Chinese eyes," and what difference to that nexus that Russell's take on Chinese defects reproduces so exactly the stereotype of George Henry Mason's 1801 book on Chinese punishments? Let us simply say that if China could be named a "problem" by one of the world's two foremost intellectuals in 1922, then the geopolitical status of China, its relation to Japanese colonialism, to modernization, the possibility it might give "to mankind . . . a whole new hope in the moment of greatest need," all spoken of in Russell's book, must be thought of as one substrate of the world-perception that simultaneously generated the perception of Chinese indifference *and* the "Chinese" logics of modernist form (*PC*, 252). This chapter has shown how closely the "problem" of China cleaves to the eyeless, earless world without subjects—the world of sensibilia generated but unperceived—that was Russell's main contribution to Woolf's modernism. If the specter of a total global indifference to human meaning can be bound to the particular indifference of nine out of ten Chinese to the suffering of a crushed dog, it is only because the Wittgensteinian language game in which they both participate relies so heavily, and still so lightly, on the appearance of China in it. Because it is precisely in the transaction between the heaviness of the history of philosophy or literary form and the lightness of the example that the Chinese referent both acquires and loses its critical legitimacy, a Wittgensteinian reminder of the importance of the rules of language games is a useful place to end this chapter: it suggests that the major project of this book will have been to describe the grammar, or metagrammar, that allows "China" to perform the philosophical and referential function that becomes it.

6 Ideologies of the Anesthetic: *Acupuncture, Photography, and the Material Image*

> In order to take the first portraits (around 1840) the subject had to assume long poses under a glass roof in bright sunlight; to become an object made one suffer as much as a surgical operation.
>
> —Roland Barthes, *Camera Lucida: Reflections on Photography*

> Suppose the image was not . . . merely an emphatic expression of language's desire to draw closer to the natural object, but a visible and material entity, a representation in a physical medium like stone or human flesh?
>
> —W.J.T. Mitchell, "Romanticism and the Life of Things," *Critical Inquiry* 28 (Autumn 2001).

The semibiographical, semipolitical essays that make up Pearl S. Buck's 1972 *China Past and Present* are punctuated by some forty black-and-white photographs. Buck and her family had left China in 1934; the photographs show a contemporary China that she had never seen personally. In the years since her depature, Buck had become the West's foremost interpreter of China, thanks to the success of her many books, fiction and nonfiction (most famously *The Good Earth* [1931]), and her charitable interventions on its behalf. But by the early 1970s, her relation with China was strained. Denied an entry visa by the Canadian embassy of the People's Republic of China (PRC) shortly before the publication of *China Past and Present,* Buck, aged 79, wrote the text knowing that it was unlikely that she would ever return to the country she loved so much, and that the only access she would have to China or the

Chinese would come through the kinds of photographs and traveler's reports she reproduced and cited in the text.[1]

China Past and Present is therefore as much an exercise in reading photographic images as it is a memoir of the nation and people Buck knew, an attempt to discern through the photographic surface the historical fate of Buck's childhood home. In this caption to a René Burri photograph of a parade in Tiananmen Square, Buck pursues that ambition with a utopian intensity:

> Sometimes these parades are military, but on this day it was not, I am glad to say, for it gives us a chance to see the faces of the people. I have studied them as closely as I can, even under a magnifying glass, trying to fathom the difference in these faces and the faces of the Chinese I used to know. There are differences. I do not see old faces here. They are handsome faces, but they do not seem happy faces. At least the crowd is well clothed and well fed. Perhaps, after all, that is enough. Perhaps it is even happiness nowadays. (*CPP*, 94)

Perhaps it is enough that the crowd is fed; perhaps the nature of happiness has changed. As Buck pores over the faces with the magnifying glass, the answers she seeks seem to dissipate before her. The glass has allowed the eye to range across the image-grain, but there is no way in to the photograph, no "fathom[ing]" of a historical difference, no vertiginous plunge into certainty. Whatever interpretation the magnifier admits through its lens threatens its own dissolution; the photographic screen, a metonymy of the faces that Buck attempts to read, indicates the possibility of depth but does not provide it. What's left is longing, a super-facial flatness in which China's final certainties are withheld, or held, in the form of an invocation, a prayer to the missing and beloved real—"alas, my beloved land, China!," she writes elsewhere (160)—whose absent presence is articulated in the photographs as both theme and form.

Buck's caption to Burri's photograph will recall George Mason's interpretive struggles with Pu Qua's images of Chinese workers and punishments. Something of the two-step between caption and image that gave Mason's *The Punishments of*

[1] Pearl S. Buck, *China Past and Present* (New York, 1971). Further references in the text are cited as *CPP*. The letter from the People's Republic of China embassy reads in part: "In view of the fact that for a long time you have in your works taken an attitude of distortion, smear and vilification towards the people of new China and their leaders, I am authorized to inform you that we can not accept your request for a visit to China" (171).

China such an interesting, tense relation to its status as a reference book appears here, reminding us that the self-evidence of the image's representational work is rarely evident enough to do without explanations (even ones as minimal as dates or captions). Buck's book, like Mason's, reminds us that such texts rarely involve "the straightforward discursive or narrative suturing of the verbal and visual," in which the "texts explain, narrate, describe, label, speak for (or to) the photographs" and the "photographs illustrate, exemplify, clarify, ground, and document the text."[2] What happens when the text can't quite explain the image, when it either foregrounds its interpretive work as the work of a body trying to read, or conceals it, is simply a more open version of what happens every time in a "failure" that goes both ways: the text can never quite explain the image, and the image can never perfectly exemplify the text. Their interactions plot the sweeps and curvatures of their interactive meanings. This mutual "failure" reminds us to approach both images *and* languages as media rather than as systems, as "heterogeneous field[s] of discursive modes" rather than "universally coded scheme[s] open to scientific explanation."[3]

Seen in this light, Buck's caption to the photograph of the Tiananmen parade—both the physical relation she describes, the poring and the magnifying glass, and the textual relation she establishes to it through her caption—opens up the larger questions of the relation between image, text, and the kinds of knowing they produce in combination that have been the subjects of a number of chapters so far. If I begin this chapter with this moment from Buck's work, then, it is to recognize first of all the complex mediatic nature of the relation between sympathy and images of suffering and thus to recall how strongly the history of a sympathetic relation to China depends on the presentation of those kinds of evidence deemed to have a privileged access to the real—be they watercolors, oil portraits, anecdotes, or medical case reports. By attending particularly to the photograph's ability to invoke an absent reality, an ability so profound as to produce the desire to stare through the photograph to the real, to insist on the ability of the photographic surface to generate the impression of depth—a verticality for which the magnifying glass becomes, in Buck's hands, a formal as well as an epistemological index—I also

[2] W. J. T. Mitchell, *Picture Theory* (Chicago, 1994), 94.

[3] Mitchell, *Picture Theory*, 97. Throughout this paragraph, I am drawing on Mitchell's work, particularly his theoretical claim that "[A]ll arts are 'composite' arts (both text and image); all media are mixed media, combining different codes, discursive conventions, channels, sensory and cognitive modes," which suggests that far more attention needs to be paid to mediatic form than has been done so far in literary criticism (*Picture Theory* 94–95). Mitchell also tackles the possible objections to his claim (95–99).

want to assert, recalling the lessons of anecdotal theory, that the work of photographic representation cannot simply be folded into a larger theory of the image borrowed from Mason and Pu Qua, but must be attended to in terms of all the specific mediatic, formal, and cultural processes through which the photograph generates its meaning.[4] For those reasons, this chapter, more than any since the first, will make as much a methodological argument about its primary object—the photograph of a Chinese man being executed in the early twentieth century—as it does a historical or interpretive one.

1. The Anesthetic and the Aesthetic

Before getting to that photograph, however, let me stay with Buck a moment longer. Late in *China Past and Present*, there appears a Marc Riboud picture of a surgical operation (figure 6.1). The scene "could be taken from an American television series," Buck tells her readers. But it "was photographed in a modern Chinese hospital in Wuhan . . . . The patient, a Chinese woman, is having a tumor removed." If this picture differed at all from something Americans might have seen on the *Marcus Welby* show, it was not so much because the hospital was Chinese as because of the medical procedure the doctors were performing. The woman on the operating table "is conscious; she is eating slices of fruit put in her mouth by a medical assistant; she feels no pain under the surgeon's knife although she has not been given an anaesthetic. Instead she is anaesthetized by acupuncture" (*CPP*, 126).

In 1973, a year after the publication of Buck's book, Susan Sontag, in Shanghai, watched "a factory worker with advanced ulcers have nine-tenths of his stomach removed under acupuncture anesthesia." Four years later, recalling the operation in *On Photography*, she wrote, "I managed to follow the three-hour procedure (the first operation I'd ever observed) without queasiness, never once feeling the need to look away." Sontag went on to compare her experience of seeing the operation in person to watching an operation on film: "In a movie theater in Paris a year later, the less gory operation in [Michelangelo] Antonioni's China documentary *Chung Kuo* [1973] made me flinch at the first cut of the scalpel and avert my eyes several times

[4]The early history of both photography and film suggests that the kinds of representation now understood as natural to those media were in fact the products of experimentation, remediation, and active discussion; see Mary Ann Doane, *The Emergence of Cinematic Time: Modernity, Contingency, the Archive* (Cambridge, 2002).

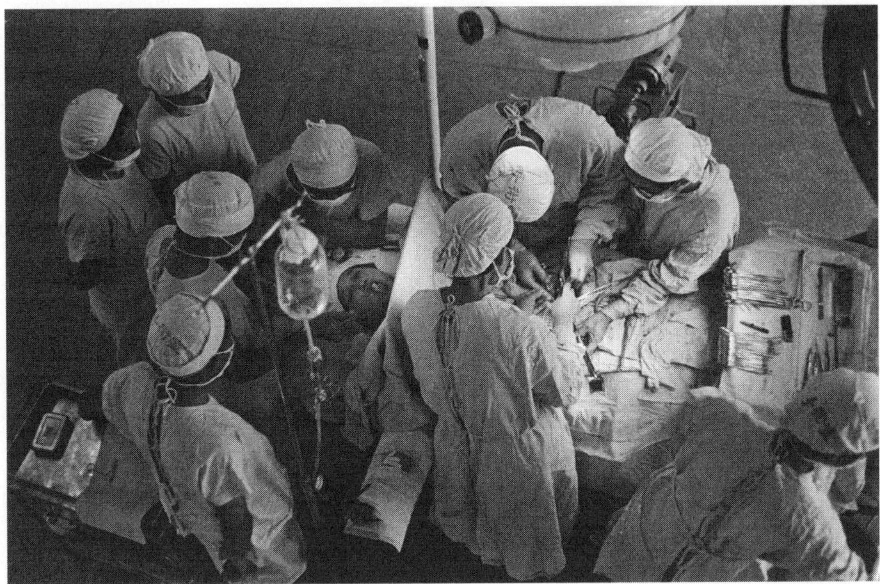

Fig 6.1 Acupuncture anesthesia. Photograph by Marc Riboud. Courtesy of Magnum Photos.

during the sequence. One is vulnerable to disturbing events in the form of photographic images in a way that one is not to the real thing."[5]

In the conjunction between these three experiences of "seeing" a surgical operation in China, each occurring within a year of the others, one witnesses first of all the success of a concerted campaign by the People's Republic in the early 1970s to advertise itself to the world as a modern nation-state. The combination of Western surgical theaters with Chinese acupuncture—what Buck calls, inimitably, the combination of "the most modern Western hygienic manner" and an "ancient" "technique centuries old"—signaled that China would become "modern" by combining Western science with Chinese values, that is, by producing modernity through rather than against China's cultural and historical heritage.[6] The anesthesia-by-acupuncture experience Riboud, Sontag, and Antonioni

[5] Susan Sontag, *On Photography* (New York, 1977), 168. Further references in the text are cited as *OP.*

[6] *CPP,* 124, 126. A report produced by the American Acupuncture Anesthesia Study Group and published by the National Academy of Sciences in 1976 attributes the development of acupuncture anesthesia in China to Mao's 1958 "directive to explore traditional Chinese medicine and integrate it with Chinese medical practice" (*Acupuncture Anesthesia in the People's Republic of China,* [Washington, 1976], 3).

disseminated to their respective audiences took place, therefore, within an international political frame in which the Chinese government exhibited its ability to care for its own people after the Chinese fashion and modeled for the countries of the world (especially those still on their way to modernity) an alternative to the developmental trajectory traced out, in those days, by the United States and the Soviet Union.

Though anesthesia was only one of the modes through which this performance took place (others included industrialization, military prowess, the elevation of folk culture to high culture, and agricultural innovation), it was in philosophical terms an especially important one. The development of anesthesia in the West had prompted throughout the nineteenth and early twentieth centuries major shifts in the human relationship to pain, changes perhaps best memorialized by the neurologist S. Weir Mitchell who, speaking at Massachusetts General Hospital on the fiftieth anniversary of "Ether Day" in 1896, announced that no future gift to humankind would be as welcome as the hour in which "hope, doubt, and fears / 'Mid deepening stillness, watched one eager brain, / With Godlike will, decree the Death of Pain."[7] No less than the Death of Pain, then, was the result of anesthesia's discovery in 1846, a discovery whose epochal pretensions were given weight by such mid–twentieth-century histories as *Victory over Pain* (1946), *Kampf gegen Schmerz und Tod* (*The Struggle Against Pain and Death,* published in English as *Triumph over Pain* in 1938), and *Man against Pain: The Epic of Anesthesia* (1945). Anesthesia was not just any old triumph, but one over humankind's oldest foe, over the very thing that might be said, for readers of Elaine Scarry, to define the human as such. As a medical practice that could replicate (or even improve upon) the "modern" solution to the problem of surgical medical care, and that had been around since long before the West's modernization, acupuncture could go a long way toward suggesting that modernity was not the exclusive property of the globalizing, post-industrial West.

[7] Cited in David Morris, *The Culture of Pain* (Berkeley, 1991), 65. Martin Pernick's history of the cultural reception of chemical anesthesia in the United States and Europe shows that the practice was met with genuinely mixed responses after its discovery in 1846, responses which kept anesthesia from being universally practiced and universally recognized as a boon to humankind until the late 1870s. As Pernick shows, many surgeries were performed without anesthesia in this period. Mitchell's 1896 poem should be taken, therefore, as representative of the attitude toward anesthesia's invention which began to dominate in the late nineteenth century and which predominates today, in which it is seen as an unmitigated good (*A Calculus of Suffering: Pain, Professionalism, and Anesthesia in Nineteenth-Century America* [New York, 1985].). One critique of the view of pain promoted by anesthetic thinking appears in Morris.

I will be worrying the conjunction of Buck's description of the Riboud photograph as a potential still from an American television series, Sontag's discussion of her experience, and the Antonioni film in the context of a broad theory of photography for the rest of this chapter. Let me begin by suggesting something about the relation between anesthesia and the photographic that will ground that theoretical connection. In an essay that revisits Walter Benjamin's famous theory of the work of art in modernity's technological age, Susan Buck-Morss explicitly connects cinematic forms of looking with the development of modern anesthesia. She suggests that the surgeon's relation to the patient changed radically when the former could perform operations without having to respond to the patient as a person. "Whereas surgeons earlier had to train themselves to repress empathic identification with the suffering patient," she writes, "now they had only to confront an inert, insensate mass that they could tinker with without emotional involvement."[8] This perceptual transformation was given physical form in the transformation of the operating "theater" at the end of the nineteenth century, when "discoveries in germ theory and antiseptics transformed the operating room from theatrical stage into a tile-and-marble, scrubbed-down, sterilized environment" in which the audience was separated from the proscenium by a glass partition. That "glass window became a projection screen," in which the "tripartite division of perceptual perspective—agent, matter, and observer—paralleled the brand new, contemporary experience of the cinema" (*AA*, 32).[9] In other words, the perceptual transformation created by the development of anesthesia and of modern surgery reproduced the agential splitting between actor, object, and observer that typified modern photography. Not for

[8] Susan Buck-Morss, "Aesthetics and Anaesthetics: Walter Benjamin's Artwork Essay Reconsidered." *October* 62 (Autumn 1992), 28. Further references in the text are cited as *AA*. Indeed, the history of surgery before anesthesia was a far less sterile thing and not just because of the development of germ theory. Operating theaters were usually located in hospital basements or on their upper floors, as far as possible from other patients, so that the ringing screams of those under the knife wouldn't be found too disturbing. Some patients refused treatment or committed suicide rather than be operated on; some aspiring surgeons abandoned their profession rather than live with their patients' suffering. For an overview of surgery before anesthesia, see Julie M. Fenster, *Ether Day: The Strange Tale of America's Greatest Medical Discovery and the Haunted Men Who Made It* (New York, 2001), chapter 2. Pernick, incidentally, cites at least six sources using variants of the phrase "boon to suffering humanity" in relation to anesthesia (290n3); "the pangs of suffering humanity," you will recall, were specifically the subject of attention from the compassionate Brits described in George Henry Mason's preface to *The Punishments of China.*

[9] As the fact that the operating space was called a "theater" prior to this transformation suggests, these changes reflect *shifts* in the mediatic experience of surgical procedure and not a new mediatization of something that had previously been "natural" or unmediated by representational codes.

nothing, then, did Benjamin compare the surgeon to the cameraman, as Buck-Morss notes: "the surgeon at the decisive moment abstains from facing the patient man to man; rather, it is through the operation that he penetrates into him. Magician and surgeon compare to painter and cameraman. The painter maintains in his work a natural distance from reality, the cameraman penetrates deeply into its web."[10]

Here, we come to the negative version of "anesthesia," the death of feeling not as triumph over pain but as capitulation to the dehumanizing gaze of modern techno-capitalism. If the spatial arrangement of the operating theater after anesthesia owed something to the codes of camera vision, or rather, if both the operating chamber and the camera lucida of the real world were in the late nineteenth century reconceived as visual spaces in accordance with the demands of new forms of perception, then both the camera and operating theater were cultural expressions of Western modernity in its most malevolent aspect. And this aspect might be said to derive the aesthetic of its looking from the anesthetic treatment of the world as a just another spectacle, the body as just another thing.

In other words, looking at Buck's photograph of an operation means looking at a photograph of something that has already been arranged photographically, partly because all looking has been transformed by the advent of the camera that organizes the world according to its perceptual rules. And this not just for the photographs: even when *witnessing* the operation, the distance created by the separation of surgical table from audience—itself a kind of anesthetizing force in relation to the potential experience of sympathetic pain, Buck-Morss writes—reflects and reproduces the experience of photographic vision. Such an account of the general relation between the camera and anesthesia suggests that every surgical scene expresses a photographic pose, because the fact of anesthetic perception (an anesthetic aesthetic) has been encoded in advance inside the camera as an apparatus.

Sontag's account of her experience in China offers an occasion for reading the relationship between modern ways of seeing and the operating theater. "One is vulnerable to disturbing events in the form of photographic images in a way that

[10] Walter Benjamin, *Illuminations,* trans. Harry Zohn, ed. Hannah Arendt, (New York, 1969), 233. Part of this has to do, ironically, with the excessive *stimulation* of modern culture, which turns out to be deadening, a position that one finds already in Edmund Burke's writing on the French revolution; see Steven Bruhm, "Aesthetics and Anesthetics at the Revolution," *Studies in Romanticism* 32:3 (Fall 1993), 407.

one is not to the real thing," Sontag had written. "In the operating room, I am the one who changes focus, who makes the close-ups and the medium shots. In the theater, Antonioni has already chosen what parts of the operation I can watch; the camera looks for me—and obliges me to look, leaving as my only option not to look" (*OP,* 169). Though Sontag may wish to differentiate her experience from Antonioni's filmic representation of it, the way she describes the operation—where like Benjamin's painter she faces the patient "man to man"—borrows all its terms from the language of cinema. Standing in the operating room, Sontag arranges her close-ups and medium shots, changes the focus of her attention. Hers is a model for live seeing already "penetrated" by the cinematic apparatus; the only argument with Antonioni is about who gets to control the camera.

The closeness between Sontag and Antonioni, their basic acceptance of a mode of looking connected to the operation's self-presentation as something suitable for photographing, is confirmed in Sontag's next paragraph. There, the separation Sontag imagines between her subjective vision and Antonioni's camera eye collapses into the objective case of the first person plural pronoun: "Nothing could be more instructive about the meaning of photography for us—as, among other things, a manner of hyping up the real—than the attacks on Antonioni's film in the Chinese press in early 1974" (*OP,* 169). The "us" at the end of the first clause herds Antonioni and Sontag into the broader category of the West, its differences erased in the comparison with that other great family of man, the PRC. Sontag devotes the book's next ten pages to showing how the controversy over Antonioni's documentary illustrates major cultural differences in both the experience of photographic technology and in politico-aesthetic modes of perception. What appeared in *On Photography's* first 168 pages to be a theory of technological and cultural modernity articulated around photography *in general* becomes, at the precise moment when Sontag mentions seeing acupuncture anesthesia in China, a theory of photography as a particularly *Western* form of experience, as an aesthetic mode suitable to a particular cultural geography. Why?

Let me back up. In 1972, Antonioni traveled to China at the invitation of the PRC government and spent twenty-two days filming the documentary that became *Chung Kuo* (*China*). The film met with a positive response at its first showing in 1973 for members of the Chinese embassy in Rome, before rapidly becoming the subject of enormous international controversy. It was extensively denounced by the PRC, which organized demonstrations against the film in China and pressured national governments to cancel public screenings (in 1975, the film could not be shown at the Venice Biennialle, though it was screened elsewhere in the city).

According to its critics, *Chung Kuo* insulted China by minimizing its industrial progress, suggesting that the Cultural Revolution was merely a sham, and presenting the country in cold, stark colors that made it look bleak and desolated. "He ignored busy motor traffic on the highways but picked only ox-carts and wheelbarrows," wrote Yang Kuei, the chairman of the Linhsien County Revolutionary Committee. "He paid no attention to big and small tractors working in the fields, but chose only a donkey pulling a stone roller. He skipped the stirring sights of collective labour and turned his camera solely on old people and a sick woman."[11] Antonioni, stung by the criticism, insisted in response that his film was an expression of interest in and even love for China and its people.[12]

Umberto Eco, writing in 1977, suggested that the film "reminds us that when political debate and artistic representation involve different cultures on a worldwide scale, art and politics are also mediated by anthropology and thus by semiology." No dialogue about international structures of social class can be opened, Eco wrote, "if we do not first resolve the problem of symbolic superstructures through which different civilizations represent to themselves the same political and social problems."[13] This clarity of this assessment of the differences between the official Chinese perspective on the film and Antonioni's suggests that what was at stake in the film was not so much its content—though there were complaints in that regard—but its aesthetic form. One of the most prominent objections involved the claim, articulated by an anonymous writer for the *Renmin Ribao* in an article translated and disseminated internationally by Beijing's Foreign Languages Press, that Antonioni's shots of a new bridge over the Yangtze River near Nanjing made it look dilapidated and unimpressive.[14] Antonioni's

[11]Yang Kuei, "Refuting Antonioni's Slanders Against Linhsien County," *Peking Review* 17.8 (1974), 13.

[12]The PRC also attempted unsuccessfully to stop showings of the documentary on Swedish and German television. For more on the controversy, see Gideon Bachmann, "Antonioni After China: Art Versus Science," *Film Quarterly* 28.4 (1975); Umberto Eco, "*De interpretatione*, or the difficulty of being Marco Polo," *Film Quarterly* 30.4 (1977); and *A Vicious Motive, Despicable Tricks: A Criticism of M. Antonioni's Anti-China Film China*, written by an anonymous *Renmin Ribao* commentator (Peking, 1974). English-language criticisms of the film appeared in *Peking Review* 17.8 and 17.11 in 1974, of which this statement by Fang Chun-sheng, a textile worker, is fairly typical: "Like all reactionaries, Antonioni has inveterate hatred for the revolutionary cause of the Chinese people" ("Textile Workers' Protest," *Peking Review* 17.8 (1974), 16.). In 2004, the documentary was publicly screened in China for the first time as part of an Antonioni retrospective at the Beijing Film Academy.

[13]Eco, 9.

[14]"In photographing the Yangtze River Bridge…the camera was intentionally turned on this magnificent modern bridge from very bad angles in order to make it appear crooked and tottering. A shot of trousers hanging on a line to dry below the bridge is inserted as a mockery of the scene"

fairly lame response—that because it was a foggy day "I had to limit myself to take shots of the bridge from closer by, and naturally, passing underneath it, the bridge appears slightly deformed"—avoided the representational questions entirely.[15]

Like Eco, who reads the controversy as the product of different cultural semiologies, themselves effects of "symbolic superstructures" operating at the level of civilizational self-representation, Sontag argues that the critiques of Antonioni's film depended on profound differences in cultural ways of seeing. "While for us photography is intimately connected with discontinuous ways of seeing (the point is precisely to see the whole by means of a part—an arresting detail, a striking way of cropping)," she wrote, "in China it is only connected with continuity . . . there are proper ways of photographing, which derive from notions about the moral order of space that preclude the very idea of photographic seeing" (*OP*, 169–70).[16] While for Eco the preference for frontal representation over foreshortening might be understood as the expression of a cultural habit that can be overcome through dialogue and discussion, Sontag makes the *Chung Kuo* controversy stand in for a much larger and possibly irreconcilable difference between continuity and discontinuity, East and West. The difference between a moral order that rules out photographic seeing entirely and one interested in discontinuity and fracture thus figures an enormous symbolic difference between a West that favors seeing "numerous variations of something" and increasing "the possibilities of meaning" and a China in which "only two realities" and two ways of looking, the right way and the wrong way, can even be acknowledged (*OP*, 173).

This is an incredibly rich and complicated set of claims, and in another book I could spend a great deal of time discussing them. As far as this book is concerned, let

---

(*Vicious Motive*, 11). A Riboud photograph of that same bridge, one of the great architectural feats of Chinese modernization in the early 1970s, appears in Buck's *China Past and Present* (113). As Buck notes, nationalist pride in the bridge's construction depended partly on the fact that it was built after the withdrawal of Soviet assistance because of tensions between the two communist countries. Another Riboud photograph, of the bridge under construction, appears in *The Three Banners of China* (New York, 1966), 96–97.

[15] Cited in Bachmann, 30.

[16] Sontag's reference to the "arresting detail" as a figure for modern aesthetics can be connected to the larger "humanitarian narrative" that organizes the Western perception of pain after the eighteenth century. Thomas Laqueur argues that the attention to detail in the modern novel and in medical case histories, which "present in purest form the amassing and ordering of vast quantities of detail so as to make real the pain of others," has an origin in the general epistemological and cultural shift that Thomas Haskell has described (Laqueur, "Bodies, Details, and the Humanitarian Narrative," *The New Cultural History*, ed. Lynn Hunt [Berkeley, 1989], 182 and Haskell, "Capitalism and the Origins of Humanitarian Sensibility," *The Antislavery Debate: Capitalism and Abolitionism*, ed. Thomas Bender [Berkeley, 1992].).

us simply note that Sontag implicitly theorizes here, once again, the possibility of a non-Western modernity, articulated as a set of aesthetic practices that allow China to consume the "goods" of Western modernity without simultaneously taking on the burden of their cultural content, just as the use of acupuncture anesthesia allowed China to show that it could produce modernity's goods in a way that was culturally Chinese: anesthesia without anesthetics, cameras without photography. Given what "photography" meant for Sontag—shifts in visual points of view, "discontinuous ways of seeing" produced by dramatic cropping or alteration of visual angles, the "hyping of the real" that occurs in the montage of photographic magazines or contemporary film—this suggested, finally, that China might have a modernity without modernism, a modernity disconnected from the set of visual practices with which it is most commonly associated in the West. Photography "in our sense," Sontag wrote, "has no place in their society" (*OP*, 174).

In the 1970s, at least, Antonioni seemed far less capable than Sontag of seeing the debate over his documentary as produced by anything other than a Chinese misunderstanding of his motives. In a 1975 interview, he defended himself against the Chinese response: "It has been said that I've denigrated Chinese children. I don't really know why. I made shots of those children while they were singing their little songs; their delicious little faces. They are really beautiful, Chinese children, and if I could, I would adopt one."[17] At the intersection of international symbolic superstructures, the willingness to adopt a Chinese child—the ultimate, and ultimately transnational, good intention, occurring here in the echo of Buck's 1949 founding of Welcome House, an organization designed to encourage the adoption of Chinese children in the United States—becomes proof against photographic violence, as though the assertion of an intention to care could undo the discontinuous ruptures of form.[18]

As Sontag suggests, however, it's precisely the difference between aesthetic form and loving care that is at stake in *Chung Kuo*. If photographic seeing cares for the world it sees by breaking it into ever-newer pieces, then anyone for whom care means being seen *whole* will experience photographic "love" as a gesture of intolerable violence, and may ask to be seen on other terms, demanding not only to choose the close-ups, but insisting that the Mr. DeMilles of the world not shoot close-ups at all. Here the dream of photography's ability to grant the planet a singular, shared mode of representation—as one optimistic journalist put it in

[17] Cited in Bachmann, 30.

[18] And perhaps it can, though it did not for Antonioni.

1840, photography would be "the first universal language addressing itself to all who possess vision and in characters alike understood in the course of civilization and the hut of the savage"—founders upon the recognition that the apparatus of "photographic seeing" that Sontag attributes to the West is not the necessary consequence of the invention of the camera.[19]

2. Geographies of the Anesthetic

How does one understand, in relation to the complex historical knot that unites photography, anesthesia, and the acupuncture operations of the early 1970s, the circulation during most of the twentieth century of photographs like the one reproduced here (figure 6.2)?[20] This picture of a man being executed at the end of the Qing dynasty, in the early 1900s, was almost certainly taken by a European. Other photographs of executions like this one—which involves the procedure called in Chinese *lingchi*, in English the death of a thousand cuts, that was discussed in Mason's 1801 book on Chinese costumes—were part of a postcard series, called *Les supplices chinois* (*Chinese tortures*), which circulated between

[19] Cited in Anne McClintock, *Imperial Leather: Race, Gender and Sexuality in the Colonial Contest* (New York, 1995), 123.

[20] Mieke Bal once told a group of people I was in that when she has to reproduce a picture she considers "pornographic," she goes to some efforts to do so without actually reproducing it "whole"—reducing it in size, cropping it in ways that reduce its force, and so forth. My sense is that too much respect for the image—a respect that would declare, for instance, that it is unethical to reproduce it at all—simply replicates the image's violence by making it into a fetish for the power of the visual (on this see Rey Chow, who asks for "a careful reading of the materiality of the images" [*Writing Diaspora: Tactics of Intervention in Contemporary Cultural Studies* (Bloomington, 1993), 40].). Such a position is fundamentally incompatible with the major goals of this chapter and this book, which aims partly to show how the "respect" granted an other (a human other, or otherness in the form of pain or violence) almost always leads to a declaration that the other can only be subject to certain kinds of simple reading. What looks like it wants to protect the other, however, ends up protecting it from things like literary reading or the aesthetic that are almost always the modes in which the one doing the protecting comes to value objects outside of the instrumental. In reproducing this image and in reading it, then, I am attempting to engage it and the scene it reproduces as well as I know how—by treating it as a member of the community of worldly texts that can be subject to historical and literary critical modes of reading (of which this book is also, finally, a member). Beyond the general theoretical argument, one might ask whether my particular reproduction of this image is ethical, that is, whether the use to which I put that image here and the reading that I do of it do not simply reproduce its violence in ways that disregard my responsibilities to the readers of this book (as members of a community to which I belong, and as members of communities to which I do not belong), or to the people the image shows. That is a real question. I am open to the possibility that I am wrong.

Fig 6.2 "The death of a thousand cuts." Courtesy of Jérôme Bourgon.

China and France in the early part of the last century.[21] Similar photographs appeared in books published in France, Belgium, and Germany between 1909 and 1926, in sources ranging from Ferdinand Joseph Harfeld's *Opinions Chinoises sur les Barbares d'Occident* (1909) to Louis Carpeaux's *Pékin qui s'en va* (1913), to Georges Dumas's *Traité de psychologie* (1923).[22] A print of this photograph belonged to Georges Bataille for most of his adult life. He refers to it in his

[21] On *lingchi*, see Timothy Brook, Jérôme Bourgon, and Gregory Blue, *Death by a Thousand Cuts* (Cambridge, Mass., 2008). On the Taiwanese artist Chen Chieh-Jen, who has used as raw material photographs of Chinese victims of violence, including this one, modifying them by inserting his own face into the photographic scene, see Joyce C. H. Liu, "The Gaze of Revolt: Chen Chieh-Jen's historical images and his aesthetic of horror" available online at http://www.srcs.nctu.edu.tw/joyceliu/mworks/mw-interart/GazeOfRevolt/GazeOfRevolt.htm; see also Michael Berry, *A History of Pain: Trauma in Modern Chinese Literature and Film* (New York, 2008).

[22] The appearance of these three books in a list should not obscure important differences in their attitudes and presentations of images of *lingchi*. In Harfeld, for instance, the images are offered as evidence of the inappropriateness of Chinese judicial punishment during a dialogue between a Chinese mandarin and a Westerner on the question of exterritoriality. The Western speaker describes an execution by crucifixion, and says, "*Avouez que ce mode de répression est un peu vif, de même que le 'ling hi,' d'ailleurs*" ("admit that this mode of punishment is a bit much, just like the 'ling hi,' for that matter" [74]). A brief discussion follows, in which the Chinese speaker suggests that the *lingchi* is not as bad as it seems, and the Westerner replies that it (and judicial torture in general) nonetheless justify the temporary extension of extraterritoriality. The dialogue segues into a discussion of *feng shui*. Though the first use of "*ling hi*" is footnoted with an elaboration and illustrated with six images, its

books *Guilty* and *Inner Experience.* It appears as an image for the first time in his work in *Tears of Eros* in 1961.

The meaning of this photograph, and even the obvious "content" of this image, depend profoundly on the context of its circulation. In a discussion of the psychology of crowds, the image instantiates; as a postcard, it titillates; as a family keepsake, it commemorates; in a newspaper report, it illustrates. Any apprehension of the image, then, begins with a circulatory context that privileges certain kinds of reading and obscures others. (A complete reading of this photograph—of any photograph—could therefore attempt to record, or imagine, all its possible and actual modes of circulation.) I would like to begin by foregrounding two of this photograph's major contexts: first its circulation as one of a number of images of this type, and thus its production of codes that belong to a broader historical class; second, its history as the subject of Bataille's writing and thought.

As an example of a class of photos, this photograph is also, one might say, a picture of an example. That is, insofar as this photograph participates in a general European interest in pictures or descriptions of Chinese torture that one can trace back to the sixteenth century, it does so because it reproduces Chinese judicial violence as a typological instance whose most profound communication is anthropological.

This communication emerges from the difference between how the photograph looks and the looking it sees. It may be banal to say that the photograph's subjects—not just the condemned man, but the crowd that bends inward toward the executioner who, seen from behind, saws at the knee—owe their arrangement in space to codes borrowed from culturally specific habits of perspective and representation, some of which are encoded in advance in the camera as a machine. Nonetheless, a reading of the photograph can usefully begin with the difference between the "perspective" it organizes and the "event" to which it refers, and the manner in which the perspective modifies the content of the event it shows. I am not suggesting that there could be an authentic or appropriate perspective on this event to which one could compare the photograph's perspective. But that the photograph as photograph already contains within itself as a condition of its own readability the difference between the how and the what: how it shows, and what it shows.

---

appearance in the text remains subordinate to the larger discussion at hand, which attempts to give voice to the legitimate grievances Chinese people might have against the West (see vii–viii).

In the photograph, the members of the crowd have arranged themselves in a physical and scopic circle around the condemned man's leg. The crowd that seems to surround the condemned man does not, in fact, surround "him"; the direction of its attention is firmly on the state-sponsored violence metonymized and embodied by the figure of executioner at work (two men in the back crane their necks to look at, what? . . . not the man's face; his leg). The photograph shows the crowd, but it also shows what the crowd does not attend to, the condemned man's face and torso. His body faces the camera. A reading of the photograph according to aesthetic codes could remark the line that follows the executioner's back, the stake, directly to the man's chest, which, as it is more in focus and less faded than his face, becomes the major focal point of the photograph itself. Because the man's chest has been cut open, it is the site of the viewer's greatest vulnerability to sympathetic pain; it is in this sense the "face" of the photograph, and its apertures stare, like eyes, back at the viewer (we do not see the faces of the executioner and his helper, both of whom have their backs to the camera).[23] The eyes of the victim's face are blank. The condemned man's body faces the camera as the face of his pain, the surface of his suffering and the violence that produces it.[24]

With its eye on this face, the photograph offers its audience the possibility of reading the man's suffering in relation to the indifference of the crowd, whose focus lies instead on what one might call the execution's technical side. The photograph sees not only the original event, located in reality's apparent zero degree, of the execution of a condemned man, but also a looking at that event which, while located in the photograph's internal referential space, nonetheless is referred to and commented on by the photograph's own regard. The gap between what the photograph shows and how it shows it can therefore be understood as folded into the internal space of its own reference. It shows an unseen showing, a given-to-be-seen that it witnesses and records, even as it also shows a failure on

[23] A reading of the chest wounds as apertures also appears in Chen Chieh-Jen's film *Lingchi*, which shows a reenactment of the scene in the Bataille photo. At one point, the camera films from *inside* the chest in order to look back at the crowd that stares at the victim's execution. For a reading of the film in the general context of historical violence in China, see Berry.

[24] Let us be clear—we are in the presence once more of a "language of agency" in relation to pain that does not show the man's pain so much as it produces metaphors that signify pain. Given that those put to death by *lingchi* were apparently given opium in order to keep them from dying too quickly from the shock produced by the pain of the flaying, it is possible that the condemned man was not feeling any pain at all at the moment the photograph was taken. The photograph does not therefore "show" the condemned man's actual pain, but rather generates sympathetic pain in the viewer.

the part of another set of looks to register the spectacle of the body as it is given to be seen: the photograph shows, that is, its own seeing and another seeing; it sees both its seeing and another, internal seeing. Among the subjects of the photograph is this difference, produced by the how of the what.

This triangular structure, familiar from the discussion of Bertrand Russell and the Chinese dog in chapter 5, can be thought in relation to Buck-Morss's theory of photography. Buck-Morss had argued that the camera's "transformation of perception" depended on the split it induced between agent (the camera), matter (the referential real world), and observer (the spectator). In this image, the photographer's gaze surgically penetrates the inert matter of Chinese life on behalf of an observer back home who will encounter China (or "Chineseness" more generally) as an anesthetized and objectified body, that is, a body that cannot intervene in its own self-production as subject. The separation between agent, inert matter, and observer occurs at the intersection of the photographer's experience of the execution as practice and the ability to record the execution in mediatic form.[25]

That separation, understood in the context of the photograph's circulation as a postcard, illustration of a foreign curiosity, generates the photograph's relation to cultural specificity. The crowd's indifference to the violence and suffering, the difference between the general look of the Chinese crowd and the single look shared by the victim and the photographer, tells the audience of the postcard not only that such terrible things happen but that some group of people can be indifferent to them. In Buck-Morrss's terms, the photograph's penetration of Chinese life (and thus its "anesthetization" of the body of the image) occurs at least partly in order to critique the anesthetized regard of the Chinese crowd, to contrast the photographer's own sensitive relation to the condemned man's pain with the crowd's anesthetized indifference. At the cultural level, then, the photograph aligns itself with an Enlightenment faith in the representationality

[25]This is fairly clear also in Carpeaux's *Pékin qui s'en va*, which registers the execution of Fou-Tchou-Li in both words and photographs: "*La foule innombrable regardait d'un oeil indifférent ce beau corps d'ivoire dont l'harmonie des formes sculpturales était vouée à la boucherie infâme*" ("The enormous crowd looked with an indifferent eye at this beautiful ivory body, whose sculpturally formal harmony was destined for vile butchery") (185). In this instance, the crowd's indifference is simultaneously directed at Fou-Tchou-Li's suffering and at his body conceived as an aesthetic object ("*beau corps d'ivoire*," etc.). Of the Bataille photograph, one might say that the crowd both fails to appreciate the victim's pain—it is anesthetized to it—and that it fails to appreciate the aesthetic perspective from which it might observe the victim as the potential subject of a photograph, a perspective shared by both the photographer and whoever observes the image. The separation between the agent and the matter is thereby doubled.

of representation and the universal value of the human, a sense that what the image shows is realistic both in the scene it shows and in the conclusions it proposes. It is precisely insofar as it does so that it, of course, does violence to the Chinese crowd by turning it into the anesthetized object of its surgical gaze. (That the execution the crowd happens to be witnessing is also a vivisection, and therefore a bleak metonym of actual surgical practice, effectively closes the interpretive circle.)

Considered as an example of a type, then, the photograph's reading of Chinese pain resembles very much Russell's, though this image, unlike Russell's story of the dog in the street, is layered over with the possibility of a fascinated, even pornographic pleasure in the destruction of a body-life, the transformation of a life into a body. In the sense that the photograph as photograph collaborates in this pleasure, it does so by turning the scene into an object, by reducing rather than intensifying the pain to which it refers; like the surgeon operating on the flesh of an inert body, the image objectifies what it acts on.[26] It is in this sense that the photograph reproduces something of the European relation to China in the modern era.[27]

[26]Perhaps the most extreme expression of such a relation to the photograph in general comes from Ernst Jünger, whose 1934 essay "On Pain" Buck-Morss cites as an instance of the total expression of fascist aesthetics. In the essay, Jünger approvingly notes the evolution of a new "human type" that he connects directly to "revolutionary fact of photography" ("Photography and the 'Second Consciousness': An Excerpt from *On Pain*," trans. Joel Agee, in *Photography in the Modern Era: European Documents and Critical Writings, 1913–1940*, ed. Christopher Phillips [New York, 1989] 208, 207.). Connecting the photograph's invulnerable eye to the new technologies of war and newly mass-mediated politics (where the "photograph is a weapon that is being used with increasing mastery"), Jünger envisioned nothing less than the development of a new "second" consciousness that would radically transform the human relation to pain: "As the process of objectification progresses, the amount of pain that can be endured grows as well. It almost seems as if man had an urge to create a space where, in a sense quite different from the one we are accustomed to, pain can be regarded as an illusion" (209–10). Here, the objectifying properties of photographic vision are turned to the production of a new generation of human beings capable of dissociating themselves from their own bodies, and thus from their own physical embeddedness in the world.

[27]James Hevia makes a different photograph of a Chinese execution figure the relationship between Europe and the West. The photograph he reproduces, taken from a booklet titled *Unique Photographs of the Execution of Boxers in China*, shows three British soldiers supervising the beheading of several men in 1900. A pillar near the execution ground, reproduced on the right side of the photograph, advertises English lessons. Hevia reads these two facts—the execution and the advertisement—as illustrations of the "hard" and "soft" sides of imperial power (*English Lessons: The Pedagogy of Imperialism in Nineteenth-Century China* [Durham, 2003], 3.). The photograph Hevia reproduces represents far more openly than Bataille's a relation to China arranged around military force and Western imperialism. Perhaps it is precisely because such a relation—that of the execution of colonial

Bataille's relation to the photograph can be read as a complete refusal of photographic objectification, an attempt to unmake both the photograph's surgical relation to its subject and the humanist, Russellian response that would condemn Chinese violence. Bataille's stature as a major figure in modern French literature and philosophy means that this superidentificatory relation to the photograph, and his reproductions of the photograph in descriptions and as image in his books, have historically produced a circuit of representation that competes with and, in certain contexts, overshadows the reading of the photograph I have pursued so far. In circles that exchange philosophy rather than postcards, Bataille, far more than the unknown person who took the picture, is the origin of its circulation. It is through his patronage that this photograph, now signifying something beyond Chinese violence, becomes "legendary."[28]

Though Bataille did not reproduce the photograph until it appeared in *Tears of Eros* in 1961, it appeared in his writing on several occasions before the war. In *Inner Experience* (1943), it provides a possible opening to ecstatic meditation:

> I had recourse to upsetting images. In particular, I would gaze at the photographic image—or sometimes the memory which I have of it—of a Chinese man who must have been tortured in my lifetime. Of this torture, I had had in the past a series of successive representations. In the end, the patient writhed, his chest flayed, arms and legs cut off at the elbows and the knees. His hair standing on end, hideous, haggard, striped with blood, beautiful as a wasp.
>
> I write "beautiful"! . . . something escapes me, flees from me, fear robs me of myself and, as if I had wanted to stare at the sun, my eyes rebel.[29]
>
> . . .
>
> The young and seductive Chinese man of whom I have spoken, left to the work of the executioner—I loved him with a love in which the sadistic

---

rebels—is so connected to the production of capitalist modernity that Hevia's photograph tells us less about the kind of *mythological* relation to China that I am exploring here.

[28] Susan Sontag, *Regarding the Pain of Others* (New York, 2003), 98.

[29] The sun's blinding light is a vital figure for Bataille, dating back to *Histoire de l'oeil* and "The Solar Anus." Eduardo Cadava, writing of Walter Benjamin, declares in a section on "Heliotropism" that "In the ancient correspondence between photography and philosophy, the photograph, related by the trope of light, becomes a figure of knowledge as well as of nature, a solar language of cognition that gives the mind and the senses access to the invisible" (*Words of Light: Theses on the Photography of History* [Princeton, 1997], 5.). On Bataille and sunlight, see James Elkins, *The Object Stares Back: On the Nature of Seeing* (New York, 1996), 103–05. On Bataille and the image, see Benjamin Noys, *Georges Bataille: A Critical Introduction* (London, 2000), 18–37.

> instinct played no part: he communicated his pain to me or perhaps the excessive nature of his pain, and it was precisely that which I was seeking, not so as to take pleasure in it, but in order to ruin in me that which is opposed to ruin.[30]

These responses present the emotional and political difficulty typical of Bataille's work. His erasure of the condemned man's life history, his passing over without comment the cultural and historical circumstances that surrounded (and legitimized) this execution, the fact that he calls the man a "patient" and "beautiful as a wasp": all these, but especially the last, occur beyond the pale of a reasonable relation to this image.

Bataille intends to resist just such "reasonableness." If he refuses to address himself to the man's particular suffering it is, Amy Hollywood writes, "because to uncover these dimensions of experience—to ask why such events occur and how they can be stopped—is to provide a narrative for them that risks covering over their sheer horror." For Bataille, "narrative and historical contextualization are . . . ways of evading the real." Any attempt to ask how to resolve this violence, to situate its causes, to trace its history, to register a protest in the name of a common humanity, replicates the violence perpetrated on the body of the speechless subaltern, forcing that body to mediate between its own pain and the sign that emerges from its readability. Any relation to the body of the tortured that aims to "provide a context in which demands for justice might be made" or make it the site of an origin that would aim to prevent its repetition erases the pain of that body, the experience of that body as a body, by making it into a historical or political sign.[31]

Bataille's reading of the photograph, which locates itself prior to any transformation of the condemned man into political use-value, attempts to interact with the image by respecting the moment it captures in its being as a moment, the man in his being as the man in the photograph. Rather than read the victim's pain in relation to the political or historical facts of state-sponsored violence, his biography, or the medical mechanics of saws, knives, and bodies, Bataille elevates the victim into a theological figure for a world beyond subjectivity, a world without self-protection or even selves at all. In this, Bataille's reading follows the theological and cultural traditions dormant in the word *supplice*, which in its earlier uses

[30] Georges Bataille, *Inner Experience*, trans. Leslie Anne Boldt (Albany, N.Y., 1988), 119–20.

[31] Amy Hollywood, *Sensible Ecstasy: Mysticism, Sexual Difference, and the Demands of History* (Chicago, 2002), 83.

Fig 6.3 George Henry Mason and Pu Qua, *The Punishments of China.* "The Capital Punishment of the Cord." Courtesy of The Huntington Library.

in French and English refers to a sacrifice that was "ceremonial in performance and transcendent in meaning," a notion embedded in European Christian culture and explicitly associated with the crucified Jesus.[32] The Christ-like arrangement of the torture victim in Bataille's photograph—or rather, the fact that this photograph and not some other one was able to become the one through which he communed with its victim—surely owes something to this cultural habit, in which "punishment was tightly connected to redemption, martyrdom to beatitude, and suffering to joy," and in fact can be seen in earlier depictions of Chinese punishment, for instance in this image, figure 6.3, from Mason's *Punishments* book.[33]

In relation to the organization of looking and seeing that presents itself as the face of a photograph on Chinese practice, or in terms of the historical mode of circulation of this photograph prior to its arrival in his hands, Bataille's response can only be a misreading. It ignores much of the photograph's referential content (the crowd, the executioners), not to mention its history of circulation, and its

[32] Brook et al., 21.
[33] Brook et al., 21.

mediatic status. But such a misreading is not necessarily false. Or rather, in reading falsely, by ignoring aspects of the photograph's referential space and its point of view, it falsifies what is already false in the photograph, refusing the anthropological gesture that leads either to a sense of cultural superiority or to a justified and prosthetic intervention in the name of an asserted common humanity. Acting as though the photograph could mediate transcendentally between himself and the condemned man, Bataille pairs a complicity with the "death" present in all photography with a genuinely violent disregard for the difference between a picture of something and the thing itself. Bataille's reading of the photograph is not therefore "photographic" in Sontag's sense; it aims to engage the photograph through a sensory mechanism that resides beyond the visual. He does not so much "look" at the photograph as commune with it.

This communion enacts its own violence, discarding the particulars of the man's history and suffering in favor of philosophical utility. As Hollywood writes, "it is precisely the distance between Bataille and the victim that enables him both to particularize the suffering other (in ways that efface the historical and political grounds of his or her suffering) and to generalize from that individual to the suffering of any and all human beings."[34] Though one can admire it for its refusal of the photograph's easy cultural superiority, then, Bataille's position is not for all that anthropologically innocent: Europeans and Americans have a long history of finding the West's ideational limit in the transformational ecstasy or suicide of a positive identification with ethnic otherness. Bataille never mentions the condemned man without mentioning his Chineseness. (In *Tears of Eros*, the photograph appears between a series of images of a voodoo ritual and the reproduction of a European painting of Aztec human sacrifice.[35]) The geographic shadow thereby cast over the argument suggests that the experience of extreme pain Bataille sees in the photograph derives its force at least partly from the fact that the picture's referential origin is China.[36] Bataille's transformation of the photo-

[34] Hollywood, 93.

[35] The placement of the image in *Larmes d'Eros* undergoes some fairly significant changes between the first and second editions. In the first edition image appears facing image a reproduction of Balthus's frankly erotic *La Leçon de guitare* (1934); whereas in the second the facing images are close-ups and other images from the execution sequence. The third edition returns to the model of the first; the only English-language edition adopts the structure of the second edition. In both cases the images of voodoo and Aztec sacrifice are the immediate surrounding context for the images of the Chinese execution. I am grateful to Jérôme Bourgon for drawing this shift to my attention.

[36] This structure is almost inevitable in the modern West: why does the Other so often grant us what we lack, restoring us to the fullness and plenitude we so desire? Because the Other is what we define as that which has what we lack. The problem occurs, as Christopher Bush has shown, when the

graph's victim from subject to insect, "young and seductive Chinese man" to "wasp," which resists the more general photographic objectification performed by the photograph in the mode of its circulation as a postcard or a foreign curiosity by remapping the man's humanness onto categories of being—the insectoid and the aesthetic—able to persist beyond his subjective death, loses some of its philosophical force as a result.[37] Bataille's relation to the man in the photograph remains "bewitched in the ambiguous circle of the sacred," that is, in the fundamental political structure of modern life.[38] The philosophical pretensions of Bataille's argument may founder, it is true, on the grounds of his failure to imagine an alternative to political life outside the pure possibility of transgression, but it may also be enough to say that they founder because the alternative they imagine to Western modernity takes as its most transgressive figure someone who Bataille cannot love without mentioning that he is from the East.

Considering now the relationship between this photograph of Bataille's and a more general theory of photography and anesthesia, one might say that Bataille's reading of the photograph attempts to overcome the photograph's anesthetizing and objectifying properties by inverting them, so that the photograph becomes in his hands the communicative path between himself as an observer and the total experience of the victim's totalizing and absolute pain, and not an (an)aestheticized look at "inert matter." Rather than diminish the experience of pain, then, the photograph seems to expand and extend it, making it possible for Bataille to merge with the referential surface rather than "penetrate" it.[39] At the same time,

---

racial other becomes the Other in general ("The Other of the Other?: Cultural Studies, Theory, and the Location of the Modernist Signifier." *Comparative Literature Studies* 42.2 [2005].). "Geographic shadow" refers to Gayatri Spivak's introduction to her translation of Derrida's *Of Grammatology*, in which she notes that "the shadow of a geographical pattern . . . falls upon the first part of the book" (Derrida, *Of Grammatology*, trans. Gayatri Spivak [Baltimore, 1976], lxxxii.).

[37] In this context, consider this astonishing sentence of Jean-Paul Sartre's, which appears in his introduction to Henri Cartier-Bresson's 1954 *D'une Chine a l'autre:* "The negroes did not concern me; I'd been taught they were good dogs; with them, we were mammals together. But the Asian scared me; like these crabs from the rice paddies which jump up from between two furrows, like the locusts which descend on the great plain and devastate everything. We are kings of the fish, of the lions, of the rats, and of the monkeys; the Chinese is a superior insect, he rules over the insects." The comparison to insects should recall the figure of the coolie, discussed in chapter 4.

[38] Giorgio Agamben, *Homo Sacer: Sovereign Power and Bare Life*, trans. Daniel Heller-Roazen (Stanford, 1998), 113.

[39] Bataille's relation to this particular photograph may be "erotic" but it is not sexual, though elsewhere, of course, Batialle is the great twentieth-century elaborator of the relationship between pain and pleasure. Karen Halttunen has placed the development of the relationship between pain and

one can argue, thinking of the geographic pattern of his subjective affiliation with the victim in the picture, that this extreme subjectification and intensification of real pain breaks through one anesthetic perspective only to adopt another one. Though Bataille's relation to the photograph cannot be considered "photographic" in the sense in which Sontag or Buck-Morss define it, his production of an alternative mode of seeing through the Chinese figure in the image—a figure which represents, in twentieth century Europe, evidence of China's connection to a pre-modern European past very much caught up in judicial violence and, thus, a relation to pre-modern primitivity that cannot be ignored (remember the other images around this one: voodoo and Aztec sacrifice) must be understood as a gesture of the same type as Sontag's division of the world into a dictatorship of the interesting and a dictatorship of the good. It is in this sense that Bataille "re-objectifies" the victim in the image, by making his philosophical significance dependent at least partially on the ethnic or national origin of the scene of which he is a part. The difficulty philosophy has registering this kind of geographic effect indicates, one might conclude, a kind of cognitive anesthesia, an inability to perceive the importance of the place that it consistently fails to perceive.

3. The *Hyle*: Intentions of the Image

Writing in 1927, Siegfried Kracauer declared with some alarm that "the world itself has taken on a 'photographic face'; it can be photographed because it strives to be absorbed into the spatial continuum which yields to snapshots."[40] Kracauer's argument, in some ways simply the more general case of Buck-Morss's reading of the operating theater, was that the world had come to arrange

pleasure, particularly as it was expressed in pornography, explicitly in contact with the same large-scale development of humanitarianism that produced the dramatic rise in European and American attention to pain beginning in the eighteenth century ("Humanitarianism and the Pornography of Pain in Anglo-American Culture," *The American Historical Review* 100.2 [Apr. 1995].). She writes: "The modern pornography of pain taking shape in the late eighteenth and early nineteenth centuries was not merely a seamy sideline to humanitarian reform literature but rather an integral aspect of the human sensibility" (304). The rise in the production of a "more modern kind of sexual writing" that included depictions of the infliction of pain, especially the flogging pornography of the eighteenth and nineteenth centuries, allowed "the spectacle of suffering . . . [to become] the dominant convention of sexual pornography by the early nineteenth century" (317).

[40] Cited in Cadava, xxvii.

itself in accordance with the demands of a particular type of photography. But Kracauer did not, Eduardo Cadava writes, simply think the world should refuse its status as a photograph. Rather he believed that "the photographic present returns eternally to the event of its death—a death that comes with the death of understanding. . . . What remains at stake for [Kracauer] is the possibility of a politics that, beginning from the presupposition of our mortality, asks us to be answerable for these deaths," deaths that included but were not reducible to the horrors of the World War I and the fatal rhythms of Taylorized industrial production.[41] To think of the man in Bataille's photograph as a figure for ecstatic transformation, as Bataille does, is to approach an ethics that attempts to be answerable to the image-death of the photograph as such by communicating with the living-death of its indexed subject.

Such readings of photographs, which return insistently to the idea that any given image is "an image of death," and argue that "conjunction of death and the photographed is in fact the very principle of photographic certitude," present us with some of the most compelling theoretical arguments about photographs available today, at least partly because their vision of a world layered over with death-images borrows from a quasi-tragic, quasi-theological reading of modernity as an era of profound loss.[42] But the relentless morbidity of such readings, despite their ring of truth, misses in its death-drive something of the living presence of the photograph as a material object, and so they are prone to produce—as they do for Bataille in this instance—incomplete or finally uninteresting readings of the photographs they care for.

In phenomenology the term *hyle* is used "to describe that which is perceived but not intended." Buck-Morss uses Edmund Husserl's example of a Dürer woodcarving of a knight to explain the concept: "Although the wood is perceived along with the knight's image, it is not the *meaning* of perception. If you are asked, what do you see? you will say, a knight (i.e., the surface image), not a piece of wood."[43] Likewise, then, with the paper that sustains the photographic print, the physical medium whose chemical malleability permits the aesthetic one its being.

Nonetheless, the photograph is never simply an image, but always an image attached to a particular material substrate that itself organizes and responds to

[41] Cadava, xxviii–xxix.

[42] Cadava, 10.

[43] Buck-Morss, 28.

historical effects and affective relations.[44] We can imagine one index of the *hyle*'s intentions if we think of the way a photographic print organizes light. The print generates a visual field "behind" and through itself, opening focal depth in a rectangle some twenty inches square, even as it beams the light it reflects forward in "front" of its surface like an inverted cone. Placed on a desk, the snapshot makes a hole in the world, and the light that emerges from this hole casts its glare over the desk entire; the photo can be picked up, handled, put face down or in a drawer, its illuminations shifting as it moves.

This relation to light belongs to the print alone. Described in language or reproduced in the pages of a book, the image is all front and no back, all surface; the focal depth it generates has no physical counterpart in the real space behind or beneath it. It retains its indexical or iconic qualities, its ability to refer to an anthropological practice or an experiential limit, but loses what allowed it to be held, to be differentiated and broken off from the world. As Elizabeth Edwards and Janice Hart have argued, an approach to photographs "that acknowledges the centrality of materiality allows one to look at and use images as socially salient objects, as active and reciprocal rather than simply implications of authority, control and passive consumption on one hand, or of aesthetic discourses and the supremacy of individual vision on the other."[45]

In following Edwards and Hart's injunction to read photographs materially, I intend to elucidate the theoretical underpinnings of the analysis of Pu Qua's paintings in chapter 2, where an attention to the circulation of the image as a commodity modified what might otherwise have seemed to be a purely formal relationship between caption and image in Mason's *Punishments* book. Instead of focusing on the photograph's status as a commodity located in the context of international trade and intercultural representation, however, I would like to discuss the photograph simply, or not so simply, as a material thing whose physical properties tend to constellate a particular set of subjective responses, to wonder how its status as an inanimate object constitutes human subjects, how it moves them, how it threatens them, and how it shapes, positively or negatively,

[44] Sontag begins *On Photography* with a meditation on the relation between photograph and image, remarking that "with still photographs the image is also an object, lightweight, cheap to produce, easy to carry about, accumulate, store" (3).

[45] Elizabeth Edwards and Janice Hart, *Photographs Objects Histories: On the Materiality of Images* (New York, 2004), 15. On the materiality of the image, see also Carol Mavor, *Pleasures Taken: Performances of Sexuality and Loss in Victorian Photographs* (Durham, N.C., 1995), and Dick Hebdige, *Hiding in the Light: On Images and Things* (London, 1988).

their relation to other subjects.[46] To put it plainly, the problem of reading I am addressing is this: How can one come to read and understand a thing that is also a sign, a sign that is also a thing, without giving short shrift either to materiality or meaning? How can one read a photograph as a picture of something, without ignoring the something upon which that picture appears?[47]

The photograph of the execution I have been calling "Bataille's photograph" was given to him, he says, in 1925. Sontag says that it sat on his desk, "where he could look at it every day."[48] Bataille's biographer Michel Surya writes that photographs of this execution "obsessed him," and that he "often spoke of them, and always kept them."[49] Bataille described this photograph twice in writing before reproducing its image in *Tears of Eros*. In *Inner Experience*, he mentions in a note that he had the photo "for a long time at home"; in *Guilty* he calls it "my photo." In *Tears of Eros* he writes, "Since 1925, I have owned one of these snapshots. It was given to me by Borel, one of the first French psychoanalysts. This photograph had a decisive role in my life. I have never stopped being obsessed by this image of pain, at once ecstatic(?) and intolerable."[50] Reading these sentences with an eye on the *hyle* of the image, it is worth recalling Benjamin's claim that "ownership is the most intimate relationship that one can have to objects." Each time Bataille mentions the photograph something in his language points directly to its belonging to him.[51]

[46] This sentence paraphrases and cites Bill Brown, who writes: "Methodological fetishism, then, is not an error so much as it is a condition for thought, new thoughts about how inanimate objects constitute human subjects, how they move them, how they threaten them, how they facilitate or threaten their relation to other subjects" ("Thing Theory," *Critical Inquiry* 28 [Autumn 2001], 7).

[47] This discussion of the photograph's material substrate owes a great deal Brown as well as to N. Katherine Hayles; what I am trying to do here is to bring together Brown's work on things with Hayles' work (especially in *Writing Machines* [Cambridge, Mass., 2002] and *How We Became Posthuman: Virtual Bodies in Cybernetics, Literature, and Informatics* [Chicago, 1999]) on literary media in order to pursue readings of the things I have been calling mediatic "substrates" or "surfaces," upon or through which representations are carved, written, chemically induced to appear, projected, spoken, played, and so forth.

[48] *Regarding the Pain of Others*, 98. Sontag lists no source for this fact, and I have not been able to confirm it elsewhere.

[49] Michel Surya, *Georges Bataille: An Intellectual Biography*, trans. Krzysztof Fijalkowski and Michael Richardson (London, 2002), 94.

[50] *Inner Experience*, 119; *Guilty*, trans. Bruce Boone (San Francisco, 1988), 38; *The Tears of Eros*, trans. Peter Connor (San Francisco, 1989), 205–206, translation modified. Jérôme Bourgon has told me in conversation that he is not sure that Bataille really owned a print of the image for as long as he claims to have in *Tears of Eros*. If he did not, the description and desire circulating around its ownership become more significant, not less, to this analysis.

[51] Benjamin, *Illuminations*, 67.

But ownership is just one gesture in a broader economy of exposure and concealment, transaction and adjudication, in which a print can be given as a gift, placed on a desk or a wall, hidden from children, shown only to special friends, fall out of an album or be dropped in a puddle or otherwise damaged or lost, protected or exposed. The *hyle* of the photograph calls out to the subject as a thing subject to the same cares or miseries as a subjective life. Rereading Bataille's descriptions of the image for clues about his relation to the print it appeared on, one sees the consistent expression of the image's material aspects, intimations that its presence in his life was governed at least partly by an ethics of possession and care arranged around the materiality of the photograph's physical being.

How does the field of visual projection indexed by the image interact with the field of auratic, possessive projection established by the photographic print? How can the print be read in its totality as image-thing? And what can the answers to those questions teach about the historical value of this particular image as it was owned by Bataille, and about the larger problematic of anesthetizing vision and aestheticized pain of which this photograph is a token?[52]

The souvenir's "double function," writes Susan Stewart, "is to authenticate a past or otherwise remote experience and, at the same time, to discredit the present. The present is either too impersonal, too looming, or too alienating compared to the intimate and direct experience of contact which the souvenir has as its referent. This referent is authenticity."[53] Bataille's photograph is a souvenir in two senses; it marks within his own history his relationship with his psychoanalyst, Adrien Borel, and thus memorializes a shared masculine bond that is itself the product of a model of medical care. And, in its reference to both the absolute terrifying pain of the condemned man and the "exotic," "primitive" temporality of late Qing dynasty China, the photograph remembers and memorializes the possibility of an "authentically human" experience, where

[52] Or even, but this is beyond the scope of this book, how do mediatic substrates become sites of international transactions of feeling designed to alter political structures or international development? Consider in this context the *Saturday Review*'s sponsorship of a World Travel Photographic Awards contest beginning in 1954, which articulated itself in these terms: "East is East and West is West and the twain shall meet in a camera" (cited in Christina Klein, *Cold War Orientalism: Asia in the Middlebrow Imagination, 1945–1961* [Berkeley, 2003], 115). The camera becomes a ground for armistice-signing, like a moving train, perhaps, a figure for movement and transformation that resolves ideological or cultural conflicts by opening up an imaginary and inhuman neutrality in the internal space of the apparatus.

[53] Susan Stewart, *On Longing: Narratives of the Miniature, the Gigantic, the Souvenir, the Collection* (Durham, N.C., 1993), 139.

"authentically human" means something like "outside European modernity," that is, outside the dissipating tensions of the "modern" present.

The authenticity physically retrieved by the souvenir as the double marker of real human experience and of genuine friendship depends largely on its status as a thing, but Bataille's souvenir was of course not just any old thing. Because his souvenir was also a photograph, the entire memorial apparatus encoded in its object-status is layered over with the fact that as an object the photograph is always already a kind of souvenir, an image that indexes and memorializes a certain moment in the past. The photograph in particular does this so intensely as to produce a linguistic slippage between what it remembers and what it is, so that people will point to photographs and say things like, "this is my son," or, "this is a man being executed in the early 1900s."[54] Even as it functions as a souvenir and is thus connected to the potential retrieval of a visible moment or an experience, the photograph is widely considered to be profoundly inauthentic, a terrifying distortion of "natural" experience whose seductive authenticity must be resisted in the name of other ways of seeing. These two functions of the photograph as the most authentic possible souvenir and as the most inauthentic distortion of the real are connected. Only because the photograph seems so authentic must its inauthenticity be loudly and widely declaimed. This double asymptote of authenticity and inauthenticity makes the photograph the perfect souvenir, since the purpose of the souvenir is to embody enough authenticity to create nostalgia in relation to an absent past, without ever embodying so much authenticity as to fully assuage the nostalgia it creates (if it could, it would simply become the experience it remembers, and thus cease to be a souvenir at all).

In relation, then, to what the image of Bataille's photograph shows, one might say that the print's production of its authenticity as object relies heavily on the extremity of the scene that it performs as image. More than that, however, one can also argue that the photograph's image of the transformation of life into death by way of the figure of the mutilated body of the condemned man figures at the level of the image the role of the photograph as thing; the print as souvenir perfectly captures the threshold between the life of the object as the fully authentic expression of a set of subjective desires (the friendship with Borel, the desire to commune with the "young and seductive" man) and the failure of the object to be those desires absolutely. In this sense, this souvenir-photograph recapitulates the dying of the

[54] Barthes gives the former example in *Camera Lucida: Reflections on Photography,* trans. Richard Howard (New York, 1981), 5.

condemned man by echoing the movement of authentic life-experience into authentic corpse-souvenir—a corpse which to be authentic as a corpse must be inauthentic as a live body. Thus, the care that Bataille offers the photograph is on one hand a monstrous inversion of the lack of care for the condemned man depicted in the image, and on the other a kind of recapitulation of precisely the process which is occurring in the image itself, in which Bataille's retention and care of the object as the threshold between experience and representation—that is, as a souvenir—reproduces in a fairly astonishing way the photograph's own retention and care of the image as an image of the threshold between life and death. Insofar as Bataille cares for the photograph, then, insofar as he protects it against loss or damage (by keeping it out of the rain, by knowing where it is), or grants it the right to mirror back to him an idealized but absent subjectivity, he does so in perfect concord not only with what it shows but also with what it is.[55]

Nothing here decides whether this concord is admirable, or obscene. But attending to the particular material qualities of the photograph, and to the specific cultural role it fills as souvenir, makes it possible to think of the photographic relation expressed by Bataille's ownership of this image as something more complex than simply "anesthetized." If we allow the care and pride in ownership Bataille exhibits in relation to this photograph to stand in for the general care and pride in ownership people tend to have in relation to things then it may not make sense to think of anesthetizing vision as objectifying at all. In an essay on the traffic of East Asian trade goods throughout the United States in the nineteenth century, Christopher Bush has juxtaposed the amount of care given to and money spent on Chinese and Japanese *objects* during the late 1800s with the amount of cultural racism and physical violence directed at Chinese and Japanese *people* in that same period. The people would have been better off, he points out, being treated like the objects. The idea that "objectifying" someone is inevitably a bad thing, which depends on the idea that people are indifferent to the feelings of

[55] Much of this analysis operates also for the postcard version of the image, but in the case of the postcard the intensity of its role as souvenir is modified by the fact of its mass reproduction, and by the movement of the postcard itself. Malek Alloula has written that the postcard sent by the European abroad "is the fragmentary return to the mother country" because it "straddles two spaces: the one it represents and the one it will reach" (*The Colonial Harem*, trans. Myrna Godzich and Wlad Godzich [Minneapolis, 1986], 4.). That prosthetic return home happens at the level of the object, not the image. Here again, the intention of the *hyle* will be missed by a reader who is not the intended recipient of its traveling message, which is tactile and physical rather than textual, though clearly the two levels operate in concert and cannot, therefore, easily be considered apart from one another; as Mitchell reminds us, all media are mixed media (*Picture Theory*, 94).

the objects they own—that they do not imbue them with subjectivity more or less independent from their own—must be revised to account for this understanding. Writing specifically on the quality of Japanese objects and the ways in which they called out to be treated, Bush suggests that we might imagine between the subject and object a "a less hierarchized, more multidirectional model in which reification, commodification, aestheticization, and racialization can be understood as historically related modalities of the relationship between abstraction and concretion (including personification)."[56]

While photographic vision may anesthetize, then, it does not, strictly speaking, "objectify," or rather, in objectifying it runs the risk of undoing the anesthetizing work implicit in its visual mode, since turning the raw material of experience into a possessable thing will open it to modes of sympathy that are in many cases more profound than the ones that bridge the gap between people. (In another historical context, as Jonathan Lamb has shown, narratives written by former slaves often adopted the conventions of the eighteenth-century genre known as "it-narratives" or "object-tales" in order to announce the transformation of chattel into person.[57]) This is not to argue that relations to things are unproblematic or simple, or to suggest that things are inevitably treated better than people (or that they should or shouldn't be). But I want to complicate theories of the photograph's anesthetizing vision that assume that the death of feeling necessarily occurs when something becomes an object to be penetrated by a surgeon or a camera eye, that is, when the agent is able to treat that which it acts on as "inert matter." Such theories misunderstand the history of human relations to inert matter as it coalesces in things and overestimate the necessity of sympathetic relations between human beings. Considered in relation to photographs of

[56]Christopher Bush, "The Ethnicity of Things in America's Lacquered Age," *Representations* 99 (Summer 2007), 85. On insects, see note 20 in chapter 4. The Chinese origin of photographs of *lingchi* is not forgotten in Julio Cortázar's *Hopscotch*, where a man named Wong carries a folded up sheet showing eight successive images of a death. But the importance of the image's materiality can also be measured by the care with which it emerges from Wong's wallet, and then is returned to it: "The piece of paper was folded in four, a black leather wallet opened its mouth like a crocodile and gobbled it up from amidst the smoke" (*Hopscotch*, trans. Gregory Rabassa, [New York, 1966], 56.). The relation between the paper and the wallet that holds it is so intense as to turn the wallet into another intermediary figure of life and death: the Egyptian crocodile-god Sobek was widely believed to be responsible both for fertility and for the punishment or rewarding of the dead. Wong's interlocutor Oliveira refers briefly to the most intense European example of the connection between sexual pleasure and Chinese torture, Octave Mirbeau's 1899 *Le Jardin des supplices*.

[57]Jonathan Lamb, "Modern Metamorphoses and Disgraceful Tales," *Critical Inquiry* 28 (Autumn 2001), 158.

people in extreme pain, like Bataille's, this suggests that readings of such photographs as the archetypical figures of photographic anesthesia, or indeed, readings of those photographs as allowing for theological identification with the other, may depend not so much on what the image contains as on the interaction between that image and the material surface upon which it appears. That same photograph multiplied thousands of times and placed in the pages of Bataille's *Tears of Eros* may provoke, as it does in me, feelings of horror and despair, but those feelings occur within the framework of my knowledge that I do not own this picture, that it is not unique, and that I am not responsible for taking care of it. In this sense, the image's de-objectification through mass reproduction, the way that it ceases to register as a single object once it is multiplied on the pages of a published book, may in fact be more profoundly anesthetizing than the initial moment of its capture on film. (Though even the mass reproduction of the object creates structures of feeling, most visibly in the form of communities of ownership; at stake here are differences within a system rather than a set of binaries aligning singularity with aesthetics, mass production with anesthesia, and so on.) The fact that Bataille owned the image as a photograph and not as a postcard thus makes an enormous difference to his relation to it, even though a complete reading of that relation would have to account, as I have tried to do, for the fact that other images like it were circulating as postcards in the years before Bataille put his photograph on his desk.

Returning to Bataille's photograph with its materiality in mind, it seems important now to try to make this analysis operate also at the level of the inside of the image, to see what happens when we come back to the image "as such" and attempt to read in its arrangement of light a relationship to the kinds of formal structures I have been attending to at the level of the print.

Originally, you will recall, the discussion of the image according to Buck-Morss's tripartite structure of observation took the photographer as agent, the execution as "inert matter," and the various audiences of the image as postcard or print as its observers, who watch passively from behind a "glass partition" as the agent-photographer penetrates the body of the real. In this relationship, the content of the image itself, its arrangement according to aesthetic (and anesthetizing) codes decided on by the photographer, becomes the intending but unperceived *hyle* of the image.

This "external" structure can be seen to repeat a structure that exists inside the image itself, so that the image seems to anticipate its own production as photograph. Considered solely from the perspective of the "standard" reading of the image as an instance of Chinese indifference to pain, the "inert matter" penetrated by the photographic point of view that organizes the image is not so much the entire field of perception as it is the behavior of the "crowd," which in its apparent indifference to the condemned man's pain illustrates the historical stereotype about Chinese indifference to suffering. It is the personality and values of the crowd as crowd (and particularly as Chinese crowd) that are the subject of the photographic "operation" that penetrates and reveals them.

If the crowd is the purely "inert matter" of the image, it is because the photographic look that establishes the image as image organizes its sympathy in relation to the condemned man. Through the sympathy established between the agent of the photograph and the victim of its violence, the photograph attempts to breach the barrier that separates agent from *hyle*. The blankness of the victim's eyes recapitulates and returns the look of the camera, mirroring the photographer's regard and allowing the camera to register in the figure whose picture it takes a symbolic opening to light. Like the observer at the surgery, the condemned man doubles the cinematic eye. But in doubling it from *inside* the sphere of perception, from inside the theater, as it were, the condemned man also comments on that eye. It is not that in this looking the blank apertures of the man's face (or even those of his bloody chest) retake the photograph as a picture of the man behind the camera, but that in offering a reflection of that look they suggest that the difference between the image and its perspectival frame is not so much the difference between "inside" and "outside" as the difference between the image's "inside" and its own internal limit.

Drawing the photographic eye, the "agent" or "perspectival frame" of its production, back into the interior of the photograph is an act of agency. Insofar as the condemned man can be said to emerge from the *hyle* of the image as agent, then, he does so only to acquire a limited power to call attention to certain features of the image. But it is precisely because its agential intervention in the photograph is so limited that this portion of the image can be said to exist as both *hyle* and not-*hyle*. On one hand the image of the condemned man is the inert and aestheticized body upon which the photograph operates; on the other it is the partial agent of the image's self-production as image. This seeming paradox, in which the "inert matter" of the image responds as *hyle* to the status of the photographer-agent by indicating the agent's similarity to itself, is a model for sympathy and likeness that moves *from* the anesthetized body of the image toward the self-confident agent who attempts to penetrate it. Just as for the souvenir, "the *possession* of the metonymic object is a kind of *dispossession* in that the presence of the object all the more radically speaks to its status as a mere substation and to its subsequent distance from the self," here, in the photograph, the *hyle* of the image reveals itself as the self-revelation of the agent inside the image whose outside it pretends to be.[58] Owning this photograph, then, is like owning a broken off and vulnerable piece of the photographer-self. The generosity of both the image and the print comes from their quiet revelation of this fact, and thus their restoration of the *hyle*'s intention to the field of perception—where it had been lying unnoticed, like the wood in the carving, all along.

4. Modernity without Modernity

On one hand, the goal of this chapter has been to produce historical knowledge: to show how certain kinds of relations to photography in the West articulated themselves with reference to the Chinese example and how these relations figured a broader connection between anesthesia and cinematic vision, the one that Buck-Morss elaborates explicitly and at length in her 1992 essay. On the other, the reading of the Bataille photograph in particular has aimed to show how the relation between felt pain and that image—itself among the most notorious representations of Chinese suffering in literary circles—could and did change depending on how the image circulated. This focus on circulation turned, finally, to a reading of the medium of the image as *hyle*, which showed that the authenticity guaranteed by the features of the *image* could be understood as partial effects of the authenticity referred to by the status of the *print* as souvenir. By attending to the *hyle* of the image as a "thing" capable of eliciting powerful subjective responses and of organizing relations between persons, I attempted to revise the standard story about how photography works by noting that for most of its history its major byproducts were not just images but things and by suggesting that a complete theory of the photograph needed to consider both those aspects of the photograph in order to read well.[59]

Insofar as the chapter can offer a model for that mode of reading, in which the intentions of both the *hyle* and the image move into the field of percep-

[58] Stewart, *On Longing*, 135 (emphases mine).

[59] The interaction between image and thing produces a kind of interpretive "interference" of the same type as the interference between image and caption, where the potential conflict in the felt difference between image and text can also become a collaboration. I borrow the term "interference" from Marsha Bryant, who uses it to refer to interactions between images and texts ("Introduction," *Photo-textualities: Reading Photographs and Literature*, ed. Marsha Bryant [Newark, N.J., 1996], 14.).

tion, it will have to return to the representations of acupuncture anesthesia with which it began. Like the postcards of Chinese executions, those representations circulated in mass mediatic form, belonging to no one in particular; though the *hyle* of their underlying physical form could be remembered by associating the image's production with the name of a particular artist, they operated largely as indexical or documentary signs. In the case of these pictures, however, one might say that the images themselves contained a picture of their own *hyle*. Insofar as the operating table figured the photographic mechanism that captured it, the subject of the image can be said to be "looking back" at the camera, registering in that regard the longstanding fraternity between their ways of seeing.

My conclusion will hinge upon that last sentence, but before I explain it, let me back up slightly. Anne McClintock has noted how in photographs taken for colonial postcards, "primitive icons and atavistic relics were arranged around sitters to metonymically signify an anachronistic relation to the technological time of modernity." In all colonial postcards, "time is reorganized as spectacle," the spectacularity of the image relying on its representation of a primitivity that registers as foreign in both spatial and temporal dimensions.[60] Part of what "colonial" representations of a certain type show, then, is the temporal gap between "primitivism" and "modernity," a gap whose immediacy can be experienced in the metropole thanks to the kinds of innovations in transportation, photographic representation, and postal delivery that are themselves the emblems of modernity whose location at the end of a narrative of historical progress they reinforce.[61] (The resulting conflation of time and space, in which the so-called primitive becomes the contemporary figure for the past of modernity's present, generates the relation between temporality and otherness so elegantly discussed by Johannes Fabian.[62])

McClintock's argument explains well the status of the image of the man being tortured to death as the potential subject of a postcard. It also clarifies

[60] McClintock, *Imperial Leather*, 125.

[61] This is true for both the acupuncture images and for Bataille's photograph, though as I will go on to suggest the acupuncture representations complicate a simple here-present, there-past temporality. In the case of judicial torture, however, the written descriptions of the execution of Damiens the regicide that open Foucault's *Discipline and Punish*, which illustrate there the movement of a judicial mechanism that is, at the moment of writing, separated from the present by an epistemic shift that makes such "punishment" unthinkable, will suggest that part of what Europeans observed in the image I have been discussing here was their *own* repressed past refigured as an *other* present.

[62] See Johannes Fabian, *Time and the Other: How Anthropology Makes its Object* (New York, 1983).

some of the Chinese complaints about Antonioni's film. Though it may have seemed silly to some in the West to complain that *Chung Kuo* showed "a donkey pulling a stone roller" instead of tractors in the fields, or ox-carts and wheelbarrows instead of "busy motor traffic," what was at stake was whether the film would function as a colonial postcard whose primary spectacle was that of China's "primitive" past, or as an advertisement for the country's "modern" present.[63] It may also explain, in turn, why there were no complaints about the documentary's surgical scene: no matter how discontinuously shot it was, no matter how much the symbolic superstructure of its representation differed culturally from China's, it nonetheless testified powerfully at the level of its content to the fact that the Chinese had "learned" how to do modern surgery. As Lu Gwei-Djen and Joseph Needham put it, "More than any other development, this acupuncture analgesia . . . has had the effect of obliging physicians and neuro-physiologists in other parts of the world to take Chinese medicine seriously, *almost for the first time*."[64]

Because the images of acupuncture anesthesia contained, by representing a surgical operating theater, a picture of the mediatic perspective that was also responsible for their global distribution, part of what was being represented back to the West in these moments was not simply the fact of modern surgery in China but China's ability to organize its internal physical spaces in accordance with the demands of modern ways of seeing. Within this context it is crucial finally to acknowledge the major difference between acupuncture anesthesia and the kind of anesthesia practiced in the West: in acupuncture anesthesia, *the patient remained awake.* Though experiments in partial chemical anesthesia (absence of feeling) and analgesia (absence of pain) produced through the use of epidural and caudal anesthetics had taken place as early as the late nineteenth century (sometimes using a mixture of tap water and cocaine), the practice of spinal anesthesia was only in the 1970s becoming commonplace in Western medicine.[65] Though

[63] Yang, "Refuting Antonioni's Slanders against Linhsien County," 13.

[64] Lu Gwei-Djen and Joseph Needham, *Celestial Lancets: A History and Rationale of Acupuncture and Moxa* (Cambridge, 1980), 5 (emphasis mine). *Celestial Lancets* is the best review of the historical moment at which acupuncture anesthesia seemed to hold the greatest medical promise. Lu and Needham review all of the objections raised by Western observers to the "magic" of acupuncture anesthesia, including the possibility that the patients were merely under hypnosis (see 226). Their discussion of acupuncture anesthesia for major surgery appears on 218–30.

[65] For a history of early experiments in the use of epidural anesthesia, see Mark G. Mandabach, "The early history of spinal anesthesia," *The History of Anesthesia: Proceedings of the Fifth International Symposium on the History of Anesthesia*, eds. José C. Diz, Avelino Franco, Douglas R. Bacon, Joseph Rupreht, and Julián Alvarez (New York, 2002).

acupuncture's production of local analgesia without unconsciousness did not, therefore, demonstrate the presence of the inconceivable, it did open the possibility that a longstanding goal of modern Western medical practice could be reached by a means whose cultural and scientific pedigree did not correspond to anything recognized as legitimate in the West. Some measure of the cultural shock provoked by this possibility was the insistent reference to the acupuncture treatment as "anesthesia," even though, as some American scientists noted, because "in no instance is sensation totally abolished or consciousness disturbed," the proper term was analgesia or hypalgesia (diminution of pain).[66] That both Buck and Sontag use the word "anesthesia" to describe the procedures they saw suggests that the cultural work done by acupuncture anesthesia had to do as much with its putative equivalence to Western medicine as to its production of a Chinese alternative to it.[67]

Perhaps the most shocking thing about the Riboud photograph is not, therefore, that the woman is anesthetized by acupuncture, but that a medical assistant is feeding her slices of fruit, an act that deftly illustrates both her lack of pain and her subjective consciousness. Patients being operated on under acupuncture anesthesia did not have to become "inert matter" for the surgeon to penetrate; rather, the surgical penetration of the body could proceed alongside the subject's remaining self-aware as subject. The fact that the patient's subjective desires could be met without interrupting the operation suggests that subjectivity, rather than becoming an obstacle to the surgical work, could co-exist with or even abet it.[68] Acupuncture anesthesia as it was represented in Western popular culture seemed to offer the possibility not simply of an equal "alternative" to chemically induced sleep but, far more than that, a new form of pain management that could undo the anesthetizing, "objectifying" effects of Western modernity by allowing the subject to be anesthetized while still remaining a subject; dissociating the body from its own pain could occur without dissociating the body from its sense of self.[69]

[66] American Acupuncture Anesthesia Study Group, 3.

[67] The authors of the American Acupuncture Anesthesia Study Group—which, you'll notice, included "Anesthesia" in its very name—preferred "hypalgesia," which indicates a diminished (but not eradicated) sensitivity to pain. In their study, Lu Gwei-Djen and Joseph Needham use the term "analgesia," though they note that "common usage, especially in Chinese foreign-language publishing, calls it anaesthesia" (221nC).

[68] By contrast: Buck-Morss quotes a nineteenth-century surgeon who notes with satisfaction that under anesthesia "the patient lies a tranquil, passive subject, instead of struggling and perhaps uttering piteous cries and moans" (28).

[69] Pernick notes that in the years between 1846 and the end of the century, some doctors and some patients refused to use anesthesia in order to secure the patient's active participation in the

Given the historical and formal connections between photographic vision and modern surgery, acupuncture anesthesia opened the possibility that modernity could be detached from the deadened, anesthetized aesthetic that it had seemed naturally to require, the alternative *medical* modernity of the acupuncture operation crossing over to become an alternative *aesthetic* modernity as well. Images of acupuncture anesthesia returned the camera's look by showing the possibility of a surgery without unconsciousness. Pain could be managed without making the body the *hyle* of the subject. To Dürer's question, What do you see?, a person looking at a human being from this perspective would be able to recognize the body and its person *at the same time*, in effect including the body, the material substrate of the subject, in the field of perception and recognition.

In showing a surgery without total objectification, these images also showed a cinematic look without photographic vision. And if vision could change—if indeed China offered, as Sontag believed it did, the experience of cameras without the experience of the photographic—then perhaps the world could have modernity without pain, industrialism without the exploitation of labor (another dream of the Cultural Revolutionary era), mass culture without the deadening effects of overstimulation. What those photographs showed at the level of the image was a new relationship between *hyle* and non-*hyle*, articulated explicitly through a body that while no longer sensitive to pain nonetheless remained aware of itself and of its desires, a body that could adopt an attitude toward its own pain that was simultaneously aestheticized—able to view itself from a objectifying and anesthetized distance—and "man-to-man," in the sense that the patient could remain awake to attend to the body as self, or to ignore it and eat fruit.[70]

The representations of acupuncture anesthesia did not, then, offer some kind of primitive return to the premodern, in which the confrontation with pain produced a fully engaged and articulated self *as* pain (and therefore no aesthetic

---

surgery, or to allow the patient to face, awake, the possibility of his or her death: "As late as 1862, it was not uncommon to find surgeons who 'expected the patient to assist in small operations,' such as probing wounds and removing bone fragments" (59). The unconscious patient was thus a potential victim as well as the potential beneficiary of the "boon to suffering humanity" that was anesthesia's discovery; some worried that the "powerlessness of the anesthetized subject would lead not merely to carelessness and disrespect but also to involuntary surgery and to unnecessary and experimental operations" (59).

[70]In some deeply ironic sense this resembles what Bataille saw in the photograph of his "beautiful" young Chinese man, though the modernity Bataille overcame in his ecstatic communion did not return, as it would in the photographs of Chinese surgeries, as yet more bland evidence for a wealthier, more comfortable world.

or anesthetizing separation between agent, observer, and inert matter), catapulting the self beyond modernity in a fantastic act of sacrifice. That was Bataille's model. Rather these images opened *inside* the field of modernity proper the possibility of an accommodation between the *hyle* and body, *hyle* and image. In these surgical "postcards," temporality became a spectacle that showed Europe the possibility of an "alternatively" modern future that would have to wait till the late 1990s to appear as the fully conscious philosophical project of the proponents of "Asian values." The latter's emphasis on the possibility of modernity without social pain (individualism, divorce, drugs, crime) would reinscribe the fascination of these images into a more recognizable and more lasting political idiom.

7 Closures

Three Examples in Search of a Conclusion

Because kindness is only the projection of defeated self-love; because tenderness can originate in perversity and tend towards violence; and because the real sense of another's loss calques upon a presentiment of the extinction of our own identity, we should worry not about extending sympathy, but that it is already too disgracefully extended.

—Jonathan Lamb, "Modern Metamorphoses and Disgraceful Tales," *Critical Inquiry* 28 (Autumn 2001), 166

In the educational model of the body's burden, I feel the pounding of my own enlarged heart.

—Shin Yu Pai, "Body Worlds," *EOAGH* 4

I am the alpha and the omega, Jesus said (or didn't say), trusting the metaphor of a closed linear system to affirm his purchase on the infinite. Academic books, no less than children of the divine, frame whole worlds between their openings and closings. Their final sutures establish—like the alphabetic omega, but less predictably—the endpoint of a line that defines the story of the book. No preface that is not also an opening to light, Eduardo Cadava writes; likewise no conclusion that does not mark the shuttering of that aperture.[1] What you see just before the curtain falls frames (closes, discloses) the ambit of its captured illuminations.

[1] Eduardo Cadava, *Words of Light: Theses on the Photography of History* (Princeton, N.J., 1997), xvii.

1. Sense of an Ending (I)

In 1983, the Austrian writer Peter Handke gave his newly published novel the title *Der Chinese des Schmerzes*, a phrase that translates into English as *The Chinaman of Pain.* The title's somewhat bewildering reversal of subject and object pushes the themes of *The Hypothetical Mandarin* to a figurative limit. There, at the limit, the West's historical concern with the suffering of Chinese people suddenly appears on the other side of the genitive mirror, presenting readers with the anticipation of a radically different mode of belonging.

As if explicitly to frustrate the sense of curiosity and wonder produced by its evocative title, *Der Chinese des Schmerzes* has almost nothing to do with China at all. In it, a middle-aged first-person narrator moves through a Salzburg brimming with infrequently expressed and ultimately impotent violence, hopping on and off buses, attending a card game, and wandering along rocky paths in the mountains outside the city, where he kills a man by hitting him in the head with a stone. He eventually comes home and tells his son a story, which seems to be the story of the novel. Along the way, the narrator has a sexual encounter with a woman he knows, or seems to know, in an upstairs room of the airport hotel. As she leaves, he asks her, not without desperation—"I was in need of being described a little"—to give him a portrait of himself.

> Then she replied: "You don't seem to be wholly present; you breathe discontent. You're kind of run-down. I desire you but I don't trust you. You have something on your conscience; not theft, or you'd be on the run. It's plain that you are outside ordinary law, and it makes you suffer in a way. I don't trust you, and I do. You are like the man in the doorway. Though very ill, he went to see a good friend. In leaving, he stopped at length in the doorway and tried to smile; his tensed eyes became slits, framed in their sockets as by sharply ground lenses. 'Goodbye, my suffering Chinaman,' said his friend." (*'Auf Widersehen, mein Chinese des Schmerzes!' sagte der Freund.*)[2]

In someone else's novel it would be possible to reconstruct from this episode a coherent rationale for the connection it asserts between Chineseness and suffering, in this context justified only by the fact that the friend's attempt to

[2]Peter Handke, *Der Chinese des Schmerzes* (Berlin, 1983), 217–18; translated as *Across* by Ralph Manheim (New York, 1986), 116–17. Further references in the text to the English edition.

smile reproduces one of the key physiognomic features of the Chinese racial stereotype.[3] But since Handke's strategy throughout *Der Chinese des Schmerzes* (and indeed in most of his fiction) is to provide the *signifiers* of interpretive depth without ever connecting them to appropriate *signifieds*, I am tempted instead to say that the scene produces interpretive desire ("why does the friend call him *der Chinese?* Why does this become the title of the novel?) precisely in order to leave it unsatisfied. The sense of pregnant but empty meaningfulness that follows the reading of such a passage, so typical of Handke's work, presents a reference to China that has failed to connect in any significant way to the poetic or narrative coherence of a social world.

That may be the reason that, when Ralph Manheim translated *Der Chinese des Schmerzes* into English in 1986, he changed its title to *Across*.[4] The shift has the effect of erasing the extradiegetic quality of the phrase "my suffering Chinaman" in the English edition, whose readers will instead spend their time attending to the novel's various crossings (literal and metaphorical: bridges, translations, and the like). I take Manheim's assertion of the title's meaninglessness—itself dependent on a completely reasonable reading of the novel as having nothing to do with Chinamen of suffering—as a confirmation, or reconfirmation, of its vital importance: the fact that its presence in the title can disappear without comment is precisely what grants the phrase, when compared to all the other features of the book, an unusual prominence. The Chinaman's erasure thus reproduces at the material level involving translations, book sales, and newspaper reviews the figurative function it had served in the novel itself, its combination of significance and insignificance—of insignificant significance—in the history of the book's international publication essentially mirroring its mimetic role in the work to which it (sometimes) gives itself as title.

Ending this book at this point, with Handke, would suggest that the historical drift of the discourse on China, sympathy, and suffering reaches in the Austria of the

[3] From this point, one might move on to the four other mentions of China in the book. In one of them, the feverish narrator dreams of a Chinese restaurant in an airport on the moon, in which human beings are slaughtered for food in front of a live audience of diners and tourists (98–99). In another, a bus driver says to the narrator, who has been making an especially verbose farewell, "Good night, Mr. Chinaman (*Gute nacht, Herr Chinese*)!" (81); there are mentions of Chinese limestone and Far Eastern calligraphy (19; 38). The first two instances seem at least to refer us to historical forms of Chinese stereotype, of which the cannibalistic violence, the verbosity, might be the extended edges. Nothing else in the novel seems to have anything to do with China at all.

[4] Ralph Manheim's view was apparently not shared by the translators of either the French or the Spanish editions, who published the novel as *Le Chinois de la douleur* and *El Chino del dolor*, respectively.

early 1980s a kind of apocalyptic finality, a transformation into the realm of the pure idea. Though such a claim need not imply that the "suffering Chinaman" in Handke's novel closes a *historical* trajectory that leads inevitably from high economic mediation (George Henry Mason, Peter Parker) to contentless figuration (Georges Bataille, Handke), the choice of Handke would establish one endpoint of a *logical* continuum leading from the material to the ideal. Between the intense economic and imperialist animations of Edmund Scott's torture of a Chinese goldsmith in Java in the late sixteenth century and Handke's virtual, or virtually empty, linkage of Chineseness and suffering, one could then plot the coordinates of every other example in the book. From such a perspective, *Der Chinese des Schmerzes* would function as the high point of the Chinese "example-effect," its reference to China appearing in the mode of total unimportance or arbitrary disappearance ("well of course Handke didn't mean anything by the word '*Chinese*'! That's why we changed the novel's title . . . ") confirming the nearly total emptiness of the Chinese example, even as it confirmed its vital and unrelenting plenitude.

2. Sense of an Ending (II)

Other closures are possible. Consider, against Handke, the biography of the Chinese modernist Lu Xun, whose decision to become a writer turned on his being shown, while a young medical student in Japan, a photograph of the execution of a Chinese spy. The scene appears for the first time in the preface to *A Call to Arms* (*Nahan*, 1922):

> I do not know what advanced methods are now used to teach microbiology, but at that time lantern slides were used to show the microbes; and if the lecture ended early, the instructor might show slides of national scenery or news to fill up the time. This was during the Russo-Japanese war [1904–05], so there were many war films, and I had to join in the clapping and cheering in the lecture hall along with the other students. It was a long time since I had seen any compatriots, but one day I saw a film showing some Chinese, one of whom was bound, while many others stood around him. They were all strong fellows but appeared completely apathetic. According to the commentary, the one with his hands bound was a spy working for the Russians, who was to have his head cut off by the Japanese military as a warning to others, while the Chinese beside him had come to enjoy the spectacle.

> Before the term was over I had left for Tokyo, because after this film I felt that medical science was not so important after all. The people of a weak and backward country, however strong and healthy they may be, can only serve to be made examples of, or to witness such futile spectacles; and it doesn't really matter how many of them die of illness. The most important thing, therefore, was to change their spirit, and since at the time I felt that literature was the best means to this end, I determined to promote a literary movement.[5]

This passage is among the most widely discussed in twentieth-century Chinese literary history. In its movement from medicine to literature, from spectatorship to writing, passivity to activity, and expatriate identity to national identification, we see the socio-cultural outlines of the Chinese intellectual's early twentieth-century turn to modernity articulated as a project of national spiritual restoration *through* literature. That this project appears for the first time in Lu Xun's autobiography as the result of his passive spectatorship of a scene explicitly not directed toward him—and that he turns that scene, or forces it to detour, so that it breaches him in a particular and particularly productive address—suggests how intimately the task of the postcolonial intellectual in early twentieth-century China was caught up in a doubled relation to violence and representationality.

The self-consciously modernizing themes of Lu Xun's narration—his frustration with the Chinese audience's "secret sense of carnival," thus his privileging of sympathy, his distaste for pleasure in cruelty, his rejection of public executions as expressions of state power—are guised, also, in an explicitly modern form.[6] As many scholars have observed, the passage's arrangement of shifting spectatorial

[5] Lu Xun, "Preface," in *Selected Stories of Lu Hsun*, trans. Yang Hsien-yi and Gladys Yang (Beijing, 1978), 2–3. A slightly more "American" and contemporary translation is William A. Lyell's, in Lu Xun, *Diary of a Madman and Other Stories* (Honolulu, 1990). Lydia Liu also translates this passage, retaining more of Lu Xun's sentence structure (the Yang translation combines a few sentences) in *Translingual Practice: Literature, National Culture, and Translated Modernity, China, 1900–1937* (Stanford, 1995), 61–62; see also Rey Chow's modified version in *Primitive Passions: Visuality, Sexuality, Ethnography, and Contemporary Chinese Cinema* (New York, 1995), 4–5. For a lengthier treatment of this scene within the context of a biographical-critical reading of Lu Xun, see Leo Ou-fan Lee, *Voices from the Iron House: A Study of Lu Xun* (Bloomington, 1987); Lee's translation of this passage appears on 16–17.

[6] David Der-wei Wang, *The Monster That Is History: History, Violence, and Fictional Writing in Twentieth-Century China* (Berkeley, 2004), 22. Chow argues in *Primitive Passions* that the shift from image to writing in Lu Xun's anecdote represents the conversion of "an older, pre-modern model of discipline and punishment by physical torture and visual spectacle to a 'progressive,' because more efficient, notion of discipline and punishment by education" (18). Hence the importance of writing as a mechanism for national transformation—the question is not of getting rid of the disciplinary

positions, with all its play of engagement with and detachment from reality, produced a complex of interpretation and intervention that became "one of the major issues of modern Chinese critical realism."[7] But the triangular narrative structure Lu Xun articulates—in which he opposes himself to the cheering Japanese students, and to the Chinese audience that has come to enjoy the execution's spectacle—also recalls the mediated narrative gaze of Bertrand Russell's description of the dog run over in the street, and the ethnographic knowledge arranged by the photographer of Bataille's beloved image. Part of my argument has been that this spectatorial relationship to suffering is itself the structural *form* of a certain modernity and that the implication of the reporter or viewer in any such scene—the degree to which any disapproving report on the cruelty of others depends on the viewer's simultaneous disavowal of and participation in the scene of violence—discloses the compromised position of the modern narrator as such. Lu Xun's production of such a position occurred as part of his lifelong dialogue with and transformation of Western texts on the Chinese character, including Arthur Smith's *Chinese Characteristics*, which Lu Xun read in Japanese translation, and Russell's *The Problem of China*, whose chapter on Chinese character appeared in *Dongfang zazhi* in early 1922, the same year Lu Xun wrote the *Nahan* preface.[8]

Though this example does not end the chronological story I tell about the history of the perception of the Chinese relationship to suffering, or confirm the assertion that something culturally or racially particular to China is responsible for that relation, it marks the movement of that discourse into the Chinese context, where, thanks partly to the influence of Lu Xun, it became a vital ideological feature of the history of Chinese modernity. This discursive shift, in which a Chinese writer begins to pose questions about the Chinese relation to sympathy that had been the province of a more general Western imperialism, constitutes something like a return: the final step in a diasporic movement whereby the traveling question arrives at home and embraces, as though for the first time, its "native" origins. The force of the Lu Xun example would in such a conception be to close a geographic circle, so that a discourse that began, more or less, in the relation between Mason and the Macartney embassy—and indeed in

mechanism of the state altogether but of "modernizing" the state by converting its disciplinary mechanisms from "hard" to "soft" ones.

[7] Wang, 24.

[8] For a lengthy discussion of these important moments in the translation and internationalization of the concept of modernity, see chapter 1 of Liu's *Translingual Practice*.

the sense of a Chinese "failure" to be modern—would find an almost natural ending point in the apparent *agreement* to that position by the most modern of modern Chinese writers.

But to gesture toward such a closure, and thus to think of the Lu Xun episode as a "return," requires us to make two mistakes: first, to imagine that a difference in intended addressees makes no difference to the social and philosophical meaning of a literary text, and second, to believe that "China" was the true *origin* of the discourse I address. On the first count, it is enough to consider that, as Lydia Liu has noted, the drama of violence represented in the scene "also unfolds at the level of reading where the reader is shocked to discover that she or he is implicated in the violence of representation by being induced to play the role of a witness to the same spectacle of horror" the scene describes.[9] The difference between Lu Xun's narration of such a scene and one by say, Russell, is that the former, directing itself toward a Chinese audience, aims to allow both Lu Xun and his readers to "emerge as subject and agent of their own history," and not simply to confirm for a Western readership the well-known cruelty of the Chinese.[10]

As for the second mistake, which takes "China" for the origin of the discourse I have described, my position is, rather, that the discursive network built up around the question of a Chinese relation to pain is most at home not in China but in the ecliptic: the virtually universal, virtually local figure that describes the cultural limit-space out of which that network *seems* to appear (and whose function is, finally, to *be* the site of that apparent appearance). This is as much as to say it is at home nowhere, or that it is at home only in the relation. Since the ecliptic marks, as I have said, the appearance of the global from the perspective of the local, the home to which it refers its Western readers will of necessity appear definitive—as definitive, in fact, as the globe itself—even though it is, from any other perspective, completely arbitrary. Its uncanny homeliness rests in the relation it establishes between those two perspectives, just as the perception of Chinese suffering that appears in the story of the Chinese execution that provides Lu Xun's career with its retroactive inauguration lies neither in the China to which it refers, nor in the West that is site to its extensive reproduction and circulation, but in the historical and narrative relation between those two epistemological and social forms.

[9] Liu, *Translingual Practice,* 64.

[10] Liu, *Translingual Practice,* 76.

3. Sense of an Ending (III)

Other closures are possible. Consider, against Handke and Lu Xun, the appearance since 1995 in the privileged cities of the globe of large-scale exhibitions of plasticized and skinless corpses demonstrating the internal functions and structures of the human body. Usually open to the muscle, sometimes to the bone, sometimes reduced to anthropomorphic collections of vascular networks, placed in yoga poses or arrested in the middle of some athletic endeavour, occasionally offering up an ironic commentary on their own bizarre ontological status, the corpses recall the extravagances of Andreas Vesalius's sixteenth-century *De humani corporis fabrica,* whose anatomical drawings leavened their moments of genuine instruction with the occasional dark joke (a skeleton leans on a shovel, with which it has just dug its own grave; this latter, then, an early example of the genre it would take the twentieth century to understand as "edutainment").

The "plastinated" bodies featured in American museums of natural history first appeared in a Tokyo exhibition called *Body Worlds.* By 2006 this exhibition and its successors had attracted over 20 million visitors and generated more than $200 million in major cities across the United States, Europe, and East Asia.[11] A number of copycat exhibits with titles like "The Universe Within" (San Francisco), "Mysteries of the Human Body" (South Korea), and "Cuerpos entrañables" (Spain), followed shortly behind the success of the original *Body Worlds,* the phenomenon threatening to surpass the commercial success of wildly popular exhibitions on the artifacts of the Titanic in the late 1990s and to exceed even the 1980s' craze for shows featuring robotic dinosaurs.[12] So the recent history of the public's museal fascination takes us from the animated fossil record to the ocean floor to the self: as though the past brought to life in the first two cases, replete with the important pleasures of seeing and touching objects once seen and touched by the dead, had been elevated to an apothetic prolepsis in which what

[11]The "plastination" process was invented by Gunter von Hagens in the 1970s and involves replacing body water and fat with liquid silicone rubber and other synthetic polymers. Von Hagens' Institute for Plastination, which I discuss below, is responsible for *Body Worlds.*

[12]For a longer discussion of these exhibits in the context of the museum industry, see David Barboza, "China Turns Out Mummified Bodies for Displays," *The New York Times,* Aug. 8 2006, also available online at http://www.nytimes.com/2006/08/08/business/worldbusiness/08bodies.html?ei=5088&en=672da5787d998daf&ex=1312689600&partner=rssnyt&pagewanted=print. Barboza's video report is available online at http://www.youtube.com/watch?v=AqKvYUO7C7w. On the arc of the dinosaur's popularity and its general cultural meaning, see W.J.T. Mitchell, *The Last Dinosaur Book: The Life and Times of a Cultural Icon* (Chicago, 1998).

the museum brings to life is the visitor's inevitable *future*, this nearly literal animation hardly troubled by the fact that such a future quite explicitly entails the visitor's becoming a corpse.

If the educational materials surrounding these exhibitions are to be believed, these displays do not, however, address the future but the present, particularly when it comes to showing a desiccated, blackened, smoker's lung or the liver of a heavy drinker, each individuated organ reminding those still and temporarily among the living to care for the precious cargo that lies beneath their coverings of fur and skin. Likewise, the whole bodies, so often posed to demonstrate athletic feats, encourage through their alienating exposition an awareness of the "miracle" and "wonder" of the human machine, while recalling the fragile, complex workings of the visitors' own personal embodiments. The *hyle* of the body has become identical with the work of art that plays across its surfaces.

The identification that allows the bodies in the exhibit to speak of and finally *for* the visitor's body depends heavily on the stripping of the corpses' skin: chemistry has removed the marks that would have allowed someone to assign these nameless, faceless physiognomies to some cultural habitus or individuated personality. The resulting hypernudity of muscle and organ, vein and bone, swathes the corpses in an anonymity so sad and modest that it verges on greatness. Small wonder that the second and third *Body Worlds* exhibitions draw for their biological material on corpses donated by visitors to the first one: to see these bodies is to want—for some people, and some of the time—to become one of them, to share in their lasting, celebrated, permanence, their "uniquely secular, material form of immortality."[13] Immortality and change for the living as well as the dead: the exhibit "profoundly changed my attitudes towards my body, towards life and death," says one visitor cited by Megan Stern. "I feel myself in a different way now, more intensely."[14] Thus is the external face reunited with what the exhibition's publicity materials call the "interior" face made of muscle and bone. This reconciliation between inside

[13] Megan Stern, "Shiny, Happy People: 'Body Worlds' and the Commodification of Health," *Radical Philosophy* 118 (March/April 2003), also available online at http://www.radicalphilosophy.com/default.asp?channel_id=2187&editorial_id=11213.

[14] As you might imagine, the exhibits have also been met with protests, including ones from religious leaders, arguing that they are deeply disrespectful to the dead. The bioethicist Ruth Guyer, speaking on *National Public Radio*, for instance, argues that the "bodies were in perverse, unnatural, mocking poses," and that visitors "yukking it up with off-color comments" indicated that "we have forgotten our moral obligations to the dead" ("A Bioethicist Takes a Peek at 'Body Worlds'," http://www.npr.org/templates/story/story.php?storyId=5640183).

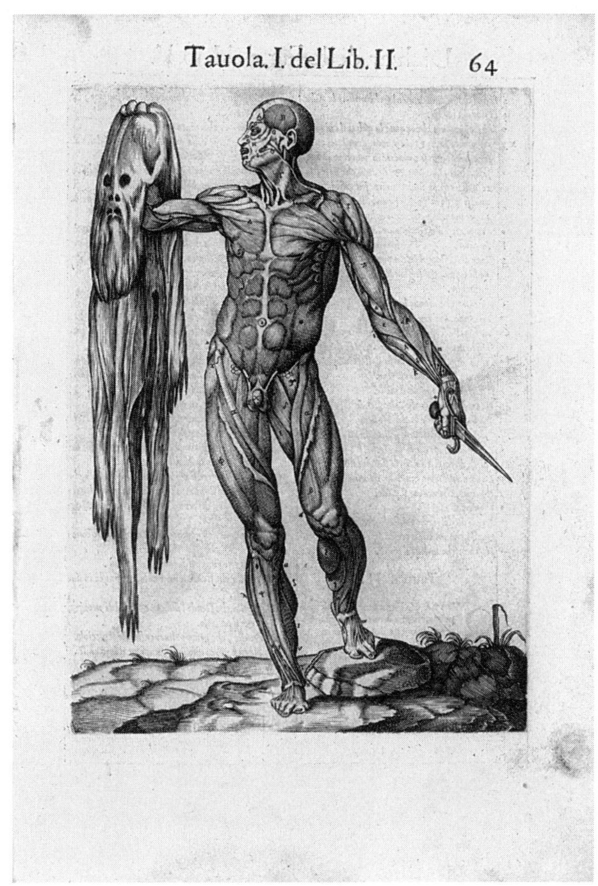

Fig 7.1 Gaspar Becerra, *A flayed man holding his own skin*, 1556.

and outside appears in allegorized form in the exhibit itself, in the posed corpse of a man who strides forward, bare and bold, his entire skin held high in his right hand: a deliberate imitation, also, and not for nothing, of a sixteenth-century anatomical drawing by Gaspar Becerra.

In the intensity of the feelings provoked by the figure the exhibit calls "The Skin Man," I read the presence of a mode of belonging to what Mark Seltzer has called "wound culture," in which the "collective spectacle of torn and open bodies and persons" emblematized by the obsession with serial killers and horror movies becomes a privileged and literalizing metaphor for the more general opening toward otherness required by the public sphere. In wound culture, Seltzer writes, "the opening of relation to others (the 'sympathetic' social bond)" appears as coterminous with "the traumatic collapse of boundaries between self and other (a yielding of identity to identification)"—meaning that the entry into culture occurs on the basis of a psychic experience defined in terms of an originary and

Fig 7.2 *The Skin Man*, 1995. Gunther von Hagens, Institute for Plastination, Heidelberg, Germany, www.body-worlds.com.

violent tearing open of the self.[15] It is the production of this awareness as social fact that makes the "public sphere" of wound culture so pathological, because all of its participants depend for their putative equality on the fantasy that such an equality—and, thus, the origin of community—stems from an originary wounding to a self-enclosed and self-sustaining self that exists prior to that public sphere.[16] Hence we are all victims, and hence there is no power and no fascination in contemporary society like those we give to and have for the wounded and the bereaved; as Wendy Brown puts it, "identity structured by this ethos becomes deeply invested in its own impotence, even while it seeks to assuage the pain of its powerlessness through its vengeful moralizing."[17]

If the structure of belonging to and engaging in the contemporary social world is defined as the function of an originary and inescapable violence (rather than as, more optimistically, the welcome healing of a festering and negative solitude), as Seltzer suggests, then we might understand exhibits like *Body Worlds* as attempts to depathologize the nature of the wound, normalizing it as the kernel of a collective identity whose "public" has expanded to the limits of the human species. From this perspective, the tremendous violence done to the corpses-become-bodies in *Body Worlds* is the material precursor of the spectators' figurative identification with them, the violence done to dead bodies imagining *avant la lettre* the woundedness of live ones. "I feel myself in a different way now, more intensely," is the mark of just such a recognition, in which empathy with the opened-up body encourages the feeling that I, like you, am wounded. The sinews and muscles holding me together, bound by the premonition of their future shattering: so identification leads back to identity. The marketing materials' reminder of "what we are: naturally fragile in a mechanized world" ties the visitor to the corpse.[18]

[15] Mark Seltzer, *Serial Killers: Life and Death in America's Wound Culture* (New York, 1998), 258.

[16] Hence, as Seltzer argues in *Serial Killers*, the obsessive return in both real life and the news and entertainment media to scenes of crime, to scenes of bloody murder, to forensic investigation, and so on.

[17] Wendy Brown, *States of Injury: Power and Freedom in Late Modernity* (Princeton, N.J., 1995), 70.

[18] This and other citations from *Body Worlds* publicity materials draw on information at http://www.bodyworlds.com. As far as identification goes, its intensity explains the reason that so many visitors to the exhibits respond by immediately signing up to become donors to them. As for the mechanized world, these lines from the exhibition catalog remind us that recent conceptions of the "natural" body draw heavily on its conceived relation to the "mechanized" world it inhabits, a cultural habit whose beginnings in obsessions with automata travels through the early twentieth century's discovery, in work like Frederick Taylor's, of the "human motor," and beyond that on to the historically belated awareness of what N. Katherine Hayles has called the body's "posthuman" condition, the latter having turned out to have been with us all along. On these topics see Daniel Tiffany, *Toy Medium:*

This is true at least in theory. In practice, the unity of this "we" proves harder to sustain, largely because the mute and vulnerable corpses have—despite the exhibits' best intentions—continued to "speak" from beyond their open graves, thereby dislocating the identificatory structure that depends on the presumption of their universality. And what they have said is this: we were once, the vast majority of us, inhabitants of the People's Republic of China.

This fact owes something to the cheapness of cadavers in the PRC, something to the large number of trained anatomists there, and something to its loose regulation of the trade in dead bodies before 2006—all of which have come together to create a major body preservation industry in the northeastern Chinese city of Dalian. None of this would matter much, however, if the provenance of the corpses used in exhibitions had not caused human rights activists to claim that both Gunter von Hagens (who operates *Body Worlds*) and Premier Exhibitions (*Bodies . . . The Exhibition*) have used cadavers from the mentally ill and from executed prisoners as material for their programs.[19] Though the accusations have never been proven, and though von Hagens won a lawsuit against *Der Spiegel* for publishing them, the fact that both the Institute for Plastination and Premier Exhibitions continue to obtain most of their cadavers and organs from China—where at least ten body preservation factories have opened in recent years to meet the worldwide demand for processed corpses—has meant that the provenance of the bodies they put on display has become the necessary armature of an exhibition's arrival in any new city: no newspaper article reviewing the exhibition is

Materialism and Modern Lyric (Berkeley, 2000); Jessica Riskin, "The Defecating Duck, or, the Ambiguous Origins of Artificial Life," *Critical Inquiry* 29 (Summer 2003); Anson Rabinbach's *The Human Motor: Energy, Fatigue, and the Origins of Modernity* (Berkeley, 1992); Martha Banta's *Taylored Lives: Narrative Productions in the Age of Taylor, Veblen, and Ford* (Chicago, 1993), Mark Seltzer's *Bodies and Machines* (New York, 1992), as well as Hayles's *How We Became Posthuman: Virtual Bodies in Cybernetics, Literature, and Informatics* (Chicago, 1999). As for *Body Worlds*, in 2003 von Hagens "issued a public appeal in Britain seeking a terminally ill volunteer who would donate his body to a 'Futurehuman' project. After the donor's death, a TV station planned to film his plastination and reconstruction as a 'Futurehuman' with 'improvements' to correct what von Hagens considered flaws in human evolutionary design" (Russell Working, "Shock Value," *Chicago Tribune*, July 31, 2005, also available online at http://www.chicagotribune.com/features/lifestyle/health/chi-0507310429jul31,1,3790747.story?page=2&coll=chi-health-utl.).

[19] Adding to these accusations, Von Hagens and Premier Exhibitions have traded a number of lawsuits around copyright and patent issues, at least partly because Premier's major supplier in Dalian, Sui Hongjin, used to manage von Hagens' preservation facility. Both von Hagens and Premier have suggested that the other is operating unethically in China; see Barboza and Stern, as well as Neda Ulaby, "Origins of Exhibited Cadavers Questioned," *All Things Considered* (National Public Radio), Aug. 11 2006, http://www.npr.org/templates/story/story.php?storyId=5637687.

complete without a mention of the disputed human rights charges, and in many cities local organizations have staged protests against the organizers without, for all their efforts, being able to stop the exhibitions themselves.[20]

Let us push a little harder on the ways in which the corpses' Chineseness interrupts the universalist and identificatory appeal to "wound culture" upon which the exhibitions' success depends. "From a cultural perspective, especially since a number of the cadavers are from China, it feels like a gross violation," activist Bettie Luke told a newspaper reporter shortly before *Bodies . . . The Exhibition* opened in Seattle. "The willful use of putting a body on indefinite display like that condemns the soul to wander the netherworld with no chance to rest."[21] Luke's objection, though reflecting personal beliefs, shows us how the corpses' Chineseness persists beyond their processing and flaying, the grammar of their posthumous torment relying on the structure of what they may have believed when they were alive. In this persistence, one finds reproduced the very mimetic impasse upon which the exhibitions depend for their pure and engrossing allure. As the promotional material for *Body Worlds* insists, the fact that each of these displayed bodies was once a unique individual is part of their collective appeal:

> Every human being is unique. Humans reveal their individuality not only through the visible exterior, but also through the interior of their bodies, as

[20]In London, for instance, members of Pity II, a group formed to protest the use of infant and fetal body parts without parental consent, demanded that the exhibition be shut down; in Amsterdam, the opening of *Bodies . . . The Exhibition* "was greeted by 21 white crosses on the sidewalk with the words 'Unknown Chinese' written on them," according to Aaron Ginsburg, who runs a website devoted to stopping body exhibitions (<http://dignityinboston.googlepages.com/presscoverage>). As Linda Schulte-Sasse has remarked, criticism directed against the exhibitions in Europe—where von Hagens has been labeled a "speculator with death" and compared to Joseph Mengele—has been far more vociferous than in the United States ("Advise and Consent: On the Americanization of Body Worlds," *BioSocieties* 1 [2006], 370–71.). Part of this difference, she argues, rests on the fact that in the United States, the exhibitions have appeared and been authorized by their museumification: not only their literal appearance in museum spaces (and not exhibition halls or converted slaughterhouses, as in Europe), but the general shift in lighting and presentation that such spaces provide (in some shows, she notes, the bodies are contextualized by appearing alongside anatomical drawings "dating back to the Middle Ages" [373]).

[21]Cited in Winda Benedetti, "Education or Freak Show? 'Bodies . . . The Exhibition Cashes in on Our Own Curiosity," *Seattle Post-Intelligencer*, Sep. 28 2006, also available online at http://seattlepi.nwsource.com/lifestyle/286689_bodies28.html. Bettie Luke's comment is mirrored by that of another Chinese-American, Fiona Ma, a member of the San Francisco board of supervisors, who told Russell Working of the *Chicago Tribune* that in "Chinese culture they have great respect for the dead and superstition about dead bodies and death. And so I know they would never consent to have their bodies displayed like this, in such a manner."

> each body is distinctly different from any other. Position, size, shape, and structure of skeleton, muscles, nerves, and organs determine our "interior face." It would be impossible to convey this anatomical individuality with models, for a model is nothing more than an interpretation. All models look alike and are, essentially, simplified versions of the real thing.

Though any distinction made between the unique and "uninterpreted" quality of the bodies in *Body Worlds* must falter on the fact that they are not only deliberately posed, but individually *signed* by von Hagens, the rhetoric presented nonetheless grasps something crucial about how the exhibitions operate. The generic "humanity" they represent through the exhibit as a whole (fragile before the mechanized world, and so forth) depends for its strength on its never actually appearing in any particular body. Only in being exactly as we "are," individually, do we represent our belonging to a community composed of other beings who are each, in their own way, exactly as they "are" as well. Whereas in models, the drive to produce a generic singularity eliminates, paradoxically, the very representative qualities that the models aim to reproduce. It is this strange combination of uniqueness and representativeness—the fact that the bodies become, in some sense, most representative when they expose their individuality—that allows the corpses in the exhibitions to retain the forms of historical embeddedness and belonging that motivates the cultural anxiety about their origins.[22] That the bodies come from China thus offers something like a return of the national and cultural particularity whose repression grounds the idealized conception of the exhibitions as being about a universally "human" anatomy defined by a generic vulnerability to an equally generic machine age.[23] The racial and national origin of the corpses, their circulation in a network of exchange that owes a great deal to differences in the national regulation of the sale of human cadavers and to the cost of certain forms of skilled labor, matters enough that the anatomical knowledge these exhibitions spread appears alongside a discourse about the methods of its acquisition and propagation, the two discourses occasionally intertwining as community activists respond to the controversy by reminding the viewing public

[22] Compare, for instance, the history and circulation of the body exhibitions with the embarrassing and violent modes of display forced upon Saartjie Baartman, known as the "Hottentot Venus," or any of the other people of African, South American, or Pacific descent forced to "perform" their racial and cultural difference for audiences in the privileged European cities of the nineteenth century.

[23] Imagine, instead, if we got an exhibit of a man who had died of cirrhosis of the liver, with a narrative explanation that he had liked to drink because it kept his mind off the fact that he had lost his job when his factory was sold to foreign investors.

that the displayed bodies are, despite the removal of the "exterior" faces that would testify to this fact, still ethnically and nationally Chinese.[24]

Whereas in other examples we have seen the ecliptic quality of the reference to China emerge from the internal representational structures of the formulations themselves—the Chineseness of the mandarin, for instance, organizing from within the frame of the hypothetical as a linguistic micro-genre the shift from politics to philosophy that rendered his Chineseness irrelevant—in this context the ecliptic appearing and disappearing of Chineseness at the limit of the human operates in the gap between the corpses' representational function and their material substance. The appeal to a universal humanity made by the bodies as representations of a norm (the norm of uniqueness) thus oscillates in a tenuous dialectic with the fact of their physical provenance. The history of the bodies' production as artifacts interrupts the mimetic effects of their representationality. The woundedness of these pseudo-corpses appears simultaneously as a feature of a universally human state of affairs and as a particular act of violence done to human subjects presumed not to have consented to their transformation into art objects. (In this sense, the exhibition repeats some of the tropes of Edward Steichen's now-notorious "Family of Man" exhibition at the Metropolitan Museum of Art in 1955.[25])

Recalling Seltzer's argument that in wound culture the violated physical boundary figures "the opening of relation to others" conceived explicitly as the *sympathetic* "social bond," it thus seems possible to suggest that the accusation of human rights abuses piled upon the cadaver exhibitions must be thought of as part of a much larger complex—one that includes the exhibitions, their pedagogical and publicity materials, the modes of their production and circulation, and the journalistic and activist armature that surrounds them—whose final determinations belong to the tripartite field of sympathy, economy, and mimesis that has organized this study. The sympathetic bond opened up by this complex would then refer us to the more general problem of an opening to otherness enacted through and represented as trauma, one highly dependent on the circulation of persons inside a field of capital production and exchange. The fact that

[24]The ethnic component is clear enough in Luke's comments. As for the national one, here is activist Aaron Ginsburg, also in the *Seattle Post-Intelligencer*: "China is not a nation of laws, and any assurances that the bodies were legally obtained is meaningless" (Benedetti).

[25]See Roland Barthes, *Mythologies*, trans. Annette Lavers (New York, 1972), 100–03, for the classic critique of the exhibition; see also Eric J. Sandeen, *Picturing an Exhibition: The Family of Man and 1950s America* (Albuquerque, 1995).

the bodies retain their history—and indeed, for some activists, their cultural background—across the veil of death recalls once again the troubled divide between the Kantian inner worth and the subjection of life to the simplifications of market pricing: the very divide in which Balzac's hypothetical mandarin also interferes.

The nearly total woundedness of the Chinese subjects in these "body worlds," now grasped as a physical allegory of the sympathetic opening to others, thus returns us to the always-deferred future of the universal human subject, whose fate it is to appear in the world always as the imperfect analogue of its ideal. But it also reminds us how frequently modern thought encounters and measures the universal against the global, the latter functioning as the flawed yardstick of the former's pretensions toward the infinite.[26] To this point, one might observe that, in the case of *Body Worlds* at least, the realm of circulation for the bodies' ecliptic Chineseness no longer follows the geographic logic that has structured so much of this book. The exhibitions' movement through an international cityscape that places Tokyo, Seoul, Singapore, and Taipei alongside New York, Cologne, and Mexico City suggests that the discourse network captured by the figure of the hypothetical mandarin has in the contemporary moment been disrupted by the new forms of production and circulation that shape the uneven geography of late capital—and thus that shifts in the shape of the "globe" as an imaginary will have their effects, also, on the universals that attempt to account for it.

Ending at this point would thus gesture toward the occlusion of one aspect of the discourse it has been *The Hypothetical Mandarin*'s task to describe, since the horizontal alignment between the East and the West that governed earlier examples in this book now seems to have been surpassed by globalization's new arrangements of space: capitalography subsuming the older geographies. Though this difference seems on the surface to presage a radical shift in the nature of the sympathetic discourse outlined so far, it may also be the case that that discourse's coherent structure can survive the loss of one or more of its major thematic features, and that changes in those features will simply indicate the kind of quasi-evolutionary changes that allow any cultural formation to retain a structural coherence and vitality over time. These shifts—never exactly closures—suggest that the possibility of transformation or revision is in fact a crucial feature of any discourse coherent enough to generate the impression of a singularity. So, that at

[26] I owe his formulation to Russ Castronvo, who said, "the global is revealed as the imperfect translation of the universal" in "How Does Democracy Taste?," a lecture delivered at the Huntington Library, San Marino, Calif., May 18, 2007.

the far end of the imagination, one can think the possibility that the discourse outlined in this book will remain viable beyond the literal presence of the Chinese example: even if some day all the plastinated corpses are those of European volunteers, and all the imaginary mandarins come from Latin America, the social forms to which they refer will retain some fossil traces of their origins in the West's geopolitical encounter with the whole, unwounded otherness it has called "China." In that originality readers of the future will discern, if they are careful, the disappearing appearance of the material substrate from which the universality of the human birthed itself in this age, and which it consumed in the moment of birthing. Like the Chineseness of Balzac's mandarin—itself a largely ignored feature of that particular hypothetical arrangement of life and capital—the Chineseness of the corpses in these exhibitions shows that it is only in the encounter between the universal ideal and the disavowed physical or linguistic material of its elaboration that the modern recognizes itself as modern. Even though the form of that recognition remains, in most cases, largely unrecognized.

4. Toward Sympaesthetics

Alexander Broadie has remarked the resemblance between Adam Smith's emphasis on the mutuality of sympathy in *The Theory of Moral Sentiments* and the process of "truck, barter, and exchange" that forms a cornerstone of *The Wealth of Nations.*[27] To this observation, we need only adduce David Marshall's comment that sympathy is "structured by theatrical dynamics that . . . depend on people *to represent themselves* as tableaux, spectacles, and texts before others" in order to suggest how closely the identifications on which sympathy depends rely, both in practice and in theory, on a notion of "exchange" that includes representational and economic dimensions.[28] The hypothetical of the mandarin is the fictional codification of that relationship, whose particular history has unfolded from the opening pages of this book.

Sympathy's economic dimensions, the degree to which an entire relation to the suffering of the Chinese was historically caught up with a set of mercantile exchanges and apprehensions of globalizing labor markets, were most carefully

[27] Alexander Broadie, "Sympathy and the Impartial Spectator," in *The Cambridge Companion to Adam Smith*, ed. Knud Haakonssen (Cambridge, 2006), 178.

[28] David Marshall, *The Surprising Effects of Sympathy: Marivaux, Diderot, Rousseau, and Mary Shelley* (Chicago, 1988), 5 (emphasis mine).

traced in the first few chapters. There, I showed how the notion of sympathetic exchange as a feature of economic exchange forced a generic violation in the structure of William Miller's typological book series, and I suggested that the texts' concealment of that violation in the "open" (which I compared to Poe's purloined letter) told us something about the difficulty of establishing the connection between European sympathy and the China trade, as well as the profound necessity for it. I followed the Mason chapter with a discussion of the medical missionary project's physical reliance on the economic wars fought between Britain and China in the mid-1800s, and that, in turn, with an analysis of the effects of coolie labor on one especially unusual piece of late nineteenth-century American fiction, each of which, I showed, adopted a structure of feeling that revealed the connection between sympathetic exchange, suffering, and transnational flows of goods and people.

The resemblances among these texts, and indeed between them and the material in the later chapters, are what led me to refer (at the end of the introduction) to their complexity as "holomorphic," a word which in mathematics refers to a function whose "character is preserved over the whole of the plane which is not at infinity."[29] As the individual case studies in the chapters have shown, the "character" preserved over the historical course that takes us from 1790 (the date of the sixth edition of Smith's *Moral Sentiments*) to the present has appeared in a wide range of genres (anecdote, novel, case study, watercolor, photograph, sculpture) and affective modes (indifference, compassion, silence, panic, appreciation), not to mention historical circumstances and geographical locations. But these differences have not seriously deranged the structural similarity that gives the examples what they have in common, that makes them in some serious historical sense a matter not of accident but of ideology. It is the role of that ideological structure as an expression of the history of Western thinking about China and modernity that this book has pursued, with the goal of forcing a recognition of its continuing presence in contemporary debates about the future of universals, economic and political relationships between the West and China, and indeed the long-term subjective orientation of a relentlessly globalized and globalizing planet.

It would not do, however, to push the holomorphic envelope too far. The crucial difference between a mathematical function and its expressions, on one

[29] As Andrew Forsyth put it in 1893, in *Theory of functions of a complex variable*, cited in the *Oxford English Dictionary* under "holomorphic, *a.*, 2."

hand, and the kind of cultural formation I discuss here, on the other, is that in the case of the former the precedence of the function over the expression is natural, while in the latter the function only appears retroactively, as the idealized form to which a series of expressions *might be said* to refer. Though the reconstruction of that function has occupied much of the project, I wish to emphasize that whatever structure has emerged from that labor is very much a fiction, showing the imaginary historical form of something that only ever comes to light in a series of essentially virtual instances. Because cultural forms, unlike mathematical expressions, are overdetermined, they are subject to a number of overlapping and competing causalities whose total contributions to the happening of any object or event do not obey a logic that allows for the assignment of percentages of responsibility, or for the easy extrication of a single causal chain from the raveled whole. My introductory discussion of the example-effect meant to admit the fact of this overdetermination into the field of play, and to suggest how the assignment of singular cultural forms to larger substructural formations always operates at the cost of a certain blindness. Accordingly, my readings have attempted in every case to gauge the chosen material along multiple lines of possibility: as, first, historical expressions of the holomorph they at least partially instantiate and, thus, as evidence for the longstanding presence of a discourse on China and the modern human; as, second, nonidentical in their resemblance, that is, as expressions of a set of variables modified by forms of historical and cultural difference, as well as differences in attitude, medium, and genre, that demonstrated the *complexity* of that holomorphic discourse over time; and as, third, expressions of kinds of cultural interest having more or less nothing to do with the question of China and the human at all, but which referred instead to, say, the relation between text and image, between native and immigrant labor, or between medical care and the suffering subject. None of these latter issues is unthinkable without China, and in writing about them here I meant to indicate the limits of a reading that would treat its examples as though they functioned exclusively to represent the book's major idea.

By the end of the chapter on Arthur Vinton, the historical relation between economy and sympathy seemed to me to have been fairly well established, largely on the evidence that emerged in the readings of Mason and Parker, in which the Western apprehension of Chinese suffering occurred in such an intensely literal relationship to problems of trade, of transnational labor, and of medical, religious, and market penetrations. At the same time, the entire question of exchange as it emerged in those chapters created a burgeoning sense of the importance of representation. A thematics of representation had appeared as early as the theorization of the anecdote in the first chapter, but it had been subsumed in the chapters on Mason and Vinton to the question of sympathy's economic function. By the time I arrived at Russell, however, I felt like the balance between sympathy's economic dimensions and its mimetic ones ought to be reversed, with the result that the last two chapters on Russell and Bataille, and especially the discussion of aesthetics and anesthesia, foregrounded the roles played by representational exchange. In both cases, my emphasis was on the manner that representationality, rather than functioning as an absent or prior idealization of interpersonal exchange to which sympathy might then be compared, tended instead to be articulated *through* acts of sympathy and suffering, as though the ability to transfer certain kinds of human feeling were the test of any representation's mimetic aptitude: the test, that is, of whether it counted as mimesis at all.[30]

Anyone wishing to think the relation between sympathy, pain and representation must contend, as I have throughout the book, with the almost nuclear impact of Elaine Scarry's 1985 publication of *The Body in Pain.* The immense sweep of Scarry's historical and geographical ambition, encapsulated in her subtitle, "the making and unmaking of the world," is fulfilled with particular vigor in her fourth and final chapter, which moves from the discussion of historically particular relations to suffering to a more philosophical treatment of the nature of all of human creativity. All making, Scarry writes, responds to the perception of pain: a chair, for instance, to the recognition that it hurts to sit on the hard ground, Promethean fire to the fact that it hurts to be cold in winter, postal services to the fact that it hurts to be alone, and so forth. All human artifacts are the mimetic "projections" of the experience of pain, the products of an initial recognition that something hurts, and the physical expression of an attempt to ease that pain for oneself or for others.

From a series of small and largely material projections, Scarry ladders up the entire scale of human creation, moving from chairs and fires to entire regimes of comfort-creating or warmth-making artifacts, seeing how they can be idealized as concepts (the idea of "the hearth," for instance) that prompt renewed activity designed to support or sustain them. So, as Scarry puts it, "the sense of protective

[30]That sympathy and mimesis might be connected is an idea as old as Aristotle's writings on theatrical catharsis, though any comparison between Aristotle and the present would have to parse the difference between the social function of catharsis in the Aristotelian theater and the more individualistic sympathetic drive in contemporary accounts of the workings of text and image. Let us observe, in any case, the difference between theories of mimesis oriented around affect and ones directed at something like verisimilitude.

unity sensorially available in a concrete shelter and in the lived patterns of family life may be greatly extended in the concept of 'polis'; and, in turn, the projective act of apprehending and holding steadily in the mind the remote concept of polis . . . may be assisted and relieved by the comparatively freestanding existence of maps, colored squares of cloth, courthouses, and verbal pledges," each of these last the material and pseudo-sentient projections of the pain or difficulty of remembering, and each enabling in its own way a further set of identifications and projections that might lead to social transformation: hospitals, aqueducts, and the like.[31] Two and a half million years after the emergence of *Homo habilis*, all this projection, reflection, idealization, and creation leads inexorably to the world we have today, which is essentially the mimetic reflection of an entire history of human suffering and of human attempts to relieve it.

Before discussing the implications of the mimetic theory that grounds Scarry's history of the species, I wish briefly to address the problem created by the ontological sweep of the claim that places sympathy at the core of human making. Generosity, Scarry writes at one point, is "embedded in the *ontological* status of human beings as creators" (*BP*, 324; emphasis mine). How can we think the *ontological* nature of human making (as grounded in the experience of pain and the timeless nature of compassion) against the evidence that other claims of the same sort can be located in a series of particular historical moments, and thus against the clear Eurocentrism of the ontological claim as such? A serious response cannot simply oppose historical evidence to philosophical argument: as Gayatri Spivak so nicely puts it, in another context in which the difference between history and philosophy is at stake, "it is not correct to think that, because 'inalienable' rights have been again and again violated, they do not exist."[32] Nonetheless, if we wish to assert the ontological generosity of all human making, and if a major consequence of such an assertion is to tie sympathy inextricably to representation (to make them, essentially, identical), we would do well to test that intuition against the lived history of the planet and, thus, to recognize the degree to which an argument like Scarry's effectively reproduces the language of epistemic violence whose existence has been narrated in this text.

Considering the historical complicity of Enlightenment compassion with violence does not mean that we invalidate its lessons or its claims. It requires

[31] Elaine Scarry, *The Body in Pain: The Making and Unmaking of the World* (Oxford, 1985), 322. Further references in the text are cited as *BP*.

[32] Gayatri Spivak (lecture, University of California at Los Angeles, Los Angeles, Calif., May 8, 2007).

instead recognizing that the geographic limits of that compassion and its historical expressions are relevant to the realm of the idea. In this context, if we imagine for a moment another way of looking at things, see making, for instance, as a way of honoring God, or see pain as the necessary if unfairly distributed presence of the worldness of the world, without returning each of these by way of metaphor to a *primary* relation to suffering, then we can imagine a planet on which, as Singapore Prime Minister Lee Kuan Yew quite seriously proposed throughout the 1990s, the suffering of any single human body were not the final referent of the political, but merely one element among many having a right to accommodation in the social system (others being family, justice, or order). The point is not that that Lee is right, nor that one should respect whatever cultural differences one finds, no matter how cruel or ignorant one finds them, but rather that the encounter with genuine difference is by definition the encounter with the initially incomprehensible, with the apparently cruel or the seemingly ignorant. The challenge of cross-cultural understanding is not that of getting along with people who like a different flavor of ice cream than you do but of getting along with people who think your eating ice cream is obscene, or who don't think that putting ice cream in your mouth involves "eating" at all—in meeting forms of difference, that is, that force one to reconsider one's most normalized assumptions about the proper relation between self and self, world and world. The project is, then, how to think the relevance of pain to the human condition while remaining aware of the evidence that suggests that pain's primary importance (and thus compassion's) has to be *taught* and *imposed*, and has historically been taught and imposed (even in the West) in collaboration with a series of other events and effects, most broadly those involving the building and narrating of the idea of modernity.

The completion of that task belongs to another book, for which this one will have functioned as something like a preface. For now, to return to the explicitly mimetic dimensions of Scarry's universalizing claim about the nature of sympathy, I wish to remark that for all the complexity Scarry attributes to the mimetic force of creative making, all the astonishing diversity of coat and fire, polis and map in the end comes down to a single representational imperative: you can make anything you'd like, but what you make will in the final instance be a representation of suffering. Such a model imposes on its mimetic objects a fairly forceful version of the representational strategy known as "realism": "though the objects [of the world] are projected fictions of the responsibilities, responsiveness, and reciprocating powers of sentience, they characteristically perform this mimesis more successfully *if not framed by their fictionality or surrounded by self-conscious issues of reality and unreality*," if, that is, they do not notice or otherwise draw attention to their own status as fictions (*BP*, 325; emphasis mine). In response to this relatively impoverished notion of the representational capacities of the pain-centered object, I would say that my task here has been, first, to demonstrate that quite often the elaborate making of a fiction is in fact precisely where the mimetic labor lies (as in the case of Mason, or Parker, or the photographer of Chinese executions), and, second, to assert that any theory of sympathetic mimesis that limits its representational functions to the range established by a restricted Lukacsian realism will miss a great deal, since in its insistence on representation's final reference to the "realness" of suffering it will be unable to imagine *other* kinds of mimetic motivations (of the type generated by, to use a literary shorthand, modernism, the Romantic, or surrealism). A sense of the world's objects as mimetic expressions of the experience of pain can therefore be expanded, this book has shown, to include a wide variety of representational strategies. Part of my project's aim has been to restore to these mimetic objects a strong sense of their representational complexity, undermining the performance of a certain realism by showcasing that realism's reliance on representational strategies, including elision, discontinuity, and paralepsis, and a series of formal and generic concerns—about the evidentiary status of the image, about the nature of allegory, or the representation of unoccupied perspectives—that consistently foreground the very issues of reality and unreality that the texts and images themselves seemed to want to pass over in silence.

This matters because if the mimetic exchange suggested by the transfer from "reality" to "representation" belongs to the general field of exchange that generates the transfer of sympathy, it is not only because sympathy always responds to the represented evidence of suffering, but because the process of sympathetic exchange itself may be far more mimetically complex than we have imagined. If sympathy is a model for mimesis, that is, and if mimesis can be shown to allow for a series of complex representational strategies (genre, movement) or tactics (metonymy, litotes), then any theory of sympathetic representationality that does not itself allow for a similarly complex set of tactics and strategies will in fact be undermining the fundamental insight of its initial recognition. The point is not only that sympathetic exchange and representational exchange are "like" each other (which they are), but that the set of mimetic strategies through which we read representations should be turned to the reading of sympathies as well, partly because it is the nature of sympathies to be complex and intertwined with history, and partly because this kind of sustained attention to the *making* of sympathy will tend to undermine the normalizing assumptions about its naturalness that make it so hard to imagine the reason that someone else doesn't feel about suffering the way you do. The readings I have done of these mimetic objects ought therefore to be understood, *mutatis mutandis*, also as readings of the sympathetic labor whereby they generated (or dismissed, or rendered invisible) their identification or disidentification with suffering, a labor that each time was no less complex and self-referential than the more obviously textual or image-oriented work that made it visible.

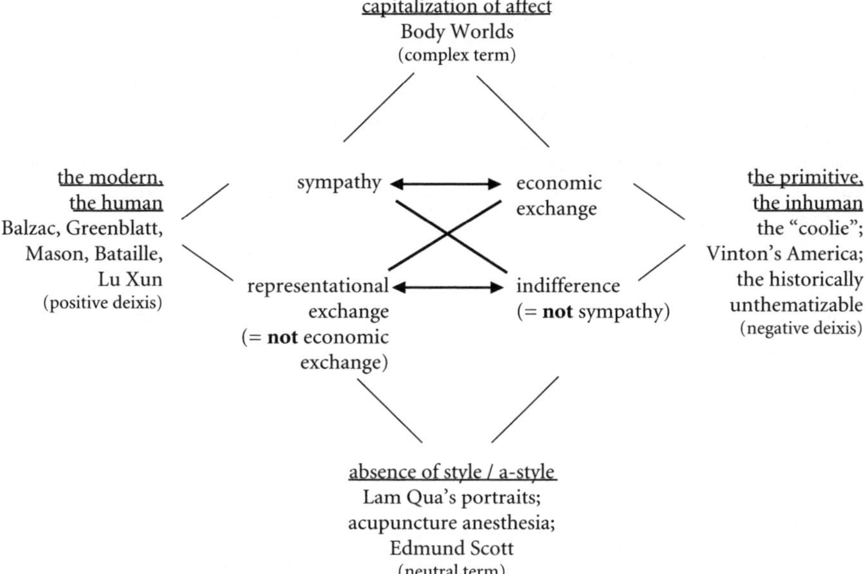

Fig 7.3 The Greimasian Square, even so.

Index